DEDICATED
TO MY WIFE
MRS. VARALAKSHMI RAJAMANICKAM

PREFACE

The scientific spirit for the study of human nature had its start as an offshoot of psychophysics in the middle of nineteenth century when Gustav Theodor Fechner (1801–1887), a German scientist and philosopher had started writing many things about mind-body problems between 1850 and 1860. Even before Fechner's time many thinkers were concerned with the relationship between the body and the soul or spirit. But Fechner had perceived this from different angle with his knowledge and experience in physics and had stated that the problem was the relationship between physical energy and its corresponding effect on mental energy. His hypothesis had been that if mind is to be studied, the physical energy that causes change in the mental energy has to be studied.

Fechner formulated several, hypotheses, designed many experiments and worked on them and came out with a new field of scientific approach called psychophysics in the year 1860. Though at the same time another German scientist, Ernst Heirich Weber (1785–1878) revealed the same view, he had not developed his idea. Fechner, for about ten years had been working on it consistently and brought out many publications. This had become the beginning of scientific and experimental approach to the study of human sensory experiences and behaviour, though attempts have been made a few years later for founding the laboratory for psychological studies by Wilhelm Wundt (1832–1920), in 1879 at Lepzig.

Subsequently, several scientists came forward in the United States and United Kingdom to start experimental laboratory for the study of various aspects of sensory experiences. Instruments for the study of various aspects of sensory responses, reaction time, visual perception, judgments, mental abilities were invented and test materials of various types were designed and validated. Time to time more and more instruments and test materials were found to be putting into use in all aspects of human behaviour. This has enriched the field of psychophysics, and modern psychophysical methods have been evolved.

Subsequently, the psychological scaling methods were also designed and put into use to study the various responses. Hypotheses have been formulated and experiments have been often designed and conducted to explore all aspects of human resources. In this way enormous amount of information were produced by the researchers in a short time and they were published in periodicals. By these means, psychophysics and psychophysical methods have been considered as accurate fields of study and can provide reliable materials to different fields of psychology.

Psychologists believed that experiments based on psychophysical and scaling methods yield accurate results. They, not only provided accurate and new information or results, but also made one to keep involved in dealing with men and matters directly and made them to see the consequence of the performance. A new student in a laboratory situation finds exciting experiences when he is tested on a new instrument and also when he conducts some experiments with such instruments. Every experiment conducted in a laboratory, whether it is based upon psychophysical or scaling methods or an experiment in other fields, yields certain new information. If one properly plans and conducts an experiment with all seriousness, it certainly would yield some new results which may be used for making out a research paper for publication in some scientific journal. It is true that experiments in the area of psychophysics or psychometry are more difficult than the experiments in other areas. But these provide the basic knowledge and experience and also confidence for conducting experiments in other areas.

In this treatise, Modern Psychophysical and Scaling Methods and Experimentation, many intricacies of the theoretical and experimental aspects are simplified and explained. Attempt has been made in this work to provide what are all a student needs in his course of study with regard to psychophysical and scaling methods and research experimentation. The controversial issues and certain criticisms discussed in some places in this book may provide some interest to the student who wishes to proceed in this subject beyond certain stages.

Chennai-40

M. RAJAMANICKAM

ACKNOWLEDGEMENTS

The author wishes to acknowledge the permission granted by the Publishers.

1. John Wiley & Sons, INC, New York for reprinting the copy right material, Figure 7 in page 17 of the book, *Psychophysics : Introduction to Its Perceptual, Neural and Social Perspects* by S.S. Stevens, Edited by Geraldine Stevens. It is Wiley Inter Science Publication, 1975.

2. The McGraw-Hill Book Company, New York, for reprinting the copy right material, Table-M : Ranks corresponding to C-Scale Values for different numbers of things ranked from Guilford's Book, *Psychometric Methods,* Second Edition, p. 577, 1954.

3. The McGraw-Hill Book Company, New York, for reprinting the copyright material, Table-5 : J., Table for converting p values to Z Scores, from D.K. Canland's *Psychology : The Experimental Approach,* 1E (1968), p. 133.

CONTENTS

differentiate the tone of a violin from the tone of a piano or veena, can

PART - I

Evolutionary Trends in Psychophysical Methods

The problem that was greatly puzzling and baffling the German, Physicist, Gustav Fechner for a long time in the middle of the 19th century was, how the functions of the mind and body should be lawfully related. He tried to study the mental energy in the same manner as the physicists study the physical energy. He had observed that since the mind was functioning in its own way, it was futile to relate the mind to the physical laws. But he constantly felt that there must be some lawful relationship between these two. Fechner had often noticed in his experiments that every time when he increased the energy of the physical stimulus there was also increase in the sensation. He also found that this relationship was in agreement with a logarithmic law. He finally observed that his efforts were wholesome and so he continued his work and evolved a general law which he called as psychophysical law and published the same in 1860 under the title of 'Elements of Psychophysics' in which he had explained the methods of determining the relationship between the mind and body. This had become the basis for the psychophysical methods.

The young scientists who were very much interested in experimental psychology found that Fechner's psychophysical methods were very much useful for them and in a short time there were large number of research papers published on psychophysics. But there were both appreciations and criticisms and on the basis of the criticisms several changes and modifications have taken place. Fechner, himself had published his revision in 1877. Soon there were new psychophysical methods by the way revision, modification and also by the combination of old methods with new methods. One of the important changes was the introduction of statistics in psychophysical methods. But all these changes and modifications were based upon the general psychophysical laws, which all contributed to make the psychophysical methods a most powerful instrument in studying the human sensory experiences.

1

PSYCHOPHYSICS AND MODERN PSYCHOPHYSICAL METHODS

ORIGIN OF PSYCHOPHYSICS AND ITS STANDING: AN INTRODUCTION

Human life, all the times, is involved in the perception of the external world through the sensory processes such as seeing, hearing, tasting, smelling and touching the objects in the surrounding areas and reacting to them according to the requirements by accepting certain things and rejecting certain things. Man is accepting or responding to certain stimuli or objects and not responding or rejecting certain stimuli or objects. The whole human life and behaviour is based upon these processes throughout the life, whether it is for fulfilling the basic needs like food, water, shelter, security for life or safety for property or for protection, construction, destruction and so on. Similar response or reaction, acceptance or rejection – all take place in the cultural and social life also. All these phenomena are explained in modern psychological studies through the fundamental principle of the relationship between the mind and body.

This may be also stated that any physical event, occurred or produced, is having a corresponding psychological reaction in an organism in a specific situation. Every physical stimulus has some energy to stimulate an organism and make the organism to react or respond to it. But every stimulus object is multidimensional in nature. An object which is used as a stimulus has several qualities or charcteristics. An organism may respond to one dimension or one quality only at a time in which the organism is interested. It is not possible to respond to all the dimensions or qualities of an object or stimulus for an organism.

A stimulus to which an organism responded may be from any source, which may be pertaining to vision, or audition, or taste or smell or touch. An organism is constantly attacked by different kinds of stimuli all the times in an environment. Do all the stimuli arouse response or reaction in an organism? No, it is not. Only those stimuli which have sufficient strength can stimulate an organism, and if the organism becomes aware of them, and if they are to its needs, then the organism responds to the stimuli quite appropriately. Individual differences are there in responding to the stimuli, which may be due to some defects in the sensory apparatus of the organism. Events of these types naturally may arouse curiosity in a person who is interested in investgating these types of events of natural phenomena which are having influence in human behaviour. Fechner, a German physicist became the champion of this phenomena and explored the nature of the functions of the physical stimuli and founded a new field of study called Psychophysics, which was later on called as the classical psychophysics.

On observing human reactions in various ways to the same type of stimuli, one who is curious of these differences may be tempted to ask the question, 'Why some individuals respond to a stimulus presented in certain situation, and why some individuals do not respond to the same stimulus in the same situation?'

One possible answer to this question is that it may be due to some defects in the sensory apparatus of the organism. Another reason may be that the stimulus might have been weak to arouse response or the organism may require still stronger physical stimulus for responding to it. A third reason also may be attributed to this event. The organism is not interested in that particular dimension of the stimulus.

In the case of human beings, it is presumed that all normal humans supposed to respond to the same level of stimulus energy. There may be some individual differences, but it may be at a very negligible level. Therefore, a stimulus which is having certain amount of physical energy only may arouse response in an organism. If so, what amount of physical energy in the stimulus is required? This is generally called the limen or threshold. The limen or threshold is defined as the smallest amount of physical energy that can arouse a response in an organism perceptibly fifty percent of the time. A limen or threshold in a sensory area can be determined only by conducting an experiment. It may be with regard to seeing a light stimulus, hearing a sound stimulus, or lifting some weights, or pricking with a pain causing stimulus. In every sensory area certain amount of stimulus strength is required to arouse a response which we call as limen or threshold. Fechner had devised methods for determining the limen which were called classical psychophysical methods. These methods were used by the psychophysicists for determining the limen or threshold. This limen is called absolute limen.

Similarly, with regard to the estimation of the quality or quantity of two similar stimuli or objects, problems arise as to whether the two stimuli are equal in quality or quantity or different? If different, which one is bigger and which one is smaller? This type of problems we are experiencing in our everyday life events. There are methods devised by psychophysicists to estimate it and there are also formulas evolved by them to solve such problems.

What amount of difference or change is required in an object to estimate that one is bigger than the other or smaller than the other stimulus or object? In this problem, two stimuli or objects are compared and judged by a person with regard to the quality or quantity of the stimuli or objects. One object or stimulus is stated as the comparative or variable stimulus or object, and the other is stated as the standard stimulus or object. To make comparative judgment and state that the comparative stimulus is bigger than the standard stimulus, it is not meant that the comparative stimulus should be too big or too small. The difference or change should be to the minimum. What minimum amount of difference or change is required in the comparative stimulus to judge it as bigger than or smaller than the standard stimulus? The minimum or the smallest difference or change depends upon the stimulus value used for comparison. The difference or change in the comparative stimulus is proportional to the value of the standard stimulus.

This proportional value is stated in a law evolved by Weber (1795–1878), a German physiologist. Weber was working on differential sensitivity and the accuracy of human perceptual differences between and among the stimuli. His experiment was, what could be the smallest difference between two weights that could be differentiated. The results of his experiment provided him the information to evolve the formula, called Weber's law. This is stated as $\frac{\Delta S}{S} = K$ where, ΔS is the difference or change in the variable stimulus, S is the stimulus intensity, and K is the constant. The constant is a fraction. It is the ratio between the stimulus intensity and the difference or change in the variable stimulus. This change in the variable stimulus is perceptible change or difference. This is also stated as the just noticeable difference 50 per cent of the time.

Fechner had reformulated Weber's law and made it applicable to all sensory areas. Fechner had worked out a constant for every sensory system and published them. The psychophysical function of Fechner's formula is : $R = K \log S$. Fechner had evolved this formula on the basis of Weber's law. Thus, psychophysics and psychophysical methods find their basis on these two general and natural observations and Fechner founded it and evolved a general formula. But the constants evolved for every sensory area on the basis of Weber's law raised several controversial issues.

One of the important issues raised by some investigators was that the constant varied in case where there were individual differences in the judgments. Fechner had rectified this by evolving the formula S = K log R, involving the logarithm in the formula. This is what the modification Fechner had made in Weber's law. Fechner's classical psychophysics and psychophysical methods have become very popular all over the world at once. A detailed discussion of this follows in the next section. But some of the followers of Fechner have become dissenters. Attempts were made by some of the dissenters to dislodge Fechner's psychophysics and tried to evolve better methods in place of them. But it resulted in demonstrating the same methods with different epithets and nothing more. Candland (1968) was surprised at these attempts and asked the question, 'Why Fechner's psychophysical law continued to be on the limelight in spite of all these criticisms?' He has answered the question himself by stating that, first of all, Fechner's psychophysical function fits into the predictions. Secondly, the functions of many of the psychophysicists have failed to fit into the predictions and none of them could demonstrate a satisfactory and acceptable mathematical rule or formula to out do Fechner's influence in psychological studies.

Therefore, it is very conspicuous that the dissenters of Fechner's psychophysics seemed to have developed certain amount of disinclination and repugnance towards psychophysics and psychophysical methods. There were also statements, constantly appeared that psychophysics is dead and gone. The reason for attributing such disfavour and disfigured statement is that Fechner's psychophysics is based upon ordinal scale. Though all psychophysical measurements involve quantitative measurements like the interval and ratio scales, the ordinal scale is considered as the weakest scale, because, in the ordinal scale measurements, one may know simply that the object X possesses the quality or quantity more than the object Y, and it does not state how much. In other words, in ordinal scale the respondent makes judgments comparatively, which are not accurately measurable judgments. But the dissenters wanted the judgments straightaway in terms of ratios, in multiples or in fractions. The crux involved in this is, that the dissenters instead of asking the respondents to make judgments of the stimuli, they wanted them to produce a scale. This is not in accordance with the basic methods of psychophysics.

However, a person,who serves as a subject in the experiment, is expert in judging the stimuli like the light and sound intensities, and in judging weights it is not possible for him to state the comparative judgments accurately in terms of ratios, either in multiples or in fractions. Another important reason is that Fechner's psychophysics is German in origin. The American psychologists during the first quarter of this century have raised protest against the systems of German origin, even Titchner's system was never spared.

As the Fechner's dissenters believed, Fechner's psychophysics was not dead. It will not die, because it makes its appearence often in most of the psychological measurements and also in the development of psychological scales. Candland, a leading American psychophysicist and psychologist had issued a strong statement that if psychophysics is dead, it would certainly return to earth at any time for performing adventurous activities. The spirit of psychophysics is so rude that it cannot be ignored. Any attempt to ignore psychophysical methodology in any form, at once the spirit of psychophysics would haunt them in the form of conscious awareness. Therefore, whether one treats it as an uninteresting, laborious and tiresome procedure or treats it as an unusually rare intellectual weapon, psychophysics and psychophysical methods occupy an indispensable place in psychological studies and they become, no doubt, the foundation of modern psychology. But because of psychophysics, modern psychology can never dream of claiming itself as the science of behaviour.

Antecedent to Modern Psychophysics

In the history of modern psychology, psychophysics and psychophysical methods have occupied such an important place that any psychological study can never be accurately conducted and explained scientifically without its aid. Therefore, psychophysics can never be neglected or omitted at any level. Psychophysics and psychophysical methods seem to be dull for those who do not comprehend it properly and apply it in their studies. Some of the Institutions in India, it appears that they deleted the portions of psychophysics from the syllabus and incorporated something under the heading psychological measurements. This is like avoiding the fundamental principles and methods of experimental psychology and resorting to something at surface level. As result of this attitude, the performance aspect or instrumentation is slowly diminishing in Indian Universities and superficial paper-pencil tests, which are not designed and developed and validated strictly according to the principles are thrusted into the experimental and research studies.

Psychological studies cannot be fully depending upon the correlational research and selection procedure alone without concentrating on experimentation using psychophysics and psychophysical methods.

The development of instrumentation in the field of psychology is indended to assess the sensory experiences experimentally. Modern instruments are very accurate in assessing human sensations, through which various behavioural anomalies could be measured.

The important procedure and expectation involved in the experimentation is that the interested variable is subjected to direct manipulation by the experimenter and the more reliable and precise results that can be obtained. This is what every scientist wants and so also the psychologist.

The psychophysics and the methods were not suddenly emerged sciences. This was the result of long incubated and contemplated efforts of Gustav Fechner (1801—1887), a physicist, theologist and philosopher. Fechner, after rigorous experimental procedures, had tried to measure mental energy in the same manner as the physicists measure the physical energy and found that it was no good of applying the same principle on mental energy. The mind was found working on its own principle and might not concord directly with the physical laws in all respects. However, after ten years of rigorous research by putting his ideas into action as to how to determine the relationship between mind and body, Fechner was able to bring out a book under the title of *Elements of Psychophysics* in the year 1860. This book has provided us with the basic principles of psychophysics and psychophysical methods.

Fechner's work has drawn the attention of many scientists who were exploring the field of experimental psychology and several papers on psychophysics have appeared in scientific journals, making use of Fechner's methods. During this time Fechner's interest was on the study of aesthetics. He started working on, how to measure beauty, and several methods were devised and used for assessing beauty, and related variables. After an elapse of 22 years, Fechner has revised his psychophysical methods which was a combination of old and new psychophysical methods and statistical techniques. This was appeared in 1882 under the title of "Revision of Cardinal Points of Psychophysics".

The psychophysical problem which was baffling the scientists for a long time was a general formula which can describe the relationship between physical stimulus and assessing the corresponding effect of that stimulus in all sensory systems. The invention of psychophysical methods has solved the crux of the problem. Hence, Fechner was considered to be the father of psychophysics. A few years earlier to Fechner's declaration of psychophysical methods, Weber had made comments on the relationship of sensory systems. According to him, each sensory stimulus has different ratio in its reaction and therefore equal stimulus ratios produce equal differences in reactions. Stevens says, that equal stimulus ratios produce equal subjective ratios. This is the essence of psychophysical laws. The word 'subjective' here according to Stevens, is referred to the judgment or reaction made by the observer. Stevens (1906—1973) is often called as the innovator of psychophysics of 20th century, the other two, Weber and Fechner lived in 19th century.

Weber has proposed, what we now call as Weber's law in 1834. He had stated that if a stimulus should become just noticeable a fixed percentage must be added. In other words, if the stimulus is small, a small amount of change need be added. If it is large stimulus a large amount of change need be added. Thus, according to Weber's law the just noticeable difference (JND) increases in direct proportion to the size of the stimulus. Fechner had accepted Weber's law and stated it as : $\Delta S/S = K$, where ΔS is the increment made in the stimulus, S is the stimulus and K is a constant expressed as a fraction. Weber's constant K indicates the assessment of sensitivity of the organisms to various types of stimulation. Thus the formula states that for each sensation there is a fraction — For example, 1:30 for weights lifted. This predicts the relationship between mind and body (psychophysical). If the given weight is 90 grams the experimenter would have to increase a weight of one-thirtieth of its original weight for a difference to be noted 50 percent of the time. Therefore, the next weight that would be judged heavier than the original weight (90) must be 93 grams. Adding one to 90, that is, 91 grams would not be judged as heavier than the 90 grams. There may be also individual differences in observation. According to Weber's ratio, the smaller the ratio the greater the sensitive modality.

Fechner (1860) had accepted Weber's law and added something new. In the experiment each time a JND is added to the stimulus and the sensation increases to the constant stimulus size. The jump of one step to another is constant and the increase of sensation also is constant. But the increase should be proportional to the size of the original stimulus. For example, if the original stimulus is 90 grams one step increase of stimulus to arouse corresponding response is 3.0. But if the original stimulus is 120 grams then the JND is 4.0 grams. Any stimulus less than 4.0 grams may not make any difference in the judgment. Similarly, the original stimulus 150 grams should have 5.0 grams as JND. In every sensation a proportion is maintained. Fechner's addition to Weber's law resulted in giving birth to a new law, called Logarithmic law. This indicates the relationship between sensation and stimulus — a relationship between logarithm and number.

The logic is that sensation depends upon both the threshold and the stimulus value (the sensation). In other words, sensation depends upon the logarithm of the magnitude or intensity of the stimulus. The important characteristic of Fechner's law is that the stimulus increases in ratio steps while the response (sensation) increases in equal steps. The stimulus continuum is having equal proportions and the response becomes equal units. Fechner had revised the Weber's law. The revised law according to Fechner is :

$$R = K \log S$$

Where R = Response, the sensation judged

K = a constant

S = Stimulus dimensions from the threshold.

The formula may be also stated in the other way :

$$S = K \log R$$

Where S = the sensation experienced by the subject (the psychological value of the stimulus)

R = the stimulus

K = a constant value.

According to this formula the strength of the subject's sensation of the stimulus varies directly as a function of the logarithm of the stimulus. Fechner has stated Weber's law mathematically as S = KS. Fechner also had included in his revision that the JND is a unit of sensation. The JND is a change in the stimulus just noticeable 50 percent of the time. Fechner had observed that the ratio obtained in the relationship between the standard stimulus and the DL (Difference Limen) is not constant. It varies sensation to sensation. Further, in order to have a just noticeable difference in the stimulus a fixed percentage must be added. What makes one to see a difference in the perception is a relative matter. In spite of individual differences, a small standard stimulus is needed only a small amount of stimulus need be added and for a large standard stimulus a large amount of stimulus be added. Therefore, according to Weber's law, just noticeable difference (JND) becomes larger in direct proportion to the size of the standard stimulus.

Fechner, had conducted experiments on the sensation of sound and the results helped him to think of a scale formation. Starting from a faint sound, so faint that one cannot hear it, he increased the intensity until one hears it clearly to the level of absolute threshold. He further increased the sound until one says, that it is louder — a louder that is called a JND, which is a next (second) step on the sound continuum.

From this place, he increased the intensity of the sound again until one hears it as louder, producing another JND. This is the third step on the ladder of intensity of sound sensation. In this way a step by step procedure was carried out until he got the loudness whose value he wanted to measure. The value according to Fechner was the number of steps on the (ladder) sound continuum and he counted the number of steps. In this procedure the problem of the size of the steps is there. Fechner assumed that all steps were subjectively equal as it is done. But if the steps were not equal in size then counting the steps find no value. Therefore, Fechner proposed to measure sensation indirectly. Instead of asking a person to make estimation of relative magnitudes of his sensation of sound he conducted many discrimination tests to measure the JND. The JND, here is nothing but one's ability to tell the nature of one stimulus from another. This may lead to some confusion when a person tries to deal with small stimulus differences. In fact, the JND is a measure of variability in sound.

Fechner had devised a unit of subjective scale, for which he measured the JND at various places along the scale (sound continuum) and then counted the number just noticeable steps. In this way he thought that he could measure the total subjective magnitude of sensation of the sound. In the subject's judgment of the small differences in steps of the sound magnitude there may be confusion and variability and this becomes Fechner's unit of measurement.

Fechner uses the word confusions which he might have meant places of uncertainty in the subject's judgments. Thurstone (1929) called it as Fechner's logic and supported Fechner's assumption that out of confusions and variability the units of measurement can be shaped. Thus, the transformation of a measure of variability into a unit of measurement became the beginning of quantification of psychophysics. But what has come as a result of these efforts is the solemnizing act of evolving a method of study – the methodology – which came to be called the classical psychophysical methods. There are three different variations in procedure in measuring the first noticeable difference (JND).

In the classical psychophysical methods the important experimental function is to compare two stimuli of the same type and the subject is asked to state when the two stimuli appear equal or different. This appears very simple. But it can also be in the other way, what happens if the subject is asked to generate his own dimensions of stimuli? What would happen if we ask the person to tell us when two lights appear equal or when one light is twice brighter than the other. By this means the subject himself produces his own scale. If so, what kind of psychophysical function it is called? This is a way of thinking different from what Fechner had suggested. Whatever different way of thinking takes place in Fechner's psychophysical methods, the simple procedure suggested by Fechner need not be masked in the name of criticisms.

Weber's ratio is concerned with the relationship between ΔS and S. These two components are concerned with physical continuum. The R (Response) continuum is made only on the physical continuum and the relationship between ΔS and S is not linear. Further, the R continuum suggested by Weber is not constant. The law does not speak about sensation. Therefore, critics like Candland (1961) say that Weber's law is not a true psychophysical law. Guilford (1954) states that classical psychophysics is an incomplete psychophysics as it did not give a scale for the response on the R continuum.

Fechner's primary interest was to study the relationship between mind and body, between physical event and corresponding psychological event. His psychological event mainly referred to sensations. Therefore, he saw in his experiments that his logarithmic law has described the relationship between physical stimulus and sensation. He tried to test the universality of his law. The experimental psychologists have followed Fechner's new psychophysical methods and found that sensory experiences could be studied experimentally. Thus, experimental procedure that could be used to solve the psychophysical problem was a long felt one and the invention of psychophysical methods has fulfilled it by providing a general formula for all sensory systems that would describe the relationship between the physical stimulus and the judgment of that stimulus.

Since the inception of the Fechner's psychophysical methods there were several formulations as the psychophysical law, but Fechners' formula was found to be still most useful formulation. The techniques used in them – the psychophysical methods, were used not only to study the thresholds and the sensory experiences (sensations) but also were used in many fields of experimental psychology. Contemporary psychologists have devised several methods for studying the relationship between the stimulus and response in various fields. But Fechner was the first to impart the psychophysical methods, hence this is called classical psychophysical methods. Fechner had provided several options in his work for deciding the method of measuring a sensory threshold. Thus, there are three methods, such as (1) method of minimal changes, (2) method of average error, and (3) method of constant stimuli. Generally, these three are called classical psychophysical methods (we shall see these three methods in detail elsewhere in this book).

Modern Psychophysical Methods

The main aim with which Fechner started his work was to establish a universally accepted làw for solving the psychophysical problems and he was able to innovate the psychophysical methods which were used by modern Experimental Psychologists all over the world for more than 140 years. After disseminating his psychophysical methods Fechner turned his attention to the measurement aesthetic values. Several scientists tried to apply and verify Fechner's procedures in their studies and found that they could not fit their data into Fechner's prediction. Hence there were severe criticisms on the Fechner's methods. Plateau (1872) after conducting experiments with light had stated that "we have no ability to judge directly the ratio of two sensations". Therefore he looked necessarily for an indirect approach for judging the light sensations. He suggested that the lightness scale could be built up by starting from zero. However, in the experiments he conducted subsequently on grey paints, the respondents who were artists were instructed to draw which should appear and lie half-way between black and white, but they looked very much alike even though they were painted under very different illuminations by eight artists in their own studies. He was not satisfied with the results and wanted to have more experiments to determine his assumption. Therefore, he asked his friend Delboeuf to carry out the experiment on a colour wheels to produce shades of grey from black and white. Delboeuf in the year 1873 conducted this experiment producing a series of intervals – equal – apperaing contrast steps. The results of these experiments seemed to harmonize better with a logarithmic law and did not support the power law proposed by Plateau. Since the conclusions of his proposition were defective, Plateau had to abandon his power law.

Fechner, while pondering over the problem as to how to connect the inner world of sensation with the outer world of stimuli and to evolve a lawful relation, it was struck in his mind that by doubling the value of the stimulus a constant increment was added to the sensation. This relation would agree with the logarithmic law. Apart from Plateau, a few more investigators who disagreed with Fechner's logarithmic law have protested from time to time and there were also some isolated instances, attempted here and there to establish different forms of psychophysical function. But there were no continuity in their works, and each worker ignored the works of his predecessors.

Meanwhile Fechner had reviewed his experiments and the arguments, made by others, carefully and convinced himself with his work. He had developed so much confidence in his logarithmic form of Psychophysical law that on seeing the protests from his dissenters, boldly resisted his critics and wrote in his book "On Psychophysical Matters" in the year 1877, that, the Tower of Babel would never be finished, because the workers could never come to a conclusion on how they should build the Tower, similarly, Fechner felt that his Psychophysical Edifice would stand for ever, because his dissenters would never come to an understanding on how to pull it down.

Fechner had expressed his real feeling and strong conviction about his Psychophysical Law and Methods. He had known it pretty well that there were Jahavahs to confuse the builders and to frustrate them. This was what happened when Stevens continued his work in dealing with the Psychophysical problems on the general Psychophysical Law and added his contributions to the classical psychophysical law and methods. Stevens created many followers and admirers. Stevens (1957, p. 8) had stated in his paper, "On Psychophysical Law", what Fechner had felt about his Psychophysical Law.

Psychophysics and Psychophysical Methods were looked upon as mere a method of determining sensory thresholds till Stevens had started his research work and visualized the field of psychphysics beyond the level of determination of sensory thresholds. Stevens had established that psychophysical methods can be used for many purposes. He demonstrated that psychophysics can be used to measure perceptual experiences on sensory channels and psychophysical scaling can be taken to the useful measurement of sensations and also he used the same methods for the study of social variables such as crime and delinquency. He had shown that how the modern scientific and industrial world is in need of psychophysical methods for the accurate study of visual and auditory thresholds.

Fechner's long felt desire was to have one general formula which can describe the relationship between the physical stimulus and the judgment of that stimulus in all the sensory systems. Steven's works and inventions were, whether in that direction or not, but his psychophysical works were extended into diverse areas. Most of his works were based upon the estimation of sensory magnitude and stimulus magnitude. One of the major contributions to psychophysics was the Auditory Psychophysics.

Subsequently in the year 1882 Fechner had revised his psychophysics under the title of "Revision of Cardinal Points of Psychophysics". Stevens remarked that Fechner was right in a sense. Because psychophysics has contributed a wealth of information about sensory systems. Psychophysical methods have been in practical use during the past 140 years, measuring sansory thresholds. Right from the time of Fechner to the time of mid-twentieth century investigators are still searching for a universal psychophysical law which is still at large. Since Fechner's critics could not find out an alternative method to replace Fechner's law, Stevens had stated that they abandoned it in favour of a more serviceable structure. Stevens was the most virulent critic of Fechner's psychophysical methods and who later on founded the psychophysical power law. We shall discuss this a little later.

Many psychophysicists made some improvements and changes in the techniques and measurement on the Fechner's classical Psychophysics. They have taken more serious steps with the view of constructing mathematical model for describing mental phenomena: Among those who tried along the way of making contribution to the task of finding out the psychophysical function, four were to be mentioned. They are Fullerton-Cattell, Thurstone, Helson and Stevens. The contributions made by these authors independently come under the heading of Modern Psychophysical methods.

1. *Fullterton and Cattell*

The contributions made by these two authors is called Fullterton-Cattell (1892) principle. This principle is based upon the discrepancies between Weber and Fechner laws. The experimental test of each law had different operations. In Weber's law we determine whether small changes in the stimulus continuum are equal or whether the ratio ($\Delta S/S = K$), K is constant. The small changes on the stimulus continuum is supposed to be noticed often equal and they are also psychologically equal. In Fechner's law the test is made with multiples of the absolute threshold stimulus. The stimulus value increases in ratio steps Sl/S0 = S2/S1 = S3/S2 = S4/S3 etc. and the response value increases in equal steps. In other words when the stimulus increases geometrically (by doubling each step) the (response) sensation increases arithmatically (in steps of constant size). According to Fechner when the response value (R) sensation is 0, the stimulus value is S0 and not S. Therefore, R = 0 and S = S0. When these values are substituted in the equation it is : $\Delta R = C\frac{\Delta S}{S} = K$. The C is the constant proportionality between ΔR and $\Delta S/S$. The S0 is the absolute threshold stimulus from where the operation begins and not at the place where (R0) response continuum meets the stimulus continuum (S). Therefore, the formula becomes: $R = K \log S$, where R = response (sensation), K = a constant and S = stimulus dimensions measured in distance from the threshold.

Thus, the psychological scale value is derived differently from Weber's laws. Fechner assumed that only when the discriminal dispersons of different stimuli are equal on the stimulus scale the two laws are related. Fechner's law is not affected by the size of the dispersons, but Weber's law is affected. In Fechner's law, while testing, we are interested only in the central tendencies of discriminal of the stimuli and we relate these to S. But in testing Weber's law the size of ΔS is directly dependent upon the nature of the discriminal processes. If the dispersons for the stimuli are not equal then the judgments on the R are not equal. Therefore, if the dispersions on the R continuum are not equal then the subjects either never perceive a difference or always perceive a difference. In the words of Fullterton-Cattell: "equally often noticed differences are equal, unless always or never noticed". This well-known generalization is called as the Fullerton-Cattell principle. Fullerton-Cattell in their studies of dispersion in psychophysics asked the subjects to reproduce a stimulus a number of times and computed the probable error of the reproductions. According to their assumption, if Weber's ratio and Fullerton-Cattell principle are correct then the dispersion should be constant. The ratio of the probable error of the mean should be constant. But this has not taken place in their studies. Instead, the mean error of the reproduction increased in direct proportion to the square-root of the stimulus. Therefore, their principle is stated thus: $\Delta S = C\sqrt{S}$, where C = constant, mean or probable error. However, in the contemporary psychological studies the refinement in techniques and measurement made by Fullerton-Cattell on the basis of their criticism upon Fechner's law did not have much attraction.

2. *Thurstone's law of Comparative Judgment*

Though attempts have been made by Psychologists sufficiently earlier for constructing mathematical models for description of the Psychophysical subject matter, a much better rational basis for psychophysical methods and for psychological measurements in general were evolved only in the second quarter of twentieth century. Not all those who criticised Fechner's law were able to come out with successful rational formula. The credit goes to Thurstone when he published his 'law of comparative judgment in 1927. The original law of comparative judgment as given by Thurstone is:

$$Rb - Ra = Z_{ba} \sqrt{\sigma_a^2 + \sigma_b^2 - 2\, rab^{\sigma}\, a^{\sigma}\, b}$$

But authors who deal with this, present it with some change in the subscript notation. Guilford presents the same law as :

$$Rj - Rk = Z_{jk} \sqrt{\sigma_j^2 + \sigma_k^2 - 2\, rjk^{\sigma}\, j^{\sigma}\, k}$$

Candland presents the same law with some change in the subscript notation as :

$$\overline{X}_1 - \overline{X}_2 = Z_{ab} \sqrt{\sigma_a^2 + \sigma_b^2 - 2\, rab^{\sigma}\, a^{\sigma}\, b}$$

Let us state the meaning of the subscript notation following Guilford. Here the Rj and Rk refer to the psychological values attached to stimuli Sj and Sk respectively.

Zjk = deviate from the mean of a unit normal distribution or standard measure distance.

σj and σk = standard deviation of distribution of Rj and Rk respectively.

rjk = coefficient of correlation between Rj and Rk.

The size of each separation Rj – Rk may be determined if the value on the right side of the equation is known. From the experimental proportion Rj > Rk, the value of Zjk will be known. The remaining three components of the equation σj, σk and rjk are unknown.

Thurstone has evolved five cases from his law of comparative judgment for the purpose of application of the law.

1. The first case is the ideal one. The law in its complete form is applied and the observer is to make repeated judgments of the pairs. In this procedure the last three components of the equation become unknown.
2. In the case of the second, the law is applied on a group of observers, in which each observer is to make only one judgment of the pairs. Here also the last three are not known.
3. In case of the third the assumption is that there is no correlation between judgments (rjk = 0) of any pair of stimuli and therefore, the last term of the equation is dropped out. Since the value of Zjk may be obtained from the experimental data and σj and σk can be determined the equation $Rj - Rk = Zjk \sqrt{\sigma_j^2 + \sigma_k^2}$ can be solved.
4. In the case of four and five the discriminal dispersions are assumed to be equal and then the law is further reduced to

   Rj – Rk = .707 Zjk (σj + σk) and to

   Rj – Rk = Zjk respectively.

Now the observable variable Zjk remains. The Rj and Rk are determined from the judgments made by the observer/observers.

According to the law of comparative judgment, the scaling operation is to start with comparative judgments of pairs of stimuli. The operational method is stated as the method of pair comparisons in which all stimuli are evaluated on a psychological scale. The stimuli are presented all in pairs to the observer and he is to judge whether the stimulus j is greater in quantity or quality than the stimulus K in some respect. The stimuli may be of similar in nature such as size, colour, weight, feeling of pleasantness, leaders, actors etc. in quality or ability. The observer judges the pairs of stimuli for a large number of times on different occasions. The data obtained in this way are given in a tabular column which is called occasion matrix. The operation is also made in the other way by asking a number of observers to make a single judgment of all the pairs of stimuli. This is presented in the individual matrix. In both cases the judgments received numerical values—the number of times each stimulus judged either greater than or smaller than the other in the pair. These values may be converted into proportions and presented in a proportion matrix and the scaling is made from this (This is explained in the pair comparison method experiment elsewhere in this book).

The method of pair comparison has certain advantages and disadvantages. The important disadvantage is that it takes too much of time and makes the judges to loose interest in the task. Secondly, if the number of stimuli are many the number of pairs become too large for judgment and the judges become wearisome in the task. For example, if the number of stimuli are 15 then the number of pairs become 190. In the case of a single observer, for preparing occasional matrix he has to make multiple of 190 judgments. Thirdly, the method also involves tedious computation work on the part of the investigator to arrive at the scale values of the stimuli. Therefore, suggestions have been made by Uhrbrock and Richardson (1983) McCormick and Bachus (1982) to reduce the number of judgments in the experimental procedures. Thurstone (1927b) himself has suggested a method to reduce the computation labour in finding out the scale values.

This method is very widely used when stimuli are presented in pairs successively or simultaneously. Apart from sensory areas it is also mainly used for determination of values of colours, designs, aesthetic values, musical notes and also for the assessment of attitudes and opinions towards races, religions, nations, birth control and family planning, prohibition, revolution and war. The method can be used also for assessing certain personality traits. The values obtained by this method are more accurate compared to other methods.

3. *Helson's Adaptation Level*

This is one of the modern psychophysical methods evolved by Helson as a reformation of Fechner's law. Helson (1947) invented it first in connection with judgments of visual qualities. The adaptation level as a principle is not limited to visual or other sensory processes, but it also applied to complex perceptual processes and to the processes of learning and conditioning. The social psychologists, of late made use of this adaptation level for describing phenomena like 'context' and 'frames of reference'. Guilford (1954) says that the adaptation level is the most promising and unifying principle. The principle is more complex. It was intended to deal with many contradictory phenomena of the psychophysical experimentations.

The classical psychophysics tried to avoid the sources of errors from the judgments. Judgments may differ or change as a result of previous experience (error of expectation, habituation). This may result from the way in which the psychophysical procedures are designed. Therefore, Helson (1947, 1948) had designed an experiment for verifying the relative influence of four attitudes of colour such as colour constancy, colour contrast, colour conversion and colour adaptation. Formerly these colour phenomena were regarded as unrelated events and shifts from one event (colour constancy) to another (colour contrast) with very little change had been obtained. Helson thought that the general problem of colour has three experimental variables such as *colour object, its background,* and the *amount of the illumination.* In the experimental condition, Helson has varied each of these three variables on a very wide ranges in many combinations and the background colour was varied in three steps like white, grey and black. For every combination of background and object colour, Helson found four varied illuminants such as red, green, yellow and blue. Therefore, judgment of the colour of the object depended upon the other variables (background colour). This result shows that the level the subject had adapted with regard to illumination partially determine his final judgment of colour. Therefore, the general conclusion is that the colour constancy event for the white light stimulus would occur when the object seen was at the adaptation level of the moment and therefore the adaptation level becomes a function of many stimulus conditions. Because of this type of function, Helson (1938, 1964) had stated that adaptation level is "a pooled effect of all stimuli impinging upon the organism both from without and within and includes residuals from past experience". Helson assumed that adaptation level is a weighted mean of all these stimuli. Therefore, the final judgment is the result of each of the judgments obtained earlier has been weighted for the prediction. Helson had generalized his findings in colour phenomena of his adaptation level and extended its application to judgments of lifted weights and conducted many experiments.

4. *Stevens Power Function*

The classical psychophysics was primarily interested in the determination of sensory thresholds or limens or stimulus value. Fechner's original interest was the philosophical problem. He wanted to study the relationship between mind and body — the physical event and the corresponding psychological event and he saw them in his logarithmic law and had described the relation between physical aspects and the related psychical aspects. Fechner's psychophysical methods provided new experimental procedures to the experimental psychologists for investigating the sensory phenomena. For more than hundred years Fechner's psychophysical methods occupied important place in text books, in laboratory experiments and in the classroom discussion all over the world. Criticisms now and then appeared stating the limitations of the psychophysical methods and why Fechner's law required improvements. But none came out with a universally accepted rational principle and a substitute for Fechner's law and methods till 1959. But how can one prove that Fechner's law and methods are not correct when the basic assumptions are logical. At this time Stevens (1953) of Harvard University was able to come out with accumulated evidences giving a basis for the long expected efforts and the transfer of Fechner's logarithmic law to his prothetic continuum. Stevens (1975) asserted that his prothetic continuum can replace Fechner's logarithmic law. Stevens power law is applied to large number of modolitics and physical stimulus is related to sensation (psychological effect). The formula for his power law is :

$$\psi = K(r - r_0)^n \text{ where}$$

ψ = psychological (sensation) magnitude of stimulus
K = a constant, depends on the unit of measurement (choice of unit)
r = Physiological stimulus
r_0 = effective threshold: point on physical scale from which measurement of effective stimulus begins
n = an exponent, varies with sensory system, from one continuum to another.

Since Stevens' intention was to make improvement over Fechner's law and Fechner founded his logarithmic law from Weber's law, Stevens' formula includes the characteristics of both Weber's and Fechner's laws. Fechner's addition to Weber's law is the measure of the threshold value from which psychological value is determined. Stevens and his colleagues have varied the n with sensory modelity. They found that a power function expresses the relationship between reports of stimulus intensities and actual stimulus magnitudes better than a logarithmic function. It may also be stated as :

$$R = KS^n$$

where R is the report of apparent magnitude

S is the stimulus magnitude measured in physical unit

K and n are experimentally determined constants.

Stevens had conducted most of his experiments on the sensation of sound. He states that sensations come to us in so many varied forms and they elude from complete description. There is no formula that can register all the richness of our daily lights and sounds, tastes and smells and feelings to which our sense organs are exposed to. But if we could make some basic distinctions then there can emerge some simple principles that would relate specific aspects of sensation to certain properties of stimulus forces. One of the important distinctions is between quantity and quality or magnitude and kind or size and sort. But there are no suitable common pairs of words that could describe them. For example, sour is different from salt but they may vary from strong to weak. Even though psychophysics is the science that can say something about the qualitative variations among the sensations, when we go from one sense modolity to another the qualities of various sensations baffle us. The various colours, sounds, tastes, smells and pressures do not fall on a continuum but they are all independent of one another. But some of the aspects of sensations which have some specific characteristics appear to fall on a continuum of some type. In such cases it is possible to order the sensations on a scale from weak to strong or faint to intense or in some other dimensions. In the case of many continua it is possible to devise a form of measurement that would be better than simply ordering them. The problem may be simplified if some set of rules become common to all perceptual continua, but that does not take place. One basic distinction can be made between two kinds of continua of the same sensation. In the case of sound, the two kinds of perceptual continua, for example can be shown by loudness and pitch. Both these continua are from sound only. The perceptual continuum loudness is an aspect of sound and it is described in degrees of magnitude or greatness of size or loudness of sound or amount of quantity. The other continuum, pitch is the highness or lowness of a sound due to vibrations of sound waves. It has a point or position. From the perceptual point of view of the sound it is a qualitative continuum. Stevens called the loudness a *prothetic* (quantitative) continuum and the pitch as a *metathetic* (qualitative) continuum. Stevens assume that these two continua are the physiological processes that seem to underlie some of the sensory continua. The metathetic continua are concerned with what and whereas the prothetic continua are concerned with how much. In the case of sound the metathetic continua include pitch, apparent position, apparent inclination and apparent proportion.

Stevens put more emphasis on prothetic continua as it provided him with satisfactory results in his efforts to measure the magnitudes. Stevens in 1953 had conducted more than 36 experiments on the sensation of sound and examined the prothetic continua and he had the same results. That is, the sensation magnitude ψ grows as a power function of the stimulus magnitude. S. Stevens thought that this kind of result happens very rarely in behavioural studies. In 1953, he was able to demonstrate a simple quantitative law under many diverse circumstances and the application of power law was able to draw the attention of many psychophysicists and how the power law is applied to both light and sound. Since then experiments have been conducted in the psychophysics laboratory of Harvard University to demonstrate a power law for taste and smell, warmth and cold, vibration and shock. Thus, a power law was evolved for every sensory continuum and what is required is only to change the stimulus magnitude with pre-determined quantity. At this development Stevens claims that his psychophysical power law has substituted Fechner's logarithmic law.

The estimation of magnitude is a very simple and most direct and most widely used method. The subjects were presented with a series of test stimuli, one at a time and they were required to give numerical estimates which should be proportional to the magnitudes of the sensations evoked by each stimulus. These numerical estimates were averaged, to provide the points of the required scale.

But Stevens' early exploration to evolve a rational method to measure sensory modelities was on the sensation of sound. In estimating the magnitude of prothetic continua Stevens followed a different method. A number of sensory scales were constructed by Stevens and Guirao (1962, 1963). A scale of loudness of a 1000 Hz. (Hz = Hertz : It is a unit of frequency, equal to one cycle per second) tone developed by means of magnitude estimation. The following instructions were given to 10 subjects (observers):

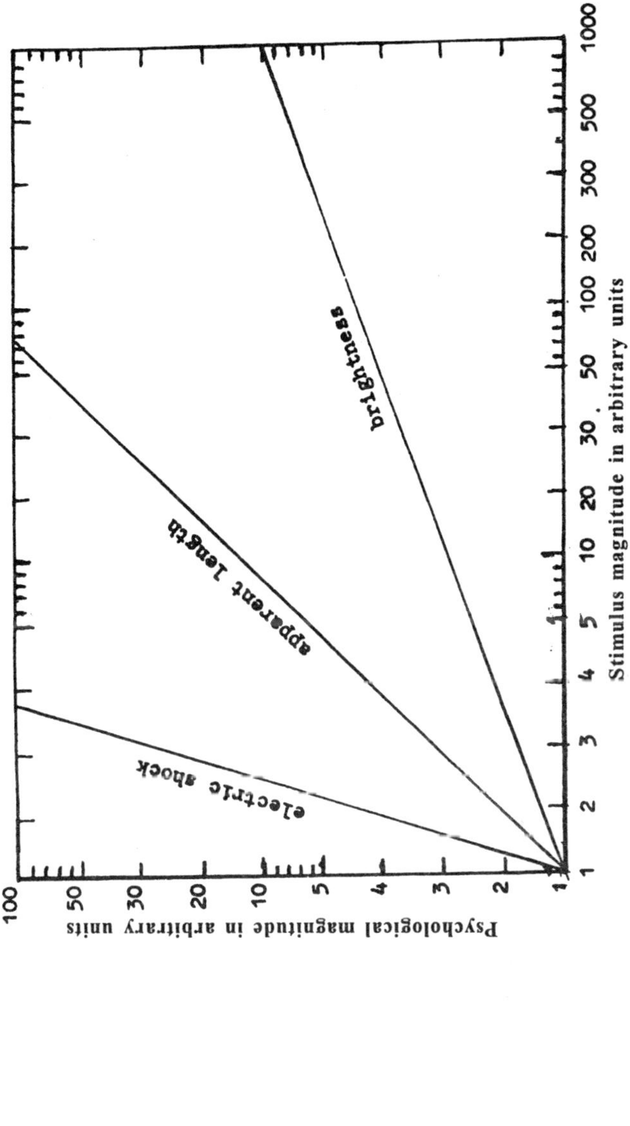

Fig. 1.1 : Three Sensory Modelities, Electric shock, Length and Brightness on log - log (Reproduced with permission from Stevens/Psychophysics, 1975, p.17, © John Wiley & Sons, INC.)

"I am going to present a series of tones. Your task is to tell how loud these tones sound by assigning numbers to them. Call the first tone any number that seems to you appropriate.

Your task is to assign numbers proportional to your subjective impressions. For example, if a tone sounds 3 times as loud, assign a number 3 times as large as the first. If it sounds 1/5 as loud assign a number 1/5 as large, and so forth" (Stevens and Guirao, 1962, pp. 1466-67).

In this experiment there were seven tones, all 100 Hz. They were all varying in intensity. They were presented twice for each subject in an irregular order. Therefore, every subject made 14 judgments for the seven tones. The geometric mean of 20 judgments of each subject was worked out for seven tones. The data obtained according to Stevens' method were plotted in a curve. Stevens found that the exponent (P) of the power function determined the curve. An exponent of exactly one provided a straight line on the graph. The sensation (output) varies directly with the intensity of the stimulus. But if the exponent was greater than one then the curve indicating the function was upward concave and when the exponent was less than one then the curve was downward. Stevens drew three curves, one for electric shock, one for apparent length and one for brightness. These three curves were having bizarre shape and not as expected.

At this stage Stevens revised his power law equation in terms of logarithm ($\log \psi = P \log \theta + \log K$) and plotted the curve on log – log coordinates. Then the curve of the power function was straight line and the curvatures disappeared (Fig. 1.1). Stevens explained the reasons for his failure to obtain the expected result and a straight line in the graph was drawn to the data obtained according to his method. According to him in the first curve the electric current produced through the fingers a sensation that grew more and more rapidly as the current increased and the brightness grew less and less rapidly as the physical intensity increased. The apparent length grew in direct proportion to the physical length. Stevens rectified this by changing the formula and data to log – log coordinates. Stevens had summed up his discovery in a single line: "Equal stimulus ratios produce equal subjective ratios". According to power function there exists a simple relation between stimulus and sensory response. This was what Fechner also stated. Stevens was able to state a general rule from this: "on all continua governed by the power law, a constant percentage change in the stimulus produces a constant percentage change in the sensed effect" (sensation). Stevens had stated that the power law reveals the relationship between sensation and stimulus (rather than judgment).

Stevens' findings became the cause of the production of many new psychophysical scales. The most interesting one is the scale of loudness based on the newly defined unit, the 'sone'. This was developed because the acoustical engineers found the decibel scale was not satisfactory. They needed a scale which could reflect more accurately the loudness of sounds to the listeners. These developments renewed the experimental interest to solve the problem that was not attempted for many years.

The psychophysical power law founded by Stevens and his colleagues is not free from criticisms. The origin and development of Stevens power law itself is an outcome of the criticism levelled against the Weber's and Fechner's laws. Though Stevens and his colleagues were successful in formulating a new psychophysical law it has not fulfilled all the requirements of psychophysical problems. D'Amato (1970) states that power function does not always fit the observed scale points. There are instances where the relation between the data and the theory becomes uncertain. Further, it is not possible to determine objectively how far the power function fits to a given set of points, because it lacks the statistical measures of goodness of it. One of the weaknesses of his power law is that the straight line of best fit is done by eye and not by mathematical means objectively. The values of the exponents elicited are not specified from the source. Another important argument is that the subjects scaling judgments appear to be determined by many more variables than the sensations connected with the judged stimuli. In one of the recent studies Paulton (1968) has observed that the central processes involving judgments cannot be understood fully in terms of the behaviour of the sense organs. The mechanism of response and the response bias should be included in the description.

Galanter's Decision Theory

The decision theory is a most interesting and a vivid account of a new approach to psychophysics. According to this theory the sensory threshold is a statistical approximation and this changes sometimes. The threshold is a statistical device but it is not referring to it fully. It is named after the founder Galanter (1962). It is also called *signal detection theory.*

The decision theory is based on a simple assumption that psychophysical measurement may be considered to be a measurement of detection and recognition of thresholds. A person is able to say that a stimulus is present. This referred to as the decision. Having perceived a stimulus the person is able to say that the stimulus has certain character. Suppose, for example you may be asked to see in front of you at a distance and say something about the approaching person. You might have seen the person moving towards you. This means a decision has been made that a person is coming. But you may not be able to determine whether the person is a man or woman. As and when the person approach towards you, you are able to say that the person is a young lady. At this stage the recognization threshold is determined. This theory emphasises the need on the part of the subject to make decisions about the stimuli and ascertains the presence of the stimuli by referring to their character. It is called decision theory.

In classical psychophysical theory also the subject makes his own decisions with 'yes' or 'no' responses. He is to state whether the subject perceives the stimulus, whether the variable stimulus differs from the standard stimulus and so on. Here, the procedure ascertains that the threshold is present and perceived. In all classical psychophysical procedures, by definition, a threshold is perceived 50 percent of the times. Since detection occurs 50 percent of the times it may be called detection threshold instead of stimulus threshold or absolute threshold. According to the decision theory the number of 'yes' responses for the stimulus threshold are the same as the 'no' responses. Equal number of times the stimulus threshold is not perceived. It is because of this some writers have stated that a stimulus threshold is a statistical device or approximation and the presence of the stimulus alone is reported and nothing more. Further, there may be physiological changes in the sensory apparatus and because of this individuals judgments also may vary. What is stimulus threshold for one person may not be for another. The earlier experience in the experimental situation makes the subject to expect that the stimulus is going to appear. But in the case of decision theory the procedure yeilds for a complete recognition of the threshold.

In an experiment, the probability that a stimulus appears and it is varied. The subject was asked to tell whether he perceives a stimulus or not. But the experimenter cautions the subject that when he watches the stimulus the probability of the appearance of the stimulus is varied from 10 to 90 percent. This means that the stimulus may appear sometimes 10 percent of the times and sometimes 20 percent of the times and sometimes 90 percent of the times. In this way the appearance may vary in between 10 and 90 percent. This procedure may reduce the chances of probability and the error of expectation may be reduced. Therefore, there are more chances in this procedure for the subject to report the perceiving stimulus correctly. This function is called *isosensitivity contour* or a response operating characteristics. It is also important to observe in the experimental situations that even when the stimulus is presented, the subject may not be reporting that he has perceived it if it was presented after some unperceivable trials.

Further, an absolute threshold is not properly defined concept with regard to its point. The subject always might say that he does not perceive the stimulus if it is below the absolute threshold and he might always say that he perceives the stimulus if it is above the absolute threshold. Therefore, there appears a region in which the probabilities of perception (response) vary due to the function of stimulus strength. In the classical psychophysics it can be observed that as and when the intensity of the stimulus increased a sharp change from no response to yes response takes place. What actually happens is that the probability of yes response increases gradually as the strength of the stimulus increases on the stimulus range. But the stimulus threshold is determined arbitrarily on the stimulus continuum (on the scale of physical energy) at which the probability is 50 percent. Galanter states that as it is, there is nothing absolute about threshold value. Therefore, the absolute threshold now may be called signal detection and 50 percent point may be referred to as the detection threshold. It is also observed in a typical experiment that when the stimulus is presented objectively high signal detection is more accurate and the proportion of errors are reduced. But when the stimulus is presented infrequently signal detection is less accurate and the proportion of errors are increased. Results suggest that detective thresholds are determined by the experimental procedures the experimenter adapts and the subject's expectations as to whether the stimulus appears or not. The motivational factors also may influence the detection thresholds.

Some of the modern psychophysicists questioned the fundamental concept the threshold. They say that it is not reasonable to speak of threshold and say that they do not believe it. Even if they accept that one such exists, there cannot be one threshold, but there should be three, one below threshold which a signal is never detected (low threshold), one at which the signal is detected with some specific degree of chances and one at which the signal is fully and always detected and perceived (high threshold). Modern psychophysicists apply similar thoughts to the problems of discrimination and scaling. That is the determination of difference thresholds and accurate expression of mathematical language of the relationship between perceptual experience and the magnitudes of physical stimuli. The subject in the experimental situation is no doubt sensitive to the stimulus energy at the detection threshold but he is also variably sensitive to many other factors. Therefore there is every reason to suppose that the determination of thresholds are also unstable. Therefore, it becomes necessary to revise the psychophysical scaling methods.

Information Theory

Modern psychophysics has opened certain new and challenging problems for investigation. This seems to be the continuation of the signal detection theory. If we associate the concepts decision and detection a third concept also is imminent, that is recognition. The problem is posed in a simple form out of several possible detectable stimuli that might have been presented which was actually presented. This refers to the amount of information the stimulus contains and the amount of information the observer can process and register at one look. Psychophysicists have found that the information theory may provide answer for this. Information theory could tell the experimenter how much information is contained in a stimulus presentation. The psychophysicist may be controlling the stimulus displays in his experimentation. In such cases it is possible for the experimenter to know how much minimum information his observer can deal with and still he can produce accurate judgments (responses).

According to information theory observers cán learn to recognize perfectly only about seven alternatives with more stimuli on a single sensory dimension such as pitch of a tone, brightness of light or weight of an object. The information recognized is a little less than three bits of information. Information depends upon the number of alternatives. Therefore, the amount of information transmitted by an occurrence may be defined as the natural logarithm of the number of alternatives. Galanter (1962) states that recognition is easier when complex stimuli are used instead of simple stimuli and the number of bits successfully managed is higher. When stimuli become more complex a process of diminishing returns occur and the absolute limit for the stimuli of any complexity is not more than 10 or 11 bits. In real life people manage many more alternatives than this. But it should be noted that the occurrence of 1 out of 10 alternatives transmit only half the information transmitted by the occurrence of 1 out of 100 alternatives. The basic idea is that the amount of information increases logarithmically as a function of the number of alternatives may be expanded to estimate the amount of information communicated in a unit of speech. For example, if a speech wave is a basic unit the amount of information contained in the wave is a function of (a) the duration of speech, (b) the range of frequency of speech and (c) the intensity. Any increase in the amount of information may occur only through these three components of speech. Psychophysical methods for measurement of speech perception have been developed by Lane and others (1961).

It is also important to know the number of alternative stimuli involved in this for evaluating the amount of information conveyed by the stimulus. An 'yes' answer to some 15 questions may elicit little information from the respondents. But for the answers 'yes' or 'no' there may be more informations and if the respondent increase the number of alternatives like 'may be' may add still more information. The 'may be' answer indicates that neither 'yes' nor 'no' is correct. In this way as the number of alternatives increase more information can be obtained from a single answer.

Thus, the modern psychophysics has gone long way from Weber and Fechner – from the determination of sensory thresholds to the measurement of information processes. The fundamental classical psychophysical laws have been challanged and the basic principles have been verified experimentally and reformulated and attempts also have been made to substitute the classical psychophysics. But with all the challanges, reformulations and substitutions historically classical psychophysics is the foundation on which much of the experimental psychology has been built.

Part - II

Classical Psychophysical Methods

The general psychophysical laws and psychophysical methods were invented by Gustav Fechner after ten years of rigorous research work. He had the strong assumption that the physical stimulus energy was having corresponding effect on the mental energy or in the sensory systems. He was able to acertain this result on observing in his research works that whenever the physical magnitude increased there was also an increase of the sensation magnitude. Therefore, he came to a conclusion that it was possible to assess the relationship between the physical energy and the mental energy and formulated several methods for determining the same. Out of several methods, three methods were considered to be more important, namely the method of average error, the method of minimal changes and the method of constant stimuli. During the course of time, these three methods were called as the 'classical psychophysical methods' because they were the foundation of experimental psychology.

In the beginning, though these three methods were used only for two important purposes of determining the absolute limen and the difference limen, later on they were used for studying various behavioural aspects. These methods were having certain significant characteristics. They were determining the absolute and difference limens very accurately. It is because of the efficiency of these methods, they were still applied with some modifications in psychological laboratories all over the world.

2

PSYCHOPHYSICAL METHOD OF AVERAGE ERROR

INTRODUCTION

The scientists who have tried to estimate the relationship between the stimulus and its effect upon the sensory apparatus have invented several experimental methods which they called as the psychophysical methods. All the psychophysical methods are associated with the problems of identifying the properties of the stimulus which the organisms perceive and to which they react. The method of average error is one of the important psychophysical methods. The aim of the method is to determine the equal stimuli by adjustment. There are several ways of deciding the strength of a sensory threshold. We shall discuss here three important methods of measuring the strength of sensory threshold.

1. *Method of Adjustment* : The respondent or the observer in this method is actively involved in controlling the variable stimulus and makes adjustments in it in comparison with the standard stimulus.

2. *Method of Equation* : The respondent here is fully engaged in equating the variable stimulus (Sv) with the standard stimulus (Ss) until both the stimuli appear to be equal in each trial. A number of such judgments are obtained from the respondent and the central tendency is taken as the stimulus value. Under the prevailing experimental condition this value is taken as the equivalent to the standard stimulus.

3. *Method of Reproduction* : This is another name for the method of average error. The respondent in this method is attempting throughout to reproduce the given stimulus to that of the standard stimulus. The important characteristic of the method is the respondent's decision, when the variable stimulus is going to be equal to the standard stimulus.

The method of average error may be called by all the three names.

Further, this method is primarily concerned with matching or equating the two stimuli, the variable and the standard, and finding out the error, resulting from the matching. Generally, in the method of average error the participant is allowed to adjust the variable or comparative stimulus until he/she considers it equal to the standard stimulus. Another feature of this method is that the method is not directly giving us the judgments. It is only referring to the treatment of results. Titchener (1905) says that this method is a gift from physics and astronomy to psychophysics. This method has been used by several investigators in various ways. Steinheil in his study, equated the lighted surface to the brightness of certain stars and called his method as method of equating variable. Fechner (1882) has introduced this method into psychophysics in his measurement of visual and tactual sensations. Later on certain alterations have been suggested by those who tried to make use of the methods.

It was Muller (1878) who first made certain alterations in the method. According to him the participant will have to adjust the variable or comparative stimulus by moving it backward and forward in the region of equality and then is trying to find out the total range of settings that can be accepted as equal. The participant, then, finds out the mid-point from the range. Kellogg and others (1929) did not permit the participant to shift the variable stimulus back and forth to make the decision that the two stimuli are equal. Instead they wanted that the participant should move the variable stimulus to the point of equality from one direction only. He/she must take pains and care in making the movement accurately and stop just when arrived at the point of equality. In this procedure the participant becomes more alert and have the least chance to commit error. The method of average error may be illustrated by presenting two stimuli to the participant. One stimulus is the standard stimulus and the other is the variable stimulus. The standard stimulus is horizontal line with arrow heads and the variable stimulus with feather heads. Though these two lines are of equal length they perceived differently and there is always some distortion of line lengths. The feaher heads and arrow heads cause some confusion, which make the perceiver to judge differently. This is an illusion and named after Muller and Lyer and it is called Muller-Lyer illusion.

While conducting an experiment with these two stimuli in half of the observations the variable stimulus should be on the right of the participant and in half of the observations on the left. These two space arrangements are indicated as R and L. In half of the observations the variable stimulus should be too great and the movement of the variable stimulus should be inward and in half of the observations the variable stimulus should be too small and the movement should be outward. This gives rise to two conditions as I and O. Thus, we have four combinations, putting space and movement conditions together, as Ro, Rl, LO and Ll, and when counter balanced we have the sequences as RO, Ll, LO, R1, Ll, RO, Rl, LO. Here there is a systematic variation in the space right and left and movement conditions (in and out). The reason for such variation is that any conclusion regarding the illusion should be general. In this type of variations there will not be any difference in the means.

Constant Error

There is every chance of committing error in the judgments. The horizontal line with arrow heads is having the chance of being judged as shorter than the line with feather heads. One purpose of the method of average error is to determine the discrepancy between the standard stimulus (Ss) and the average of the judgments made by the participant. This measures the extent of the illusion. This is called main constant error in the experiment. When we present two physically equal stimuli 'A' and 'B' to a participant, he/she does not always perceive them as equal. Even though the physical characteristics of the stimuli are the same, he/she may report with a difference. If such judgments are due to the variable stimulus it is imperative that the standard stimulus is overestimated sometimes and underestimated sometimes. However, frequently we find a systematic tendency on the part of the participant towards overestimation or underestimation. Such a systematic tendency is called constant error. In the case of horizontal lines with feather heads and arrow heads the deviation is in a fixed direction and it may be a negative deviation.

Let us say that the mean of the judgments is Mj which is greater than the standard stimulus (Ss). This means the standard stimulus (Ss) was always judged as greater than the Variable stimulus. In other words, there has been a general overestimation of the feather heads and general underestimation of the arrow heads. This is what the experimenter generally expects. The constant error may be denoted as $Mj - Ss = Ec$, where

Mj = mean of the judgments
Ss = value of standard stimulus
Ec = Constant error

Space Errors and Movement Errors

There are also two other constant errors. They are called space error and movement error. The space error is the difference between the means for R and L observations. The R refers to right and L refers to left.

The movement error is the difference between the means for O and I. The O stand's for outside movement and I for inside movement.

In some experiments the space and movement variations are more important. But they are rarely significant statistically. If the space and movement variations are statistically significant then there would be four constant errors of the illusions. There will be four means, two for space (R and L) and two for movement (O and I). If each of these means vary from the standard stimulus significantly then there are four constant errors. Error here refers to the extent of fluctuation in judgments.

In any experimental situation judgments may be influenced systematically by the spatial positions of the stimulus whether it is on the right or left of the participant. Thus, the space error becomes a constant error.

Similarly, in any experimental situation judgments may be influenced systematically by the movements of the stimulus whether it is moved inside or outside. In this way the constant error of movement error is caused.

The constant errors are due to systematic tendencies and they should not be dismissed by saying that they are the inaccuracies of judgments. They need to be corrected. The psychophysicists are very much interested in these as they find dependable correlation between certain conditions of stimuli and judgments.

The method of average error has certain advantages and also certain disadvantages. It is considered to be a best method in certain cases. While discussing the merits and demerits of this method psychophysicists have varied views. Generally, in the method of average error the participant is observing and comparing two stimuli. Actually he is not making comparative judgments. He/she is to produce equivalent appearing stimuli. In the method of average error we are concerned with participant's adjustments (Sj) and their mean (Mj) and not all the quantities the variable stimulus (Sv) are undertaken.

In the method of average error, in the experimental situation we come across another error called motor error. There is every possibility for the participant to commit this motor error while making adjustment in the apparatus. Sometimes the participant may be moving and adjusting the apparatus without proper control. This may perhaps lead to overestimation or underestimation of the standard stimulus which may expand the dispersion of judgments.

Advantages and Disadvantages

The method of average error when compared with other psychophysical methods has certain practical advantages :

1. In this method in every trial we get a measurement whereas in other methods several trials are required.
2. There is economy of time on the part of both the experimenter and the participant in this method.
3. This method is more useful wherever measurements are to be made in a limited time.
4. Since discrimination between the standard stimulus and the variable stimulus is made by action on the part of the participant it is considered to be the most natural method.
5. Titchener says that in all psychophysical methods judgments involve some kind of action. The participant makes atleast verbal type of action. But in the method of average error the participant's muscular activity is involved and the participant actively makes adjustment of the stimulus. In other psychophysical methods the participant must take the stimuli as they come to him/her. He/she is not permitted to make any change in the stimuli even if he/she wished.
6. Since the participant has got the liberty to adjust and control the stimuli the participant may develop a favourable attitude towards the method. In other psychophysical methods this condition does not prevail.
7. In the method of average error, since the participant actively cooperates with the experimenter there is always some benefit in it.

With all these advantages the method of average error has certain disadvantages. Muller and others have criticised this method.

1. In using the muscular activity there is always certain amount of uncertainty of the hand. The measurement depends upon this. There are several things under the phenomenon of uncertainty of the hand.
2. The participant makes the adjustment by moving the variable stimulus. But always there are instances of occasional inability on the part of the participant to stop the moving apparatus at a particular point. Though it is possible to avoid this by providing the participant with certain instruments to control it, the handling of such instruments need accurate skill.
3. The errors of movement and the errors of perception cannot be ruled out in this method. Fullerton and Cattell (1892) ascertain

these errors after conducting many experiments. According to them the participant will not be satisfied with his judgments however carefully he/she makes the adjustment and whatever time he/she takes. After the participant has made an adjustment of a stimulus, the experimenter asks him/her to say whether the stardard stimulus and the variable stimulus appear equal. We can find at this stage that any one who had been a participant in this experiment will agree that the moment he/she ceases the adjustments he/she may notice that the two stimuli are not equal. This kind of vacillation may arise in any participant. Titchener calls this as muscular contamination and this could be minimized if the apparatus is easily and accurately adjustable.

4. Guilford (1954) states that there is an inherent characteristic in this method which puts certain limitations upon the usefulness. This he called as the constant time error. In the experimental situation when the standard stimulus and the variable stimulus are presented in succession they must be in the same time order, Ss than Sv. When there are many stimulations, the time order is not maintained and there is often a negative time error. As result of this the standard stimulus is always overestimated. If this error is statistically significant the negative time error can be balanced by reversing the time order, which may be positive time error as in the case of space and movement errors.

Classical Psychophysical Method and Method of Average Error

Among the psychophysical methods,only in the method of average error the respondent is allowed to manipulate the variable stimulus. The method is applied very usefully in the study of visual extent in the Galton's Bar experiment and in the measurement of geometric illusions. The other areas in which this method can be applied are in the study of total attributes, pitch and intensity, in the study of bodily movements and in the study of problems of memory.

According to Fechner the method of average error can be used to determine the difference limen (DL). Actually it is the probable error (PE) of a distribution that has been taken as the DL. The probable error is somewhat proportional to the difference limen and it measures the respondent's sensitivity. Further, Weber's law also can be verified by using the method of average error through the measures of dispersion.

The method of average error is one of the three classical psychophysical methods designed by Fechner in the last quarter of nineteenth century. The other two classical methods are the method of limits and the method of constant stimuli. Fechner has developed these methods for evaluating the change in the mental energy (perception) which was accompanied by a change in the physical energy (stimulus). Fechner originally was concerned with the psychophysical methods as means of measuring the human perceptual process. But later on they were used for the purpose of determining the sensory thresholds. The experimental psychologists who followed Fechner's new psychophysical methods have found that these methods provide experimental procedures quite appropriate for their purpose and they thought that they could investigate the sensory systems very accurately. In determining the absolute and differential thresholds in other psychophysical methods the control and change of the stimulus is absolutely in the hands of the experimenter. In psychophysical experiments, however, there are certain problems which could be attacked by allowing the participant to have the control over the stimulus. In this case, the method of average error is more suitable.

This method is also known as the method of adjustment, the method of equation and the method of reproduction. The distinguishing characteristic of this method is that the participant plays the active role in the procedure and he/she decides when the variable stimulus is equal to the standard stimulus. The participant performs the task of adjusting the variable stimulus until it appears equal to the standard. Thus, the participant handles and manipulates the instrument until he/she is satisfied.

The stimulus may be anything like two verticle lines or one verticle line and one horizontal line, or a shade of colour, or intensity of sound. Thus, the method of average error is primarily concerned with matching of two stimuli and working out the difference between the standard stimulus and the variable stimulus which may be stated as the 'error' which is resulting from the matching. Since the method of average error is having certain advantages, which the other psychophysical methods lack, it is very widely applied in perceptual experiments. Frequently, the method is used to obtain the difference limen (DL) in psychophysical determinations. Every adjustment, in comparison with the standard stimulus, the participant made in the instrument is a measurement of point of subjective equality (PSE). Suppose, for example, in an experiment with two horizontal lines, the standard stimulus (line) is 300 mm long and the participant adjusts the variable line once at 302 mm and once at 298 mm. Each of these two adjustments provide us with an estimate of the PSE. The estimate of PSE is the average of many such adjustments made by the participant. The average adjustment is supposed to be almost equal to the standard stimulus. But it never happens. Some of the participants' adjustments may be always greater than the standard and in the case of some may be smaller. The first is positive deviation (over estimation) and the second is negative deviation (underestimation). One cancels out the other. That is, one average error cancels out the other average error. Therefore, this method is called average error.

An experimenter wants to determine the extent of illusion using the method of average error. The Muller-Lyer illusion can be used to illustrate the method of average error. The amount of distortion of the lengths of line in every judgment can be measured. In the Muller-Lyer illusion there are two horizontal lines, one is the standard stimulus (A) with 'arrow heads' and the other is the variable stimulus with "feather heads" (B). Both the lines are equal in length. But the line with feather heads will be perceived by the participant to be longer than arrow heads line.

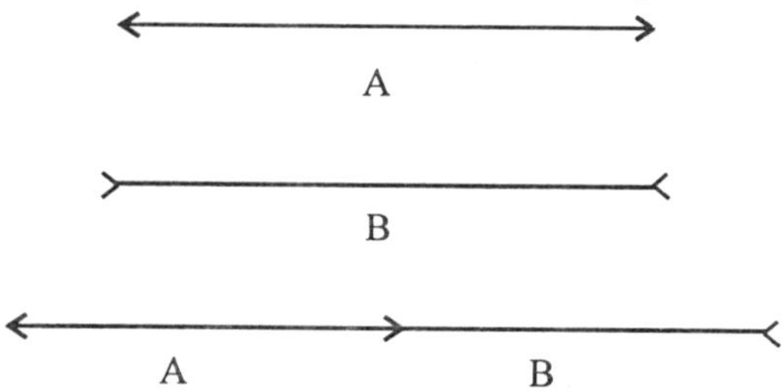

An apparatus, having this principle as the basis, may be designed and constructed to perform the experiment in which the participant may be allowed to adjust the feather heads line (B) to perceive the two lines equal. The experimenter can find out how close the participant comes to match the two lines from the scale fixed behind the illusion board. The experimenter should take certain precautions while collecting data in the method of average error. The direction to the participant for the adjustment should be varied. In half of the trials the variable stimulus should be set with a value considerably longer than the standard and in half of the trials it should be set considerably smaller than the standard. In this situation the participant should begin his adjustment towards matching both the stimuli equal on successive trials, one from above the standard and one from below the standard. This is the general condition to be followed in all trials. But there are also two other conditions. They are (1) space condition, and (2) movement condition.

In half of the adjustments the variable stimulus should be on the right of the participant and in the other half on his/her left. These two space arrangements are indicated as R and L respectively. In half of these two space conditions the variable stimulus should be too long, longer than the standard stimulus so that the participant should move the variable stimulus inward (i) to match it with the standard stimulus. Thus, the participant by way of adjustment moves the variable stimulus in half of the trials from right (R) and in half of the trials from left (L). In the other half, the variable stimulus is set too small on the right in half of the trials, and too small on the left in half of the trials, so that the respondent by the way of adjustment should move the variable stimulus outward (O). In this way we have four combinations of canditions, RO, RI, LO, and LI. The space conditions R and L and the movement conditions O and I may be counter balanced on the basis of number of trials the experimenter sets. In this procedure the extent of illusion may be general and the space and movement variations do not make much difference in the means, because the extent of illusions are counter balanced in this arrangement. However, the mean of the judgments (Mj) would be always smaller than the standard stimulus (Ss). This is what the experimenter expects in this experiment. The arrow heads line is always underestimated than what it actually is.

EXPERIMENT - 1 : Determination of equal stimuli by the method of Average Error

Problem : The purpose of this experiment is to determine the extent of visual illusion in the Muller-Lyer Illusion Board by using the method of avarage error.

2. METHOD

Respondent : Choose a person who has no knowledge about this experiment and describe his/her characteristics such as age, sex, qualifications, physical type, deformities if any, whether wearing eye glass etc.

Materials : Muller-Lyer Illusion Board, metre scale, paper and pencil.

Description of the Material : The Muller-Lyer Illusion Board is designed and manufactured by some firms in India. The Board is made up of wooden plank about 45 cm long. Two iron rods are about 30 cm long vertically fixed on a wooden stand. In between the two iron rods the illusion board is fixed. The illusion board is detachable from the iron rods, and can be fixed at different levels. On the front surface of the board, white sunmica sheet is fastened. In the white sunmica sheet a red line is drawn in the centre, the left end with arrow heads and the right end with feather heads. In the centre of board there is a small grooved sunmica segment with a handle. This is devised in such a way that it can be moved from one end to the other end through the illusion board. In the segment there is a red line with feather head. This feather head is in line with the long line on the board in such a way that there is one "arrow heads" line and also one "feather heads" line. By moving the segment with feather head forward and backward we can change length of the arrow heads line and also the feather heads line. On the back side of the wooden board there is scale segmented into millimetres. In the Muller-Lyer illusion apparatus the standard stimulus is 160 mm in length with arrow heads.

Procedure : The experiment should be conducted in a well illuminated room. The participant should be made to sit in front of the work table on which the Muller-Lyer illusion board is placed. The experimenter first of all should check the board whether it would be easily handled as directed. The experimenter in advance should prepare a table in his/her record note book for noting down the judgments. The table should have two space and two movement conditions with the sequence of RO, LI, LO, R1, LI, RO, RI and LO. Then the experimenter should give the following directions.

"I am going to set this apparatus so that one line is obviously longer than the other. I want you to move and adjust the longer line so that both the lines should appear equal in length. When you believe the two lines are equal remove your hand from the apparatus. You should not pull back the segment at any time. You must always push it in and so as to be certain that you do not over-push the segment beyond the point where you think the lines to be equal. You will have to carry out 10 trials. When I say, 'ready go', you must start pushing and adjusting the feather heads line equal to the arrow heads line. Now, ready go."

Then the participant should begin his/her task and the experimenter should watch whether the participant goes according to the procedure. When he/she is satisfied that both the lines are equal then the experimenter should check the scale behind the illusion board and note the difference if any between the two lines in mm in his/her record notebook. Then the experimenter should move the segment and make the variable stimulus (feather heads) longer than the standard stimulus once again. Then the experimenter should ask the participant to push and adjust line again and note down the difference. The experimenter should continue the same procedure till the participant completes all ten trials on the right in (RI).

In the next stage the experimenter should push the segment inside so that the variable stimulus (feather heads line) is too small and then should give the following directions to the participant :

"Look at the lines. This time you will have to do the task little differently. The feather heads line looks very short. You will have to pull the segment and adjust so that the two lines are equal. You must only pull the line to be equal with the other line. You must not pull too much and then push the segment inside. When you are fully satisfied that the two lines are equal remove your hand from the apparatus. You will have to carry out ten trials as you did previously. Now, ready go."

The experimenter should watch the participant whether he/she is carrying out the task correctly. When the first trial is completed the experimenter should note down the difference from the scale in 'mm' in the respective column RO. In the same manner the participant should carry out ten trials and the difference in length between the two lines should be noted down.

In the next stage, the standard stimulus with arrow heads should be on the right side and the variable stimulus should be on the left side. For which the wooden board with the segment should be removed from the rods and sets (left to the right and right to the left). Now the experimenter should set the variable stimulus too short on the left and the participant should pull the segment out to make the two lines equal. The experimenter should give the following directions to the participant.

"Now the feather head line is on the left and too short. You will have to pull the segment out and make the two lines equal as you did previously. You should perform ten trials. Now, ready go". The results of the ten trials should be entered in the column LO.

After completing ten trials the experimenter should set the variable stimulus longer than the standard stimulus and the participant should push the longer line inward to make it equal to the standard line. Again ten trials should be performed and the results should be entered in column L1.

In the next stage, the experimenter should reset the illusion board again as before, having the standard stimulus on left and the variable stimulus on the right. Now the variable stimulus is set with medium length neither too short nor too long but longer than the standard stimulus. The experimenter should ask the participant to push the line inward to make it equal to the standard line. Ten trials should be performed and the experimenter should make a note of all the judgments in column Ll. Then the experimenter should set the variable stimulus smaller than the standard stimulus. The participant now should be asked to push the variable stimulus and make the two lines equal. Ten trials should be taken and the judgments should be noted in the column RO.

Now, again the illusion board should be reset and the standard stimulus should again on the right. The experimenter should reset the variable stimulus with medium length but longer than the standard stimulus. Then the experimenter should ask the participant to push the variable stimulus and make it equal to the standard stimulus. Ten trials should be performed and the judgments should be recorded in the Column Ll. Lastly the experimenter should set the variable stimulus smaller than the standard stimulus, not too smaller, but medium. Now the participant should pull the variable stimulus slowly to make it equal to the standard stimulus. There should be ten trials and the results should be entered in the column LO. Now the experiment is completed with two space conditions R and L and two movement conditions O and I and consequently there are four combinations as RO, Rl, LO and Ll. When these four conditions are counter-balanced we have the sequences as RO, L1, LO, Rl, Ll, RO, R1 and LO and for each sequence there are 10 trials and a total 80 trials. The settings were randomised with too large, medium and too small lengths of the variable stimulus. There were 4 ascending and 4 descending series. The sequences may be randomized and may be in any order.

3. RESULTS

The observer's judgment of the standard stimulus is given in Table 2.l. In all, there were 4 ascending series (RO, LO, RO, LO) and four descending series (Rl, Ll, Rl, Ll). Thus, we have eight conditions. The means for R and L spaces and the means for O and I movements were worked out. The main aim of this experiment is to determine the discrepancy between the standard stimulus (arrow heads) (Ss) line and the average of the participant's judgments (Mj). This is the extent of illusion. This is the main constant error (Ec) of the experiment.

The formula to find out space error is: $\frac{Mr - M1}{2}$

Mr = Mean of the right space.

Ml = Mean of the left space.

The formula to find out the movement error is: $\frac{Mo - Mi}{2}$

Mo = Mean of the outward movement

Mi= Mean of the inward movement.

The formula to find out the constant error is : Mj – Ss = Ec

Mj = Mean of all the judgments

Ss = Standard stimulus

Ec = Constant error.

Table 2.1 : Showing the participant's judgment of the standard stimulus in space and movement conditions in the Muller-Lyer illusion experiment. Size of the standard stimulus is 160 mm.

Trial No.	RO mm	LI mm	LO mm	RI mm	LI mm	RO mm	RI mm	LO mm	Total Mean in mm
1									
2									
3									
4									
5									
6									
7									
8									
9									
10									
Total									
Mean									

Table 2.2 : Showing the means of judgments in the Muller-Lyer experiment for space and movement conditions and for the total.

	Condition				
	Space		Movement		Total
	R(mm)	L(mm)	O(mm)	I(mm)	mm
M					
O					
OM					

The experimenter can collect the group data from the whole class and the same can be given in Table 2.3. The group data should be the extent of illusion of the individual participants. The mean for the group can be worked out and the individual's, means may be compared with group mean.

Table 2.3 : Showing the extent of illusion for the group in the Muller-Lyer illusion experiment.

S.No.	Name	Extent of illusion
1.	M.V.	
2.	M.B.	
3.	A.S.	
4.	P.S.	
5.	R.K.	
6.	T.K.	
7.	C.B.	
8.	A.T.	
9.	G.G.	
10.	P.K.	
11.	P.V.	
12.	K.R.	

4. DISCUSSION

Discuss the results obtained in the Muller-Lyer illusion experiment. State the extent of illusion whether it is due to overestimation or underestimation. State whether the result is in accordance to the assumption of the experiment. The standard stimulus with its 'arrow heads' line should be underestimated in comparison with the variable stimulus ('feather heads'). Compare the space error with movement error and state which is greater and also state the reason. Is the constant is greater than the space error and movement error, if so, why? Explain. While performing the trials were there any variations in your participant's judgments trial to trial. State the possible reason for this. Was the extent of illusion in the ascending series varied from descending series in your participant's judgments? In the group data where your participant stands in the extent of illusion? Whose judgment was nearest to the standard stimulus and whose judgment farthest from the standard stimulus? Find out the reason. How many of them above group mean in the judgments? Compare your result with the results of previous studies. Compare the results on the basis of age, sex, physical deformities of the participants.

5. CONCLUSIONS

1. State whether your result is in relation to the assumption of the experiment.
2. State the level of judgment of your participant, whether he/she was nearer to the standard stimulus.
3. What is the extent of illusion of your participant?
4. What is the extent of illusion of the group?
5. Do individuals differ on the basis of age or sex or physical deformities?

3

PSYCHOPHYSICAL METHOD : Method of Minimal Changes - I

INTRODUCTION

The method of minimal changes is another psychophysical method as the end results are on physical values. This method is also known as the method of limits, method of serial exploration and the method of just noticeable differences. The method of minimal changes is used for two purposes, one is to determine the absolute limen and the other is to determine the difference limen. The assumption in this method is that a human observer can identify a just noticeable difference (JND) when he/she observes one such thing. Therefore, Weber made first the variable stimulus (Sv) equivalent to that of the standard stimulus (Ss) and then varied the variable stimulus in small steps either by increasing it or by decreasing it till the observer reports that he/she could see the difference (JND).

In this procedure of method of minimal changes adapted by Weber, a small change was suggested by Fechner. This is not only starting the variable from physical equality and then changing in small steps to physical inequality, but also from physical inequality to equality. Accordingly the variable stimulus (Sv) either it is definitely larger than the standard stimulus or smaller than the standard stimulus and then either variable stimulus is reduced in smaller steps or increased in smaller steps till the subject observes the two stimuli are equal. By this means this method brings out an idea or conception of just not noticeable differences (JNND). Guilford (1954) says that these two methods (JND, JNND) are yielding two different measures of difference limens. According to him the second method (JNND) always yielded a smaller limen than the first (JND). It is also true that both the methods do not yield the correct limen. But the correct limen lies in between these two limens. This was noticed by Muller and stated that the difference limen is an ideally calculated statistical value and not an observed value psychologically. Wundt had analysed this method in an important characteristic way. That is, the stimuli are presented to the observer in a serial order. By this process the observer comes to know the way in which the stimuli were arranged and could predict whether it is in the increasing order or in the decreasing order. Thereby the observer has a chance to relax his attention and when the limen is approached, his attention is also inereased to the maximum level. This procedure creates a favourable attitude on the subject in the experimental situation.

Constant Errors of Habituation and Expectation

It will not be possible for us to make psychological measurements very accurately. However, carefully experiments are conducted the measurement may vary from time to time and place to place. It mainly depends upon the observer's attitude and disposition. It is observed by some experimental psychologists that Wundtian procedure leads to the errors of habituation and expectation. In the case of error of habituation the observer is likely to give the same judgments for long time in any series. For example, in descending series he may start giving the judgment as greater, greater and greater and may continue to give the judgment as greater even if the limen is approached and the stimulus become smaller. However, we cancel out the error by obtaining the mean from the average of JNND and JND.

There is also another constant error in Wundtian procedure. It is called the error of expectation. Here the observer is alerted and his attention is greater. He is influenced by the suggestion given by the experimenter and develops strong expectation. Therefore, the observer may report a change in the stimulus. This tendency would make the measurement smaller than the stimulus. That is, the observer would say that change has occurred in the stimulus even though there was no change in the stimulus. He may report just noticeable difference (JND) both in the ascending series and descending series. But the series of ascending and descending would cancel out the constant error of expectation as in the case of habituation.

The Stimulus Error

This stimulus error is also interferring in the experimental situation. This has been pointed out by Titchener. This error is with regard to the presentation of the two stimuli as equal or unequal in the experimental situation. At the beginning of the series Ss and Sv are shown as equal to the observer but varied later on. In such situations the observer considers his two experiences with Ss and Sv as equal in the first case, and his two experiences with Ss and Sv are uneuqal in the second case. But if the observer did not know that the two experiences (Ss and Sv) are equal he would consider that the two experiences are unequal. If the observer knows that the two experiences are unequal he would consider that the two experiences are equal. This error can be avoided to some extent by changing the relationship between Ss and Sv haphazardly, that is not known to the observer.

A method has been suggested by Titchener to avoid this error by allowing the observer to continue the judgment till he reports a second change in the judgment. That is, by setting the variable stimuli definitely greater or smaller than the Ss and the experimenter continues the series even when O stops as smaller or greater. This method has been called the method with part knowledge.

It was Wundt in the year 1880 introduced the method of minimal changes. According to his method the stimuli were presented in serial order. The respondent also known the arrangement of the stimuli as to whether it is an increasing difference or decreasing difference. Taking the respondent to know the whole arrangements is the significant characteristics of Wundt's method. Since the respondent knows the specific change that is taking place, he relaxes his attention for few seconds and increases his attention to the maximum level as the point of limen is reaching. By this means the respondent need not pay maximum attention for every stimulus presented, but he becomes alert as the limen is approached. The respondent knows when the increasing and decreasing series start and when the series starts with equality. Similarly, the experimenter also knows the physical equality. This method is called method of complete knowledge.

EXPERIMENT-2: Determination of Absolute Limen by the Method Minimal Changes

Problem : The purpose of the present experiment is to determine the absolute limen or threshold using the method of minimal changes. The specific problem of this experiment is to determine the distance necessary to see the two lines separated by 1/3 of a millimeter as two lines.

2. METHOD

(a) Participant : Find out a subject who has no knowledge of the purpose of this experiment for the individual data. State the participant's age, sex, class etc. State whether he is using eye glass. For the group data collect data from other experiments.

(b) Apparatus : A circular disc having two black lines of the same length

and the same dimension drawn with 1/3 of a millimetre apart, a metre scale, chin rest, chalk piecer (Appendix-A).

Description of the Apparatus : The circular disc is fixed to a stand. The disc is covered with a white paper of the same size, so that the participant should not see the lines in the disc before starting the experiment. There are two black lines in the disc having the length of two centimetres. The thickness of the line is 1/3 of a millimetre. There is white interspace of 1/3 of a millimetre between the two lines. This type of material is also used in the visual acuity tests. The two black lines are drawn in a circular disc of 10 cm diameter.

(c) Procedure : The experimenter should make the required arrangements for the experiment. A room with sufficient amount of illumination should be chosen. Since the stimulus disc is varied in distance the experimenter should measure the distance and make marks of the places on the ground with a chalk piece where it is to be moved step by step. The observer should be seated comfortably and his head should be rested in a chin rest without any inconveniences. The experimenter himself should test this condition first. Care should be taken to see that there is no distracting force or interference in the situation. The disc that is fixed to the stand, should be kept in front of the observer 180 cm away. It should be in line with the observer's eyes. Before starting the experiment the experimenter should point out to the observer where the (stimulus) disc will appear.

The stimulus card (disc) should be kept in a fixed position first. Then the stimulus (disc) should be presented to the observer through a series of trials in which the distance between the subject and the stimulus should be varied in small steps of 20 cm. Both ascending and descending series should be used. The ascending series should be started with a stimulus well below the threshold at 60 cm. Increase its magnitude (distance) in small steps of 20 cm in successive trials until the subject could observe and report the two lines as one.

In descending series, start with a stimulus well above the threshold at 300 cm and decrease the distance between the subject and the stimulus in small steps in successive trials until the subject could observe and report the two lines as two lines.

Several trials of ascending and descending series should be used for the determination of the threshold. The ascending and descending series should be alternated according to a pre-arranged sequence (i.e. with varying distance) to avoid the constant errors of habituation and expectation. The length of the series should be varied in each time. There should be ten ascending series and ten descending series. It should be carefully observed that the white cover paper of the stimulus card (disc) should be removed only at the time of starting the experiment. It is better to have 11 ascending and 11 descending series.

The following instructions should be given to the participant. "Please see, a circular card is fixed to a stand. There are two verticle parallel black lines with a white interspace between them. I will be moving the stand in small steps and the distance will be increasing from the starting point in some trials and the distance will be decreasing in some trials from the starting point. Your task is to observe carefully the two lines and to report it. If you see *'two'* lines in the card say 'two'. If you see *'one'* line in the card say 'one'. Try to observe the card as carefully as possible. You will have to keep your chin in the chin rest and should not move your head to other sides till everything is over. Please make it a point to report what you could actually see in the disc and do not give assumed report."

3. RESULTS

N.B. : For the purpose of illustrating this experiment, some data obtained from an experiment conducted on an earlier occasion is used here. This experiment was conducted with a circular disc. The distance between the stimulus and the participant was taken as the determining factor of the participant's judgment of the stimulus variable, the black lines at the centre of the circular disc. The distance between the stimulus and the participant varied from 60 cm to 300 cm. The experimenter varied the stimulus by moving in small steps upward from 60 cm in the ascending series and moved the stimulus in small steps downward from 300 cm. Eleven ascending and 11 descending series were taken. On the whole there were 22 series. The distance was stepped by 20 cm. Thus, there were 13 steps and the middle position was at 180 cm, six above the mid-point and six below the mid-point. The mean distance in judging the two black lines was taken as the limen.

The responses of the participant are presented in Table 3.1. The sequence of the series are given in a counter balanced manner. The small changes in the distance was in centimetres. Two was written in the record sheet when the participant reported as two and one when he reported one. The series was stopped as soon as the participant reported change from two to one and from one to two. Limen was estimated for each series taking the mid-point between the two distances where the change was occurred.

Table 3.1 : Showing the entries of the judgments in the Experiment of the Method of Minimal Changes for determining the Stimulus Limen.

S. No.	Stimulus Values in cm	Types of series																									
		A	D	A	D	A	D	A	D	A	D	A	D	A	D	A	D	A	D	A	D	A	D	A	D	A	D
1	300		1		1		1		1		1		1		1		1		1		1		1		1		2
2	280		1		1		1		1		1		1		1		1		1		1		1		1		2
3	260		1		1		1		1		1		1		1		1		1		1		1		1		2
4	240		1		1		1		1		1		1		1		1		1		1		1		1		2
5	220	1	1	1	1	1	1		1		1	2	1		1		1		1		1		1		1		2
6	200	1	1	1	1	1	1	1	1	1	1	2	1	2	1		1		1	1	1		1		1		2
7	180	2	1	2	1	2	2	2	1	2	1	1	1	2	1	2	1	1	1	1	1	1	1	1	1	1	1
8	160	2	2	2	2	2	2	2	2	2	2	1	2	1	1	2	2	1	1	2	1	1	1	2	2	2	
9	140	2	2	2	2	2	2	2	2	2	2	1	2	1	2	1	2	2	2	2	2	2	2	2	2	2	
10	120	2		2		2		2		2		1		1		1		2	2	2	2	2	2	2		2	
11	100	2		2		2		2		2		1		1		1		2		2		2		2		2	
12	080	2		2		2		2		2		1		1		1		2		2		2		2		2	
13	060	2		2		2		2		2		1		1		1		2		2		2		2		2	
Limen in Distance		190	170	190	170	190	190	190	170	190	170	190	170	170	150	150	170	150	150	170	150	150	150	170	190	170	190

A refers to ascending series. The Experimenter increases the distance between the participant and the simulus in 20 centimetre every time.
D refers to descending series. The Experimenter decreases 20 centimetre between the participant and the stimulus every time.

Computation of Absolute Limen and the SDs and SEMs

The absolute limen or the stimulus limen is the average of the limens obtained from the 22 different series of both ascending and descending. The limens for ascending and descending series are obtained separatoly for the purpose of comparison between the two series. Further, the limen of the first ten series and the last ten series also are worked out separately. These four measures of limen and the limen for the all series are presented in Table 3.2. The standard deviation (SD) and the standard error of the mean for all the four series and for the whole data are also computed and presented in Table 3.2. The standard error of the mean is obtained by applying the formula :

$$\frac{\sigma}{\sqrt{N}}$$

Computation of the Mean Difference and the t Test

The mean difference between the ascending and descending series and the mean difference between the first ten series and the last ten series are presented in Table 3.2 below between the measures of ascending and descending series and between the first ten and last ten series. In the next step the standard error of the mean difference between the first ten and the last ten series are worked out by applying the formula $\sqrt{SEM_1^2+SEM_2^2}$ and presented just below the mean difference in Table 3.2. The 't' test is worked for the mean difference between the ascending and descending series and for the mean difference between the first ten and thc last tcn series and entered below the SEM Diff. of the respective measures.

Table 3.2 : Showing the mean, standard deviation, standard errors of the means the SEM Diff and the 't' test for different condition of the experiment.

Measures	All data (N—22)	Ascending series (N—11)	Descending series (N—11)	First 10 series (N—10)	Last 10 series (N—10)
Mean	171.36	178.18	164.54	182.00	156.00
SD (σ)	15.51	17.27	12.32	9.80	9.16
SEM (σ M)	3.31	5.21	3.71	2.95	2.90
Difference			13.64		26.00
SEM Diff			6.17		4.14
't' test			2.21		6.28
Level of sig.			P > 0.05		P > 0.01

For the ascending series the mean is little higher than the whole data 178.18, the SD is 17.27 and the SEM 5.21. The mean for the descending (164.54) lower than the ascending series. The SD is 12.32 and the SEM is 3.71. These two dispersion values are smaller compared to the ascending series. The mean score difference between the ascending and descending is 13.64 and the t test (2.21) shows that the difference between these two series is significant at 0.05 level.

The mean for the first ten series is 182.00 and the SD is 9.8 and the SEM is 3.10. The dispersion measures are considerably lower compared to the whole data and to the ascending and descending series. The last ten series is having the mean of 156.00 with the SD of 9.16 and with the SEM of 2.90. There is much difference in the mean score between the first ten and the last ten series (26.00) and the t value is 6.28 which is significant at 0.01 level. The mean limen is worked out and presented in the first column. It is 171.36 cm with a standard error of 3.31 and the SD is 15.51. If the group data is available from other experimenters they can be collected and presented in Table 3.3. The group data in Table 3.3 should be consisted of the limen for the whole series, the contant errors of expectation, habituation, the learning effect and also the fatigue effect. The group mean can be worked out. A bar diagram or a polygon graph can be drawn to the group data.

Table 3.3 : Showing the limen for whole series, the strength errors of the participants under different conditions of the experiment

			Mean difference					
S. No.	Name	Mean Limen	Ascend-ing	Descend-ing	Diff-erence	First 10 series	Last 10 series	Diff-erence
1	B.S.	171.36	178.18	164.54	13.64	182.00	156.00	26.00
2								
3								
4								
5								
6								
7								
8								
9								
10								
11								
12								
	Mean Limen							

4. DISCUSSION

The aim of this experiment is to determine the absolute or the stimulus limen by presenting a circular disc to a participant at different distances and asking him to judge whether he/she perceives one line or two lines in the disc. Since the two lines are having a small interspace between them to the size of 1/3 of millimetre, it is distance that could facilitate the perception. If the stimulus is at a smaller distance the person can see two lines and if the stimulus is moved far he/she can see only one line. At what distance the change in judgment takes place and this distance is supposed to be the absolute limen.

In this experiment according to the procedure the limen is determined in five conditions. One limen at ascending series, one at descending series, one at the first ten series, one at the last ten series and one for the whole series. These five limens vary considerably among them. The middle position in this experiment was 180 cm which is the standard. The limen of first ten series alone is little higher (182.00) than the standard. A11 other limens are smaller (170.36, 171.18, 164.54 and 156.00) than the standard. While examining the difference between the means for the ascending and descending series we can understand the effects of the serial order. The difference between these two series is 13.64, which is statistically significant at 0.05 level (Table 3.2). This indicated the strength of error of habituation since the mean of the ascending series is higher than the descending series. There are several sources of variation. The humans' perceptions of the physical world do not always correlate correctly with actual physical judgments. The participant's judgment of the stimulus values did not agree with the real physical value. There are several factors which are having influence in the judgments. Hence, the participant has committed the error of habituation. It is because the participant has been making the same report as 'one' a number of times continuously and he has made the same report even though the same report is no longer is applicable to report as one and he suddenly aware of it and reported as 'two' and thus made the error of habituation.

While examining the difference between the effects of learning and fatigue, the mean is higher for learning (182.00) than the fatigue (156.00). The difference between these two effects (first ten series and last ten series) is 26.00. This difference is statistically significant at 0.01 level since the learning effect is extremely higher than the fatigue effect. The dispersion values 9.8 and 9.16 of these measures show that there were not much deviation in the judgments. The more judgments the participant made the more difference between the learning and the fatigue effect has occurred. The mean of the learning effect is more close to the standard than the other four means, while the fatigue effect is found to be decreasing.

One of the reasons for the increase of the fatigue effect is that the stimulus needs very careful observation for making judgments as the interspace between two black lines is very small, 1/3 of a millimetre. It is because of this the participant's judgments as two and one ranged within 150 cm and 190 cm distance and as and when he made more judgments, the judgments nearing the last ten the distances were only 150 and 170 cm distance.

It is this effect that has made the limen to bring down to 171.36 for all data. Therefore, the sample is excess in favour of the errors in the judgments of the stimulus compared to the standard was smaller in ascending series and the errors in judgments were higher in descending series. It might be also due to the expectation of the participant that the line may appear to him at distance as one.

If the group data for this experiment are available individual's errors of habituation and the fatigue effect may be compared. The mean for all data may be used to compare the individual's stand in every series. In which series the mean is higher for the group and in which series it is lower, can be stated and discussed. How many of the participants have obtained higher mean than the group mean and how many have obtained lower than the group mean also may be stated and discussed. Critically analyse this method and state the advantages and disadvantages of it.

5. CONCLUSIONS

The mean stimulus or absolute limen as judged by the participant is 171.36 cm. The limen for ascending series is 178.18 cm and for the descending series is 164.54 cm. The limen for the first ten series is 182.00 cm for the last ten series is 156.00 cm. The mean difference between the ascending and descending series is significant at 0.05 level and the mean difference between the first ten and the last ten series is significant at 0.01 level. The participant has committed the error of habituation. The fatigue effect also was higher.

If the group data is available work out the mean. State on whose case the error of habituation is higher and in whose case it is lower. Also state the mean for the all data and also for the other four conditions.

Appendix - A

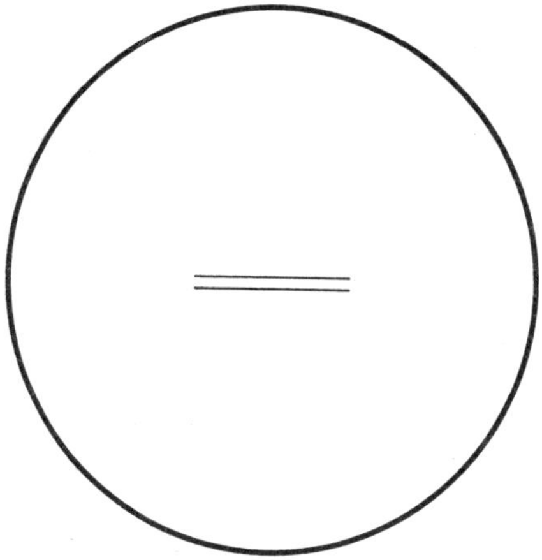

Appendix - B

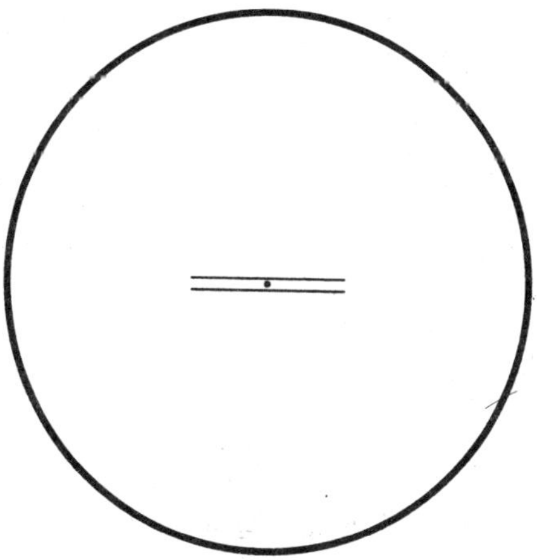

4

PSYCHOPHYSICAL METHOD : Method of Minimal Changes - II

INTRODUCTION

The earlier psychologists, till the last quarter of 19th century were studying the events of conscious experience and behaviour was the outcome of conscious experience for them. They were able to get only very little information from this. When Gustav Fechner invented psychophysics and psychophysical methods in 1860, psychologists started making use of Fechner's psychophysics and psychophysical methods for studying conscious experience. It was also observed that the conscious experience was the result of the sensation caused by a physical stimulus. Physical stimulus may be handled or manipulated in such a way that a person is made to respond or reach to it. A physical stimulus may be having varied intensities, from the lowest to the highest point. Therefore, a physical stimulus may produce a reliable experience or sensation which can be assessed by suitable methods. This was the state of starting point of experimental psychology and enormous amount of enquiries were made following Fechner's psychophysics and psychophysical methods.

The fundamental basis on which psychophysics developed, was, to evolve a general law that can work between the qualities of physical stimulus and the sensory experience. There were several methods invented to test the general psychophysical law. But the methods invented by Fechner alone remained in the field. The three psychophysical methods which Fechner had put into use were, the method of average error, the method of minimal changes and the method of constant stimuli. All these three methods were used for two purposes. One purpose was, whether a physical stimulus that can arouse response or reaction in an organism can be assessed reliably. Or, whether a person can state the presence or absence of the conscious experience, the sensation when a physical stimulus of certain intensity was manipulated on him. The second purpose was, when two stimuli of equal intensity were presented to an individual, can he judge and state whether they are equal or different in magnitude, or whether one can differentiate two similar sensations experienced.

The psychophysical methods were used for estimating these two aspects, the magnitude of the stimulus and also the sensation. One of the methods, the method of minimal changes is widely used in the experimental psychology for estimating the absolute limen and the difference limen. This method is easy for the experimenter to conduct experiments and also for the responded to make judgments and report. This method is also called the method of limits, method of serial explorations and the method of just noticeable differences.

This method is named after the procedure adapted in conducting the experiment. The variable stimulus is moved in small steps in the procedure in both ascending series and descending series. Further, the movement of the variable stimulus is very much limited. As such it is called method of limit. The difference between the standard stimulus and the variable stimulus is only just noticeable difference. Since the difference limen is obtained by presenting the variable stimulus serially and the respondent also makes judgments serially for every presentation, it is also called method of serial exploration.

Differential Limen

The psychophysical method of minimal changes is used here for determining difference limen (DL). The operation of this method is little different from the method we have stated in the earlier experiment. In the determination of difference limen the two stimuli, one the standard or constant stimulus and the other, the variable stimulus are presented to the observer at the same time.

The absolute limen is a measure of absolute sensitivity, but the difference limen is a measure of differential sensitivity of the observer. The differential sensitivity is the sensory ability of the observer to discriminate the differences between the two stimuli presented simultaneously. The differential limen, therefore, refers to the smallest stimulus difference that can be perceived between the two stimuli fifty percent of the time. It is the minimum difference possibly perceived between the stimuli on a quantitative variable or qualitative variable, that is detectable. Generally, all psychophysical methods originally were developed as the methods for determining thresholds.

The difference limen, therefore, may be defined as the smallest stimulus difference that is observed fifty percent of the time. It is stated as fifty percent from the theoretical point of view, but from the operational point of view it is 75 percent of the time or more than 50 percent of the time. The word limen is a German word, the meaning of which is threshold. It is the limit below which a given stimulus cases to be perceptible. Threshold or limen is a statistical average even in the case of an individual person.

The experimenter, in the determination of difference limen, first presents a standard or constant stimulus and a comparative stimulus simultaneously. Here the observer has to say whether the magnitude of the sensation aroused by the comparative (variable) stimulus is greater than or lesser than or equal to the sensation aroused by the constant stimulus. It is possible that the same constant errors of habituation and anticipation that we discussed in the earlier experiments may occur in the determination of different limen.

EXPERIMENT 3: Determination of Different Limen for Visual Space by the Method of Minimal Changes.

Problem : The purpose of this experiment is to determine the difference limen (DL) for visual space making use of the method of minimal changes and also for determining the Weber's ratio.

2. METHOD

Participant : Choose a person who has no knowledge of the purpose of this experiment for the individual data. State the person's age, gender, qualification etc., state whether he is wearing eye glass etc. For the group data collect data from other experimenters.

Apparatus : Aubert Diaphragm, chin rest, metre scale.

Description of the Apparatus : The Aubert Diaphragm is an apparatus used to present a variable stimulus in the psychophysical experiments. It is designed by Aubert and named after him. A black square metal sheet of 1½' x 1½' in size is fixed to a rectangular stand. At the centre of the metal sheet there is a square apperture of 4" x 4" in size. Close to the black sheet a white metal sheet with black background is attached from behind to the stand. The white sheet is visible at the 4" x 4" apperture at the centre of the black sheet. The area of the white sheet can be increased and decreased by turning the knob that is fixed at the centre of the lower frame of the stand. The knob can be turned clock-wise and anti-clockwise directions. At the back of the board on the left frame there is a pointer and a linear scale. The pointer indicates on a linear scale the size of the variable square. A standard stimulus is another separate instrument used along with the Aubert Diaphragm in the experiment. It is a square white metal sheet of 4" x 4" in size with black background mounted on a stand. The variable stimulus is to be placed both on the right and left sides of the standard stimulus.

Procedure : The experiment is to be conducted in a properly lighted room. The participant should be made to sit comfortably in front of the Aubert Diaphragm board at a distance of 8' (with the help of a metre scale, the experimenter should measure the distance and seat the participant). This distance should be maintained as constant for all the observations. The participant's chin should be rested properly on the chin rest. The variable stimulus should be placed by the side of the standard stimulus in such a way that the two white squares in both stimuli should appear at the same height from the point of view of the participant.

In half of the observations the variable stimulus should be kept on the right of the standard and in another half it should be on the left of the standard.

In half of the observations, the variable stimulus should be infinitely larger than the standard and it should be gradually reduced by 1/10 of an inch on the linear scale by turning the knob. This procedure is called the descending order.

In the other half of the trials the variable stimulus should be infinitely smaller than the standard and it should be gradually increased by 1/10 of an inch on the scale by turning the knob. This procedure is called ascending order. The starting point under all conditions should be randomized from trial to trial. The experimenter should prepare a response sheet (Table 4.1) and keep ready to enter the responses of the participant.

The following instructions should be given to the participant: "Please see that there are two white squares in front of you. The size of one square is fixed and the other can be varied. The size of the white square on the larger board (pointing out the board) can be changed by manipulating the knob, whereas, the white square on the smaller stand is constant. I shall be changing it in smaller steps. The size of the white square will be increasing in some trials. Therefore, your task is to observe the two squares carefully every time and report how the white square in the larger board appears to you in comparison with the white square in the smaller board. If it appears larger say 'larger', if it is equal, say 'equal' or if it is smaller, say 'smaller'. Try to be as careful as possible and make accurate judgments."

The reports of the participant should be entered in Table 4.1. In every trial the manipulation of the knob should be terminated when the participant reports the judgment of inequality either by saying larger or smaller. A plus (+) mark should be entered in for every report as larger, an equal (=) mark for every report as equal and a minus (—) mark for every report as smaller. The participant can be dispensed with as soon as all the trials are over.

3. RESULTS

N.B. : The results presented here are obtained from an experiment conducted on an earlier occasion. They are given here and discussed as a model.

The judgments reported by the participant are summarised in Table 4.1. In each series of judgments there is an upper limit at the transition from the larger to equal judgments and a lower limit at the transition from the equal judgments to the smaller judgments. This range of equality of judgment covered a span of 2 difference limen (DL). That is, from the point of subjective equality, one DL higher and one DL lower. The aim of this experiment is to determine the difference limen by using the Aubert Diaphragm.

Computation of the Differential Limen

In the experimental procedure we assume that each observation supposed to provide an estimation of the differential limen (DL). The experimental procedure also yields the determination of interval of uncertainty (IU). The interval of uncertainty is the area between the upper limens and the lower limens. If an experimenter uses only two responses in the experimental procedure then, there is no IU. But when three responses are allowed an area appears and this area is known as the interval of uncertainty. The range of judgments of equality of IU covers a span of two DLS. That is, one DL higher from the PSE and one DL lower from the PSE. Therefore, one half of the interval (IU) is taken as the DL. Hence 2 DLS are estimated for each occasion. The IU is calculated by substracting the mean of the T-values from the mean of T+ values. The DL is determined by using the formula .5(IU) or by dividing the (IU) difference by 2. Thus we have :

The mean of T+ = $\overline{X}$ T+ = 4.08125

The mean of T− = $\overline{X}$ T− = 3.94375

The IU is ($\overline{X}$ T+) − ($\overline{X}$ T−) = 0.1375

The DL = .5(IU) or $\frac{IU}{2} = \frac{0.1375}{2} = 0.06875$

The differential limen in this experiment is 0.06875 and the same is presented in Table 4.2.

Model

Table 4.1 : Showing the observations made by the participant to determine the Difference Limen in the Method of Minimal Changes.

Order / S / Values	1	2	3	4	5	6	7	8	9	10	11	12	13	14	15	16	M
	VR	VR	VR	VR	VL	VL	VL	VL	VL	VL	VL	VL	VR	VR	VR	VR	
	d	a	d	a	a	d	a	d	d	a	d	a	a	d	a	d	
4.6	+					+								+			
4.5	+		+			+			+					+		+	
4.4	+		+			+		+	+		+			+		+	
4.3	+		+			+			+		+			+		+	
4.2	=	+	+	+		=	+	+	+		+			=		=	
4.1	=	+	+	+	+	=	=	=	+	+	=	+	+	=	+	—	
4.0	—	=	=	=	+	—	—	—	=	+	=	+	+	—	+	—	
3.9	—	—	=	—	=	—	—	—	=	=	—	+	+	—	=	—	
3.8	—	—	—	—	—	—	—	—	—	—	—	=	=	—	—		
3.7	—	—	—	—	—	—	—	—	—	—	—	—	—		—		
3.6		—		—	—		—			—		—	—		—		
3.5		—		—						—		—			—		
3.4		—		—											—		
T +	4.25	4.05	4.05	4.05	3.95	4.25	4.15	4.15	4.05	3.95	4.15	3.85	3.95	4.25	3.95	4.25	4.08125
T –	4.15	3.95	3.85	3.95	3.85	4.05	4.05	4.05	3.85	3.85	3.95	3.75	3.75	4.05	3.85	4.15	3.94375
PSE	4.20	4.00	3.95	4.00	3.90	4.15	4.10	4.10	3.95	3.90	4.05	3.80	3.85	4.15	3.90	4.20	4.0125

VR = Variable stimulus on the right. VL = Variable stimulus on the left. T + = Threshold above the standard. T – = Threshold below the standard.

Computation of Point of Subjective Equality (PSE)

The point of subjective equality is the central tendency of the judgments made by the respondent. This is often computed when we want to work out the limens. The PSE may be computed in all three psychophysical methods as this is the mid-value of the judgment between the two limits. The point of subjective equality is determined by adding the means of the T+ values and the means of the T–values and dividing it by two. This yields an average of the place where the T+ and the T– change to equality. This difference between the PSE and the standard stimulus is considered as the constant error (CE). Since the PSE may be extended on either side of the standard, the CE may be either positive or negative. If the CE is positive the respondent has overestimated the quality of the comparative stimulus and if negative he has underestimated the comparative stimulus.

The point of subjective equality (PSE) is determined by working out the average of the two means of the judgments. The two means of the judgments are $\overline{X}$ T+ and $\overline{X}$ T–. The formula for determining the PSE is :

$$\frac{(\overline{X}\,T+)+(\overline{X}\,T-)}{2}$$

Applying the formula to the data : $\dfrac{4.08125+3.94375}{2} = 4.0125$

the PSE 4.0125 is obtained and presented in Table 4.2.

Table 4.2 : Showing the summary of the individual's judgments in the experiment of the determination of the Difference limen by the method of minimal changes

Participant	DL	PSE	CE	Weber's Ratio	Fechner's law
PK	0.06875	4.0125	0.0125	0.01734	4.0119

Determination of Constant Error

In the method of minimal changes there is every possibility of the occurrence of the constant errors of habituation and anticipation.In the ascending and descending series these errors may occur. But Wundt was of the view that the errors of habituation occurring in ascending series are cancelled out by the descending series. The respondent, however, is careful in his observation and judgment, there is a tendency in him to give the same judgment every time and his sudden awareness may change the judgment. The just not noticeable difference (JNND) might have been quite close to the level of equality, but the respondent might have failed to notice it and reported as before without change. When the respondent was waiting for the just noticeable difference (JND), on becoming aware of it, it would be more than just noticeable difference. Thus, the constant errors of habituation occur. Similarly, in the case of descending series the respondent gets ready and judges it even before the equality occurs. Thus, the constant error is determined by the formula: CE = PSE – St. Applying the formula to the data we get the CE = 4.0125 – 4.000 = 0.0125 (Table 4.2).

Determination of Weber's Ratio

In the determination of Weber's ratio the two values required are the difference limen (DL) and the point of subjective equality (PSE). These two values are already determined. The Weber's law states that the just noticeable increment in a stimulus is proportional to the standard stimulus. In other words, it is also stated that the small equally perceptible increments in the R correspond to the proportional increments in S. If a change is to occur in R (response) the S (stimulus) must be changed in certain ratio. Therefore, the equation of Weber's law is $\Delta S = KS$. Where Δ is an increment in S, K is the constant and S is the stimulus. The common form of the law is :

$$\frac{\Delta S}{S} = K \quad \text{(Delta S by S is equal to K)}$$

The K is constant and it is called Weber's ratio. According to Weber, K is constant to any kind of sensory response. Weber's experiments were conducted by the method of the first noticeable difference (JND).

Therefore, an operational statement of this finding is that the DL is a constant fraction of the stimulus.

In this experiment for the determination of Weber's ratio, we require two values, the DL and the PSE. The DL is used as a numerator and the PSE is used as a denominator. The ratio here is computed with these values. The formula is :

$$\frac{DL}{PSE}$$

Thus, we get the value : $\frac{DL}{PSE} = \frac{0.06875}{4.0125} = 0.01734$ (Table 4.2).

Verification of Fechner's Law

Fechner has accepted Weber's law and expanded it and formulated the psychophysical law. Fechner's law is an improvement over Weber's law.

Fechner has observed that the relationship between the standard stimulus and the DL is not a constant ratio as the function is not linear and also it is not applicable to all sensations. Fechner has noticed in his experiments that different sensations require different ratio of DL. Therefore Fechner evolved a formula involving the logarithm. The formula is: S = K log R, where S is the sensation experienced by the respondent from the stimulus (Psychological value), R is the stimulus value and K is the constant value. According to Fechner the strength of the sensation of the respondent to the stimulus varies as a function of the logarithm of the stimulus. This is the general law of Fechner. In this experiment the formula to verify the Frechner's law is $\sqrt{\overline{X}T+)\ (\overline{X}T-)} = \sqrt{4.08125 \times 3.94375} = 4.0119$. The obtained value is presented in Table 4.2.

Table 4.3 : Showing the Means, standard deviations, the standard errors of the means and the t ratio under different conditions and also for the whole data in method of minimal changes for determining the difference limen

Measures	Series order		Space arrangement		All data
	Ascending	Descending	VR	VL	
Mean	3.931	4.094	4.031	3.393	4.0125
SD	0.089	0.946	0.127	0.326	0.1215
SEM	0.318	0.016	0.045	0.115	0.0304
t ratio	4.556		.3055		

Since the series order and the space arrangements seem to be giving different judgments, it is tried to see in the treatment of the results whether these conditions have any influence in the means. Therefore the means, standard deviations, standard errors of the means and also the t ratios are also worked out. The conditions are, the ascending and descending series, and the variable on the right and on the left of the standard stimulus. The means between the ascending and descending series should differ. The t value is found to be (4.556) highly significant at one percent level ($P < .01$). The difference in the case of descending (4.094 – 4.00 = .094) is found to be higher than the ascending (4.00 – 3.931 = .069) series. This shows that the error of anticipation is higher than the error of habituation in this experiment (Table 4.3).

In the condition of space arrangements the mean is found to be higher (4.031) than the standard stimulus (4.00) when the variable stimulus was on the right, whereas the mean is lower (3.993) than the standard stimulus (4.00) when the variable stimulus was on the left. But the difference is greater (4.031 – 4.00 = .069) when the variable stimulus was on the right.

Whereas the difference is very small (4.00 –3.993 = .007) when the variable stimulus was on the left. The mean difference between these two conditions (4.031 –3.993 = .037) is very small and it is not significant. Unlike the series order the space arrangements seem to have yielded better judgments (Table 4.3).

If the group data are available from other experimenters they may be entered in Table 4.4. The mean for all the values may be worked out and the data may be discussed comparatively with special reference to the DL, PSE and CE and in the case of the series order and space arrangements. Every individual may be compared with the group mean.

4. DISCUSSION

The main purpose of this experiment is to determine the differential linear (DL) by the method of minimal changes by using the instrument called Aubert Diaphragm. In the process of determining the differential limen it becomes necessary to determine various other values like the point of subjective equality (PSE), the interval of uncertainty (IU), the constant error (CE), determination of Weber's ratio and verification of Fechner's law.

Table 4.4 : Showing the DL, PSE, CE, Weber's Ratio and Fechner's Law from the Group data in the Method of Minimal Changes Experiment

S.No.	Name	DL	PSE	CE	Weber's Ratio	Fechner's Law
1	P.K.	0.06875	4.0125	0.0125	0.01734	4.0119
2	M.S.					
3	R.K.					
4.	P.V.					
5.	B.M.					
6.	S.V.					
7.	M.R.					
8.	K.R.					
9.	N.B.					
10.	S.K.					
11.	T.V.					
12.	U.K.					
	Mean					

The variable stimulus was placed on the right of the standard stimulus fifty percent of the time and on the left fifty percent of the time for eliminating the space error. Similarly, the descending and ascending series were carried out alternatively to equalize the constant errors of habituation and anticipation. It is because of these procedures the upper mean 4.08125 is very close to the standard stimulus 4.00 with a difference of .08125. The lower mean 3.94375 also is very close to the standard with difference of 0.05635. The PSE is 4.0125 with a very small difference of 0.0125 from the standard stimulus.

The difference limen is determined as 0.0685 for a stimulus of 4.00 inches square. The respondent was able to judge the difference on the variable stimulus even if there was a change of 0.0685 of an inch. The small DL is the indication that the respondent has made his judgments more accurately the variable stimuli in comparison with the standard stimulus. The lower DL (3.84375) is found to be having smaller difference with the standard stimulus (.05625) than the upper DL (4.08125) which is having the difference of .08125 with the standard stimulus.

The PSE (4.0125) is having very small negligible difference of .0125 with the standard stimulus. This again confirm the conclusion made earlier with regard to the accuracy of judgment of the variable stimulus by the respondent. The constant error is determined as .0125 which is very small in an experiment of this type.

The constant error (.0125) is the difference between the point of subjective equality and the standard stimulus (4.0125 — 4.00) occurred in ascending and descending series. The Weber's ratio $\frac{\Delta S}{S} = K$ is also determined in this experiment. This is found to be 0.01734. The Frechner's law is applied to the data and it is found to be 4.0119.

Generally, the judgments in different conditions vary. Some may have significant difference due to the constant errors and in some cases the difference may not be significant. In this experiment the means of ascending and descending series are compared and the t test is applied. It is observed that the means of these two series differ significantly at 0.01 level since the t value 4.556 is high. The mean (3.93) of the ascending series is lower than the standard stimulus (4.00). But the mean of the ascending series (4.094) is higher than the standard stimulus. The mean difference of 0.163 yield at ratio of 4.556 which is highly significant.

The mean difference between the two space arrangements also is tested to see whether the space differences have any effect in the means. It is observed that the mean of the variable on the right (VR) (4.031) is found to be higher than the standard stimulus (4.00), while the mean of the variable on the left (VL) (3.393) is found to be lower than the standard stimulus. The difference between these two means is very small (0. —38) and hence the t value (.3055) is not significant at any level. Therefore, the space arrangement did not cause much difference in the means of the two spaces. The space arrangement in this experiment is found much better than the series order.

If the group data were obtained from other experimenters, they may be discussed relating the group mean with every other participants. The highest and the lowest DLs may be stated and who has obtained these DLs. How many of the DLs are above the group mean and how many are below the group mean? If reasons are available they may be stated. State whether the gender and age had any influencing effect in the determination of the DL.

Similarly, state whether there is any difference between the group mean and the individual means in the case of PSE and the CE. State the highest and the lowest PSE and the CE and who has obtained these. State whether there is any specific reason for such results.

Mention the group mean for Weber's ratio and Frechner's law and state whether there is any deviation from the group mean, if so, how much. Whether the deviations are tolerable. On the whole in the group, whose data, i.e. the DL, PSE and the CE are consistant and reliable and whose data are not reliable.

5. CONCLUSIONS

The DL of the participant P.K. is .06875, PSE is 4.0125, and the CE is 0.0125. The Weber's ratio is 0.01731, and the Fechner's is 4.0119. The judgments of this participant as far as possible are accurate and reliable. The constant errors of habituation and the anticipation is found to be higher in the case of series order than that of the space arrangements.

From the group data, state the highest and the lowest DLs and the CEs and who are those obtained such results. State how many DLs and CEs are above the group mean and how many below the group mean.

5

PSYCHOPHYSICAL METHOD : Method of Constant Stimuli-I

ABSOLUTE LIMEN : AN INTRODUCTION

The method of constant stimuli is one of the psychophysical techniques used for the determination of various sensory thresholds. The method is also called constant stimulus differences and the method of right and wrong cases. This method is mostly applied to determine the absolute limen (AL) and difference limen (DL) and also for other purposes like determination of equal sense distances, equivalent stimuli and for the determination of psychological constants. This method differs from other psychophysical method, the method of limits. In the method of limits the stimuli are presented in the serial order, but in this method the stimuli are presented in a random order, by which the errors of habituation and the errors of anticipation can be eliminated.

In applying this method any sensory stimulus may be chosen for the determination of absolute limen. It may be with regard to touch or pain causing stimulus or sensation of pricking pain, any auditory stimulus with varying intensities, or lifted weights or even any visual stimulus. If it is a painful stimulus, it should be the pricking pain and it should be perceptible by the person who serves as a subject. It may be also causing a sensation of touch by sharp ends. Thus, the stimulus may be causing varying sensations like 'one touch' or 'two touches' which the person should be able to feel and identify it. Therefore, the first step in applying the method of constant stimuli is, choosing a stimulus of a specific sensory area and the number of stimuli. Normally, the number of stimuli should be in odd numbers, like five, seven, nine or it may be from five to nine. The stimuli should be presented in such a way that it should be perceived as nil or zero at the lowest level and at the highest level the stimulus should be perceived all the times or 100 percent.

In the method of constant stimuli the same stimulus is presented to the respondent a large number of times. Generally, in this method it is 100 times, in some cases it is 50 times and the responses are obtained from the respondent. The type of response expected is whether the stimulus has aroused the appropriate sensation in each trial or not. In every trial the stimulus presented to the respondent is determined randomly. Every stimulus is presented equal number of times. The procedure is adapted with the aim that each stimulus should elicit the appropriate sensation 50 percent of the time. This is the value of the absolute limen (AL) or threshold. According to this procedure, an absolute or threshold should elicit the appropriate response in a person 50 percent of the time. Therefore, an absolute limen may be defined as the minimum amount physical energy or stimulus which can arouse a response or sensation in an organism in a perceptible manner.

In the case of sound, the lowest intensity which a tonal stimulus can arouse an auditory sensation in an organism may be stated as the auditory threshold or limen. The concepts limen and threshold refer to the same physical energy that can arouse a response or sensation in an organism to the extent of making the organism to be aware of it.

The Linear Interpolation Procedure

In the psychophysical methods,various procedures are employed in determining the absolute limen or threshold. We shall discuss some four procedures and explain how through which the absolute limen is determined. The absolute limen in the linear interpolation procedure is calculated from the responses obtained from the respondent in an experimental situation. The linear interpolation procedure is very much useful in estimating the median or absolute limen. The simplest procedure of determining the absolute limen is the use of linear interpolation between two proportions, one above the limen and the other below the limen. The absolute limen may be also determined by the graphic interpolation method by plotting the cumulative frequencies and the stimulus values in a graph. The general formula for determining the absolute limen by this method is :

$$L = S_s + \frac{(S_g - S_s)(.5 - P_s)}{p_g - p_s}$$

where L = the limen or threshold

S_s = Stimulus value immediately smaller than the limen

S_g = Stimulus value immediately greater than the limen

p_g = Proportions of the judgment as two immediately greater than the stimulus

p_s = Proportions of judgments as two immediately smaller than the stimulus

The limen lies at p —.5

By placing the experimental data in the respective cells the absolute limen can be calculated. The method of linear interpolation has one disadvantage in determining the absolute limen. This method does not make use of all the data of the experiment in determining the absolute limen. It uses only two proportion values, one above the limen and one below the limen obtained in the experiment. But the method is simple and easy to work out the limen.

Spearman's Procedure of Arithmetic Mean

This procedure also is very simple which can be used for the determination of absolute limen. This procedure was designed by Spearman (1908) for estimating the absolute limen. He named it as the method of right and wrong cases and the absolute limen can be determined without the Gauss' formula. It is assumed that every time when the stimulus is applied in the experiment the value of the limen is judged either above the limen or below the limen. For example, if the stimulus value is 10 mm and if the respondent reported as two, then the limen falls below the stimulus value 10 mm. But, if respondent reported the stimulus value as one, then the limen falls above the stimulus value 10 mm.

Though this method is simple and easy in the experimental situation, one problem involved in this method is that sometimes errors are likely to occur in the judgments. Few of the judgments are more likely to fall below the last stimulus value. In such cases the Sheppard's correction can be applied assuming that there are some tail responses occurred in the experiment. But it is not advisable to depend upon always on the Shappard's correction since the limen rarely may fall below or above the last stimulus values. For example, if we use 7 stimulus values, we may assume that the limen may fall on the middle stimulus value 9, and we can see that there are three stimulus values on either side of the middle value 9, such as 6, 7, and 8 on one side and 10, 11, and 12 on the other side. There is no chance to issue here that the limen may fall above the stimulus value 12 or below the stimulus value 6. Therefore, the assumption may be applied only in relevant cases and not in all cases.

Woodworth's Summation Procedure

The summation procedure was formulated by Woodworth (1938) for estimating the absolute limen. Therefore, this procedure can be applied to the data obtained by the method of constant stimuli for the determination of absolute limen. According to this procedure there are two equations for computing the mean or absolute limen. In the summation procedure we utilize the successive cumulative frequencies. The application of the procedure is based upon the general procedure. This procedure is best applied when the range of the stimuli is highly wider enough so as to produce the end proportions as 0.0 and 1.00. By this arrangement, therefore, we may take it for granted that the ends are 0.0 and 1.00. The summation procedure, thus is quite suitable for computing the mean or absolute limen from the data obtained in two point threshold experiment. The equation for computing the mean or the absolute limen is :

$$M = S_g - .5i - i\Sigma p$$ (i) Where the proportion of the stimulus judgment value is 1.00

$$M = S_0 + .5i + i\Sigma q$$ (ii) Where the proportion of the stimulus judgment value is 0.00

According to these two equations whether the proportions of the stimulus value is 1.00 and 0.00 or not, we will have to assume like that.

The i = refers to the size of the stimulus interval. This may be 1 mm.
The p = is the proportions of the judgments as two.
The q = is, 1 — p.

The experimenter can apply these equations for determining the absolute limen (AL) in the psychophysical method of constant stimuli. The Woodworth's Summation method also includes two equations for determining the standard deviation (σ) of the data.

The equations are :

$$SD(\sigma) = i\sqrt{2\Sigma cp - (p)^2 - \Sigma p}$$ (i) Where the proportions of the stimulus value is 1.00

$$SD(\sigma) = i\sqrt{2\Sigma cp - (q)^2 - \Sigma q}$$ (ii) Where the proportions of the stimulus value is 0.00

where i = is the size of the stimulus interval
p = is the proportions of the judgments as two
q = is 1−p
cp = is the cumulated proportion value from low to high of p value
cq = is the cumulated proportion of q from top (low) to bottom (high).

Newhall's Normal Interpolation Procedure

This is another procedure applied for determining the absolute limen (AL) in the method of constant stimuli. It was Newhall (1928) who first proposed this procedure in connection with calculating the threshold or limen. This procedure is supposed to be an improvement over the linear interpolation procedure. The hypothetical view is that a cumulative normal curve can be evolved in the psychometric function by relating the p to S. For this the important process involved in this is the transformation of the p values into corresponding standard measure values or deviate values. This transformed value is indicated by the letter z. Therefore, it is assumed that the relationship of z to S should be always linear. The absolute limen according to Newhall's interpolation procedure is that the S value and the corresponding z value should be always zero (0). The z value or the deviate value ranges from — 1.00 through zero (0) to + 1.00. These values S and z can be obtained by the interpolation process. This value falls in between the two stimulus values which are on either side of the zero, one value is having the plus (on the right) and the other value is having minus value (on the left). The formula of the normal interpolation procedure is having two equations. They are :

$$L = S_s + \left(\frac{-Z_s}{Z_g - Z_s}\right) i \qquad \text{(i)}$$

$$L = S_g - \left(\frac{Z_g}{Z_g - Z_s}\right) i \qquad \text{(ii)}$$

where L = Absolute limen or threshold

S_s = Stimulus value smaller than the limen

S_g = Stimulus value greater than the limen

Z_s = Standard measure or deviate value of S_s

Z_g = Standard measure or deviate value of S_g

i = Interval between two stimuli.

EXPERIMENT-4 : Determination of Absolute Limen (AL) by the Method of Constant Stimuli

The Problem : In our everyday life we are having experiences of estimating certain material quantities without actual measurement. We may estimate them either with less quantity (weight) or with more quantity (weight). But when we actually weigh it in a weighing machine we may come to know whether our estimation is correct or not correct. Similarly, in the case of judging the length of a piece of cloth, a piece of rod, or distance between two places, or judging the intensity of sound, or hot or cold temperature, or judging the nature of sensation on the skin and so on are the instances we come across in our life either for our personal matters or in matters of others. In psychophysical experiments also we conduct experiments on some persons and study whether they are capable of judging or estimating the strength of certain stimulus. In psychophysical method, the method of constant stimuli is often applied for estimating the strength of a stimulus and also for estimating a stimulus threshold that can arouse a response in an organism or in a person.

Aim : The aim of this experiment is to determine the absolute limen (AL) by the method of constant stimuli.

2. METHOD

Respondent : Choose a person who has no knowledge of the purpose of this experiment and collect the personal information about the person such as age, gender, qualification, occupation, monthly income and so on. Also find out whether the person has any physical defects like hard of hearing, eye defect or wearing eye glass or any skin disease, etc.

Apparatus

The instrument required for this experiment is the Aesthesiometer and blind goggles.

Description of the Apparatus : There are several types of aesthesiometer. It is better to choose the vernier type of instrument which can be easily adjusted to millimetres. This aesthesiometer consists of two sharp ended needles of adjustable type. One sharp needle can be moved forward and backward and the distance between them can be varied as desired by the experimenter.

The blind goggles is a blind fold of spectacle type. The respondent should wear it at the time of conducting the experiment. On wearing this the person cannot see anything outside.

Procedure

The experimenter should make the respondent to be seated

comfortably in a well illuminated room where there is no disturbance of any type. Then the respondent should be blind folded with the goggles. One important matter the experimenter should bear in mind is that the respondent should not be aware of the instrument, the aesthesiometer. It should not be seen by the respondent at any cost. Then, the area should be selected on the palmer side of the fore- arm of the respondent. The area should be marked with pen into one inch square. Thus, having selected the area on the skin on which the limen or the absolute threshold is to be determined, the experimenter should give some preliminary trials with the aesthesiometer to determine roughly the transition zone within which the absolute threshold or the limen lies. While conducting the trial touches, the judgment should be always two touches.

In the method of constant stimuli the selection of the number of stimuli is an important aspect. The number of stimuli should be in odd numbers like, 5, 7, 9, 11, and so on. In selecting these stimuli, trials should be conducted. It is to be noted that the smallest stimulus value should arouse 5 percent of two touches and the greatest stimulus value should arouse 95 percent of two touches. The middle stimulus value should be close to the absolute limen or threshold. After conducting the trials with the stimulus values, five or seven stimulus values ranging from 7 to 11 may be selected for this experiment. The difference between two stimuli should be one millimetre. The five stimulus values with one millimetre difference among them are 7 mm, 8 mm, 9 mm, 10 mm, and 11 mm. If seven, they may be 12 mm and 13 mm. The experimenter should apply each stimulus for 3 seconds on the circumcribed area of the skin in a random order or in some pre-arranged order until each stimulus is applied 100 times. The experimenter should note down the respondent's judgments in a tabular column.

If the judgment made by the respondent is two, then the experimenter should write the number 2 just below the respective stimulus, if the respondent reports as one, then the number 1 should be written. During the course of presenting the stimulus the experimenter sometimes should use one needle instead of two. This should be done as a check on the respondent's sensitivity. If by chance, the respondent reported as two, then care should be taken to caution the respondent to be careful and attentive to the touches. The judgments as 'two' obtained in this manner from the respondent for all the stimuli should be presented in Table 5.1 for computing the limen. When everything is ready, the experimenter should give the following instructions to the respondent.

"Please listen here. I shall prick your forearm gently with a needle a number of times. Sometimes the prick will be with two needles and sometimes with one needle. Observe carefully the touching experience on your skin of the forearm and tell me each time after the prick whether you have been pricked with two needles or one needle. When you experience two say 'two' and when you experience one say, 'one'. Now I shall start it."

After giving these instructions the experimenter should start the trials and note down the responses at once in the columns of the Table 5.1 as two or one as reported by the respondent. Each stimulus should be presented 100 times in some random order which was already arranged by the experimenter.

An Altenative Method

According to the psychophysical law the number trials for each stimulus should be 100 times. But, this appears to be a very laborious task on the part of the experimenter and also on the part of the respondent to have 100 trials of the same stimulus in a random order. If the number of stimuli are 5 the trials become 500, if it is 7 the trials become 700. Therefore, some psychometricians like, D'Amato suggested to have 20 or 10 trials with the same stimulus in a random order. Some others suggested 50 times. Then the number of trials may be converted into percentages. However, the number of stimuli should not be less than 5.

In the determination of absolute limen or threshold, the number trials may be decided by the experimenter himself/herself. To have the number 100, or 50, or 20, may be left to the experimenter at the experimental situation. But it is always better to stick to the law, instead of taking any risk. As soon as the trials are over, the blind goggles should be removed and the respondent may be permitted to go away.

3. RESULTS

The reports of the judgments obtained from the respondent in the two point threshold experiment are in Table 5.1. This data is obtained from one of the experiments conducted earlier and the same are presented here for illustration. In this illustration all the calculations are shown systematically. The number of judgments made by the respondent as 'two' are counted and entered at the bottom of Table 5.1. The same judgments are converted into proportions and entered in Table 5.2.

Table 5.1: Showing the judgments made by the Respondent in the two point Threshold Experiment. Entries indicate the number of judgments as 'Two'

S. No.	7 mm	8 mm	9 mm	10 mm	11 mm
1					
2					
3					
4					
5					
6					
7					
8					
9					
10					
11					
12					
13					
14					
15					
16					
17					
18					
19					
20					
..					
..					
..					
90					
91					
92					
93					
94					
95					
96					
97					
98					
99					
100					
Total	2	6	28	32	26

Calculation of Absolute Limen bv the Linear Interpolation Procedure

The absolute limen is calculated from the number of judgments given in Table 5.1.There are several methods to determine the absolute limen. Some of the important procedures are applied here and the absolute limen is elicited by the respective methods. Every procedure has a formula or equation and the equation is applied for estimating the absolute threshold. The size of the limen is verified with the limen obtained by other procedures. The formula according to the linear interpolation procedure is :

$$L = S_s + \frac{(S_g - S_s)\ (.5 - p_s)}{p_g - p_s}$$

The formula is already explained in the preceding pages.

Table 5.2 : Showing the responses and the proportions of the judgments in the Two-point Threshold Experiment with Aesthesiometer

Stimulus Separation (mm)	7	8	9	10	11
Number of responses as TWO	2	6	28	32	26
Proportions of judgments as two	0.02	0.08	0.36	0.68	0.94

The two point limen is the stimulus that is judged 50 percent of the timc as two. In the experimental data presented in Table 5.2, it is clear that the limen falls in between the stimulus values 9 and 10 mm. It can be observed that the linear interpolation is between the proportions 0.36 and 0.68. The limen falls at the proportion of 0.50. This means that the limen lies on the way of 14/32 on the stimulus interval between 9 and 10 mm. The formula discussed in the preceding section is applied here for determining the limen. Thus :

$$L = 9 + \frac{(10-9)\quad(.5-.36)}{.86-.36} = \frac{1\,(.5-.36)}{.32} = \frac{.14}{.32} = .44$$

$$L = 9 + .44 = 9.44$$

The limen as determined by the linear interpolation procedure is 9.44. This value can be verified by other methods with the same judgments reported by the respondent, using the frequency distribution method for the responses to the respective stimulus values. Now, let us determine the limen by using the Spearman's procedure of arithmetic mean.

Determination of Absolute Limen by the Spearman's Procedure

We are supposed to get the same value 9.44 by this procedure. According to Spearman the limen falls below or above every stimulus value used in an experiment. For example if a stimulus value is 7 mm and if the respondent reported that he/she had received one touch, then the limen is above 7 mm. If the stimulus value is 11 mm and if the respondent reported that he/she had received two touches, then the limen falls below the stimulus value 11 mm. The result is applicable to all the stimulus values used in the experiment. In the case of the stimulus value 7 mm if the respondent reported two touches for two times out of 100 times, then it indicates that 98 times the respondent received one touches, which means that the limen falls above 7 mm. But the respondent also reported that he/she had received two touches two times, which indicates that two times the limen falls below 7 mm. In the case of the stimulus value 8 mm the respondent reported 6 times as 'two' touches, indicating that 94 times the limen falls above 8 mm and 6 times below 8 mm. This also means that two of the limens fall below 7 mm and 6 limens fall below 8 mm. The other responses for the respective stimulus values may be interpreted in the same manner. There are 28 limens falling between 8 and 9 mm, 32 limens falling between the stimulus values 9 and 10 mm and 26 between the stimulus values 10 and 11 mm. But there are 6 limens falling above 11 mm. There are two limens falling below 7 mm. Therefore, we have to assume that 6 limens are falling between 11 and 12 mm and two limens are falling between 6 and 7 mm. We understand from this that on either side there is a tail end. Though these two incidents of tail ends have not taken place in the experimental situation, the tail judgments may be divided into frequencies as 4 and 2. This type of tail assumption is necessary for Spearman's procedure of arithmetic mean. We can proceed further with this assumption to work out the limen and the data are presented in Table 5.3.

Table 5.3 : Showing the computation of two-point threshold according to Spearman's procedure of arithmetic mean

Stimulus Values (mm)	Frequency f	Deviation Value (x')	fx'	fx^2
12 – 12.9	2	+3	+6	18
11 – 11.9	4	+2	+8	16
10. – 10.9	26	+1	+26	26
9 – 9.9	32	0	0	0
8 – 8.9	28	– 1	– 28	28
7 – 7.9	6	– 2	– 12	24
6 – 6.9	2	– 3	– 6	18
Σ	100	0	– 6	130

The highest frequency distribution falls between the stimulus values 9.0 and 9.9. The middle value of which is 9.5. Let us compute the absolute limen having the middle stimulus value 9.5, as the limen is expected to fall above this value or below this value. This is decided by the deviation value (fx'). This value is minus 6 (–6). This value is -6 of 100 as the N is 100. by dividing –6 by 100 (–6/100) we get –0.06. Therefore we have to deduct –.06 from 9.5 to get the limen, 9.5 – .06 = 9.44. Thus, the absolute limen according to this procedure is also 9.44 mm.

The standard deviation and the standard error of the mean also can be worked out in this procedure. The formula for SD is $\sqrt{\frac{fx^2}{N}}$

$$\sigma = \sqrt{\frac{130}{100}} = 1.14$$

The formula for calculating the SEM is $\frac{SD}{\sqrt{N}} = \frac{1.14}{\sqrt{100}} = 0.11$

It is to be noted that according to the procedure of Spearman, the frequencies of responses are treated as non-cumulative distribution. In this procedure we will have to make the tail assumptions on either end systematically. The original frequencies are 94 in total (Table 5.2). But in this case we are having tail assumption by extending the tails by one step on either end and add 6 more judgments to make it 100. As result of it Spearman's arithmetic mean itself becomes the limen and it is found to be 9.44. Acually in the two-point threshold the judgments as 'two' will be going on increasing as and when the number of stimuli are increased step by step in succession. As such we cannot expect a frequency distribution of statistical type unless we make tail assumption on either end. With all these changes Spearman's arithmetic mean by uncumulated distribution is fully in agreement with the limen as obtained by other methods.

Woodworth's Summation Procedure

The summation procedure is applied to the same experimental data given above, for determining the absolute limen. In Woodworth's summation procedure the proportions of the stimulus range is to the extreme ends like 0.0 to 1.00. The procedure is already discussed in the preceding section. We are using the two equations for estimating the absolute limen. In one equation the smallest of the stimuli of the experiment is used for determining the limen, and in another equation the greatest of the stimuli of the experiment is used in determining the limen, unlike Spearman's method of arithmetic mean. The equations are repeated.

They are : $M = S_1 - .5i - i\,\Sigma p$ (i)

$M = S_0 + .5i - i\,\Sigma q$ (ii)

Woodworth's summation procedure provides us one additional information like the Spearman's arithmetic mean. It is the standard deviation (σ). There are two equations corresponding to the equations given above for estimating the limen. The equations for estimating the SDs are :

$$SD\,(\sigma) = i\sqrt{2\,\Sigma cp - (\Sigma p)^2 - \Sigma p} \qquad \text{(i)}$$

$$SD\,(\sigma) = i\sqrt{2\,\Sigma cq - (\Sigma q)^2 - \Sigma q} \qquad \text{(ii)}$$

The two equations are applied on the data obtained in an earlier experiment for estimating the limens. The same proportions that we have obtained earlier are again used here and from the proportions other measures are evolved as given in Table 5.4. The absolute limens are computed from these measures and the same measures are used for working out the standard deviations.

Table 5.4 : Showing the estimation of Absolute Limen using Woodworth's Summation procedure

Stimulus Values	Responses as Two	Proportions (p)	q(1-p)	cp (cumulated)	cq (cumulated)
11 mm	26	.94	.06	2.08	0.06
10 mm	32	.68	.32	1.14	0.38
9 mm	28	.36	.64	0.46	1.02
8 mm	6	.08	.92	0.10	1.94
7 mm	2	.02	.98	0.02	2.92
	94	2.08	2.92	3.80	6.32

Applying the equation (i) the limen is worked as follows :

$$L \text{ or } S_1 = 12 - .5(1) - (1)2.08 = 12 - (.5) - (2.08) = 9.42$$

Applying the equation (ii) the limen is worked out here :

$$L \text{ or } S_0 = 6 + .5(1) + (1)2.92 = 6 + .5 + 2.92 = 9.42$$

The standard deviation (σ) is worked out using the equation (i)

$$S_1 = SD = 1\sqrt{(2)\,3.80 - (2.08)^2 - 2.08} = 1\sqrt{7.6 - 4.33 - 2.08}$$

$$SD = 1\sqrt{7.6 - 4.33 - 2.08} = 1\sqrt{1.19} = 1.09$$

$$\text{SEM for the limen is } \frac{0}{\sqrt{N}} = \frac{1.09}{\sqrt{100}} = 0.109 = 0.11$$

The standard deviation using the equation (ii)

$$S_0 \quad SD = 1\sqrt{(2)\,6.32 - (2.92)^2 - 2.92}$$

$$SD = 1\sqrt{12.64 - 8.53 - 2.92} = \sqrt{1.19} = 1.09$$

$$\text{SEM for the limen is } \frac{0}{\sqrt{N}} = \frac{1.09}{\sqrt{100}} = \frac{1.09}{10} = 0.109 = 0.11$$

Newhall's Normal Interpolation Procedure

Let us now test whether Newhall's normal interpolation procedure would fetch the same absolute limen for the same data as given by the other procedures. The Newhall's procedure appears to be similar to the linear interpolation procedure. The important process involved in this procedure is the transformation of proportions (p) into corresponding deviate values (z). This is indicated by the letter z. The assumption is that the relationship between the stimulus value and the z value is more or like a straight line. One important point in this procedure is that the z value for the limen is always zero (0) and on either side there are standard measure values (z). On the left the z value is negative (minus) and on the right the z value is positive (plus). This procedure can be applied to the same data and the limen can be determined.

Table 5.5 : Showing the determination of absolute limen by using Newhall's Normal Interpolation procedure

Stimulus Values (mm)	7	8	9	10	11
Response as Two	2	6	28	32	26
Proportions (p)	.02	.08	.36	.68	.94
Deviate Values (z)	– 2.05	– 1.41	– 0.36	+0.47	+1.55

The formula, with the deviate values, we discussed earlier is applied here to the same data for determining the absolute limen using the smaller and greater stimulus values.

$$L = 9 + \left(\frac{+0.36}{+0.47-(-0.36)} \right) 1 = 9.43$$

$$L = 10 - \left(\frac{+0.47}{+0.47-(-0.36)} \right) 1 = 9.43$$

In the case of using the smaller stimulus value 9, we have to add with 9 the value obtained from the equation. Therefore, the minus value —0.36 becomes plus. The demominators become plus values when the bracket is removed. Therefore, we have to add both the denominators (0.47 + .36) and divide the numerator +0.36 in the first equation. In the second equation also the denominators 0.47 and 0.36 become plus values on removing the bracket. Therefore, they are added, and the added value divides the numerator 0.47. Since the stimulus value is greater in the second equation we have to deduct the obtained value from the equation. Thus, the absolute limen in both equations is the same 9.43. These values do not make much difference from the limen obtained by using other procedures. The limens are almost the same in all the procedure. The results obtained in all the four procedures are presented in Table 5.6 and the results are compared.

Table 5.6 : Showing the Absolute Limen obtained by using four procedures from the data collected by the method of constant stimuli

S. No.	Name of the Constant Method	Limen value	Standard deviation	Standard error
1	Linear Interpolation Procedure	9.44	---	---
2	Spearman's Arithmetic Mean	9.44	1.14	0.11
3	Woodworth's Summation Method	9.42	1.09	0.11
4	Newhall's Normal Interpolation Procedure	9.43	---	---

The four absolute limens, that are estimated by using the four important constant methods, presented in Table 5.6 do not vary very much among limens. The four methods that we have used here are devised by various psychometricians as constant methods of different types. All the four methods yielded almost the same value with very negligible differences. Among the four methods, the first two methods yielded the same value (9.44). Woodworth's summation method yielded a little smaller limen (9.42), and the Newhall's method yielded a limen of 9.43, which does not make much difference from the limens of other methods. The differences of 0.02 and 0.01 in the limen value in the two-point threshold experiment cannot be considered as serious differences among the limen values.

It is also better to estimate the standard deviations and the standard errors (SEM) to know the accuracy with which the experiment is conducted. But we could estimate the SDs and the SEMs only for the Spearman's and Woodworth's methods and not for other two methods as they do not provide sufficient information. Therefore, from the data as obtained by these methods, we can conclude that the experiment is conducted successfully without much dispersion values.

The experimenter can collect the group data, the four limen values obtained by applying the four methods, from other experimenters and present them in Table 5.7. The group mean for the limens for each method can be worked out separately. The group mean of the absolute limen in each method can be compared with the limen of the individuals. The highest and the lowest limens also can be examined. How many of them in the

Table 5.7: Showing the absolute limens of the group as obtained by using the four procedures of the constant method in the Two-point Threshold Experiment

S. No.	Name	Linear Interpolation Procedure	Spearmen's Procedure	Woodworth's Procedure	Newhall's Procedure
1.	P.K.	9.44	9.44	9.42	9.43
2.	A.S.				
3.	V.P.				
4.	M.S.				
5.	K.R.				
6.	B.V.				
7.	D.J.				
8.	C.S.				
9.	G.G.				
10.	T.V.				
11.	R.A.				
12.	E.P.				
Mean					

group had the limen higher than the group mean and how many had the lower limen than the group mean ?

Find out and state whether there are any abnormal deviations in the individuals' judgment of absolute limen and find out the personal reasons, if any.

4. DISCUSSION

There are several procedures to estimate the absolute limen from the data obtained by the method of constant stimuli. Four of the important procedures are applied here for determining the absolute limen and the four limens obtained by the four methods are compared. The purpose of this experiment is to determine the two-point tactual threshold by the method of constant stimuli using the instrument called aesthesiometer. The limens as presented in Table 5.6 for all four procedures in the case of one person indicate that there is not much difference between any two limens. From the data it can be understood that since all the four procedures yielded almost the same value and the SDs (1.14 and 1.09) and the SEMs (0.11 and 0.11) are also very small and negligible, we can conclude that the limens obtained by all four methods are accurate and the respondent is also found to be very sensitive to the touches of the needles of the aesthesiometer.

The experimenter on obtaining the group data from other experimenters and entering them in Table 5.7, and on working out the mean, can discuss the results relating the individuals to the group mean. The experimenter should discuss specifically his/her respondent's absolute limen in comparison with the group mean and with other individuals. What sort of experience the experimenter has gained by conducting this experiment by using the constant method ? Is the constant method more laborious and time consuming compared to other methods or more interesting and yields more experimental knowledge ? State,whether there is any constant error that might have occurred in the experimental situation. Discuss also the merits and demerits of the method of constant stimuli.

5. CONCLUSIONS

State the size of the absolute limen obtained from the judgments made by your respondent. Is it accurate or smaller or greater than the group mean? Is your respondent very sensitive to the touch sensation? Do you find any scope to improve this method? If so, state it.

6

PSYCHOPHYSICAL METHOD : Method of Constant Stimuli - II Determination of Differential Limen

DIFFERENTIAL LIMEN : AN INTRODUCTION

The determination of differential limen by the method of constant stimuli is an alternative method to the method of minimal changes for determining difference limen or threshold. This method is also called method of constant stimulus differences. The differential limen (DL) is a stimulus difference which establishes a point at which the two stimuli presented should appear to be different from each other. Psychophysics, therefore, here is mainly concerned with perceived difference between two stimuli, that is, where the two stimuli appear differently in an experimental situation.

Hence, differential limen may be defined as the smallest stimulus difference that is determined by an observer 50 percent of the time when presented. But operationally the stimulus difference is perceived 75 percent of the time. The difference limen is determined by the method of minimal changes and also by the method of constant stimuli. In both the methods a standard stimulus is required in addition to the variable stimulus for the purpose of comparison. Therefore, in each trial a pair of stimuli, one the standard (St) and the other the variable (Sv) are presented to the observer simultaneously and the observer's task is to judge by comparison whether one of the stimuli is greater than or lesser than the other. Therefore, the difference limen is intended to determine the point at which the two stimuli appear with some difference. It is concerned with determining the perceived difference between two stimuli.

In the method of constant stimulus differences one important point the experimenter should bear in mind is, the selection of the variable or the comparison stimuli. The variable stimuli should be in odd numbers like, 5, 7, 9, 11 and so on, in order to have the standard stimulus at the middle of the variable stimuli. The physical value or the quality of the standard stimulus and the middle variable stimulus should have the same value.

The number of stimuli below the middle stimulus and above the middle stimulus should be of the same number, two on either side or three on either side of the middle stimulus. The stimuli should be selected in such a way that the largest stimulus should yield approximately 95 percent of the judgments as greater and the smallest stimulus should approximately yield 5 percent of the judgments as greater or 95 percent of the judgments as smaller. The experimenter should make certain preliminary trials and ascertain this and get satisfied himself/herself at the time of selecting the variable stimuli. The judgment values of the stimuli should have symmetrical looks on either side of the values of the standard stimulus. In certain experiments as far as possible the observer should be instructed to use only two categories of judgments like greater and smaller and the category of judgment equal is avoided.

The basic principle involved in the method of constant stimuli is that it should have two types of stimuli, one constant (standard), and the other comparison (variable) stimulus. The method is quite suitable for psychophysical experiments. Two reasons are attributed for its suitability. One is, when the experimenter finds it difficult to vary the comparison (variable) stimulus in small steps all the times. The other reason is, when the experimenter wants to determine the limen on the basis of large number of judgments.

In the method of constant stimuli there are certain differences between the determination of absolute limen and the differential limen. In the case of absolute limen one stimulus (aesthesiometer) with varied distances is used one after one one hundred times, whereas in the case of differential limen a pair of stimuli, one standard and the other comparison are presented at the same time one hundred times in random order.

In the determination of difference limen by the method of constant stimuli, there are two more important measures involved. They are (1) interval of uncertainty (IU), and (2) the point of subjective equality (PSE). The difference limen (DL) is determined only from the interval of uncertainty and the point of subjective equality. The point of subjective equality is determined from the stimulus immediately greater than the limen and the stimulus immediately smaller than the limen. Therefore, these two measures should be dealt with.

Interval of Uncertainty

In the determination of difference limen the mean falls between the upper limen and the lower limen. The area between the greater limen (Lg) and the smaller limen (Ls) is called the interval of uncertainty, the IU. The true limen is supposed to fall in between these two measures and the distance is divided by two for obtaining the true limen. There is a limen for the upper limit and a limen for the lower limit. There cannot be two limens. But the upper limit and the lower limit are not the same. There are two measures. Therefore, it is presumed that since the limen is not at any one of the fixed place, it becomes a doubtful area. The limen may be somewhere in between these two measures and any specific point is not correct. Therefore, the distance between the two measures, the upper limit (the greater limen) and the lower limit (Smaller limen) is named as the interval of uncertainty.

The smallest amount of limen that can cause change in the judgment of the respondent may be stated as the difference limen. The interval of uncertainty may be defined as the doubtful area or the distance lies between the upper limit or greater limen and the lower limit or smaller limen in the judgment made by the respondent. This doubtful area or interval of uncertainty may vary from trial to trial. Generally, in decending series the IU may be higher, and in ascending series the IU may be lower. Therefore, the distance between the upper limit and the lower limit is divided by two for every trial and the mean of the whole series is taken as the interval of uncertainty. The interval of uncertainty we come across in all the three psychophysical methods, namely in the method of constant stimuli, method of minimal changes in the determination of difference limen and in the method of average error in the determination of DL, but it is very rarely used for this purpose.

Point of Subjective Equality (PSE)

This is another measure worked out from the experimental data while determining the difference limen. The respondent in the experimental situation is asked to judge the variable stimulus in comparison with the standard stimulus and report whether the two stimuli appear equal. But the respondent does not always judge the variable stimulus equal to the standard stimulus. Sometimes the variable stimulus is judged as greater and sometimes as smaller. It is possible that in the decending series there may be more number of greater judgments, few number of judgments as equal and few number of judgments as smaller. In the ascending series there may be more judgments as smaller, few judgments as equal and few judgments as greater. This may occur every trial. Therefore, the mid-point between the upper limit and the lower limit in every trial is taken as the point of subjective equality (PSE). Then the mean of the ascending and decending series is taken as the measure of the respondent's point of subjective equality (PSE). The PSE is the arithmetic mean of the upper limit and the lower limit. The PSE is worked out in the determination of difference limen in the method of minimal changes and in the method of constant stimuli. These two measures can be avoided if we resort to only two types of judgments.

EXPERIMENT 5: Determination of Difference Limen (DL) by the Method of Constant Stimuli

Problem : There are instances in our everyday life to compare objects, persons, places and even time and state whether they are equal or greater or smaller in size, length, width, height, weight, circumference and so on. In competitions, sports activities we may be made to make small changes to win the game or competition. In shooting, archery, and billiards more accurate comparative judgments are needed. Small changes in movements in accordance with the previous events are to be made in these games. It is true that some persons can make the required small changes or movements very accurately and some may make more mistakes and loose their games and competitions. This skill can be tested in the psychological laboratories. The psychophysical and the scaling experiments provide some scope for testing such skills.

Aim : The aim of this experiment is to determine the difference limen or threshold and the point of subjective equality (PSE) applying the method of constant stimuli.

2. METHOD

Respondent : Choose a person to serve as a respondent, who has no knowledge about this experiment. State the person's age, gender, qualification, occupation, salary etc., also state whether the person wears eye glass or has any physical defects.

Apparatus

This experiment requires simple materials. It requires eight white cards with one thick black line drawn at the centre of the cards with varying length in each card. One card is used as the standard stimulus whose length of line is 5 centemetre. The other seven cards are used as comparative stimuli. The seven cards are having lines of varying length ranging from 4.7 cenetimetre to 5.3 centimetre with a difference of one millimetre from card to card. Thus, the length of lines in the 7 cards are 4.7 cm, 4.8 cm, 4.9 cm, 5.0 cm, 5.1 cm, 5.2 cm and 5.3 cm. The experimenter can prepare this test material himself/herself. A laboratory metal stand with a clamp is also required.

Procedure : The experimenter should first of all check whether the test materials are ready with him/her. The respondent should be seated comfortably in a well illuminated room, where there is no disturbance of any type. The experimenter should sit with the test materials about 7 feet away from the respondent. The experimenter should have the response sheet (Table 6.1) wherein the length of 7 variable stimuli lines are entered.

The standard stimulus card with 5 cm length should be fixed in the clamp of the stand in front of the respondent. The experimenter should sit close to the stand since he/she has to display different variable stimuli every time. The standard stimulus is already fixed in the clamp of the stand and the variable in a random order should be kept at least two feet away from the standard stimulus. All the 7 cards should be shuffled after every exposure to the respondent. The set of 7 cards should be shown to the respondent 100 times, so that the relative size of every stimulus may be judged by the respondent 100 times. The standard stimulus should be on the right of the variable stimulus in half of the observations (50 times) and on the left in half of the observations (50 times). At the time of starting the experiment the following instructions should be given to the respondent

"I am going to show you two cards at the same time, having a thick black line at the centre of each card. Please look at this (showing the standard stimulus fixed in the stand) card. Now I will show you another card, (showing one variable card at two feet away from the standard stimulus card). Now you see two cards,each is two feet apart. Look at them carefully and tell me how they appear to you. Compare the black lines in the two cards and tell me whether the line on the left (variable stimulus) is equal to the line on the right or longer or shorter. Now I shall start and you will have to judge the lines and report to me." Having given these instructions the experimenter can start exposing the variable stimulus one by one in a random order by the side of the standard stimulus.

There are difference of opinions among the psychometricians with regard to the type of responses. It is, whether to have two types of responses or judgments as greater or lesser or to have a third response or judgment, as equal or doubltful. Thurstone (1927) states that if equal category of response or judgment is excluded, then the analysis is very much simplified. Because if the respondent is permitted to have a doubtful or equal judgment it becomes complicated one. The respondent may not concentrate on the correct judgment of the variable stimulus, whether the variable stimulus is greater or smaller. The respondent may simply state, 'doubtful'. D'Amato (1970) agrees with the view expressed by Thurstone. But Guilford (1954) suggests that the third category of response, equal or doubtful is essential. But we shall have the third category of judgment in this experiment, 'equal' as it facilitates the calculation of point of subjective equality (PSE).

There is also difference of opinion with regard to the number of judgments made by the respondent. D'Amato suggests 20 or 10 judgments are sufficient in the case of determination of difference limen. Others suggest 50 trials or judgments, whereas Guilford suggests 100 trials or judgments. The reason is that with 7 variable stimuli the number of judgments or trials are 700. It is tiresome for both, the respondent and the experimenter. For example, if a trial takes a minimum of 30 seconds, for 700 trials it takes 350 minutes, which means nearly six hours. It is a difficult task for the respondent and for the experimenter. In such case the experiment can be conducted in two sessions.

As and when the respondent makes judgments and reports, the experimenter should note down carefully in the response sheet, the reports made by the respondent. The respondent is required to make three alternative judgments as greater or smaller or equal. The set of 7 cards should be presented in a random order, each 100 times. Thus, there are 700 judgments and these are to be entered in Table 6.1.

3. RESULTS

The judgments made by the respondent on each variable stimulus 100 times for 7 variable stimuli are presented in Table 6.1. The data given in Table 6.1, is obtained from one of the experiments conducted earlier and the same is presented here for the purpose of illustration. In this illustrative example all the calculations involved in the determination of difference limen are shown. In Table 6.1, the three category of judgments as reported by the respondent, are entered for every variable stimulus at the bottom of the Table. For want of space only the total of the reports are given here and not every report.

The total number of judgments as larger, as smaller, as equal are worked out and given at the end of the Table 6.1. These are the basic data from which the other measures are worked out. The limen for greater judgments and for smaller judgments are worked out separately by using the linear interpolation procedure and presented in Tables 6.2 and 6.3. According to this procedure there are two limens, one for the greater judgments and one for the smaller judgments. It is because of the equal or doubtful judgments that we get two limens. If the equal or doubtful judgments as suggested by Thurstone is omitted then, there is no chance for two limens in this experiment.

But psychometricians suggest that in one way it is good, because we are taking into account the middle value, that lies in between the two limens.

Table 6.1: Showing the comparative judgment made by the respondent for determination of Difference Limen by the method of Constant Stimuli Standard Stimulus — 5 cm

Trials Random Order	Intervals of comparative stimuli (7)						
	4.7 cm	4.8 cm	4.9 cm	5.0 cm	5.1 cm	5.2 cm	5.3 cm
1							
2							
3							
4							
5							
6							
7							
8							
9							
10							
11							
12							
13							
14							
15							
16							
17							
18							
19							
20							
..							
..							
..							
90							
91							
92							
93							
94							
95							
96							
97							
98							
99							
100							
No. of G	6	16	25	36	56	70	90
No. of E	2	10	19	32	20	12	4
No. of S	92	74	56	32	24	18	6

NB : G = Greater judgment, E = Equal judgment, S = Smaller judgment.
100 judgments were made by the respondent for each stimulus.

The formula for determining the difference limen is the same one used in the previous experiment for determining absolute limen.

$$L = S_s + \frac{(S_g - S_s)\ (.5 - p_s)}{p_g - p_s}$$

where L = stands for the limen
S_s = Stimulus immediately smaller than the limen
S_g = Stimulus immediately greater than the limen
p_s = Proportions immediately smaller than limen
p_g = Proportions immediately greater than limen

Table 6.2: Showing the proportions of judgments of the comparative stimulus judged as greater than the standard stimulus and computation of limen by the linear interpolation method.

Stimulus separation in cm	4.7	4.8	4.9	5.0	5.1	5.2	5.3
Proportions of judgments made as greater	.06	.16	.25	.36	.56	.70	.90

$$DL = 5.0 + \frac{(5.1-5.0)\ (.5-.36)}{.56-.36} = \frac{(0.1)(0.14)}{.20} = \frac{0.014}{.20} = 0.07$$

$$DL = 5.0 + 0.07 = 5.07$$

Table 6.3: Showing the proportions of judgments of the comparative stimulus as smaller than the standard stimulus and the computation of limen by the linear interpolation method.

Stimulus separation in cm	4.7	4.8	4.9	5.0	5.1	5.2	5.3
Proportions of judgments made as smaller	.92 (.08)	.74 (.26)	.56 (.44)	.32 (.68)	.24 (.76)	.18 (.82)	.06 (.94)

$$DL = 5.0 + \frac{(5.0-4.9)\ (.5-.44)}{.68-.44} = \frac{(.1)(0.06)}{-.24}$$

$$DL = \frac{0.006}{0.24} = 0.025$$

$$DL = 4.9 + .025 = 4.925 = 4.93.$$

These are the calculations involved in determining the difference limen. By way of determining the DL we have also worked out various other measures like the limen for greater judgments and smaller judgments, the interval of uncertainty, the point of subjective equality and the difference limen. All these are presented in Tables 6.2, 6.3 and 6.4.

The point of subjective equality and the difference limen are calculated from the greater limen and the smaller limen and presented in Table 6.4. The interval of uncertainty falls between the greater limen and the smaller limen. The difference limen is obtained by dividing the IU by two (IU/2).

Table 6.4 : Showing the limens (greater and smaller), the interval of uncertainty, the difference limen, and the point of subjective equality

Process	Lg	Ls	IU	DL	PSE
Linear Interpolation process	5.07	4.93	0.14	0.07	5.00

$$PSE = \frac{Lg + Ls}{2} = \frac{5.07 + 4.93}{2} = 5.00$$

$$IU = Lg - Ls = 5.07 - 4.93 = 0.14$$

$$DL = \frac{IU}{2} = \frac{0.14}{2} = 0.07$$

The point of subjective equality is generally taken as the arithmetic mean of the doubtful judgments. In this experiment the doubtful judgments fall between L_g and L_s (5.07 and 4.93). The arithmetic mean of these two judgments is 5.00. This procedure of determining the PSE is in accordance with Spearman's arithmetic mean of the uncumulated distribution and Woodworth's summation processes. The distance between the L_g and L_s (5.07 and 4.93) is the area of doubtful judgments (5.07 – 4.93 = 0.14) and one-half of this interval is taken as the difference limen (0.14/2 = 0.07).

The group data may be collected from other experimenters and presented in Table 6.5. The group data may be consisted of the measures Lg, Ls. Interval of uncertainty, the Difference limen and the point of subjective equality. The mean values for all the measures may be worked out and the data should be interpreted and discussed.

Table 6.5 : Showing the greater limen, smaller limen, interval of uncertainty, difference limen and the point of subjective equality

S.No.	Name	Lg	Ls	IU	DL	PSE
1.	P.V.	5.07	4.93	0.14	0.07	5.00
2.	K.S.					
3.	M.S.					
4.	S.L.					
5.	M.R.					
6.	K.R.					
7.	T.S.					
8.	V.R.					
9.	A.G.					
10.	B.V.					
	Mean					

4. DISCUSSION

State the aim of the experiment, and state how the method of constant stimuli is considered as more accurate compared to other methods. State and discuss how your respondent was reacted in the experimental situation. State and discuss whether his/her judgments were falling more on greater or smaller or on the equal or doubtful area. Did you observe any error in the judgments? If so, has he/she tried to correct it? Discuss your respondent's nature of judgments in relation to the measures of difference limen, greater judgments, smaller judgments, the point of subjective equality and the doubtful judgments. State and discuss how the doubtful judgments serve as a check on the more of greater and smaller judgments. Some state that it serves some practical purpose. Critically discuss the statement.

State your respondent's measures (in figures) and compare them with the group mean. Is he/she above the group mean or below the group mean, state it and discuss in relation to other individuals. How many in the group judged the Lg, Ls, the DL, the IU, and the PSE much above the group mean and how many much below the group mean? Is there any abnormally greater and smaller judgment? State the reasons, if any for such abnormal judgments. Did you find the influence of gender, age, physical defects, qualifications and the SES in the judgments ? If so, explain it.

Is the experimental procedure and the experience having any relevance to actual life of an individual? Discuss it in relation to everyday events of human life.

5. CONCLUSIONS

State your respondent's DL, IU and PSE. Has he/she judged the stimuli greater than the actual size or smaller than the actual size of the stimuli ?

Has the group over estimated the stimuli or under estimated the stimuli?

Are there more over estimation or under estimation ?

State where your respondent stands in the group in the judgment of the stimuli in general?

Part - III

Modern Psychophysical Scaling Methods - I

Psychophysics and psychophysical methods were widely used in experimental psychology and also in various other areas for research purposes. The methods underwent to certain revisions time to time according to the problems for which the investigators used them in their researches. Though Weber and Fechner were the founders of psychophysics and psychophysical methods, in the second quarter of this century many modern scholars applied these methods in their studies and made lots of contributions to the development of these methods. There were revisions, modifications, and changes in the original methods, but the studies were made based upon the general psychophysical laws. Fullerton and Cattell have brought out a revision in the general psychophysical laws. Thurstone has developed an attitude scale, which he called as 'Psychophysical Method of Equal Appearing Interval'. Following this many attitude scales were developed later on in different forms.

Then there were several modern developments based upon psychophysics and psychophysical methods and they were all called psychophysical sacling methods. Some of the modern developments are, Thurstone's law of comparative judgments, Helson's adaptation level, Stevens' power function, Calander's decision theory and the information theory, Stevens' psychophysics of audition, and Lane's psychophysics of speech perception. All these are further developments in psychophysics and psychophysical methods. The psychophysical scaling methods are little different from the classical psychophysical methods in the sense that the results are not obtained from the physical stimulus, but from the judgments made by the respondent. Therefore, the results are from the psychological continuum. For every change in the physical continuum there is a change in the sensory continuum and values are evolved for physical stimulus.

7

MODERN PSYCHOPHYSICS AND PSYCHOPHYSICAL LAWS IN SENSORY AREAS

PSYCHOPHYSICS AND ITS MODERN DEVELOPMENT: AN INTRODUCTION

Modern psychological experimentation, strictly speaking, finds its origin in Fechner's psychophysical laws and methods. Though its origin is more than hundred years, its longevity is not felt as new methods based upon it are evolving time to time. We may even state that Fechner's psychophysics is rejuvenated in various ways by inventing new methods, having it as a source of information, and adding to it enormous amount of information, and extending its scope in various applied areas of psychology.

As Sigmund Freud once stated, when there were some criticisms on his psychoanalysis, it is for his followers to nourish the mental health tradition with new research findings and attend to its vulnerability. Fechner also might have felt that it is for the coming generation to continue the torch and invigorate his psychophysics with scientific spirit and temper and make it a full-pledged science. Whether Frechner has wished like that or not, many investigators have made notable contributions to its growth and development and psychophysics has become an invisible and invincible living spirit. Many considered it as the scientific source of inspiration.

The contemporary developments that have taken place in psycho-physical and scaling methods were all evolved from the principles of psychophysics invented by Fechner and on the contributions made by the later psychophysicists like Fullerton Cattell, Thurstone and few others, following Frechner's principle.

Though it is often stated that the earlier studies were mainly on sensory areas, it was the sensory experiences that were behind the whole human behaviour. Variations in studies took place later on in the areas of application. For example, the sensory experiences like, seeing, hearing, tasting, smelling and touching are used not only for personal experiences, but also for the development of various human resources. All the scientific inventions and discoveries find their roots only on the human perceptual processes like seeing, hearing and touching. The more accurately we perceive the characteristics of an object or an event the more information we obtain from it and utilize them for the efficient survival of human race.

Therefore, the perceptual processes or the sensory processes that the psychophysics studies very accurately should be viewed with a very wider perspective. The studies made by the psychophysicists on the sensation of sound and the characteristics of sounds are in no way less than that of the studies made by physicists and the musicians. The psychophysical studies of the dimensions of sensations and the determination of visual, auditory and other thresholds revealed that how accurately psychophysics studies the stimulus variation in sensations. The results of these studies, specifically in the areas of vision and audition have contributed to the development of knowledge and life aspects.

Progressive Development of Modern Psychophysics and Methods

The early psychophysicists like Fechner have made more notable contributions in the field psychophysics of vision than any other sensory fields. But the studies made in the sensory field of audition were not falling back of other studies. The early and the later psychophysicists have spent much of their times in sensory psychology for the obvious reason that it is the basic for the psychological fields like, the developmental psychology, physiological psychology, personnel and industrial psychology, consumer psychology, selection and placement, training and comprehension, military psychology and medical psychology. But because of the discovery of psychophysical laws, so much development has taken place in the field of psychology.

The psychophysical laws always try to relate the stimulus qualities to the corresponding response levels. Whether the judgments are based upon physical continuum or psychological continuum, the psychophysical law stresses the procedures involved in the measurement of physical stimuli and the responses elicited by them either in the physical continuum or response continuum, should be measurable. The psychophysicists have established this phenomena. Any physical stimulus may arouse a corresponding response.

The early psychophysics by presenting a physical stimulus expected a specified response in a physical continuum by way of judgment made by a person, which was stated as the sensory response by the person, though we called it later on as psychological judgment. The stimulus might have been of visual type, or auditory, or cutaneous, kinesthetic or organic or stimulus to chemical senses like smell or taste. Studies and contributions in these sensory areas or sensory systems have become the basic for all areas. There cannot be any accurate study or measurement in any applied area without applying any of the psychophysical laws. Any psychological study or measurement, which involves the use of stimulus dimensions and response to psychological judgment or measurement, is based upon the basic psychophysical laws. Therefore there cannot be any iota of psychological measurement or study by disregarding the basic principles of psychophysics.

Psychophysics and Dimension of Sensation

Psychophysics is defined as the study of the relationship between the stimulus and the corresponding response on the sensory modalities. Psychophysics extends its study on several areas such as the properties of the stimuli which revealed in the dimensions of sensations, noticeability of the stimuli, that is the minimum energy required to arouse sensation, the minimum amount of change required in the stimuli that can be perceived, and the scaling of sensory dimensions. But it was also observed that the studies of these areas were complicated as there were different dimensions in each sensation which caused different problems. Therefore, psychophysicists tried to solve these problems by inventing new methods and techniques. Psychophysically, it is observed that every sensation has several dimensions, such as qualities, quantities, intensities, extensities, changeableness and so on. For example, the dimension of auditory sensation are pitch (frequencies), loudness (amplitude), noise, tone and so on. The sense of hearing involves the pitch which is a qualitative dimension, loudness the quantitative dimension. Similarly every sensation has such dimension. Every dimension or modality has qualitative differences. These qualitative differences are determined at the neural level. The nervous system is mainly responsible in differentiating the dimensional qualities of every sensation. The common characteristic of the nervous system is, to transmit the electrochemical impulses to the brain centres. These sensory impulses of all sensations terminate at the cerebral cortex. For example, any impulse or group of impulses reaching the auditory are in the temporal lobe of the cerebral cortex causes auditory sensation. Similarly, any impulse reaching the occipital lobe of the cerebral cortex causes visual sensation. Thus, the quality of any sensation is determined by the respective area of the cerebral cortex.

The cerebral cortex is directly stimulated by the impulses. These impulses from a specific sensory receptor system pass through the respective path ways and reach the respective cerebral cortex area. In this way we hear something as a result of the stimulation of the auditory receptor cells in the basilar membrane of the ear. These stimulations are brought about by sound energy striking on the eardrum through the ossicles to the basilar membrane. Similarly, we see something as a result of the stimulation of the visual receptors in the retina area of the eye. Generally, this stimulation is aroused by some light energy striking on the retina area. Therefore, we may state that any sound energy when stimulates the temporal cortex of the brain may evoke the sensation of sound. In the same manner any light energy when stimulates the occipital cortex of the brain may arouse the sensation of vision.

Generally, the pressures on the tympanic membrane, tappings on the head or back of the ear may serve as stimuli for activating the auditory area of the brain and may arouse a form of hearing. Any disturbance or damage in the normal functioning of the brain may evoke some false hearing, which may be called delusions and hallucinations. All these may be accounted for the general perception of auditory sensation or visual sensation. But how the variations in qualities or modalities are determined and the different qualities are perceived? What part of the temporal cortex of the brain differentiates the varied qualities or intensities of the sound or pitch? What part of the occipital cortex differentiates the different qualities in vision? This is a problem raised on sometimes. An answer in the case of auditory sensation is provided to this problem at the end of the discussion of the inner ear. This can be a general answer to all the sensations which mainly depends upon the nature of threshold.

Psychophysics and Sensory Thresholds

The neural fibres of every sensation has a threshold. All the neural fibres are not having the same strength at all the times and the same level of threshold. The neural fibres of any sensation may have varying thresholds. The stronger the stimulation the greater the number of individual thresholds. The weaker the stimulation, the smaller the number of thresholds. For example, in the case of auditory sensation, when few impulses are generated at the nerve fibres due to low sound, at every vibrations the impulses are sensed as weak sounds. Greater amplitudes cause more impulses which are sensed as louder noise. This is how the qualities are differentiated in every sensation. Therefore, in determining thresholds for quality, intensity, extensity and duration in any sensory modalities psychophysical methods are used.

The threshold for each sensory attribute may be determined. There is a threshold for every quality, quantity or intensity, extensity and duration. The thresholds may be absolute, differential, terminal. The psychophysical methods are applied in determining all these thresholds. Changes in physical energy referring to the quality, intensity, extensity and duration, can bring out changes in the responses of the receptors by stimulating them. Humans can report these changes in their perception of every modality by attending to them systematically. Then the amount of physical energy can be compared to the level of sensation reported by a person. The relationship between the changes of physical energy and the sensation caused by the physical energy is not always linear. It is also possible that sometimes, specifically in some sensation, small stimulus change cause change in sensation, and sometimes to cause the same level of change in sensation, larger stimulus change is required. The change of physical energy that is required for the sensation and the sensation resulted should be measured separately and compared. This is what we do in psychophysics and this type of measurement can be done in the case of all sensations. An equation is evolved between physical stimulus and the response to the stimulus.

In these type of measurements, psychophysicists generally determine the various thresholds. The types of thresholds that we determined in psychophysical methods are mainly the absolute threshold (AL) differential threshold (DL) and terminal threshold (TT). In absolute threshold, we come across two kinds of threshold such as lower or stimulus threshold (LT) and the upper or terminal threshold (TT).

Absolute Threshold

A stimulus has normally two characteristics, one is the detectability and the other is discriminability. A stimulus which lacks these two characteristics is not a stimulus. The words, limen, threshold, stimulus are used to indicate the amount of energy involved in the stimulation of an organism or to arouse some sensation. Limen is a Latin word which means threshold or doorsill or doorway. Threshold means the strength at which a stimulus just perceived or the minimum intensity or value of a stimulus that will produce a response or specified effect. Limen is a Latin word, Reiz is a German word. Threshold and limen are used in place of one another.

Threshold is a German word, the meaning of which is stimulus. Thus limen, threshold and stimulus are used interchangeably. The minimum amount of stimulation that can be detected by an organism in a suitable condition may be stated as the threshold.

Stimulus, according to Woodworth (1952), is any force acting on a receptor and making it active, and any kind of acitivity aroused by a stimulus can be called a response. Therefore, a stimulus arouses an activity or makes one active. Murphy (1964) also states in the same manner that a stimulus is anything that excites a receptor. Murphy states that the amount of stimulation required to elicit a response is called threshold. According to him a low threshold easily calls out a response, but with high threshold the response is called out with difficulty. Kimble *et el.* (1985) state that absolute threshold is the weakest stimulus that it can be detected in any sensory system. It is the smallest amount of physical energy that can produce a sensation in any sense. Psychophysics tries to answer the question, how weak or small a stimulus, a person can detect, and how small difference in stimulation or how small change in a stimulus, a person can detect? In all the psychophysical experiments answers are elicited to these two questions.

With regard to the definition of absolute threshold Hilgard *et el.* (1975) clarify certain doubts that arise in defining the absolute threshold. They define absolute threshold as the minimum physical energy required to activate a given sensory system, but not satisfied with this. According to them the type of definition is somnewhat inappropriate because the experimenter is not arriving at a single intensity of the stimulus, sometimes detected and sometimes not detected and thirdly, it is always detected. Thus, there is no detection, partial detection and full detection. Having this psychophysical formation in mind, a definition of absolute threshold that can be accepted without any criticism can be that the stimulus value or intensity at which the stimulus is perceived or detected fifty percent of the time. This definition may be applied to all sensory modalities.

The absolute threshold may be determined by presenting the stimulus with certain smallest value or intensity to the participant and he/she may be asked to state whether the stimulus is perceived or not. If it is not, next bigger intensity of the stimulus may be presented. This procedure may be continued till the participant detects the stimulus intensity fifty percent of the time. If it is perceived 50 per cent of the time any further increase in the intensity of the stimulus may result in complete detection. Therefore, the presentation may be stopped as soon as the P detects the stimulus value 50 per cent of the time, which is to be accepted as the absolute threshold. This procedure of determining absolute threshold even though may be applicable to all sensory modalities, it is more applicable in the case of audition. In the case of audition in determining the absolute threshold the upper range is the terminal range. The absolute limen of this kind is statistically calculated figure. If the stimulus is at too high place, it cannot be detected more than fifty percent of the time. If the sound frequency is too high the threshold cannot be detected in the case of auditory sensation.

Generally, threshold means the absolute threshold, even if the word absolute is not mentioned, it is implied. The stimulus value is detected 50 percent of the time. This involves 50 per cent on the average of the detection. A greater energy may have higher percentage of detection and a weaker energy may have lower percentage. Therefore, an average should be 50 per cent. Further, threshold may vary person to person and also in the same person it may vary from time to time. There are also other factors like physical fitness of the person, motivation, interest and so on may have influence in the determination of absolute threshold. The psychophysical function involved in this may be demonstrated in a curve by plotting the percentage of detections on ordinate and the units of physical energy on the abscissa and the absolute threshold may be determined from the curve.

Differential Threshold (DL)

We have discussed above one characteristic of the stimulus, the detectability in which the determination of absolute limen or threshold is involved. The other characteristics is the discriminability of a stimulus. This involves in determining the threshold of a sensation. The psychophysical function involved in this is the relationship between strength of stimulation and intensity of sensation. Differential or difference threshold means the smallest amount of stimulus difference that is detectable most of the time. Psychophysically, it is 50 percent of the time. How to distinguish one stimulus from another if they are of the same type? It is only from the difference that exists between them. What is the minimum or the smallest amount of stimulation required to tell that the two stimuli are having difference? That difference is stated as the difference threshold. Psychophysically, it is termed as just noticeable difference (JND). The JND refers to the amount of change in the stimulus. But Leukal (1968) state that the difference should be perceived 75 per cent of the time.

Difference threshold, therefore, may be defined as the smallest difference between two stimuli that can be perceived or detected reliably. Difference threshold mainly refers to the accuracy with which we perceive or detect the differences among the stimuli. Thus, thresholds are fixing the transition zones. The absolute threshold passes from no experience to some experience and the difference threshold passes from no change or difference to change or difference. Psychophysicists tried to evolve certain generalizations from these psychophysical functions. One generalization they have observed was that the minimum perceptible difference in the stimulus is proportion to the intensity of the stimulus. This may be also stated that in order to produce a just noticeable increase of sensation, the strength of the stimulus must be increased. This is in a constant ratio to the original value of the stimulus. Weber (1795 — 1872) has established this ratio with lifted weights, which is called Weber's law and the fraction is called Weber's fraction or ratio. Weber's law states that the difference threshold increases with the increase of the original intensity proportionally. The law is AS = KS or $\frac{\Delta S}{S}$ = K. Where S refers to the original stimulus, ΔS refers to the increase of the smallest weight, that can show difference in 10 grams, is one gram. By adding one gram to 10 the difference can be detected. Whatever the weight is, the same proportion of weight should be added to find out the difference limen and the ratio is $\frac{\Delta S}{S}$. Thus, for lifting the weights like 10, 20, 30 grams, an increase of one gram is added to 10, 2 to 20, 3 to 30. But if weight stimuli are 100, 200, 300 and so on, then the amount of weight added as a difference limen should be in the same proportion. In the case of 10 grams the ratio is $\frac{1}{10} = 0.1$, for 20, $\frac{2}{20} = 0.1$, for 30, $\frac{3}{30} = 0.1$. The same is applied to 100, 200, 300 and so on. $\frac{10}{100} = 0.1$, $\frac{20}{200} = 0.1$, $\frac{30}{300} = 0.1$. This constant is for weight. Similarly there are different constants for different sensations. There are several deviations from Weber's ratio. Some have observed that there are individual difference and hence the range of ratio for lifted weights was found to be from $\frac{1}{20}$ to $\frac{1}{100}$.

Weber's law was elaborated and made it as a general law by Fechner (1801—1887). Fechner developed the Weber's law to state the relationship between changes in the stimulus value and the sensory perception of these changes. He restated the law as S = K log R.

where S= refers to sensation perceived by the participant (the perception of change)

R= refers to the stimulus value (R stands for Reiz the German word for stimulus)

K= refers to the constant multiplier.

Fechner proposed his law on the sensational level (S). The intensity of sensory experience is called the logarthmetic function of stimulus intensity.

In Fechner's law the R includes the intensity of physical stimulus and the absolute threshold. The Weber-Fechner law was developed for measuring and generalizing the relationship that was existing between the stimulus changes and the corresponding sensation and the perception of the same, the changes. In studying these relationships the psychophysical methods are applied. These studies answered two important psychophysical questions as stated earlier. What is the smallest difference between two stimuli that can be just perceived or what is the smallest amount of stimulus or threshold that can produce noticeable difference? This is with reference to what we call the difference threshold or difference limen (DL). The second question the psychophysical studies answered is, what is the smallest amount of stimulus that can produce sensation of response. This is with regard to absolute threshold or absolute limen (AL).

The psychophysics and psychophysical methods were widely used in the earlier days by psychologists in the experimental psychology for determining the sensory thresholds of auditory, visual tactual and gustatory areas. Later on they are used in mental measurements, and in the construction of attitude scales.

Terminal Threshold (TT)

The terminal threshold refers to the intensity of stimulation. When the intensity of stimulation increased there is a change in the sensation. Though sensation increased when the intensity of stimulus was increased, it will not be a sensation for measurement. It will be very much annoying and painful sensation in the case of sound, in the case of light there is a glaring and the fibre reaches its terminal point. The stimulus energy is increased, but the sensation is not increased. The increase of stimulus energy effects the sensation or receptors. In visual area the terminal threshold is the brightest light and the most intense sensation the person experiences. In the further increase of stimulus energy, the person does not see the light appearing brighter. The person makes errors in reporting his sensations and the experimenter records errors in varying the stimulus as the stimulus light is not correct. In determining the difference limen in psychophysical methods the experimenter has to determine the point of subjective equality (PSE). The experiment involves comparing the variable stimulus with the standard stimulus. The experimenter asks the participant to judge whether the variable stimulus is smaller, equal or greater compared to the standard stimulus. The experimenter starts with lowest level and goes on increasing the size of the variable stimulus. Thus, there are three types of judgment, smaller, equal and greater in the trials of ascending series, and the judgments are greater, equal and smaller in the trials of descending series. In both series the experimenter comes across the terminal limen or threshold. The experimenter ceases to continue the trials any further after reaching the terminal point. In any further continuation of the trial he will get the same judgment. Thus, in this type of experiment we come across two types of thresholds, one is the lower threshold (LT) in which the variable stimulus is smaller and the other is the upper threshold or terminal threshold (TT) in which, the variable stimulus is greater. This type of terminal thresholds we come across in the method of minimal changes in determining the difference limen or threshold. In these type of experiments there seem to be two terminal thresholds. One is with the stimulus of greater intensity and the other is the stimulus with weaker intensity. Terminal means forming the end, there is no further move beyond that point. The experimenter does this at two extreme points and therefore there are two terminal thresholds. Hence terminal threshold need not be attributed only to the highest physical energy of the stimulus, both the lower and the upper thresholds are terminal thresholds.

Auditory Threshold

We hear with our ears everything what is audiable, just like what we see with our eyes everything that is visual. If we want to know anything about the sense of hearing it is important that we must know something about the physical energy that provides the stimuli for our sense of hearing. The physical energy, the sound is generally considered to be the auditory threshold or stimulus. The auditory threshold, the sound is produced in some form which we hear in the form of speech, musical tone, or from the striking some solid body like the bell or some metal. Sounds are produced by humans, animals, birds, or even natural events like wind, thunder, earthquake, running water, sea waves and so on. Sounds are produced in radio and television also. Thus we hear the sounds in innumerable ways in our everyday life. These sounds may be classified as smooth sounds (tones) or harmonious, sounds, discordant or harsh noise. We like to hear some sounds and dislike to hear some sounds. What we normally dislike is stated as noise. These sounds and noises have certain distinctive characteristics like the (1) loudness or intensity, (2) pitch, and (3) timbre.

1. *Loudness or Intensity*

Loudness may be defined as a measurable auditory sensation related to intensity or amplitude of the sound wave and measured in terms of sones. Sone is a unit of loudness equal to an intensity of 40 decibels. Loudness is normally associated with the amplitude or the width of the vibrations produced by the sounding body. Loudness is the strength or intensity of the sound wave, includes the extent of compression and rarefaction. The loudness or intensity of sound is stated in terms of decibels (dB). The decibel is a unit of measure related to the physical pressure. The human ear is very much sensitive to the frequency range of 500 to 4000 hertz. Human voice can range from 100 to 3500 hertz. Prolonged exposure to sounds above 90 decibels may cause permanent deafness, and painful experience may be caused in the eardrum to sound intensities above 120 decibels.

2. *Pitch*

Pitch is a single quality of hearing. It is a sensation of hearing which changes with the change of frequency of tone. Pitch is also defined as a hearing attribute or quality mainly depends upon the frequency of sound waves. A tone, which may be vocal or musical sound, may be described as low, medium, or high in pitch. A singer's voice (tone) may be high pitched, his assistance's voice may be low pitched, another of his follower's voice may be medium pitched. The pitch is always associated with the frequency of vibration, that is, how rapidly, the sound generating source moves to and fro. In other words, the pitch of a tone mainly depends upon the speed of the vibration of the sounding body. Some kind of frequency analysis is made in human hearing. In that way, pitch is related to frequency. A slow vibration frequency (or rate) produces a low rolling tone and rapid vibration frequency (or rate) produces a high tone. The lowest tone which a normal human ear can hear distinctly is from 20 vibrations per second (20 CPS). This tone will be heard as a low humming (murmuring) sound. The upper limit is 20,000 cycle per second (CPS). These very high tones are heard as screeching sounds. Vibration frequencies above 20,000 can be heard as a tone by some animals. But in man it is a very annoying and painful sound upon the eardrum. This range, 20 to 20,000 contracts with the age of humans at the high end. As we grow older sensitivity to high tones is gradually reduced. But the sensitivity, over the middle ranges for music, voice and common noises, is not damaged. The acuity of hearing can be tested with an instrument called audiometer. The loss of hearing, and the extensity of hearing may be assessed.

3. *Timbre*

Timbre refers to the quality of tone of sounds that distinguishes one voice from another. It may be also stated as the tonal quality of sounds that enables us to differentiate one kind of sound from another if they are of the same basic frequency. This mainly refers to musical notes, specially of instrumental music that are producing the same note. Generally, timbre is the complex of overtones which enables the listeners to identify the source. We are able to differentiate the tone of one instrument from the tone of another instruments played with the same fundamental tone. The listener can differentiate the tone of a violin from the tone of a piano or veena, can differentiate the tones between the flute and the pipe.

When there is a complex tone of several instruments with fundamental tone, any one of the tones may be having higher pitch. This is higher pitch of one of the tones is called overtone. The frequencies of the overtone are multiples of the fundamental tone. A violinist or pianoist may begin the fundamental tone at 400 Hertz or CPS, and the listeners can hear it. But at the same time the strings of the instrument may vibrate also in parts or segments which may be exactly at half, one-third, one-fourth or one-fifth and so on of its whole length. Such vibrations or frequencies produce overtone of a high pitch. The fundamental tone is 400 hertz and the segmented string produce the frequencies of 800, 1200, 1600 hertz so on. Each musical instrument may produce different frequency vibrations and cause different overtones. But the peaks and valleys of the fundamental tone are maintained.

Though the fundamental frequency is simple, the complex tone may vibrate with more than one frequency. In any complex tone with a fundamental frequency the overtone frequencies are 200, 300, 400 and so on. Thereby overtones or harmonies are produced which determine the timbre of the sound and timbre depends upon the number of overtones, frequencies intensities related to the fundamental tone. The whole length of the piano string produces the pitch of the fundamental tone and it also vibrates in parts which produce the new tones having varied frequency rates. There are additional new tones which add unique characteristics to the fundamental tone, are called overtones. The first overtone is produced by the vibration frequencies of half of the string. Other overtones have the frequency rates in times of the fundamental tone and all these additional new tones or overtones have higher pitch than the fundamental tone.

Any tone or sound wave-form may be breaking down into its components and these components are single pure tones with varying frequencies. There are more complex sound waves with many frequencies not having relation with one another. Such complex unrelated sound waves produce noises. A sound can be produced without any pitch which may contain all the frequencies. But noises are called white noises which are composed of sound waves of all the frequencies. Therefore, we may state that in a complex overtone the timbre of a tone does not indicate us whether the tone is produced by a violin or a piano or some other instrument.

Therefore, we may conclude that loudness or intensity is generally combined with the amplitude of the swing of the sound wave from the sound producing source. The pitch is associated with the frequency of swinging of the sound wave. The timbre is associated with the quality of the sound that distinguishes one voice or musical instrument from another voice or instrument.

8

MODERN PSYCHOPHYSICAL SCALING METHOD

Method of Pair Comparisons

INTRODUCTION

The method of pair comparison has been classified as one of the psychological scaling methods. Some psychophysicists state that it is a psychophysical method. The reason for such classification is that the final results are not stated as the values on physical scales. They are on psychological scales. When we assign numerical values to objects, events and mental phenomena it becomes a scale. A ruler is a scale which consists of continuous series of intervals. Objects and events are determined in terms of the intervals on the ruler. Strictly speaking, in psychophysical methods all physical values are determined only from psychological functions. For example, seeing and judging the visual stimulus values hearing and judging the auditory stimulus values and so on. It is only assigning numerical values to mental events. It is also possible to place all our behaviour on some scale. When a person is asked to make his preference between the objects A and B, he makes his preference on the basis of the value of the object and thereby he provides us with two values on the preference scale. Scales are important in all the measurements because the properties of objects should be given numerical value and without numerical value there is no scale. But the accuracy of the scales may differ from scale to scale and from property to property on the basis of the techniques used as there are several errors interfering in the experimental situation.

Types of Scales

A scale is a class of measurement. It has certain well defined characteristics. Stevens (1936) and Torgerson (1951) have independently classified the scales. According to them, there are four types of scales. They are nominal scales, ordinal scales, interval scales and ratio scales. These sales are explained in detail elsewhere in this book. But for clarifying the main subject matter, the scales are briefly stated here. The student at this stage should know something about the type of scales and how they are used in psychophysical studies.

1. *The Nominal Scale :* The word nominal means naming. The nominal scale is supposed to be the lowest of all the four scales. We use number in this scale to indicate a class of objects. For example, we can state a group of soldiers as Division 1, Division 2 and so on. But in every division there should be the same number of soldiers. The numeral is used here as a symbol, as a discriminatory symbol. In place of numeral, letters of alphabet also may be used. The numerical or letter may be assigned to qualitative variable. For example, 'students' is a qualitative variable having two categories as men students and women students and we may assign to them the alphabets or the numerals Ms and Ws or 1 and 2 respectively. These symbols discriminate the variables. The number indicates only the difference and not the magnitude of the objects or persons.

2. *The Ordinal Scale :* The nominal scale as we saw above involves qualitative measurement. But, the rest of the three scales involve quantitative measurement. Among the three quantitative scales the ordinal scale is not so strong and accurate. It makes only comparative judgments in the measurement. For example, four weights such as W_1, W_2, W_3, W_4, were arranged at random and a person may be asked to arrange them in the rank order from heaviest to lightest. Here the weights are used only to judge the order of their ranks. The actual weight of the object is not known. But at the same time the objects are identified and measured on an ordinal scale. That is, an order of the objects has been made. Therefore, the ordinal scale is a type of scale that judges the relative position of an object and not the magnitude of the object, or the difference between two objects.

3. *The Interval Scale :* In the previous two scales we do not bother about the magnitude of the differences in measurement. But the interval scale is mainly concerned with the magnitude of the difference that separates two objects. In interval scale the objects are ordered with respect to a quantitative attribute and also the correct magnitude of the differences that separate the objects.

4. *The Ratio Scale :* This is the last of the scales, but possesses all the qualities of other three scales and in addition, it has certain special qualities.

In this sense, it is supposed to be the highest form of scale. Ratio scale has units of measurements and a zero point. The ratio scale refers to a level of measurement. The method of constructing a ratio scale is to start with a zero point and plot equal units and by multiply each unit by a constant that should yield equal ratios. In a sense it is a way of making a comparative judgments. For example, A and B are measured and judged as A is twice as heavy as B, X is twice as long as Y. These measurements may be given numerical value presented in ratios. For example, A weighs 20 gms, and B 10 gms. It is stated as $\frac{A}{B} = \frac{20}{10} = \frac{2}{1}$. In the method of ratio judgment it is stated as the method of multiple stimuli. If you reverse it (1/2) it is called the method of fractionation.

Psychophysical Scaling Methods

The psychophysical scaling methods are considered to be alternative scaling procedures. Guilford (1954) calls these as psychological scaling methods, whereas Amato (1968) calls this as psychophysical scaling. In psychophysical scaling methods responses are produced under two classes. The first procedure is called *estimation procedure*. According to this procedure the observer is presented with one or more stimuli and he is asked to give the estimate orally or by some means. It is with reference to the magnitude of the sensations aroused by the stimuli. In this procedure the stimuli presented are fixed throughout the experiment. Therefore, it is called estimation procedure.

The second is *response procedure* which provides some freedom to the observer. He can vary the stimuli at his disposal and produce sensation on himself according to the direction given by the experimenter. On certain occasions the experimenter also adjusts the variable stimuli on the observer's instruction. The stimuli may be varied on certain physical dimensions. The second procedure is also called production procedure.

In all the psychological scaling methods we could see these two characteristics. The most often used psychological scaling methods are methods of pair-comparisons, method of rank order and rating scales. These methods are used in a variety of situations to solve various problems. These methods produce data on ordinal or interval scales.

The fundamental principle of the method of pair comparison is that stimuli are presented to the observer always in pairs, and the observer is required to select the member of the pair which possesses more or less quality to be judged. The other way is, which one of the pair is greater in quantity than the other in some particular respect.

The Method of Pair Comparison

The method of pair-comparison is a psychological scaling method in the sense that it differs from the classical psychophysical methods. Here the stimuli are to be judged on a psychological scale and not on physical scale. The stimuli are presented to the observer in pairs and his task is to judge whether one of the pairs is better in quality or quantity than the other in some respect. Unlike the psychophysical methods the observer has to give his judgments in two categories and not three. He must guess and state which is better. Since large number of pairs are presented to the observer he may judge all the pairs for large number of times. In this respect this method is quite similar to one of the psychophysical methods, the constant method.

In this method a single subject may judge the same pairs of stimuli several times. This provides measures of dispersion in the individual judgment. But, several subjects also judge the same pairs of stimuli to provide a measure of dispersion in the group judgment.

This method has certain advantages over other methods. The stimuli are always presented in pairs and so there is a chance for counterbalancing in the values of the stimuli. This procedure therefore has a chance of eliminating time error and space error that we find in other methods. Another advantage of the method is that it permits more reliable data when large number of stimuli are presented to the observer.

In the method of pair comparisons sometimes we can use three stimuli and the method is called method of triads. The observer may be asked to select the best among the three or the least of the three. The formula necessary for comparison in this case is

$$\frac{(N-2)(N-1)N}{6}$$

where N refers to the number of stimuli.

Thurstone's Law of Comparative Judgment

The method of pair comparison rests on a law formulated by Thurstone, and it is named after him, as 'Thurstone's law of comparative judgment. It runs like this :

$$Rj - Rk = Zjk\sqrt{\sigma_j^2 + \sigma_k^2 - 2V_{jk}\sigma_j\sigma_k}$$

Rj and Rk refer to psychological values attached to the stimuli j and k. Zjk refers to measure of deviation from the mean of a unit of normal distribution. (σ j and σk refer to the standard deviation of distributions of Rhj and Rhk. Rjk refers to co-efficient of correlation between the distributions of Rhj and Rhk.

According to Thurstone there are five cases with respect to the applications of the law of comparative judgment. But, usually the case V is often applied in the experimental situations as it is simple. Here the discriminal dispersions are equal. The law, therefore, is stated as Rj — Rk = Zjk. Here the assumption is that σj stands for both σ j and σk as σj is equal to σk and therefore they are dropped in the law.

The method of pair comparison is applied whenever stimuli are presented in pairs. It may be simultaneous or succession. People differ in their preferences with regard to certain objects when their qualities are not directly measured. Its important use has been in the determination of affective values and aesthetic values, colours, designs, musical notes, names of nationalities, individuals, groups, food cooked. This method is considered to be very accurate when compared to other methods like rating scales. This method needs every item should be compared with every other item. This would make the total number of judgment pairs $\frac{N(n-1)}{2}$. This means, if the number of stimuli are 10, the total number of pairs are $\frac{10(10-1)}{2} = 45$. If we apply this procedure when the number of stimuli are large the method would become very unwieldy and time consuming. Another disadvantage of this method is the computational labour. The data are required to be posted in several tables after every step to arrive at the scale values.

Variation of the Method : Reducing Number of Pairs

When the number stimuli are large, the number of pairs become too many and it would become a very laborious task for the experimenter and for the observer. Therefore, a method has been suggested to reduce this task without sacrificing the accuracy of the method. It is by establishing appropriate rank order of the samples.

Reducing the Labour in Computing the Scale Value

Guilford (1954) has suggested a procedure to reduce the labour involved in the computation of the scale value. The important part of this process involves in finding out the mean of the proportion of judgment for every stimulus as compared with every other stimulus. The scaling is worked out from these proportions.

EXPERIMENT 6: Determination of Scale Values for a Set of Stimuli by the Method of Pair Comparisons

Problem : The purpose of this experiment is to determine scale values for a set of stimuli provided by the method of pair comparisons.

2. METHOD

Participant : Choose four persons who have no knowledge of the purpose of this experiment and collect their personal information such as qualification, age, gender and whether any of them is having any physical defects.

Material : A list of seven names of famous English Poets, namely 1. Shakespeare, 2. Milton, 3. Wordsworth, 4. Coleridge, 5. Shelley, 6. Keats and 7. Byron. The material also may be seven names of famous cinema stars, or seven eminent political leaders, or seven paintings having different aesthetic values.

The seven names of the poets are combined in all possible pairs and two names are written in each slip. Thus there are two names in every slip. Thereby it has become 21 (7 x 6 ÷ 2) pairs. The sequence of pairs are carefully arranged in a scheme that is followed in any pair comparison procedure. The pairs are arranged in such a way that every name is made to appear equally often on the left and also on the right. The positions of the names in the slips on the left and on the right are alternated. On the basis of this principle, the pairs of the names are arranged in the order given below and written in slips.

1. Shakespeare — Milton, 2. Wordsworth — Coleridge, 3. Shelley — Keats, 4. Byrbn — Shakespeare, 5. Milton — Wordsworth, 6. Coleridge — Shelley, 7. Keats — Byron, 8. Shakespeare — Coleridge, 9. Byron — Milton, 10. Shelley — Shakespeare, 11. Wordsworth — Keats, 12. Coleridge — Byron, 13. Shakespeare — Woardsworth, 14. Milton — Coleridge, 15. Wordsworth-- Shelley, 16. Keats — Shakespeare, 17. Shelley — Milton, 18. Byron — Wordsworth, 19. Coleridge — Keats, 20. Shelley — Byron, 21. Keats — Milton.

But there is every possibility of occurring space error in this type of pairing. Therefore, in order to avoid the space error in the method of pair comparisons every names is made to appear on the left and also on the right and no name appeared in successive pairs. That is, if a name appeared on the left in one pair in the next time that name is made to appear on the right. But spacing is maintained in pairs to see that a stimulus is kept apart as far as possible and as conditions permitted. Therefore, all the pairs are arranged according to this plan and the number of pairs are 42. This arrangement is made for the convenience of the experimenter. Thus, the seven names are arranged into 42 pairs as follows :

1. Shakespeare - Milton
2. Wordsworth - Coleridge
3. Milton - Shakespeare
4. Coleridge - Wordsworth
5. Wordsworth - Milton
6. Shakespeare - Coleridge
7. Shelley - Keats
8. Milton - Wordsworth
9. Coleridge - Shakespeare
10. Keats - Byron
11. Milton - Shelley
12. Shakespeare - Wordsworth
13. Byron - Keats
14. Milton - Coleridge
15. Wordsworth - Shakespeare
16. Coleridge - Milton
17. Shelley - Shakespeare
18. Milton - Keats
19. Wordsworth - Shelley
20. Byron - Milton
21. Shelley - Wordsworth
22. Shakespeare - Keats
23. Milton - Byron
24. Coleridge - Shelley
25. Keats - Shakespeare
26. Wordsworth - Byron
27. Shelley - Coleridge
28. Keats - Milton
29. Shakespeare - Shelley
30. Byron - Wordsworth
31. Coleridge - Byron

32. Shelley - Milton
33. Wordsworth - Keats
34. Byron - Coleridge
35. Keats - Shelley
36. Shakespeare - Byron
37. Coleridge - Keats
38. Byron - Shelley
39. Keats - Coleridge
40. Shelley - Byron
41. Keats - Wordsworth
42. Byron - Shakespeare.

Procedure : When the experimenter was ready with his material, he made the participant seated comfortably in a well illuminated room. The other three were kept in the next room. The experimenter kept the participant at his table in front of him. The following instructions were given to the participant.

"I am going to show you two names of famous English poets in a slip and your task is to tell me which name you prefer out of the two names. There are going to be 42 pairs in 42 slips and you will have to judge and state your preference of the name in each pair. I am going to show you these 42 pairs 25 times and every time you will have to tell me the name you prefer among the two. Now we are starting the work. Either you can tell me the name or indicate it in the slip shown to you."

Then the experimenter showed each slip with two names for few seconds to the participant. He has shown the slips one by one. When the participant made his judgment and told the name, the experimenter at once noted down the name by making a tally mark in a matrix prepared for this (Table 8.1). When all the 42 slips were shown, each 25 times and obtained the responses from the participant the experimenter has dispensed with the participant. Then the experimenter carried out the same procedure in obtaining the responses for 42 pairs 25 times from the second participant, then the third and fourth. The experimenter has maintained four response matrix for four participants in order to avoid confusion between responses of different participants.

On obtaining the responses of the preference of the names of the poets from all four participants, the experimenter has consolidated the judgments by putting the judgments of all four and presented in Table 8.3. The operational procedure in detail follows.

Table 8.1 : The Tally marks show the frequencies of the preferences of the stimuli (Poets) made by one judge (each 25 times) of the 42 pairs in the method of pair comparisons

Name	Shakespeare	Milton	Wordsworth	Coleridge	Shelley	Keats	Byron
1. Shakespeare	—	38	40	42	36	34	38
2. Milton	12	—	34	32	24	22	20
3. Wordsworth	10	16	—	26	22	18	16
4. Coleridge	8	18	24	—	20	16	14
5. Shelley	14	26	28	30	—	24	22
6. Keats	16	28	32	34	26	—	24
7. Byron	20	30	34	36	28	26	—

Operational Procedure of tallying the Preferences

In Table 8.1 seven names of famous English Poets are written both in rows and in columns, the same names in the same order. These names are made into 42 pairs and each participant has to choose the desired name in the pair 25 times. The experimenter shows each time two names in a slip and if the participant chooses the first name, a tally mark is made against the first name in the row under the second name. Instead, if the second name is choosen then a tally mark is made against the second name in the column under the first name.

For exemple, in a slip the two name are Shakespeare and Milton. If Shakespeare is choosen a tally mark is made against the name Shakespeare in the row on the right under the name Milton. Istead, if Milton is choosen by the participant, a tally mark is made against Milton on the left in the column under the name Shakespeare.

Between Shakespeare and Wordsworth, if Shakespeare is choosen a tally mark is made against Shakespeare in the row on the right under the name Wordsworth. But if Wordsworth is preferred, then a tally mark is made against Wordsworth on the left in the column under the name, Shakespeare. Thus again, between Shakespeare and Coleridge, if Shakespeare is preferred a tally mark is made against Shakespeare on the right in the row under the name Coleridge. But if Coleridge is preferred, then a tally mark is made against Coleridge on the left in the column under the name Shakespeare.

In the same way, between Shakespeare and Shelley, if the name Shakespeare is choosen, a tally mark is made on the right in the row under the name Shelley. But if Shelley is preferred then, a tally mark is made against Shelley on the left in the column under the name Shakespeare.

Similarly, between Shakespeare and Keats, if Shakespeare is choosen a tally mark is made against the name Shakespeare on the right in the row under the name Keats. But if Keats is preferred then, a tally mark is made against Keats on the left in the column under the name Shakespeare. Between Shakespeare and Byron if Shakespeare is preferred, a tally mark is made against Shakespeare on the right in the row under the name Byron. But if Byron is preferred, then, a tally mark is made against Byron on the left in the column under the name Shakespeare.

The same procedure is followed in comparing and judging every name on the left in column by the names given in the row on the right top. As there is no comparison between the same name, *i.e.*, between Shakespeare and Shakespeare, the diagonal cells are empty. In this procedure all the 42

Table 8.2 : Showing the preferences made by one Judge of the 42 pairs of names of seven famous English poets, judging each pair 25 times in the method of pair comparisons

Names	Shakespeare	Milton	Wordsworth	Coleridge	Shelley	Keats	Byron	Σ
1. Shakespeare	—	38	40	42	36	34	38	220
2. Milton	12	—	34	32	24	22	20	144
3. Wordsworth	10	16	—	26	22	18	16	108
4. Coleridge	8	18	24	—	20	16	14	100
5. Shelley	14	26	28	30	—	24	22	144
6. Keats	16	28	32	34	26	—	24	160
7. Byron	20	30	34	36	28	26	—	174
Σ	80	156	192	200	156	140	126	1050

Table-8.3 : The Tally marks show the frequencies of the preferences of the stimuli (Poets) made by 4 judges 100 times (each 25 times) of the 42 pairs in the method of pair comparisons.

Names	Shakespeare	Milton	Wordsworth	Coleridge	Shelley	Keats	Byron
1. Shakespeare	--	(172)	(176)	(184)	(124)	(116)	(108)
2. Milton	(28)	--	(116)	(124)	(88)	(84)	(76)
3. Wordsworth	(24)	(84)	--	(108)	(76)	(80)	(74)
4. Coleridge	(16)	(76)	(92)	--	(72)	(68)	(64)
5. Shelley	(76)	(112)	(124)	(128)	--	(96)	(90)
6. Keats	(84)	(116)	(120)	(132)	(104)	--	(94)
7. Byron	(92)	(124)	(126)	(136)	(110)	(106)	

cells in Table 8.1, are filled with tally marks except the 7 diagonal cells.

This part of the experiment is explained in so detail because some experimenters find it difficult in making entries in the appropriate cells and they often find that the sums of the corresponding cells do not tally. In the method of pair comparisons if the number of stimuli and the number of judges are many, the choices become numerous and the frequency distributions in each cell do not easily tally. To avoid the problem involved in this process an easy method is suggested in this way.

In Table 8.2, the data of the preferences made by one judge of the 42 pairs of the poets 25 times are presented for illustration. Similar data were collected from the preferences of all four participants and presented in Table 8.3.

With regard to the experimental procedure Culler (1926) has proposed the use of variable stimulus as the standard stimulus and every stimulus should be compared with every other stimulus as in constant method. In this procedure every stimulus becomes a standard and also a comparative or variable stimulus. What is applicable to constant method is also applicable to pair comparisons. Guilford (1954) has proposed that each pair should be judged 200 times by a single participant. Thereby we can find in each row in the matrix, the judgments of one standard stimulus vary from row to row. Since the number of pairs in this experiment are 42 in number it is better to judge each pair for 100 times by four participants, each judging the 42 pairs for 25 times. Thus the 42 pairs are judged 25 times by four persons making it 100 times.

RESULTS

The data treated statistically and presented in Tables here, were obtained from an experiment conducted on an earlier occasion. The results of the experiment are explained and discussed for illustrating the various procedures involved in the method of pair comparisons experiment based upon Thurstone's law of comparative judgments. Certain difficult issues are simplified and illustrated.

Treatment of the Results

The stimuli used in this experiment were seven famous English Poets. By presenting every poet in the first place or on the left and also in the second place or on the right 42 pairs were evolved. The procedure was already explained. The 42 pairs were judged by four participants and each one has judged each pair 25 times. Thus, there were 100 (4 x 25 = 100) judgments and each pair was judged one hundred times. Each participant has made 1050 (52 x 25=1050) judgments. The judgments made by a participant in preference of one stimulus over the other were entered by a tally mark in Table 8.1. The total judgments for an individual participant were 1050 and they were checked (Table 8.2).

The judgments made by all four participants were put together in Table 8.3. The judgments were entered in Table 8.4 and they were checked in rows and in columns. The total judgments of 42 pairs, each judged by four participants 100 times constituted 4200. Thus, Table 8.4 consisted of the data of the number of times all the names were preferred by the participants. The preferred names were given in columns and the comparison names in rows.

The next step was to work out the proportions for the number of preferences (Table 8.4) and present them in Table-8.5. This is called proportion matrix. The proportions were rearranged in rows and in columns. The rearrangement of the proportions of the judgments of every stimulus in columns and rows in an increasing order is a confusing task. It is very difficult to rearrange them in increasing order in rows and columns as the numbers do not fit in an increasing order. But one way of simplified procedure of doing this is to sum up the rows and giving rank order from highest to lowest for the rows and lowest to highest for the columns. First, the names of the poets were written from top to bottom in columns and then from left to right in the rows. According to the results of this experiment, the order of names given in the beginning from Shakespeare to Byron was thoroughly changed. The rearranged order of the names on the basis of the sum of proportion values are (1) Shakespeare, (2) Byron, (3) Keats, (4) Shelley, (5) Milton, (6) Wordsworth and (7) Coleridge, Shakespeare was placed in the first rank, Coleridge in the last rank and others in between these two names (Table 8.5). Now, in Table 8.6 the proportions of the judgments were arranged in increasing order in columns and rows. The values were checked in rows and in columns and they coincided.

In the next step the proportions were converted in deviate values or z values using the conversion table (Woodwoth,1954) and they were presented in z matrix (Table 8.7). In the conversion Table, if the proportion value is greater than .5 then the z value is having positive sign (+) and if the proportion value is smaller than .5 then the z value is having negative sign (–). It is important to note that the upper right portion of the matrix is identical with the lower left portion of the matrix numerically, if the positive and negative signs are omitted.

Table 8.4 : Showing the preferences made by four participants of the 42 pairs of seven English poets, each pair judged 25 times (25 x 4 = 100) in the method of pair comparisons

Name	Shakespeare	Milton	Wordsworth	Coleridge	Shelley	Keats	Byron	Σ
1. Shakespeare	—	172	176	184	124	116	108	880
2. Milton	28	—	116	124	88	84	76	516
3. Wordsworth	24	84	—	108	76	80	74	446
4. Coleridge	16	76	92	—	72	68	64	388
5. Shelley	76	112	124	128	—	96	90	626
6. Keats	84	116	120	132	104	—	94	650
7. Byron	92	124	126	136	110	106	—	694
Σ	320	684	754	812	574	550	506	4200

Table 8.5 : Showing the proportions of the preferences made by four participants of the 42 pairs of seven English poets, judging each pair 25 times by the method of pair comparisons

Name	Shakespeare	Milton	Wordsworth	Coleridge	Shelley	Keats	Byron	Σ	Rank
1. Shakespeare	—	.86	.88	.92	.62	.58	.54	4.40	1
2. Milton	.14	—	.58	.62	.44	.42	.38	2.58	5
3. Wordsworth	.12	.42	—	.54	.38	.40	.37	2.23	6
4. Coleridge	.08	.38	.46	—	.36	.34	.32	1.94	7
5. Shelley	.38	.56	.62	.64	—	.48	.45	3.13	4
6. Keats	.42	.58	.60	.66	.52	—	.47	3.25	3
7. Byron	.46	.62	.63	.68	.55	.53	—	3.47	2
Σ	1.60	3.42	3.77	4.06	2.87	2.75	2.53	21.00	
Rank	1	5	6	7	4	3	2		

Table 8.6 : Showing the proportions rearranged in the increasing order in Rows and Columns

	1	2	3	4	5	6	7	
Name	Shakespeare	Byron	Keats	Shelly	Milton	Wordsworth	Coleridge	Σ
1. Shakespeare	.50	.54	.58	.62	.86	.88	.92	4.90
2. Byron	.46	.50	.53	.55	.62	.63	.68	3.97
3. Keats	.42	.47	.50	.52	.58	.60	.66	3.75
4. Shelley	.38	.45	.48	.50	.56	.62	.64	3.63
5. Milton	.14	.38	.42	.44	.50	.58	.62	3.08
6. Wordsworth	.12	.37	.40	.38	.42	.50	.54	2.73
7. Coleridge	.08	.32	.34	.36	.38	.46	.50	2.44
Σ pi > k	2.10	3.03	3.25	3.37	3.92	4.27	4.56	24.50

The rows and columns of the matrix were summed up and the sums were summed up and entered on the right end of the last row. This value is Σ zjk and the sum of the sums is zero (0.00). The Σ zjk values in the rows were divided by the number of stimuli, seven and entered below the values of Σ zjk in columns. This value is Mzjk, the mean of the z values of the stimuli. These values were summed up and it is found that they are also zero (0.00). It is observed in Table 8.7 that four of the mean values are negative and therefore a meaningful zero point is evolved by making the highest negative value (—.661) as zero. This value is .661, and this is used as a constant and added with all other means and all the values are converted into positive values ranging from 0.00, .437, .535, .550, .786, .921, and 1.048. These values are taken as the scale values of the stimuli. The treatment of the data is stopped at this stage. Authors like Guilford (1954) suggested that the smaller values which were less than 1 (one) should be made greater than one and this could be ohtained by using a constant multiplier. But since the constant multiplier is not available within the limit of this experiment conducted, the Rj (Response) values are accepted as the scale values.

DISCUSSION

The aim of this experiment is to determine the scale values for seven stimuli by the method of pair comparisons. The stimuli were the names of seven famous English poets and they were presented in pairs to the participants and were asked to judge and indicate the name he/she preferred among the two in a slip. The seven stimuli were made into 42 pairs and four participants judged each pair 25 times and thus there were 4200 (42 x 4 x 25 = 4200) judgments made by four persons. The judgments were treated statistically and presented in Tables. The judgments made by one participant is given in Tables 8.1 and 8.2. The total numbers given in each cell of Table 8.1 shows the preference the participant has made of the name of the poet 25 times. The names in the columns on the left are standard stimuli and the names at the top in row are the comparison stimuli. In the first row Shakespeare is compared with every other poet. In the tabulation of the responses, if the person preferred Shakespeare to the second name Milton a tally mark is made against Shakespeare. Instead, if he/she preferred the second name, Milton, a tally mark is made against Milton in the second row. Between the names, Shakespeare and Milton the participant has preferred Shakespeare 38 times and Milton 12 times when he/she judged 42 pairs 25 times. Between the names Milton and Wordsworth the person

Table 8.7 : Proportions converted into z values, the Means and the Scale values of the seven stimuli (names of the poets)

Name	Shakespeare	Byron	Keats	Shelley	Milton	Wordsworth	Coleridge	Σ
1. Shakespeare	0.00	+0.10	+0.20	+0.31	+1.08	+1.18	+1.41	+1.28
2. Byron	-0.10	0.00	+0.08	+0.13	+0.31	+0.33	+0.47	+1.22
3. Keats	-0.20	-0 08	0.00	+0.05	+0.20	+0.25	+0.41	+0.63
4. Shelley	-0.31	-0.13	-0.05	0.00	+0.15	+0.31	+0.36	+0.33
5. Milton	-1.08	-0.31	-0.20	-0.15	0.00	+0.20	+0.31	-1.23
6. Wordsworth	-1.18	-0.33	-0.25	-0.31	-0.20	0.00	+0.10	-2.17
7. Coleridge	-1.41	-0.47	-0.41	-0.36	-0.31	-0.10	0.00	-3.06
Σ Zjk	-4.28	-1.22	-0.63	-0.33	+1.23	+2.17	+3.06	0.00
MZjk	-0.611	-0.174	-0.076	-0.061	+0.175	+0.310	+0.437	0.00
Rj	0.00	.437	.535	.550	.786	.921	1.048	4.714
Rank on the basis of Rj	1	2	3	4	5	6	7	

preferred Milton 34 times and Wordsworth 11 times while judging 42 pairs 25 times. Each name appeared 6 times in the first place and 6 times in the second place after every 6 pairs of the other names. Thus, it was arranged in such a way that the same name did not appear successively in two pairs. Therefore, the space error in this procedure was avoided. In 300 judgments (6+6 x 25) this participant preferred Shakespeare 220 times and others 80 times. On the whole he/she preferred Milton 144 times, Wordsworth 108 times, Coleridge 100 times, Shelley 144 times, Keats 160 times and Byron 174 times (Table 8.2).

On consolidating the preferences made by all four participants, each judging all seven names 25 times, made the total preferences 100 (4 x 25). It is observed that Shakespeare, on whole, was preferred 880 times out of 4200 judgments, Milton was preferred 516 times, Wordsworth 446 times, Coleridge 388 times, Shelley 626 times, Keats 650 times and Byron 694 times. All the four participants in a total judgments of 4200, given first preference to Shakespeare, second preference to Byron, third to Keats, fourth to Shelley, fifth to Milton, sixth to Wordsworth and seventh place to Coleridge (Table 8.4).

In the next stage of the treatment, all the preferences of the participants for the seven names of poets were converted into proportions (Table 8.5) and they were rearranged in an increasing order on the basis of the preferences (Table 8.6). The order of the names on the basis of preferences is, Shakespeare, Byron, Keats, Shelley, Milton, Wordsworth and Coleridge. It appears that the four participants who took part in this experiment have known more about the first four names and known moderately about Milton and little about Wordsworth and Coleridge (Table 8.6).

The response values (Rj) are used here as the scale values (Table 8.7) and these values range from 0.00 to 1.047 in the order of preferences by the participants. The lowest value represent the highest and the highest value respresents the lowest preference. Therefore, the order of the preferences from the first to the last is : 1. Shakespeare, 2. Byron, 3. Keats, 4. Shelley, 5. Milton, 6. Wordsworth, and 7. Coleridge.

In the method of pair comparisons, the preferences made by the participants of the seven names of famous English poets presented in figures in Tables 8.5, 8.6, and 8.7 are the results of this experiment. In the final stage, these figures are reduced to only seven figures as scale values of the stimuli. In the treatment of the data, the preferences of the seven poets made by the four participants; we were not having any idea about the position of the seven poets, in the beginning. But a stage has reached in the process of the treatment of the data that the ranks of the poets have automatically arrived at from the preferences. The final ranking of the names of the poets is highly surprising though the name of the poet, Byron was in the last place of the list. In the final stage the name has come to the second place, next to Shakespeare. The order of the names placed in the beginning is thoroughly changed in the final stage. This seems to be the characteristic of the method of comparative judgments.

CONCLUSIONS

The preferences made by the four participants of the seven names of famous English poets (stimuli) resulted in evolving the scale values for seven stimuli. The result has given a rank position to every poet from first to last. The rank positions are : 1. Shakespeare, 2. Byron, 3. Keats, 4. Shelley, 5. Milton, 6. Wordsworth, and 7. Coleridge.

9

MODERN PSYCHOPHYSICAL SCALING METHOD : Method of Rank Order

INTRODUCTION

The method of rank order is one of the important psychometric methods very widely used in psychological experiments. This method has been classified as one of the psychophysical scaling methods. The basic principle of this method is that a stimulus can be placed in only one place, whether it is in the first place or in the second place or in the last place, it is assigned only one place.

This method has certain similarity with the method of paired comparisons, but little different from the paired comparison method. In the method of rank order all the stimuli are presented to the respondent simultaneously and he/she has to place them in different places on the basis of the quality of the stimulus. The respondent can judge the quality of the stimulus in whatever manner he/she wants. But in the method of paired comparison only two stimuli are presented at a time and the respondent has to choose the one that he/she prefers out of the two every time. The method of rank order forces the respondent to discriminate the stimuli as much as possible as in the method of paired comparison. In the method of rank order the respondent has the liberty to manipulate any stimulus in whatever manner he/she wants, whether the stimulus refers to the member of a human group, or arts, or artistic designs, advertisements, jokes, or the quality of materials. Objects ranked by a number of respondents are placed in a pooled rank order. Scale values are assigned to the stimuli as in the case of interval scales.

The method of rank order is also having some resemblance to the method of successive categories. The resemblance refers to the arrangement of the stimuli by the respondent along some psychological continuum. In the method of successive categories the respondent is required to place a stimulus in a category and more than one stimulus may be placed in the same category. But in the rank order method only one stimulus is in a category or rank, that is, the rank whether it is the first rank or second rank or the last rank. Here the respondent should not place or give the same value to more than one stimulus. One stimulus should go into only one place.

But when a set of stimuli were judged by a large number of judges the rankings of the stimuli may vary from person to person. Some may place a stimulus in the first rank and some place the same stimulus in the second rank or in third rank and some may place the same stimulus in the last rank. In such cases the rank values of the stimuli cannot be determined by ordinary method. Therefore, Guilford (1954) has suggested the normalized rank order method for determining the scale values of the stimuli.

The normalized rank order method is based on the principle that in any population, the representation or the sample or judgment may fall into normal distribution. Most of them fall near the middle portion in a crowded manner and then thinly distributed at the ends. But in the rank order method every stimulus finds a place independent of other stimuli irrespectve of its quality or magnitude. But if we compare the quality of the stimuli some may come close and some may go far away. In other words, the distance between the stimuli A and B may be closer and the distance between the stimuli B and C may be wider. In this way the distance between various stimuli may vary. This shows that the rank does not indicate the correct position of the stimulus.

Suppose, for example, four horses are running in a race and four places they occupy in ranking. The horse C may come first in 20 seconds; B in 22 seconds, A in 40 seconds and D in 42 seconds. The time difference between the first and second is 2 seconds and between B and A is 18 seconds and between A and D is two seconds. On the basis of the positions when we rank these horses we do not take into account the difference in speed in seconds. The horse B (22 seconds) is just one rank higher than the horse A (40 seconds) because of its position. But the difference between the horses B and A in running speed is much greater than the difference between the first and the second and between the third and the fourth.

Therefore, in judging the objects and ranking them only one person cannot pay proper attention on the quality of all the objects or persons to be ranked. It is better to have a minimum of the same number of persons as the number of stimuli are, and the stimuli or objects should be presented in different order for every person. By this method we counterbalance the problems.

Variations in the Methods in Scaling from Ranks

We may face a problem in finding out the scale value of a stimulus if the number of ranks are many. It is not possible to make complete ranking. In such case it is better to have a modified method of scaling. The method suggested by Guilford (1954) is scaling from the first ranks. The stimuli may be too many and the observers may lack the power of discrimination to judge the stimuli. If such problem prevails the observers may not be interested in the task. Therefore, it is better to select the best five or ten objects and rank them out of the N ranks.

Method of First Choice

This is one of the variation methods evolved out of Fechner's method of choices. The value of the object is judged by the number of first choices made by the number of judges. But this may be useful only for ranking and the scale values cannot be determined. The method of first choices is limiting the cases, where, the case, k = 1. Because of this, the scaling from the first k ranks is better. It is not reasonable to determine the scale value of some stimuli by using only the judgments in rank 1, and any attempt to determine the scale value is not stable.

EXPERIMENT-7: Determination of Scale Values for a set of Stimuli by the Rank Order Method

Aim : The aim of this experiment is to judge the aesthetic values of a set of 12 paintings and to determine the scale values and the rank order of the paintings on the basis of the aesthetic qualities.

2. METHOD

Participants : Choose 10 to 15 persons who have willingness to serve as the respondents in this experiment and collect their personal information such as age, gender, qualifications, occupation, socio-economic-status, whether any of them having any physical defects like eye defects or sense of hearing.

Materials : The materials required for this experiment are paintings, or names of the persons of outstanding personalities, names of great scientists, or famous film stars or heroes or heroines selected from popular themes of Indian Classics. In this experiment the material used is a set of 12 contemporary artistic paintings, which includes landscapes, humans (faces or full figures), animals, birds, and designs etc. These 12 paintings are serially arranged and indicated by the alphabetical letters, A, B, C, D, E, F, G, H, I, J, K, and L. It is better not to give serial numbers like 1,2,3, etc., because the respondents may mistake these numbers as the order of the ranks of the paintings (Appendix A).

Procedure : The experimenter should get ready as many test sets as the number of persons participating in this experiment to reduce the amount of time involved in this. If they are available as the number of persons, it can be used as group test. If only one set is available it can be used as an individual test and the same test material can be repeated on all respondents one by one.

The person/persons may be seated comfortably in a well illuminated room where there is no disturbance of any type. Then the following Instructions should be given to the respondents :

"I am going to give you a set of 12 paintings and your task is to see and examine each of them very carefully one by one and arrange them top to bottom or first to last on the basis of the aesthetic values you find in each of them. The painting you judged as the best among the 12, should be placed at the top as the first rank, and the painting you judged as the second best should be placed in the next in the second place. Similarly, the painting you judged as the third best should be placed in the third place. In the same manner all the 12 paintings should be judged on the basis of the aesthetic values and placed in the respective places. The painting you judged as having the least aesthetic value should be placed in the last, in the 12th rank. The paintings should be arranged in the order from 1 to 12 on the basis of the merit. A painting should be given only one rank and no two paintings should have the same rank.

I will give you a piece of paper in which you should write down the alphabetical letter given at the top of the painting and the rank you have assigned to it and also should write down briefly the reason for placing it in the first place or in the second place or in the last place. Whatever suitable reason you find for placing it in a particular rank may be written there. There is no time limit. You can take your own time, no hurry. When I say ready go, you can start working on it. When the work is over, you must handover them to me in the same order you have arranged. Before starting the actual work you will have to provide certain personal information asked far in a profoma."

Then the experimenter can distribute the personal information proforma and on collecting them, the test materials can be handed over to the respondent/s. When the respondents are ready, the experimenter can give the order, "Ready, go".

The experimenter should maintain a stop watch or clock, indirectly, to find out how much time each person is taking to complete the task. After collecting the paintings which were arranged in the rank order, the experimenter may allow the respondents to go away. If the test is administered individually the same material may be given to another person and then to a third person and so on. On collecting sufficient number of responses, the experimenter can start tabulating the responses in a Table.

An experiment conducted elsewhere on an earlier occasion according to the procedure is used here as an example. The data obtained from that experiment are treated statistically for the purpose of illustration.

This experiment was conducted in a classroom situation to find out the scale values of 12 (stimuli) contemporary paintings. The experiment was conducted in four sessions at the rate of 3 and 4 postgraduate students in each session and the total number of students who took part in this test were 13. This procedure was followed as there was only one set of test material. Since this method needs more number of responses for determining the scale values of 12 paintings the respondents should not be less than the number of stimuli used in the experiment. The persons who serve as judges should be 12 and above. Hence, 13 students' responses were collected. The stimuli were 12 paintings with varied aesthetic values of landscapes, humans, animals, birds, interior decoration and so on.

3. RESULTS

The experiment was conducted as an individual test on 13 students in four sessions. Each respondent has arranged all the 12 paintings in the rank order on the basis of the aesthetic merits of the paintings from top to bottom. Thus, the top one received the first rank and the bottom one received the last rank and others placed in between them.

The rank order given by the participant VL to the 12 paintings is given below:

Painting : (Stimuli)	C	F	A	B	K	L	J	H	I	G	E	D
Rank :	1	2	3	4	5	6	7	8	9	10	11	12

The ranking given by the all 13 students for the 12 paintings are presented in Table 9.1. The respondent VL has placed the painting C in the first rank and placed the painting D in the 12th rank. All others were placed in between these two (1 and 12). The individual rankings for each of the 12 paintings were presented in Table 9.1. It can be observed that each person has given the ranking to every painting in his own way. There were no two persons giving the same ranking to all the stimuli. The stimulus C received the first rank only from 9 persons. The stimulus A received the first rank from only two persons and the stimuli F and K received first rank only from one person. Though every student has given different ranking to different stimulus from first rank to the last rank, when the rankings were pooled and tabulated (Table 9.2) it can be observed that the stimuli A, C, F and K alone were given first rank by one to nine persons. The other stimuli B, D, E, G, H, I, J, and L were not given the first rank by any one of the participants. So also the stimuli D, E, and I alone were placed in the last rank. It is because, in a group some may give the same rank to several stimuli.

The results presented in Table 9.1 showed that how the individual's judgments of aesthetic values vary extensively in ranking of 12 paintings from 1 to 12. The Σ fjì is Nn (13 x 12) = 156. The rankings given by all 13 students were summarised and presented in Table 9.2. The frequency of ranks for each painting show interesting results.

In the next step the proportions were worked out for the ranks assigned by all the participants.

$$\text{The formula is } p = \frac{(Ri - 0.5)\,100}{n}$$

Where Ri stands for the rank value of the stimulus i in the reverse order as 12 to 1 and n indicates the number of stimuli ranked by the respondents. Here, we need the middle area of the objects ranked. It is worked out by deducting 0.5 Irom each rank. The p is the centile value which indicates the area of the object in the normal distribution. The p values are worked out for all the stimuli. The p value for the rank Ri 12 is :

$$\frac{(12-0.5)100}{12} = \frac{1150}{12} = 95.8, \text{ and for the rank}$$

$$\text{Ri 1:} \quad \frac{(1-0.5)\,100}{12} = \frac{50}{12} = 4.2$$

Table 9.1 : Showing the Rank Positions of Each of 12 Paintings assigned by 13 Students by Rank Order Method

S. No.	Judges	Ranks assigned by 13 judges to each of 12 Stimuli A to L												
		A	B	C	D	E	F	G	H	I	J	K	L	Σ
1.	VL	3	4	1	12	11	2	10	8	9	7	5	6	12
2.	GT	3	4	1	11	12	2	10	9	8	7	6	5	12
3.	NL	3	4	2	12	11	1	10	9	8	7	6	5	12
4.	DV	6	3	2	10	12	4	11	9	8	7	1	5	12
5.	VK	3	4	1	11	12	2	10	9	8	6	5	7	12
6.	SR	3	6	1	12	11	10	9	8	7	5	4	2	12
7.	RR	4	3	1	10	11	12	9	8	7	6	5	2	12
8.	BM	2	4	1	12	9	10	6	11	7	8	5	3	12
9.	ER	1	4	3	12	9	2	10	11	8	7	6	5	12
10.	MS	1	4	2	11	12	3	9	8	10	7	6	5	12
11.	PS	3	2	1	12	11	4	9	10	8	7	6	5	12
12.	KM	6	3	1	11	12	2	9	10	8	5	4	7	12
13.	SR	4	2	1	12	11	3	10	9	8	7	6	5	12
	Σ	13	13	13	13	13	13	13	13	13	13	13	13	156

The same procedure is followed in finding out the p for all the ranks. Thus, the p values for the ranks ranged from the lowest 4.2 to 95.8.

The next step is to find out the C values for all the ranks. The correct rank order is given in the column under ri in Table 9.2. The second column Ri in Table 9.2 is the reverse of the rank order (12 to 1).

The formula is : $Ri + ri = n + 1$ or $Ri = n - ri + 1$

$$= 12 + 1 \text{ Or } 12 = 12 - 1 + 1$$

The C values are determined for each rank from the Table-M (Guilford 1954, p.577) (Appendix B). These values can be traced by putting the finger on the column extreme left of the Table-M, on the number which

Table 9.2 : Showing the Frequencies of Ranks as given by 13 students the Proportions, the C Values and the Mc Values for 12 Paintings

ri	Ri	1	2	3	4	5	6	7	8	9	10	11	12	Σ	P	C
		A	B	C	D	E	F	G	H	I	J	K	L			
1	12	2	0	9	0	0	1	0	0	0	0	1	0	13	95.8	8
2	11	1	2	3	0	0	5	0	0	0	0	0	2	13	87.5	7
3	10	6	3	1	0	0	2	0	0	0	0	0	1	13	79.2	7
4	9	2	7	0	0	0	2	0	0	0	0	2	0	13	70.8	6
5	8	0	0	0	0	0	0	0	0	0	2	4	7	13	62.5	6
6	7	2	1	0	0	0	0	1	0	0	2	6	1	13	54.2	5
7	6	0	0	0	0	0	0	0	0	3	8	0	2	13	45.8	5
8	5	0	0	0	0	0	0	0	4	8	1	0	0	13	37.5	4
9	4	0	0	0	0	2	0	5	5	1	0	0	0	13	29.2	4
10	3	0	0	0	2	0	2	6	2	1	0	0	0	13	20.8	3
11	2	0	0	0	4	6	0	1	2	0	0	0	0	13	12.5	3
12	1	0	0	0	7	5	1	0	0	0	0	0	0	13	4.2	2
Σ fji		13	13	13	13	13	13	13	13	13	13	13	13	156		
Σ fjic		87	82	100	32	36	77	46	48	54	66	74	78	780	M=5,	
Mc=Rj		6.7	6.3	7.7	2.5	2.8	5.9	3.5	3.7	4.1	5.1	5.7	6.0	60	SD=1.66	

$$SE_M = \frac{SD}{\sqrt{N}} = \frac{1.66}{\sqrt{13}} = \frac{1.66}{\sqrt{3.6056}} = 0.46$$

indicates the number of stimuli used in the experiment. In the case of this experiment the number of stimuli are 12, and also the number of stimuli to be ranked. While moving the finger from this number 12 towards right, stop at the number which indicates the rank number (ri, 12). Above the rank number you can find the respective C value 2 for the rank 12 and this can be entered in Table 9.2 on the column under C against 12 (ri). Every rank has a C value. In some cases 2 or 3 ranks may also have the same C value. The C values are from 1 to 9 only. The same procedure may be adapted in finding out the C values for all the ranks (ri) from the Table-M and entered in Table 9.2 under the letter C. In this case with 12 stimuli, all the C values can be found in the same row against the number of stimuli ranked, 12 in Table-M.

For example, in this experiment for the case of rank 1, (ri) the C value is written in the cell just below the letter C in the column. It is 8. For the ranks (ri) 2 and 3 the C value is 7, for the ranks 4 and 5 the C value is 6, for the ranks 6 and 7 the C value is 5, for the ranks 8 and 9 the C value is 4, for the ranks 10 and 11 it is 3 and for the 12th rank the C value is 2.

Then the next step is to find out the Σfjic value for all the stimuli. This value for every stimulus is obtained by multiplying the frequencies found in the columns of the respective stimulus by the C value of the rank (ri), and summing up the products for each stimulus and entering the same in the row against Σfjic. For example, in Table 9.2, the frequencies for the stimulus A are 2, 1, 6, 2, 0, 2, 0, 0, 0, 0, 0, and 0. There are five frequencies and they are in the rows or ranks against 1, 2, 3, 4, and 6 respectively. In the rest of the ranks there are no frequencies and they are zeroes. Against each frequency in the last column C, the C values for the ranks are given. Each frequency is multiplied by the corresponding C value and the sum is entered in the row at the bottom of the Table 9.2 against Σfjic under each stimulus.

For example, the stimulus A has the Σfjic value as 87. This is obtained by multiplying and summing up the frequencies by the respective C value 8, like (2 x 8) + (1 x 8) + (6 x 8) + (2 x 8) + (2 x 8) = 87. Thus the Σfjic values for all the 12 stimuli are obtained. The sum of the sums of the columns (Σfjic) are equal to 5Nn (5 x 13 x 12 = 780). It is because the total frequencies of Nn (13 x 12) 156 and for the whole matrix is (5Nn) (5 x 13 x 12) 780. The mean of the total frequencies, that is for the whole data of the matrix is (780 ÷ 156 = 5) 5, and the mean of the C values is (60 ÷ 12 = 5) also 5. Then the Σfjic values for each stimulus is divided by the total number of respondents 13, which resulted in obtaining the Mc = Rj value for each stimulus. This is the mean value (Mc) and also the response value (Rj) for each stimulus.

Thus the obtained Mc (or Rj) values for the 12 stimuli are , A:6.7, B:6.3, C: 7.7, D:2.5, E:2.8, F:5.9, G:3.5, H:3.7, I:4.1, J:5.1, K:5.7, L:6.0. The total value is 60.0 which is also the total sum of the C value, and the mean of the Mc values is 5. The standard deviation of the Mc values is 1.66.

The treatment of the data can be stopped at this stage and the Mc (mean) values or the Rj (response) values can be accepted and treated as the Scale Values. But it is also suggested to apply a transformation equation by which a meaningful zero point can be obtained. This is also stated as the constant. The Mc values are multiplied by this constant and the multiplied values form a better basis for comparing different scale values.

But Guilford (1954) has suggested that it is not necessary that we should go so far to the Rc values and therefore we may have the final values in the form of Mc or Rj levels. Further in the rank order method treating the experimental data by a constant, the final (Rc) values sometimes result in fraction (less than one) or even may have minus values as in the case of pair comparisons method. In order to avoid such occurrences therefore, some scholars suggested to accept the Mc or the Rj values as the scale values of the stimuli. The Mc values have also revealed clear ranks to the stimuli. Therefore, the mean values (Mc) or the response (Rj) values are used for comparing the stimuli. Thus, the rank order of the stimuli as determined by the scale values (Mc) from the first rank to the last rank is : C-7.7 (1), A-6.7 (2), B-6.3 (3), L-6.0 (4), F-5.9 (5), K-5.7 (6), J-5.1 (7), I-4.1 (8), H-3.7 (9), G-3.5 (10), E-2.8 (11), and D-2.5 (12).

The stimulus C is judged and placed in the first rank by the participants and the stimulus D is placed in the last rank, 12th.

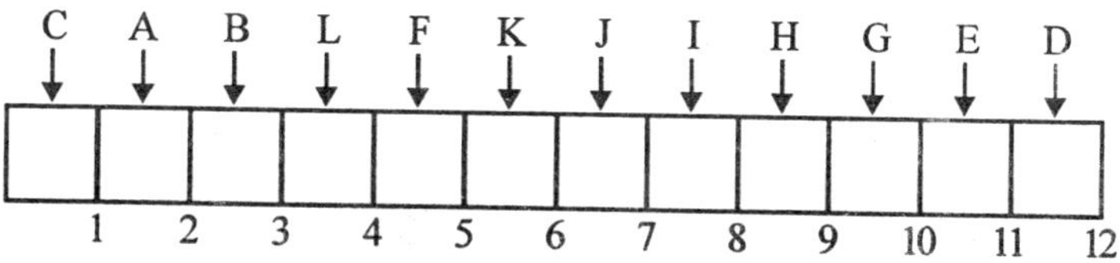

Fig. 9.1 : The rank positions of 12 stimuli from first rank to the 12th rank on the basis of the scale values.

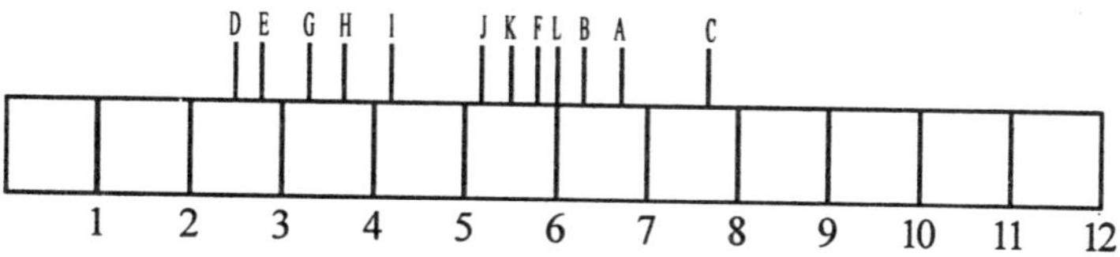

Fig. 9.2 : The normalized rank positions of 12 stimuli from the lowest rank to the highest rank on the basis of the scale values.

In ranking the 12 stimuli a person may arrange them in an order on the basis of his liking of the aesthetic values of the 12 paintings and his/her ranking should range from 1 to 12. A person may place the stimulus A in the first rank and the stimulus D in the last rank. But when 13 persons rank 12 stimuli on the basis of the quality of the paintings every one may judge the quality of a particular painting in his/her own way. Therefore, the stimuli do not get the same rank from every judge. One person may place the stimulus A in the first rank, another person may place it in the third rank, a third person may place it in 5th rank, a fourth person may place it in the last rank. Thus, there is every possibility that a stimulus may be getting a first rank or third rank or the last rank. Therefore, a stimulus may be placed distributively from first rank to the last rank. When a group of stimuli are ranked by a group of persons the stimuli may be placed from the first rank to the last rank. If every one gives one rank to a stimulus how to ascertain the rank position of a stimulus? It can be done only by pooling all the judgments made by all the persons together for all the stimuli.

The first step is to work out the frequency distribution of the ranking judgments made by the judges for every stimulus. Then while coming to the stage of working out the scale values (Mc) there may be deviations in the judgments made by some judges. These deviations are called discriminal dispersions. But we need not bother about these deviations. The normalized rank order assigns a rank position to every stimulus on the basis of the scale value. The distances between the stimuli are not equal. As the scale values go away from the mean 5.0, the intervals between the stimuli are increasing. The scale values of five of the stimuli fall on the left of the mean which are lower than the mean value and seven of the stimuli fall on the right of the mean which are higher than the mean value. The standard deviation of the mean is 1.66. The deviations range from -2.5 to +2.7. It is also observed that few of the ranks are close together, little away from the mean on the right (Fig. 9.2). The scale values are plotted in a curve and it is almost a straight line.

DISCUSSION

The aim of this experiment is to determine the scale values (Mc) of 12 paintings by the method of rank order. A set of 12 paintings consisted of various scenes like the natural settings, animals, birds, humans in different backgrounds, humans in different moods. These paintings reveal various types of aesthetic beauties in different dimensions in attractive colours. Each painting is judged by 13 persons according to his/her taste, experience and knowledge about paintings. All the individual judgments are put together and the scale values (Mc) of the 12 paintings are worked out according to the procedure. It can be observed that the scale values are ranging from the lowest 2.5 to the highest 7.7. In other words, what is considered to be the best liked painting by the whole group has the scale value of 7.7 and the least liked painting has the scale value of 2.5. These paintings are not in the same order as they were presented to the students in the beginning for judging the values. The order of the paintings are changed after the judgments made by 13 students. The rank order is determined by the scale values. Thus the the rank order of the paintings on the basis of the quality of the aesthetic values as judged by 13 persons is, C, A, B, L, F, K, J, I, H, G, E, and D. These paintings are presented to the judges in the alphabetical order from A to L. But in the judgment, the order is thoroughly changed. The aesthetic values of the paintings were perceived and judged by the judges differently.

The students who served as judges in this experiment have found it very difficult to judge and rank them in the correct order from 1 to 12. They have taken much time than they expected to do the task. All of them have taken about 45 to 60 minutes to decide the ranks. Some of them were going on changing the order 3 or 4 times to arrive at a final conclusion. Some of them expressed that they could not easily decide the ranks of the 12 paintings as each one appeared good in one way or other.

The painting that was judged by the group as the first is C (7.7), the painting of humans, animals and birds in a natural setting. This painting is an expression of a romantic love scene in a natural environment. There are humans, animals and birds all look in a pleasant moods. Nine judges placed this painting in the first rank, three judges placed it in the second rank and one in the third rank. Hence, this painting was given the first rank by the whole group. Most of the judges stated that it is a very difficult painting, every leave in the tree and in the plants were painted clearly.

The painting A (6.7) was given the second rank. It is a painting of a tiger in a natural environment. This painting received the first rank from two persons, second rank from one, third rank from six persons, fourth rank from 2 persons and sixth rank from 2 persons, though this painting did not receive first rank from more than 2 persons, more than nine persons placed this painting above the fourth rank. It is these ranks that have brought it to the place of second rank. Almost all of them have stated that the painting is very natural and it is just like seeing a real tiger in a bush.

The single human figure painting B (6.5) is placed in the third rank. This is an old man's expression of his feelings of expectation. He is seriously waiting for something else that is far away. Two judges placed this painting in the second rank, 3 in the third rank, 7 in the fourth rank and one in the sixth rank. Ten judges placed this painting above fourth rank which pushed this to the third rank. Many of the judges have stated that that this painting is very natural.

The painting that has received the fourth rank is L (6.0). This is an interior decoration. Two judges have given second rank to this painting, one third rank, seven have given fifth rank to this, one sixth and two seventh rank. All the judgments are above 7th rank. Most of the judges have said that the painting is not only beautiful, but also painted clearly and attractively.

The fifth painting F (5.9) in rank is the Chinese couple. This is placed in 5th rank in the consolidated judgments of 13 judges. This painting reveals the Chinese culture and tradition through a man and woman who seem to be in a pensive mood. Ten judges placed it above 4th rank, 2 placed it in the tenth rank and one in 12th rank which resulted in putting this painting in the 5th rank. Many of the judges have said that the painting is reflecting the Chinese culture in true sense with the real Chinese expressions.

The stimulus K (5.7) is the painting of a natural scene of a sea-shore with the blue sea and sand area. One person placed this in the first rank, 2 in the fourth rank, 4 placed it in fifth rank and 6 placed it in sixth rank. In the consloidated judgments this painting received the sixth rank. The judges generally stated that this painting looks more natural and beautiful.

The 7th rank is given by the judges to the stimulus J (5.1) which is the animal rhinoceros in a natural physical environment. Two of the judges placed it in 5th rank, two in 6th rank, 8 judges in 7th rank and one placed it in 8th rank. Therefore, this painting falls just below the middle position in ranking.

The stimulus I (4.1) is placed in 8th rank by the judges. This is a painting of a group of animals, zebra. The animals are seen in fast moving posture, which is the expression of survival of the animals, that is, they are fastly moving for safety. Three of the judges placed this painting in third rank, 8 placed it in 8th rank, one in 9th rank and one in tenth rank. Some of the judges have stated that it looks natural. This falls below the middle position in ranking.

The stimulus H (3.7) received the 9th position in the consolidated ranking. It is painting of a gymnastic posture. It is observed that most of the judges have placed it below the 7th rank. Four judges placed it in 8th rank, 5 in nineth rank, 2 in l0th rank and 2 in 11th rank. Therefore, the group ranking brought it down to the nineth rank. Some have stated that the exposition of the body is exciting.

The stimulus G (3.5) is the painting of humans, men and women seem to be in festival mood. This painting is placed in 10th rank by the 13 judges. It may be a marriage function, probably a betrothal. Many of the judges felt that the imagination and the painting of the humans look very pleasant. One of the judges placed it in sixth rank, 5 placed it in nineth rank, 6 in 10th rank and one placed it in 11th rank. Most of the judges palced it below eighth rank.

The painting of an electronic world E (2.8) is placed in 11th rank. The electronic world is imagined in the form of a cricket game. This painting is an expression of anxiety and nervousness. It is a scientific imagination to show how men are in the state of stress and tension. Just like every player in the match is put into severe anxiety to catch the ball when the bowler throws the ball, the scientists hit the world by their instruments and waiting anxiously for the result. Since the meaning of the painting is very difficult to comprehend the judges placed it in 11th rank. Most of them placed it below tenth rank except two who have placed it in 9th rank.

The stimulus painting that is placed in the last rank (12th) is D (2.5), which is a painting of a honey bird at a flower, trying to suck honey. Some have stated that it is a very simple painting, but looks very natural. All the judges have placed it below the rank of 9. Two of them placed it in 10th rank, 4 in 11th rank and seven placed it in 12th rank.

The evaluation made by the judges of the paintings seem to be somewhat rigid as the scale values did not go above 7.7. They had very average understanding of the aesthetic values of the paintings. Since some of the judges were graduate students, not having much understanding about paintings, they could not assess the aesthetic values of the paintings which expressed different emotional levels. But the students who served as judges in this experiment have shown much interest in evaluating the aesthetic beauty of the paintings. If this experiment is conducted on a large population with the same paintings there may be some variation in the ranking of these paintings and the change may be in the positive direction, the scale values may be higher than this and the deviations may be reduced. It is presumed that in any other field of study, the higher the sample the lower the dispersion values, the higher the accuracy of the results. The standard error in this experiment is (1.66 ÷ 3.6056) – 0.46, which seems to be little higher for this type of experiment.

CONCLUSIONS

The painting of a romantic scene in a natural setting with animals and birds has been ranked as the first by 13 judges. The painting of a honey bird has been placed in the last rank. The order of the paintings on the basis of the ranking made by 13 judges is C, A, B, L, F, K, J, I, H, G, E, and D. But these paintings were presented to the judges in the alphabetical order from A to L. Some of the important reasons the judges have stated are that they are beautiful, pleasant, exciting, natural, more realistic, difficult painting and so on.

Note : The method of rank order experiment may be conducted with any material having aesthetic values. It is better to have less than twelve materials, having different values. The materials may be paintings, drawings, photographs, or eminent personalities, Cinema heroes or heroines.

Appendix-A

Painting-A

correctly. We may judge certain things correctly but not always and everything. Not only in seeing, but also in hearing, smelling, and touching we are judging things with some error. What amount of error we commit in judging things? The psychophysical experiments assess this as accurately as possible. The method of average error in particular makes accurate test of human capacities to discriminate small differences. The extent of error that occurs in the approximate judgment made by individuals can best be measured by the method of average error. The method of average error was introduced in the field of psychophysics with the view of studying the precision in the visual observation or testing the accuracy in matching two stimuli of the same types.

The participant, in this experiment is asked to judge the standard length by adjusting the variable stimulus. In this procedure the standard stimulus is constant and the variable stimulus is adjustable backward and forward or inward or outward. The participant is expected to make a number of judgments by asking the experimenter to move the variable stimulus to the level of the standard stimulus. In every judgment the extent of error is noted down. The mean of all the errors in the judgments is taken as average error. Sometimes he may judge the standard stimulus as greater than the variable stimulus and sometimes he may judge smaller than the variable stimulus. All deviations from the standard are considered as errors. The method of average error is already explained with Muller-Lyer Illusion Board. But, here, this is a different type of apparatus. In the Muller-Lyer Illusion Board there is an assumption that the feather head stimulus should be judged as greater than the arrow head stimulus and arrow head should be judged as smaller than the feather head stimulus. But in this experiment even though the method is the same (method of average error) the apparatus is different and the participant is to make a comparative judgment of the standard stimulus. In the Muller-Lyer Illusion Board the participant himself moves and adjusts the apparatus. But in the Galton bar experiment the experimenter makes the movement and adjusts and the participant gives direction for moving and stopping. It is because, in the Galton's bar experiment the participant should sit at a distance af one metre away from the apparatus as the Galton's bar itself is one metre long. This is one important difference between the two.

EXPERIMENT-8: Assessing the accuracy of judgment, using Galton's Bar

Problem : Assess a person's accurate judgment of the standard stimulus by adjusting the variable stimulus in a linear magnitude by the method of avarage error.

2. METHOD

Participant : Choose a person who has no knowledge about this apparatus and the task involved in this experiment. Collect relevant personal information from him such as, age, sex, qualifications, occupation, physical deformities, if any, whether wears eye glass, etc.

Materials : Galton's Bar, Chin Rest, Spirit level, Two metal stands with clamps.

Description of the materials : The Galton's Bar was designed by Sir Francis Galton, a British Psychologist in his anthropometric laboratory for the purpose of measuring sensory acuteness and judgment. The original Galton's Bar apparatus had a bell at the back which indicated that the person is committing a mistake in the judgment when variable pointer was moved more than the standard stimulus. Secondly, it was intended to judge only short distances. Thirdly, the participant himself was made to move the variable stimulus. Fourthly, the person should make the variable stimulus double the distance of the standard length. The original instrument had certain disadvantages. Therefore, certain improvements were made in the original apparatus and the procedure also was modified. Here we are using the modified procedure on the improved medel. Galton's bar is one metre (100 cms) long and about 10 cms width. It is fixed in a frame made of steel sheet. On one side there is a metre scale. This is experimenter's side, On the other side of the bar is the white stretch linear dimension and at the centre at 50 cm there is a vertical black line. This means that the bar is divided by this vertical line into two part 50 cms on the left and 50 cms on the right. This is the participant's side. There are two moving pointers with handle for moving them to outward and inward positions. One moving pointer is used as standard and the other is used as variable. The standard length is 20 cms and it is 20 cms away from the vertical line (the centre) either on the right or on the left. The one metre long bar is made to rest on two stands with clamps, one stand on the left a few cms away from the left end and the other stand on the right a few cms away from the right end. The clamps are used to tighten the bar on the stands. The Galton bar is to be kept 100 cms or one metre away from the participant. The bar should be parallel to the ground and this should be adjusted with spirit level. The participant's chin should be placed on the chin rest. Now the Galton Bar is ready for operation.

Procedure : The participant should be made to sit in a well illuminated room comfortably and should rest his/her chin on the chin rest. The experimenter should set up the Galton bar at a distance of one metre away from the participant and adjust the height of the bar to the level of the participant's eyes. He should also use the spirit level and test whether the bar is parallel without any slanding on any side. The white portion of the bar with a vertical line on the centre should be on the participant's side. The participant should have clear and full visibility of the white linear dimension of the bar. Since the bar is one metre away from the participant he/she cannot handle or operate the instrument as in the case of Muller-Lyer Illusion Board. Therefore, only the experimenter should handle and operate the instrument. First he should fix the standard pointer 20 cms away from the vertical line (centre) in the bar or at the 30th cm on the right of the participant. The scale behind the bar reads 1 to 100 cms from left to right. Therefore, the first 20 trials should be taken by keeping standard on the right of the participant. The experimenter should prepare the Tables and keep ready for entering the readings for the trials. When everything is ready the experimenter should give the following instructions to the participant :

"Please see at the Galton Bar in front of you at a distance of one metre. You see the vertical line on the white linear stretch and from the line on the right at a distance there is a fixed pointer. This is standard length. On the left at some position there is a movable pointer on the linear dimension few centimetres away from the vertical line. Now you can judge the distance between the vertical line and the standard line on the right and tell me how far I should move the pointer on the left towards the vertical line to make it equal to the standard line. I will be moving the pointer and when you find the two lines, one on the left of the vertical line and the other on the right of the vertical line appear to you equal, say 'stop'. Even after stopping if you are not satisfied with your judgment you can ask me to move on any side you want. But see that the lines should appear to you equal. When I say ready, you must get ready to judge the lines."

Then the experimenter should set up the variable pointer as he/she has planned at a point either too short or too long. He should take 20 readings 10 with too shorter and 10 with too longer positions. First he/she may start at too shorter distance at 55th cm. How the distance at 55 cm is too shorter? Because the standard length is fixed on the right between 30 cm and 50 cm. The variable (movable) pointer is fixed at 55 cm. Hence the distance between the 50 cm (one end of standard length) and 55 cm (where the variable pointer is fixed) is only 5 cms. This means he/she is moving the pointer outward. At this stage the experimenter should ask the participant: "Now please tell me the direction in which I should move the variable pointer to make the two lines equal". The participant should say that it should go on the 'left' (the participant's left). Having obtained this answer, the experimenter should tell him: "Now, as you said I am moving the pointer slowly towards your left and tell me where I should stop".

The experimenter moves the variable pointer from behind the bar and when the participant says, "stop" he should stop at that place and at once note down the distance from the scale behind the bar. Having taken one reading with too shorter distance, now, the experimenter should set up the variable pointer at a place too long, longer than the standard line. This means that it should be far away from the centre (vertical line) on the left. It should be at 95th cm in the scale. Then the experimenter should ask the participant: "Now please tell me in which direction I should move the pointer to make the two lines equal". The participant should say that it should move on to the 'right'. Having obtained this answer the experimenter should tell the participant : Now, as you said I am moving the pointer toward the right and tell me where I should stop according to your judgment". The experimenter from behind the bar moves the variable pointer till the participant says "stop". Then he should stop and make entry of the distance from the scale behind. The experimenter has completed one trial with too shorter position and one trial at too longer position. In the same manner alternatively the experimenter should take readings of 10 trials with variable too shorter and 10 trials with variable too longer and make entries in the record note book. The too shorter and the too longer positions need not be the extreme ends as mentioned here as 55 cm and 95 cm. The position can be fixed anywhere in between, but always shorter than the standard line and longer than the standard line.

The next step is to change the position of the standard length to the left of the participant. The standard pointer should be set between 50 cm and 70 cms. on the left of the vertical line. The procedure is exactly the same as the previous trials except that the standard length is on the left and the variable pointer is on the right. The experimenter in this position should take 40 trials, 20 trials with the variable pointer too shorter than the standard and 20 trials with variable pointer too longer than the standard.

This means that for 20 trials the variable pointer should be set at too shorter a distance at 45th cm in the scale and for 20 trials variable pointer should be set at too longer a distance at 5th cm in the scale. The too shorter and the too longer positions of the variable pointer may be set at random and the sequences should be noted down in the record note book. Having set the apparatus for the changed position, the experimenter should give the following instructions :

"Please look at the Galton Bar. The position of the standard line is changed from your right to the left and the variable pointer is on the right". After ascertaining this fact and getting approval of the participant the experimenter should set the variable pointer at too shorter distance at 45 cm in the scale and ask the participant to tell him to w hich direction he has to move the variable pointer to make the two lines equal. The participant should say that it should move on to the 'right'. After obtaining this answer the experimenter should tell the participant, "now, as you said, I am moving the variable pointer to the 'right' and tell me where I should stop moving according to your judgment". The experimenter, then moves the variable pointer outward, to the right from behind the Galton Bar slowly till the participant says "stop". The experimenter should stop moving and make a record of the distance from the scale behind. Then the experimenter should set the variable pointer at too longer position at 5 cm and ask the participant to say to which direction he should move to make the two lines equal. The participant should say that it should move on to the 'left' to make the two lines equal. The experimenter should now tell the participant, "as you said, I am moving the variable pointer to the left and tell me where I should stop according to your judgment". The experimenter moves the variable pointer from behind the Galton bar till the participant says, "stop". Then the experimenter should stop and make the record of the distance from the scale. The too shorter and too longer positions need not be the extreme positions as mentioned here as 45 cm and 5 cm. The positions can be anywhere in between but always smaller than and greater than the standard length.

The too shorter and too longer positions should be alternatively repeated till 20 trials for each position are completed. Then the experimenter should go to the last stage in which the standard length should be placed once again on the right and the same procedure should be repeated. There should be 20 trials, 10 for too shorter variable and 10 for too longer variable. The readings should be noted down. As soon as everything is over the participant may be allowed to go away. The participant may be asked to give his/her introspective report. He/she may be asked to state whether he/she has followed any specific principle in making the judgments.

3. RESULTS

The experimenter should work out the extent of error for each trial by finding the difference between the standard length and the judgment made by the participant and present the scores in Table 10.1 for the first stage.

Table 10.1 : Showing the individual data of the first stage having the standard length on the right of the participant in the Galton Bar Experiment

Stage 1: Standard length on the right (20 cms) between 30 and 50 cms.							
	Variable too shorter				Variable too longer		
Trials	Variable set at cm	Judged dis- tance in cm	Extent of Error in cm + or –	Trials	Variable set at cm	Judged dis- tance in cm	Extent of Error in cm + or –
1	55 cm			1	95 cm		
2	56 cm			2	94 cm		
3	57 cm			3	93 cm		
4	58 cm			4	92 cm		
5	59 cm			5	91 cm		
6	60 cm			6	90 cm		
7	61 cm			7	89 cm		
8	62 cm			8	88 cm		
9	63 cm			9	87 cm		
10	64 cm			10	86 cm		
	Mean				Mean		

The second stage of the experiment is to have the standard length on the left of the participant. The number of trials are 40, of which 20 with variable too shorter and 20 with too longer. The extent of error should be worked out by finding out the difference between the standard length and the judged distance. The extent of error should be indicated either as positive or negative with plus and minus signs. The results should be presented in Table 10.2.

Table 10.2 : Showing the individual data of the second stage having standard length on the left of the participant in the Galton Bar Experiment

Stage 2: Standard length on the left (20 cms) between 50 and 70 cms							
	Variable too longer				Variable too shorter		
Trials	Variable set at cm	Judged dis- tance in cm	Extent of Error in cm + or –	Trials	Variable set at cm	Judged dis- tance in cm	Extent of Error in cm + or –
1	2	3	4	5	6	7	8
1	5 cm			1	45 cm		
2	6 cm			2	44 cm		
3	7 cm			3	43 cm		
4	8 cm			4	42 cm		
5	9 cm			5	41 cm		
6	10 cm			6	40 cm		
7	11 cm			7	39 cm		
8	12 cm			8	38 cm		
9	13 cm			9	37 cm		
10	14 cm			10	36 cm		
11	14 cm			11	136 cm		
12	13 cm			12	137 cm		
13	12 cm			13	138 cm		
14	11 cm			14	139 cm		
15	10 cm			15	140 cm		
16	9 cm			16	141 cm		
17	8 cm			17	42 cm		
18	7 cm			18	148 cm		
19	6 cm			19	144 cm		
20	5 cm			20	45 cm		
	Mean				Mean		

In the third and last stage the standard length is set on the right of the participant again and the variable pointer on the left. The same procedure what is done in the first stage is repeated here again and the results are to be presented in Table 10.3. Work out the extent of error for the variable too shorter and for the variable too longer and indicate it whether it is positive or negative with plus and minus signs.

Table 10.3 : Showing the individual data of the third stage, having standard length on the right of the participant in the Galton Bar Experiment

Stage 3: Standard length on the right (20 cms) between 30 and 50 cms.							
	Variable too shorter				Variable too longer		
Trials	Variable set at cm	Judged dis- tance in cm	Extent of Error in cm + or –	Trials	Variable set at cm	Judged dis- tance in cm	Extent of Error in cm + or –
1	55 cm			1	95 cm		
2	56 cm			2	94 cm		
3	57 cm			3	93 cm		
4	58 cm			4	92 cm		
5	59 cm			5	91 cm		
6	60 cm			6	90 cm		
7	61 cm			7	89 cm		
8	62 cm			8	88 cm		
9	63 cm			9	87 cm		
10	64 cm			10	86 cm		
	Mean				Mean		

Work out the average error for the two conditions (standard length on the right and standard length on the left) for all 80 trials and also for the trials with variable too shorter and for variable too longer for all 80 trials.

Find out the constant error for the three stages separately. Determine the constant error for outward and inward movements variable too longer of the variable pointer and present them in Table 10.4.

Table 10.4 : Showing the average error for two conditions and two movements and the constant error in Galton Bar Experiment

Stage	Standard length on right	Standard length on left	Average error	Outward movement	Inward move- ment	Average error
I stage 20 trials						
II stage 40 trials						
III stage 20 trials						
Average Error/ Constant Error						

Collect group data from other experimenters and present them in Table 10.5. Collect the average error for the conditions and also for the two movements and the constant error. Work out the average error for the whole group for two conditions and two movements and the constant error in the whole experiment in 80 trials.

Table 10.5 : Showing the group's average error and the constant error in Galton Bar Experiment

S. No.	Name	Standard on right (Average)	Standard on left (Average)	Outward move (Average)	Inward move (Average)	Constant error (in 80 trials)
1.	P.V.					
2.	K.R.					
3.	M.S.					
4.	T.V.					
5.	B.R.					
6.	S.M.					
7.	R.V.					
8.	S.L.					
9.	M.R.					
10.	T.S.					
11.	V.B.					
12.	M.B.					
	Average Error					

Explain the extent of error in all four positions for the individual and also his/her constant error in all 80 trials.

4. DISCUSSION

After examining the scores of your participant state where his error is higher and where it is lower. State whether the standard length is overestimated or underestimated. If so, in what condition overestimation occurred and in what condition under-estimation occurred. Whether the error is greater in the inward movement of the variable pointer or in the outward movement. State the reason for this. What is the constant error of your participant? Compare your participant's errors with the group's average error. Where he/she stands? Are his/her judgments are better when compared to the judgment of the group?

In the group whose judgment is the best and nearest to the standard length and whose judgment is worst and far away from the standard. Galton has invented this apparatus for psychometric experiments particularly for determining the accuracy of visual judgments. How many of the persons in the group judge the standard length accurately by visual perception. Though this experiment comes under one of the psychophysical methods called, the method of average error it has little different function from the method of average error and cannot be equated with Muller-Lyer Illusion Board which is used for estimating the average error. Therefore, the interpretation of the results should be in accordance with Galton's idea in designing this instrument.

For Galton (1889) the judgment made by a person in this instrument is the indication of the level of acuteness of the sensory system and it is related to the general intellectual ability of the individual. He says that so far as the information through the senses go to the brain and the sensory apparatus is more accurate the individual can judge things accurately. The more the person is endowed with the general intelligence the more accurately he uses his sensory apparatus in judging things.

Therefore, the results obtained in the Galton bar experiment not only reveals the individual's ability to judge the standard length on the linear dimension, but also shows the acuteness of his sensory apparatus and his general mental abilities. Discuss whether your participant had any improvement in the subsequent trials. State whether the participant has applied any specific principle in making the judgments.

The experimenter, therefore, from the personal information obtained from the participant can also judge his/her other characteristics in this task.

5. CONCLUSIONS

1. State your participant's ability to judge the standard length from the extent of error he committed in the Galton Bar experiment.
2. State whether there was any improvement in his judgment by reducing the extent of errors in the subsequent trials.
3. In the group how many of them have the constant error below the group mean and how many above the group mean.
4. State whether any other factors had any influence in the judgment of the standard length.

11

MODERN PSYCHOPHYSICAL SCALING METHOD : Sensitivity and Adaptation

INTRODUCTION

The light rays entering the eye must have sufficient energy and also should set upon the retina sufficiently longer to evoke excitation in the photorecepters for producing visual sensation of sight. The minimum amount of light energy required to produce light sensation depends upon the absolute sensitivity of the eye. The smaller the amount of light the lower the absolute threshold. This means higher sensitivity of the eye. The threshold value of radiant energy for the eye is extremely low as the sensitivity of the eye surpasses all other sensory apparatuses.

If we want to determine the maximum sensitivity of the eye, certain things must be investigated. The sensitivity depends upon the part of the retina on which, rays of light fall. The spot on which the light rays fall must be sensitive to day light. The colour vision occurs in the area of retina where the cones of the eye are closely packed together in the region of fovea. The sensitivity is lower if the rays of light fall far away from the fovea region and closer to the periphery of the retina.

Sensitivity and Adaptation

The eye is very sensitive to changes in the brightness of light. The highest differential sensitivity of the eye can be seen under conditions of moderate brightness. The differential sensitivity of the eye increases with the increase in its sensitivity during dark adaptation in the wider visual field. The differential sensitivity is lower in the peripheral region than in the central part of the retina. The brightness differential threshold is lower in binocular vision than in the monocular vision. The sensitivity of the eye varies very widely due to variations in the intensity of illumination.

In our everyday experience we observe what is happening when we pass from a brightly lighted room to a dark room. We do not see anything in the dark room first and then gradually and slowly we come to see everything in the room. We gradually adapt ourselves to the dark room situations. This process of adaptation of the eye to the dark room situation is due to the increased sensitivity of the eye. This process is called dark adaptation. On the other hand if we pass from darkness to bright light area, the eye is exposed to light after a long period of darkness. At first even very faint light seems exceedingly bright and blinding. It takes few minutes for the eye to develop ability to see objects in the lighted area. This is called light adaptation.

In the dark adaptation, during the first 20 to 30 minutes of darkness the stimulus threshold declines rapidly. Then the decline takes place slowly. The threshold is fully established strongly after a period of 60 to 80 minutes. But according to studies it is found that the adaptation continues through out the period of darkness. Both the rods and cones in the retina area show adaptation. Dark adaptation takes place faster in the fovea region than in the peripheral area. Studies on dark adaptation revealed that it varies with the conditions and disorders the eye develops. This has some influence in the other eye also. If the stimulation of white light increased in one eye the sensitivity in the other eye is increased. But in the case of colour, when one eye is stimulated by real light, the sensitivity of the other eye declines. Among the colours the yellow light produces low depressive effect. Adapting ability of eye declines due to oxygen deficiency, age and fatigue.

In light adaptation, the sensitivity of the eye decreases with the expenditure of the retinal photosensitive substance. During the course of light adaptation sensitivity declines rapidly in the first few seconds and then it declines slowly and at last reaches a steady level.

Excitation and After effect

The light stimulation which causes excitation in the visual sensory apparatus does not disappear immediately after the light stimualation ceases to exist. The excitation persists for some more time. The study of after images produces clear evidences. For example, if we fix our eyes on a bright electric bulb and close our eyes we can see the image of stimulus. The after images are of two types, one is positive and the other is negative. The positive after-image fully reflects the real stimulus. The negative after-image has the reverse relationship with the object. The white object becomes dark and the dark becomes white. After images exist only for a fraction of a second and not static. Actually the physiological mechanisms of after-images are based upon the after effects which persist in the sensitive elements of the retina area.

Flashes of light generally leave after effect in the visual apparatus. If the flashes are gradually increased frequently then there is a moment called fuse. Then the sensation is not continuous, it is twinkling of light. There are a number of interruptions in the light for every second and because of this the *flickers* (rapid flashings of light) become fused. This psocess is called *fusion frequency*.

The Flicker Fusion Frequency

This flicker fusion frequency can be demonstrated in a simple experiment. In a round disc have half black and half white equally and rotate it as fast as you can. We can see that the black and white colours disappear and the disc looks uniformly grey. There is neither white colour nor black colour. The brightness of white and black colours in the rapid movement of the disc loose their identity and is represented in the mean of the sum of luminous effects which is seen as grey. We do not see where white ends and black begins and *vice versa* as the disc moves fastly. Interruptions are not perceived. Therefore, if the interruption rate is very high the sensation becomes as constant as stimulation is continuously presented. The same principle is applied in the motion picture display. The motion picture reels consists of only still photos. How is that we see movement of the persons and objects and actions? The stills of photos are presented so fastly on the screen at a rate of 24 stills per second as to appear that there is continuous movement of the characters. The fusion frequency also depends upon the intensity of the light stimulus. The motion picture demonstrations somewhat exceeds the fusion frequency.

We know that visual acuity is a test of spatial thresholds for the eye. But the eye has also temporal (tissue) thresholds. The measurement of temporal threshold for the eye is called the critical flicker fusion frequency (CFF) (Leukel, 1968). This phenomenon has aroused considerable interest to psychologists. Therefore, let us now turn to psychological interpretation of the flicker-fusion from the physiological and optical interpretations. What is flicker-fusion? If a bright light is put on and put off quite number of times, say 10-15 times for a second then the eye is able to distinguish when the light was on and when it was off. The photo receptors in the retina area and the optic nervous system are able to state the presence and the absence of the light. But at the same time if we change the frequency of times of the on and off of the light so rapidly the receptors in the retina area are not able to act so rapidly as to distinguish the onset and the termination of the light. The on and off rotation is so fast that the sensation of light in the eye becomes constant. For example, a standard light is provided at 60 Hz. The light can go on for 60 times and go off 60 times. This on and off of the light goes on so rapidly that the light is perceived constantly without any break. The threshold may be changed that the rate of firing is such as to produce a constant sensation or a light sensation of blinking. The sensation felt by the person is that the light is blinking. The person sees the winking of the light.

This type of thresholds may vary due to the function of illumination, wavelength and other characteristics which may affect the thresholds. The point at which the light is appearing as constant in contrast to flickering is called critical flicker fusion (CFF). Due to certain physiological changes such as oxygen deficiency the critical flicker fusion may vary. Particularly the schizophrenic state is said to have effected the critical flickerfusion (Candland, 1968). According to Buhler's (1961) study it has been found that the critical flicker fusion (CFF) and the flicker fusion threshold (FFT) may serve as predictors of stress in patients. Further, the critical flicker fusion is associated with the problems of colour vision and the physiology of the retina of the workers. The flicker fusion is more a practical function in the field of motion picture.

Psychophysical Method and FFT

The psychophysical method of minimal changes can be used for the determination of flicker fusion threshold (FFT). The psychophysical method of measuring the flicker fusion threshold is not free from contradictory views. There are wide differences in the individual studies similar to other visual measures in respect of the kinds of controls used for intensity. But the one important component that determines the critical flicker fusion is the rate of flickering. This is shown in terms of number of cycles of light exposed for a second. One cycle is composed of one onset and one termination. But the number of cycles may be altered and the light way be on longer than it is on off. The reverse also is possible. Therefore, the agreement between the two aspects, light and dark of the flicker is the light-dark ratio (LDR). In the studies of critical flicker fusion (CFF) the light-dark ratio (LDR) is employed 50 percent. The stimulus is present half of the times.

In the function of LDR there are two variables, one for low intensities, and one for high intensities. If the intensity is increased the number of flashes also must be increased. This involves that the higher the intensity of the stimulus the greater the number of cycles per second should be.

But this proportion differs for various hues and also increases with age of the person and also has something to do with intelligence. There is low correlation between the CFF and the standard tests of intelligence (Leukal, 1968). We know that the CFF is referring to the rate at which light should flicker on and off in such a way that the eye should not see the termination of the light and should see a constant and steady light. Generally the neon or fluorescent lights, on their usual speed of 60 cycle per second of current supply flicker 60 times per second of their intensities. But we are not aware of it because of their intensities.

It is because of the functioning of other characteristics of the visual system flicker fusion varies. The retina area which is stimulated by light is a critical variable. For the CFF the peripheral area has lower threshold than the fovea region. It also varies due to other variables. Granit and Harper (1930) have demonstrated that in the fovea region if the area stimulated is smaller than the flicker fusion is higher in the fovea region. Another study made by Hecht (1938) shows that if the intensity is higher in the fovea region there is higher critical flicker fusion than the peripheral region. The electrical recording of the flicker fusion from the retina and the cortex was successfully made by Lindsley (1958). The cortex, according to Lindsley, was the first part to cease when the frequency become too fast.

The critical flicker fusion is also a measurement of visual acuity. It is concerned with the effects of duration of stimuli and not with location. It is concerned with temporal effects and not spatial. The Benham's top experiment is very simple and easy to explain the critical flicker fusion principle. This demonstrates the mystery of the visual system with regard to the appearance of colour in the disc.

The Benham's top consists of only a round disc with half black and half white. This has been already stated in different context. The Benham's disc has four sets of three curved lines in sequence in the white half. When the disc is rotated at an appropriate speed coloured rings are appearing around the centre. The yellow, red or orange appear nearest to the centre and the lines on the outer area appear blue. Thus, Benham calls as the magical trick. He claims that it can produce colour out of no colour in the disc. This is one of the important functions of the critical flicker fusion.

An electronic flicker fusion apparatus has been designed to determine the critical fusion and flicker thresholds and also the effect of fatigue in the central nervous system. This apparatus is very much in use in most of the psychological laboratories in India.

The flicker-fusion apparatus was originally developed for Indian Railways in India. It was used for lot of research purposes in the field of flicker-fusion. This has been used for long time in the studies of physiology of vision. But in recent times the apparatus is used in the study of physiological pathological stresses and medicine. The flicker fusion frequency (FFF) was considered as a retinal function for long time. Therefore, it was not used for the measure of physiological stress situations. For the first time this apparatus was used by R.H. Lee in the study of physiological stress situation to study effects of anoxia and on fatigue of central nervous system. This was also used to study circulatory metabolic and cerebral diseases in patients.

The flicker originally was obtained by passing a beem of light by a perforated rotating disc. Since there were difficulties in obtaining flawless measurement in this method the electronic device was formulated for the study of light and dark ratios and the brightness of light sources. The electronic methods of producing flicker is up-to-date and reliable. The advantages are absence of noise, vibration, easy operation and production of sequence of wave light stimuli.

Flicker means a wavering unsteady light or flame, also quick movement, flashing up and die away by turns.

Fusion means the action or process of focusing or estinguishing or being melted. It is the steady light source.

Frequency means state or condition of being crowded. The fact of occurring often or being repeated in short intervals.

The flicker threshold is the lower and the fusion threshold is the higher. Since the apparatus has both characteristics of flicker and fusion, it is called flicker-fusion apparatus.

Increasing and Decreasing Rate

The FFF is usually measured by going from low rate to up to the point of fusion (fusion threshold). It can also be measured by starting from high rates with sensation of continuous light and decreasing the rate down to the appearance of flicker (flicker threshold). The fusion threshold is higher. The difference represents largely a disguised reaction time which depends to a large extent on the speed of acceleration or declaration and the initial rate of light flashes.

Since most investigators have worked with increasing rate it is suggested that this procedure be used for the purpose of uniformity. Since no known differences in researches were obtained in physiological stress situations or diseases when both were employed it is better to discard one of them. The FFF has been expressed in terms of cycles (flashes) per second.

The point of fusion can be measured with considerable accuracy with repeated trials on the same individual.

In the absence of other known factors such as the changes in the rate of increase in the speed of flickers during continuous exposure it appears that the subjective estimate of fusion has changed rather than the condition of subject, since different results may be expected when the subjects concentrate on the sensation of flicker or the sensation of fusion. Knox (1950) has found that when the subject was giving the report, if fusion was emphasised in the instruction the FFF first lowered and when the emphasis was placed on flicker the values of FFF were higher.

Grumbeaum was able to observe these psychological elements involved in the determination of FFF. In the psychophysical sense this might be stated as the errors of expectation and errors of habituation.

EXPERIMENT-9: Determination of Flicker-Fusion Threshold and After Image and the Effects Fatigue on the Central Nervous System

Problem : The purpose of this experiment is (a) to determine the critical fusion threshold and the critical flicker threshold and (b) to determine the effects of fatigue on the central nervous system and on FFF.

2. METHOD

Respondent : Choose a person who has no knowledge about this experiment and collect certain personal information from him/her such as age, sex, qualifications, whether free from visual defects, and any other physical deformities, etc.

Apparatus

Electronic Flicker-Fusion apparatus with viewing chamber and interconnecting cable, stop clock, voltage stabilizer, blind goggles and number columns in a sheet.

Description of the Apparatus : The flicker-fusion apparatus is an electronic instrument requires power for operation. It is made up of two separate units. The first one is the central unit and the second one is the viewing chamber. These two units should be connected at the time of operation.

1. *The Central Unit* : This is a rectangular box, having the size of 12½"

length and 7½" breadth and 4" in height. It has four parts such as (a) an 'on-off' switch, (b) a brightness control switch, (c) an alternative and simultaneous switch, and (d) a frequency dial.

(a) *The on-off switch :* This switch is fixed at the right hand side of the panel and used to apply power to the instrument. It also controls a panel lamp to indicate the on-off position.

(b) *The brightness control switch :* This is a four-way light switch. It enables the operator to select four different light intensities like 25, 50, 75 and 100. Under ordinary condition this switch is left at 50 brightness level.

(c) *Alternative and simultaneous switch :* This switch is seen on the face of the control unit. It has two-way action. The operator can choose either the alternative or the simultaneous mode of operation. In the alternative position the light flashes will appear alternatively on the left and on the right eyes. In the simultaneous position both the lights will go 'on' and 'off' simultaneously.

(d) *Frequency dial :* The frequency dial is seen in the centre of the control unit. The dial indicates a frequency of the flashes in cycles or seconds. It consists of two parts, namely circular dial and a small circular window. The dial indicates the unit position of the frequency and the window indicates the position of the frequency in the unit of tens. For example the cycle 45 is shown as 4 in the small window and 5 or 50 in the dial. The frequency can be varied between one and 100 cycle per second.

2. *Viewing Chamber :* It is also a small rectangular box having the size of 5" (length) x 4 ½" (breadth) x 2" (height). On one side of the unit there is a leather hood and a binocular shaped part with two glasses. On the other side there is a four-way connecting point. This viewing chamber is connected to the control unit through a four-way interconnecting cable. During the operation the leather hood of the viewing chamber completely covers the subject's eyes and the subject could see a single circle of light spot.

3. *Procedure :*

1. Keep the apparatus steadily on a table close to the power point.
2. Connect the viewing chamber to the control unit through the inter-connecting cable.
3. Ensure that power is in off position through on and off switch.
4. Connect the main cable to the control unit to the 220 volt A.C. power point through voltage stabilizer.
5. Put on the power switch and see that the power on indicator is lit. Now the apparatus is ready for the operation.

6. On the front panel of the control unit select the intensity of light by pressing one of the percentage switches (25, 50, 75 and 100). Even though normally 50 intensity is used, the experimenter can select any percentage like 25 or 75 or 100 percent.
7. Keep the light switch at simultaneous position (SiM) and adjust the frequency knob "0-100 HZ" to 10 HZ.
8. Make the subject to sit comfortably in front of the apparatus and ask him to hold the viewing chamber with leather hood as close to his eyes as possible.
9. Ask the subject to see through the two glasses and report the variation in the light stimulus.
10. Put + mark for the presence of fusion and — (minus) mark for the presence of flicker.

(i) *Determination of Critical Fusion Threshold*

(1) To determine the critical fusion threshold turned the 0-100 HZ knob on the control unit uniformly increasing in the frequency of flicker of light sources. Carry out this until the subject reports the fusion. This means, there is no more flickering but there is a steady light source.

(2) Now note down these readings.

It is critical fusion frequency. The critical frequency is the fusion frequency. Take five trials.

(ii) *Determination of Critical Flicker Threshold*

(1) To determine the critical threshold set the 0-100 HZ knob at 80. This can be varied from 60 to 80.

(2) Then ask the subject to look through the viewing chamber.

(3) Decrease the frequency of light source uniformly by turning the 0-100 HZ knob until the participant reports a flicker effect of the light source. Now note down the reading on the 0-100 HZ knob. This is the flicker threshold. Take five trials.

(iii) *Effect of Fatigue on CNS*

After recording the data of the 5 trials give a mental task (calculation work) to the subject. The participant should be blind folded and should be put up in a restricted posture. Ask the participant to add the given numbers (2, 3, 4, 5) as fast as he can for 30 seconds (the same mental fatigue test should be conducted in the same manner with 30 trials for 15 minutes. After the mental task was over continue the flicker fusion frequency test once again on the same participant in the same manner. Take five trials and record the data.

3. RESULT

Present the individual data in Table 11.1. It is the flicker threshold and fusion threhold and the difference. Give the number of calculation and number of errors the subject has made for 10 minutes in the mental task in the restricted posture in Table 11.2.

Give the fusion threshold and flicker threshold, obtained after the mental task in Table 11.3 and find out the mean.

Table 11.1: Showing the flicker fusion threshold in the Flicker-Fusion Apparatus by the method of minimal changes before Mental fatigue test. [The Experimenter should operate the Brightness Control switch from higher percentage 100 or 80 or 75 to lower percentage in small steps and from lower percentage (20 to 25, 30, 35, 40, 45, 50) to higher percentage) (D - descending order; A - ascending order]

S. No.	Serial order/FFT	D	A	D	A	D	A	D	A	D	A
1	5.00	+	+	+	+	+	+	+	+	+	+
2	4.80	+	+	+	+	+	+	+	+	+	+
3	4.60	+	+	+	+	+	+	+	+	+	+
4	4.40	+	+	+	+	+	+	+	+	+	+
5	4.20	–	+	+	+	+	+	–	+	–	–
6	4.00	–	+	–	–	+	–	–	–	–	–
7	3.80	–	–	–	–	–	–	–	–	–	–
8	3.60	–	–	–	–	–	–	–	–	–	–
9	3.40	–	–	–	–	–	–	–	–	–	–
10	3.20	–	–	–	–	–	–	–	–	–	–
11	3.00	–	–	–	–	–	–	–	–	–	–
	Threshold	4.3	3.9	4.1	4.1	3.9	4.1	4.3	4.1	4.3	4.3
	Mean Threshold	before fatigue mental test									4.15

Table 11.2 : Showing the individual data in the mental fatigue test (Restricted posture)

Trial No.	Number called for	No. of additions	No. of Errors	Trial No.	Number called for	No. of additions	No. of Errors
1	2	3	4	5	6	7	8
1	6			16	21		
2	8			17	18		

Table 11.2 (Contd.)

***Table 11.2** (Contd.)*

1	2	3	4	5	6	7	8
3	10			18	19		
4	7			19	22		
5	9			20	24		
6	11			21	26		
7	13			22	23		
8	12			23	25		
9	14			24	27		
10	16			25	28		
11	18			26	29		
12	13			27	32		
13	15			28	33		
14	17			29	30		
15	20			30	31		
	Mean						

Important Note : The mental fatigue test should be conducted according to the same procedure adapted in the test of assessing the effects of continuous mental work Exp. No.). The restricted posture should be followed. The same numbers 2, 3, 4 and 5 as used in the mental fatigue test should be used here also and the experimenter can call any number for a trial to begin the additions. Each trial should go for 30 second continuously adding to the number the experimenter called for and there should be 30 trials for 15 minutes. For 30 trials 30 number the experimenter can call for, from which the subject start adding, 2, 3, 4, and 5. For example the numbers may be 6, 8, 10, 7, 9, 11, 14, 13, 15, 16, 19, 14, 16, 17, 20, 21, 18, 19, 22, 24, 26, 23, 25, 27, 28, 29, 32, 33, 30, 31. The called number need not be in the serial order.

Table 11.3: Showing flicker, fusion threshold in the Flicker-Fusion Apparatus by the method of minimal changes after mental fatigue test (The Experimenter should perform in the same manner as he did before the mental fatigue test)

S. No.	Serial order/FFT	A	D	A	D	A	D	A	D	A	D
1	5.00	+	+	+	+	+	+	+	+	+	+
2	4.80	+	+	+	+	+	+	+	+	+	+
3	4.60	+	+	+	+	+	+	+	+	+	+
4	4.40	+	+	+	+	+	--	+	+	+	+
5	4.20	--	+	--	+	--	--	--	+	--	--
6	4.00	--	--	--	--	--	--	--	--	--	--
7	3.80	--	--	--	--	--	--	--	--	--	--
8	3.60	--	--	--	--	--	--	--	--	--	--
9	3.40	--	--	--	--	--	--	--	--	--	--
10	3.20	--	--	--	--	--	--	--	--	--	--
11	3.00	--	--	--	--	--	--	--	--	--	--
	Threshold	4.30	4.10	4.30	4.10	4.30	4.50	4.30	4.10	4.30	4.30
	Mean Threshold before fatigue mental test										4.26

(D - descending order; A - ascending order)

Table 11.4 : Showing group data of the Flicker-Fusion experiment determining the effect of mental fatigue in the CNS

S. No.	Name	Flicker-Fusion Mean threshold before Mental fatigue task	Flicker-Fusion threshold after mental fatigue task	Difference	Mental fatigue	
					No. of calculation (Mean)	No. of Errors (Mean)
1	K.R.	4.12	4.26	0.14	16.0	3.6
2	B.V.	4.28	4.32	0.04	15.0	2.5
3	M.S.	4.17	4.20	0.03	16.0	2.6
4	R.V.	4.16	4.24	0.08	10.0	3.9
5	T.V.	3.93	4.00	0.07	12.7	3.4
6	M.R.	4.50	4.56	0.06	17.2	3.5
7	P.V.	3.96	4.10	0.05	16.0	3.2
8	R.M.	3.94	4.16	0.22	13.5	4.0
9	K.M.	4.26	4.30	0.04	16.0	3.2
10	R.S.	4.41	4.63	0.22	16.0	4.2
11	S.R.	3.90	4.10	0.20	15.0	4.0
12	N.K.	4.20	4.30	0.10	14.4	3.5
	Total	49.83	51.17	1.25	177.8	41.6
	Mean	4.15	4.26	0.10	14.8	3.46

Note : The Flicker-Fusion threshold increased after the mental fatigue test. The difference is positive for all the participants. Therefore the mental fatigue test had definite effect upon the central nervous system of the participants. Further, those who committed more errors in the mental fatigue test had higher threshold after the test.

Collect group data for these three kinds of data and present on Table- 11.4. Find out the difference between the Flicker-Fusion threshold before and after the mental fatigue test and also the means for all measures. Give suitable statistical treatment and analyse the result.

4. DISCUSSION

Discuss the three categories of the individual data. What kind of reaction did you observe in the subject? Is there much difference between the fusion threshold and flicker threshold before and after mental task?

What is the nature of the subject's mental work? Is it slow or fast? At what stage he commits more mistakes? Did he find much difference between the fusion threshold and flicker threshold after mental work? What amount of difference do you find before mental work and after mental work? Discuss the results in these lines.

5. CONCLUSIONS

Is your subject experiencing mental fatigue? Is it having any effect upon CNS and FFT? Where the individual stands in the group data? State all these in the conclusions.

12

MODERN PSYCHOPHYSICAL SCALING METHOD :
Perception of Size – Size Constancy

PERCEPTION OF SPACE AND SIZE

The objects that we see in the outside world occupy some space. Any matter, having a body must occupy some space. We also occupy some space on the earth. Space is unlimited. It is three dimensional in its characteristics. All material objects are located only in space. Space is discussed in philosophy and different kinds of space have been explained. Here we are discussing about the physical space. All the psychological experimentations are possible only in the three dimensional physical space and objects can be also located. The perception of space is a complicated process and it includes many things. In perceiving space psychologists always depend upon sensory systems, because we depend upon our eyes to see, upon the ears to hear, upon the nose to smell and so on. Perception of space includes perception of objects, distance, shape, colour, size and so on. Here we are concerned with the perception of size.

It is quite obvious that the perception of space, perception of distance, and the shape are closely related to the perception of size. They all come under the law of visual perception or visual angle. According to this law, objects become smaller and smaller when recede more and more away from the eyes. The decrease of the objects in size is proportional to the distance from the perceiver. But objects do not decrease in size. Their physical sizes are always constant. The receding objects look smaller and smaller because of the mechanism that takes place in the eyes of the perceiver. The image of the object in the retinal area is becoming smaller as the perceived object is going away. If the object is quite close to the perceiver, then the retinal image is bigger, but as and when it recedes more and more away the retinal image is becoming smaller and smaller and the object also looks smaller. Further object at a distance seen from left or right or in some other angle does not look in the same original shape. It gives different shape. Objects on the mountains look very smaller because they are located at a great distance. Still they go away to a greater distance we see every thing blurred, unlcear and we do not see any object clearly. We see objects only over a considerable range distance. Therefore, size constancy may be defined as the tendency to see the familiar objects with their original sizes irrespective of their distance. It may be also stated that we do not reduce the original size of an object even though it is far away from us and look smaller at the time of seeing.

Constancy means maintaining the same, something not changing. This is applied to our perceptual process like perception of object, perception of shape, perception of colour and perception of size and so on. Objects maintain their original characteristics and they are not altered by factors like distance, position, or illumination. We see many things in our everyday life as evidences for size constancy. For example, the aeroplane we see as a huge flight on the ground, but when it flies in the air it looks like a kite or an eagle. A motor car on a highways looks like a small toy at a long distance and when moves closer and closer towards us we see it a big car. Animals on hills, men in fields, birds in the sky all look smaller. But they do not shrink in size and nor loose their shape at any position. The round wheel of the motor car at a distance does not look round. It looks like oval shaped. Actually the wheel is round, but at a distance gives a oval shape. We can quote hundreds of evidences like this to show the size of the objects do not shrink to any level at whatever distance they are. They maintain their shape and size.

We have already mentioned above that objects look smaller and smaller as and when they recede more and more away. It is because of the size of the image of the object in the retinal zone getting smaller. This can be illustrated by a geometric figure. Hold an object in front of you, say, a rectangular card board having the height of 12 inches and a width of 4 inches close to your eyes horizontally. Look at the image of the object in your eyes. Move it away from your eyes to a distance of two feet. The object does not look smaller to you. But what is happening in your eyes? The image of the 4 inches object in the retinal area is double the size of the image of the same object at 2 feet away. The object at 2 feet away is not reduced in size, but the size of the image in the retinal area is half of the size to the same object presented close to your eyes. Look at the image in the retinal area for the same object presented at different distances (Fig. 12.1).

People judge objects by their true size and therefore see them as remaining constant in size irrespective of their distance. It is true that we also judge objects as smaller at a distance, but not as small as the retinal

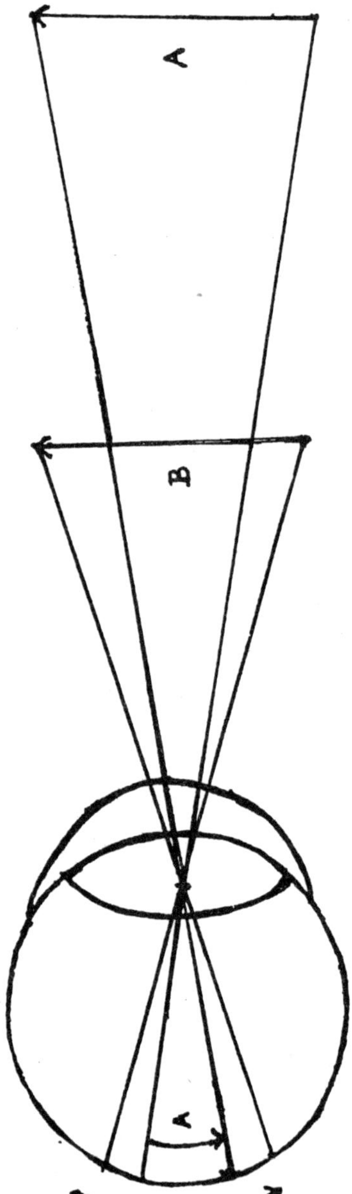

Fig. 12.1 : Size of the object and Retinal Image.

This Figure is the geometric illustration showing the relationship between the physical size of an object and its size in the retinal area. The figures A and B represent the objects of the same size. In the retinal area the size of the object A is half of the size of the object B. The greater the distance between the lens of the eye and the object the smaller the image in the retinal area.

images. There is certain amount of compromise between the size of the object and the size of the perspective. The size constancy operates upon the cues of the distance and upon our familiarity with the object. The more reliable information we get about the distance of the object, the perceived size is more close to the actual size of the object. But the more familiarity we establish with the object the more we perceive actual size of the object regardless of the distance.

The difference in the retinal image may occur to any difference in the distance to the object. For example, we see a two-storey building at 200 feet away and similar building at 50 feet away. There is difference between these two retinal images. We are aware of the fact that one building is 200 feet away and another 50 feet away. In spite of difference we are still aware that both the objects are buildings and they are of the same height and size. The different sizes of the retinal images do not lead us to see that the two buildings are of different heights and sizes. Since we are also familiar with buildings of different types and heights we are not mislead in this case. But if we do not get any cues to distance and to the size, or if they are eliminated and if we are not familiar with the objects, the buildings, then the images in the retinal area do not provide us with any information. Several experiments have been conducted on size constancy by Bower (1966), Turnbull (1961), Gibson (1950), Gramer (1923), Boring (1946). Gardner Murphy (1964) says that sometimes men of equal size seem to differ greatly, because we are influenced by contexts which we cannot help. Only the cues of the contexts provide information about varying distances.

Woodworth (1952) says that noice finds it very difficult to make a drawing or painting from nature in representing the shape and relative sizes of objects. The novice, if he draws two men of the same height, one standing ten feet away from him and another twenty feet away, cannot make them of the same size in his drawing. If he does, there is something wrong in his drawing. He must know that the man stands far away is much less in height in the field view and the height should be reduced in the picture than the man who is standing ten feet away. The size of the picture he draws depends upon the real height of the person and distance between the observer and the man. This is also applicable to the shape of the objects.

A man standing in a play ground, is looking at the real scene around him. He uses first the signs of distances of the objects and persons around him and in the field far away. He perceives the spatial relations between objects and persons and the relative distances of various objects and persons. Certain objects may look lying closer to him, but when he approaches, he has to move longer than what he thought. For example, a ball lying at distance on the ground may look very close, but actually it is not, because on the plain ground he could not use any signs of distance unless there are objects and persons in between him and the ball. He could not adjust himself to the spatial relations in the situation.

Experimentally Determining the Size Constancy

Generally, as one looks at an object, he not only sees the shape and size and other characteristics of the object, but also sees the distance and the cues for the distance. With these he sets the distance of the object. When he draws a picture using all these cues the size of the picture becomes the real size of the object. The observer or the painter, however, may not be accurately perceiving the real size of the objects and their distances. In one of the experiments conducted by Sheehan (1932) the subjects were tested how far they are consistently judging the size of the objects. The subjects were 25 college women students and they were asked to look down a long table on which there were two circular grey discs, one five feet away and the other ten feet away. The disc at 5 feet was 4 inches in diameter and the one lying at 10 feet might be larger or smaller. The size was not mentioned. The subjects were asked to judge which disc looked larger. The experimenter kept the farther disc going on changing till the size was looked of the same of the near by one by the subjects. The real size to be exactly equal, requires the farther disc to be of 4 inches in diameter. But to be exactly equal the stimulus size demands the farther disc to be of 8 inches in diameter. The judgments were varied among the subjects to a greater extent, but the average judgment was for a disc of 4½ inches in diameter. This result was very close to the real disc and there was more objective equality.

When we perceive the size of an object we can judge and measure it only with respect to some standard reference. In our every day life we may come across several such judgments and measurements. We might have said on some occasions that the size of this shirt is quite fit to me or it is bigger than my size and so on. If two persons were asked to judge and state the size (height) of a book shelf in a room at a distance of l0 feet away from them. Both may not give the same measurement, one may say, it is six feet height and another may say 6½ feet. Each one is judging with his own experience or with the help of the cues available in the situation. Every one gives his own judgment. It is private. But we must make the perceived size explicit and general or a public.

Experimenters in this field are of the view that the perceived sizes vary with the subjects' familiarity with the objects and also the type of attitudes they have developed towards the object. An uncritical approach facilitates correct judgment on the part of the subject. Apart from the experience or familiarity the individual differences play important role in the perceived size consistancies. For example, a person's age, sex, intelligence, experience, qualification, occupation and so on may have determining effect in perceived size consistancies.

From the preceding discussions we can understand that the perceived size is depending upon the distance, size of the rational image and the environmental factors that facilitate the perception of the size in the field. From this a proportional relationship can be evolved between the retinal image and the distance between the eye and the object. Emmert has evolved a generalized-law involving these components. This is known as Emmert's law. It is well known that objects look smaller and smaller when they recede more and more away. According to Emmert's law both the size of retinal image and the distance between the eye and the object should be taken into consideration. Any one factor independently cannot give us the correct information required by us. If the retinal image alone is operating in size constancy then the after image should remain constant at all varied projected distances. But it is not taking place. If the distance alone is operating in this process by altering the size of the after images with increased distance then the size of the after image should diminish in its size. Therefore, the Emmert's law takes into account the combined effectiveness of the size of the retinal image and the distance and its related information between the eye and the object.

Therefore, there is a tendency in human being to perceive the objects as they are in their original size and shape. The difference in the size of the retinal image does not lead us or misguide us to perceive the objects with different size and shape. But what is heppening in the perceptual process is that we get the information about the distance of the objects. An object is regarded as constant when it is perceptually constituted as a permanent one and also stable. In spite of some differences the object is permanent and therefore constant. The inclination to perceive the object in its usual or original size is called size constancy.

We may see objects in different positions. We know the correct positions of an electric lamp post, a post box on the road. If they were in a slanting position or in a horizontally lying position we identify them as lamp post and post box and we know what should be their correct positions on the road. They should stand vertically. Similarly, a vase lying upside down, a man standing on the horizontal bar with his head down all are perceived by us in a right manner by relating the figure or object to the ground. In using language we come across many instances of perceiving the names and words wrongly spelled and typed and read them or correct them as they should be. This means that we have a tendency to perceive objects in their original position even if they are not in the correct position or shape.

It is true that sometimes the cues we receive may not be adequate to identify the object's carrect position. In such cases it is better to use several cues like, distance, light, size, shape, shade, brightness, illumination, texture, colour and other characteristics in spite of our experience about the object.

EXPERIMENT-10 : Determination of Variations in the Perceived Size of the Object by Modern Psychophysical Scaling Method

Problem : The real size of the object at a distance is not perceived by us correctly as they are. Nearby objects look larger whereas the distant objects look smaller. Why this variation takes place in our seeing the objects? Therefore, this is to determine the variations in perceived size of the object at different positions and to verify whether the distance is having any effect in the perceived size of the object.

2. METHOD

Participant : Choose a person who has no knowledge about this experimant and the apparatus. Collect the person's personal information such as age, sex, qualifications, occupation, income, whether he/she has any physical deformities, and so on.

Material : The Aubert Diaphragm Instrument, a standard stimulus, metal stand with adjustable clamp, chin rest, metre scale, chalk pieces.

Description of Aubert Diaphragm : The Aubert diaphragm is a black board made of metal sheet fixed in a rectangular stand. The size of the metal sheet is 1'6" in height and 1'4" in width. At the centre of the black board there is an aperture of 6" x 6" size. At the back side close to the black board a white metal sheet is fixed. There is a knob fixed at the centre of the lower frame of the board. By turning the knob clockwise and anti-clockwise the size of the white sheet can be enlarged and reduced. This white sheet is used as the variable stimulus in this experiment. At the back of the board there is a linear scale and a pointer which will indicate the size of the variable stimulus (white sheet). The standard stimulus is a white square having the size of 4" x 4" painted on a black metal sheet of 8" x 8" in size. This sheet is fixed in a metal stand by a clamp. The Aubert diaphragm is named after the inventer, Aubert.

Procedure : The experiment is conducted in long well illuminated room. It may be treated as binocular function, with both eyes. The participant should be seated comfortably and there should not be any furniture or other objects on the sides or in the front of the participant. The experimenter should measure the distances 3 feet, 6 feet, 9 feet and 12 feet with the scale and make a mark of the same. The Aubert diaphragm should be kept 12 feet away from the participant. The standard stimulus which is fixed in a stand should be kept 3 feet away from the participant on the left at the same height as that of the Aubert diaphragm. The white square in the disphragm and the white square in the standard stimulus should be on the same line in the view of the participant's eyes. The white square of the variable stimulus is at 45° slanting position. Therefore, the standard stimulus also is fixed in the clamp at 45° slanting.

The experimenter should test this by asking the participant whether he is able to have a clear visual view of both the standard and variable (white square in the diaphragm) stimuli. If he/she is having the clear view of the stimuli, then the experimenter should put a chin rest under the participant's chin, so that he/she will not be turning easily or raise or sink his/her head. The experimenter should test the Aubert diaphragm by turning its knob whether it works well. The experimenter should also prepare and keep ready of the Table for making entries of the participant's perceived judgments. The ascending and descending orders of the variable stimulus and the receding and approaching series of the standard stimulus should have entered in his record note book.

The experimenter should make a note that in half of the series the standard stimulus should be on the left and in half of the series it should be on the right side of the participant. In half of the observations the variable stimulus should be larger than the standard stimulus and the size of the variable stimulus should be reduced in amall steps of .2". This constitutes the descending order. In the other half of the observations the variable stimulus should be kept smaller than the standard stimulus and it should be increased in small steps of .2" by turning the knob. This constitutes ascending order. The sequence of the series should be ordered in counter balancing manner as shown in the Table 12.1. The starting point under all conditions should be randomised from trial to trial in a pre-arranged order.

The standard stimulus is then moved from 3 feet to 6, 9 and 12 feet successively. At each of these distances the judgments from the participant should be obtained. After having got the participant's judgment at the last position 12 feet, it is desirable to decrease the distance successively from 12 feet to 9, 6 and 3 feet. In this way there is a receding series and approaching series. The experimenter first can start with receding series. In this series the variable stimulus is at 12 feet away and the standard stimulus is at 3 feet away from the participant on the left side. Having planned the experiment as above the following instructions should be given to the participant:

"Please look at a distance, (showing the variable stimulus) one rectangular black board. At the centre there is one white square at 45° slanting position. This is called variable stimulus. At your left close to you (showing the standard stimulus) there is one black sheet with a white square in the centre fixed to the stand. This is called standard stimulus. Now your business is to look at them and say whether the variable stimulus, the white square in the rectangular board at a distance appears equal to the standard stimulus, kept on your left. If both appear equal say "equal", if the white square in the rectangular board looks larger, say "larger", if it looks smaller say "smaller". Look at them carefully and make correct judgment. When I say ready go, you must get ready and give me your judgment."

The report of the judgment should be entered in a Table. For a report of larger a plus sign (+) should be entered, for the smaller a minus sign (—) should be entered. The series should be stopped as soon as the participant's report is changed from plus (+) to equal (=) or from minus (—) to equal (=). Since the experimenter changes the size of the variable stimulus by increasing and decreasing in small steps the method may be called method of minimal changes. The experimenter first starts with ascending order in receding series, then descending order and then secondly the ascending and descending orders in approaching series. It is important that while the experimenter changing the variable stimulus he should keep the participant's attention on a point at the table in front of him. Now the experimenter keeps the variable stimulus at a position smaller than the standard stimulus and wanted the participant to judge it and asks him:

"Now, tell me, how the white square in board looks to you. Whether it looks equal or greater or smaller?"

On getting the report from the participant he makes entry in his record notebook and operates the knob and increases the square by .2".

"Now tell me how it looks?"

The participant makes his judgment and gives his report. In the same manner the experimenter should continue the procedure till the participant changes his report from minus (—) to equal (=) or from plus (+) to equal (=).

Then the experimenter should operate the knob and keep the variable stimulus greater than the standard stimulus and ask the participant to make the judgments. After 5 trials of ascending and of descending orders the experimenter should change the position of the standard stimulus from left to right side of the participant and continue the same procedure for 5 trials of ascending and descending orders. It may be 3 ascending orders and 2 descending orders or *vice versa.*

Next, the experimenter should change the position of the standard stimulus from 3 feet to a position of 6 feet and continue the procedure with ascending and descending orders, 5 trials with standard stimulus on the left and 5 trials on the right.

Then, the experimenter should go to the next distance 9 feet and continue the same procedure and then to the last position 12 feet and continue the same procedure. Now the receding series is completed. That is, the distance from 3 feet to 12 feet is over. At the last position both the standard and the variable stimuli are at the same distance of 12 feet. In the next stage, the approaching series should be started. The experimenter, keeping the variable and the standard stimuli at the same distance of 12 feet and take 3 ascending and 2 descending trials keeping the standard stimulus on the left. Then the standard stimulus should be on the right for 2 ascending and 3 descending trials.

Then the position of the standard stimulus should be moved forward to 9 feet distance having the standard at the left and right and after taking 5 trials at 6 feet distance and should move lastly to 3 feet distance. When all the trials are over the participant may be asked to give his introspective report as to the procedure he followed in judging the size of the variable stimulus. Then he may be allowed to go away.

3. RESULTS

The reports of the judgments of the ascending and descending orders of the receding and approaching series should be presented in Table 12.1. The mean estimate of each condition should be worked out for each of the 4 distances separately and presented in Table 12.2. Work out the average judgment for each distance and for the whole distance. Verify whether there is any difference between the standard variable and the average judgment.

Collect the group data with reference to the two orders and two series and find out the average judgment and also the difference between the size of standard stimulus and the average judgment and present the data in Table 12.3.

Table 12.1 : Showing the perceived size of the object by the individual in the size constancy Experiment by the Method of Minimal changes Size of Standard Stimulus 4" x 4"

Size of variable Stimulus		Receding series										Approaching series									
		Standard on the left					Standard on the right					Standard on the left					Standard on the right				
		A	D	A	D	A	D	A	D	A	D	D	A	D	A	D	A	D	A	D	A
Standard at 3 Feet	3.0																				
	3.2																				
	3.4																				
	3.6																				
	3.8																				
	4.0																				
	4.2																				
	4.4																				
	4.6																				
	4.8																				
	5.0																				
	+																				
	–																				
PSE Mean																					
Standard at 6 Feet	3.0																				
	3.2																				
	3.4																				
	3.6																				
	3.8																				
	4.0																				
	4.2																				
	4.4																				
	4.6																				
	4.8																				
	5.0																				
	+																				
	–																				
PSE/Mean																					

Table 12.1 (Contd.)

Table 12.1 (Contd.)

Size of variable Stimulus		Receding series										Approaching series									
		Standard on the left					Standard on the right					Standard on the left					Standard on the right				
		A	D	A	D	A	D	A	D	A	D	D	A	D	A	D	A	D	A	D	A
Standard	3.0																				
at	3.2																				
9 Feet	3.4																				
	3.6																				
	3.8																				
	4.0																				
	4.2																				
	4.4																				
	4.6																				
	4.8																				
	5.0																				
	+																				

PSE Mean																					
Standard	3.0																				
at	3.2																				
12 Feet	3.4																				
	3.6																				
	3.8																				
	4.0																				
	4.2																				
	4.4																				
	4.6																				
	4.8																				
	5.0																				
	+																				
	—																				
PSE/Mean																					

Table 12.2 : Showing the mean of the perceived size of the object in the size consistency Experiment at various positions. Size of standard variable is 4" x 4".

Distance in Feet	Receding series		Approaching series		Per devied Mean Size	Diffe-rence
	Ascend-ing order	Descend-ing order	Ascend-ing order	Descend-ing order		
3 Feet						
6 Feet						
9 Feet						
12 Feet						
Perceived Mean Size						
Difference between St and VS.						

Computation of the Amount of Error in the Perceived Size of the Object

The application of the method of minimal changes to the determination of error in the perceived size is illustrated by means of an experiment conducted by using the apparatus, Aubert Diaphragm. The size of the standard stimulus is 4" x 4". In the experiment there are ten ascending orders and ten descending orders, one receding series and one approaching series and 4 different distances, such as 3 feet, 6', 9' and 12 feet. The starting point for ascending orders are varied from 3.0" through 5.0" and for the descending orders from 5.0" to 3.0". A plus (+) sign is recorded when the participant reports 'greater' and a minus (–) sign is recorded for the reports 'smaller' and equal sign (=) is recorded for the reports "equal". The participant's report of judgment changes from greater to equal in the descending order and from smaller to equal in ascending order. The point at which the change of report takes place is the judgment and the experimenter should stop the series and go for the next. To illustrate this point the reports of the participant are given in two of the columns in Table 12.1, one for ascending and one for descending and the perceived size of the object also is given in two columns. The ascending order starts at 3.0". The participant reported 'smaller' a minus sign (—) is recorded. The experimenter is going on increasing the size like 3.2", 3.4", 3.6", 3.8"

Table 12.3 : Showing the group data of the size constancy Experiment, the difference between the standard and the perceived mean (St: 4" x 4")

S. No.	Name	Receding Series — 4 Distances		Approaching Series — 4 Distances		Perceived Mean Size	Difference between St and Vs
		Ascending order 4 distances	Descending order 4 distances	Ascending order 4 distances	Descending order 4 distances		
1.	R.V.						
2.	M.S.						
3.	P.K.						
4.	B.V.						
5.	K.R.						
6.	M.R.						
7.	P.V.						
8.	P.C.						
9.	A.R.						
10.	T.V.						
11.	V.R.						
12.	S.V.						
Perceived Mean							
Difference							

and so on till the participant reported a change like "equal". Then the series is stopped and one equal sign is marked. The descending order starts at 5.0". The participant reported greater and this is recorded with a plus sign (+). Then the experimenter is going on decreasing the size by small steps till the participant reported "equal". This is recorded as equal (=) and the series stopped. Then next ascending order started and continued in the same manner till all 20 trials are completed. When the participant reported "equal" either in the ascending or descending order the experimenter should stop the series. The mean judgment of the size of the object is worked out by adding all ascending separately and all descending separately and the mean of the judgment of receding series and approaching series separately. Workout the mean for each distance separately. Find the difference between 10 ascending order and 10 descending orders.

4. DISCUSSION

Discuss the results obtained in the size constancy experiment for the individual. State where your subject commits more errors in judging the standard stimulus? Whether it is in the ascending order or descending order? Whether it is in the receding series or approaching series? State the values of the average judgment and compare them with the size of the standard. State whether the overall average judgment is greater than the standard size or smaller than it. Discuss the amount of error in the overall judgment. State whether the perceived size is nearest to the real size. The assumption is that there is a tendency to perceive the correct size of the object in human beings. State to what extent your subject performed the task of perceiving the size accurately.

State whose judgment of the size of the object in the group data is more accurate and state the amount of error. Whose judgment is having greater difference between the average judgment and the real size of the object. Compare your subject's perceived size with that of the group. State what is the mean of the perceived size of the object for the groups and state how many above average and how many below the average. On the whole what is the tendency of the group. Discuss the rational means used by the subjects in making the judgments. What do you understand from the introspective data of your subject and others. Were you able to find out any factor that determines the correct judgment of the size of the object?

5. CONCLUSIONS

1. Has your subject's perceived size in agreement with the actual size of the object? If there is any difference, state it.
2. While comparing the perceived size of your subject with that of the group where he/she stands?
3. Whether the error of his/her judgment is above the group mean or below the group mean.
4. In which order and series he/she committed more mistakes?
5. Whether there was any influencing effect in his/her perceived size of the object.

Note : The Aubert Diaphragm which is available in India is fitted with Inches Linear scale. If necessary it can be converted into metric system - centimetre - millimetre.

13

RERCEPTION OF COLOUR :
Tracing the Colour Zone

Perception of Object and its Qualities

Perception is fundamentally connected with matters or objects outside of the organism. It is something making the organism to be aware of the presence of the object. The organism objectifies its sensory experience in perception, Therefore, perception has reference to objects, situations and their relationships. Once the sensory experience is identified and objectified the organism develops a tendency to perceive the same without any change or modification. It is because, for the organism the object is permanent and stable, the organism perceives always the usual characteristics of the object such as the shape, size or colour. Normally human beings have a tendency to see the objects in their original colours. There may be certain hinderances in the situation to their original colours. With all that, we see objects in their original colours. We see the clear sky as blue, the sea as blue, the bright light as white, the coal as black and so on.

Once we become aware of the object outside of us we never fail to identify it with its characteristics. We see every object with some colour. Colour is one of the qualities of an object. The world in which we live is full of different colours. We are in the midst of constantly changing brilliant colours and shades of colours. The properties of the perceived colours are manifold. In all the perceptual processes of vision, the eye is the most important apparatus. The eyes are connected with the inter-brain and with the occipital lobes of the cerebral hemispheres through their sensory nerves and the optic nerves. The eyes receive the stimuli which are passed on to the inter-brain and to the cortex through the optic nerves. In the cortex area, processes are taking place which make the objects to recognize by grouping and patterning. The cortex near the primary visual area, the occipital lobe, is concerned with controlling the facts presented to the eye. Before we go into the determination of colour vision and the perceptual processes it is better to know the parts and the mechanism of the eye to have a clear view of the functions.

Parts of the Eye and its Mechanism

We see objects in the outside world with all their qualities like their size, shape, distance and colour. In between our eyes and the objects the environmental space is filled with light with all its characteristics. What is taking place in the eye when we see an object needs the understanding of the *visual psychophysics*. How the light reaches the eye determines the colours that are seen? The psychophysics of visual phenomena include several things like the visual dimensions of hue, brightness, saturation, visual sensation, acuity, phenomenon, cues for depth and distance, constancy and colour vision. The eye is a sense organ (Fig. 13.1). It is made up of different kinds of tissues and each tissue has a role to play in the response of the eye to light. Vision is a chemical reaction which occurs in response to radiant energy, the light. The light is a vibrating energy. It

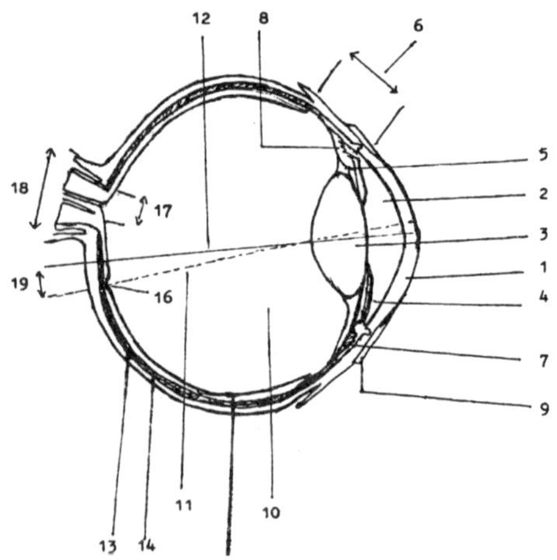

Fig. 13.1 : Cross-section of the right eye ball : Diagrammatic illustration of the parts.

1. Cornea
2. Anterior Chamber
3. Lens
4. Iris
5. Posterior Chamber
6. Ciliary Body
7. Ciliary Muscle
8. Ciliary Processes
9. Conjunctiva
10. Vitreous Body (Fundus)
11. Visual Axis
12. Optic Axis
13. Sclera
14. Choroid Coat
15. Retina
16. Fovea
17. Optic Disc
18. Optic Nerve
19. Yellow Spot

forms a part of the electromagnetic spectrum of wavelengths. The human visual system is such that as soon as the energy, the light, reaches the point, where the chemical conversion takes place, it is changed into an object, the light is transfigured.

It is not easy for us to state definitely about the subject matter we study under the headings of the psychophysics of vision and the physiology of human eye as quite number of studies are made now and then and new findings are revealed in the area of visual perception. But, let us accept what is prevalent at present about the psychophysics of vision.

Layers (coats) of the Eye

The human eye mainly is made up of jelly like substance looks roughly round like a ball. It is functioning like an optical instrument registering objects exposed to it like a camera. The human eye roughly can be compared to a camera in its functions. The eye-ball is consisting of three layers superposed upon one another. They are : (1) the sclerotic coat or sclera, (2) the choroid coat and (3) the retina.

1. *The sclerotic coat or sclera* is a tough non-transparent outer fibrous tissue of the white part of the eye. It prevents light entering the eye except through pupil. The sclerotic coat continues and joins with cornea at the front of the eye. The anterior portion of this coat forms the transparent cornea. The sclera develops the trunk of the optic nerve at the posterior portion through which the optic nerve enter the eye-ball.

2. *The choroid coat* is the middle layer lays under the sclera of the eyeball. The choroid coat continues round the eyeball like sclerotic coat and gradually merges into the ciliary muscles on either side. It contains many blood vessels for nourishing the other tissues of the eye. It is dark coloured. The most anterior part of the vascular (choroid) coat is a ring shaped strip called the iris which fringes the pupil.

3. *The retina* is the third inner layer, unlike the other two layers, covers only a two-third part of the interior surface of the eyeball, except the front part of the eye ball. The retina is like the sensitive plate of the camera, but differing from the photographic plate as the plate has to be changed after every exposure. It has a complex structure and it contains sensitive elements to light.

When we see an object, light rays from the object entering the eye through a circular opening called *pupil* (pupillary opening). On either side of the pupil there is coloured iris. The *iris* is a smooth muscle structure which regulates the size of the pupil. It is the contractions of the iris that open or close the pupil to regulate the amount of light entering the eye. The iris is corresponding to the adjustable diaphragm of the camera. There is a curved transparent outer tissue called cornea in the front of the eye ball that when light first entering the eye encounters the cornea. The *cornea* is a transparent outer tissue in front of the eye-ball. The cornea does the job of focusing in such a way that the lens brings complete light rays to focus on the retina area.

The light must pass through the aqueous humor and the vitreous humor, the lens, and through some tissues of the retina to the photo-receptors to get them stimulated. The *aqueous* humor is a fluid like substance fills the anterior and posterior chambers of the eyeball. The *anterior* chamber is the cavity, a small hollow space of the eyeball that lies between the cornea and the iris and the *posterior chamber* is the cavity, a small space that lies in between the iris and the lens. *The vitreous humor* is a jelly like substance that fills the large interior cavity of the eyeball that extends from the lens and ciliary muscles back to the retina area of the eyeball. Both the aqueous humor and the vitreous humor absorb some light rays and scatter others as the lens and the cornea do. There is a structure called *suspensory ligament* which attaches the ciliary muscles and the lens in the eye on either side. The contraction of the ciliary muscles relieves the tension in the suspensory ligament and causes the lens to thicken. The thickening lens focuses light on the retina from nearby object. For the light of the far away object the lens becomes thinner. But the distance between the lens and the retina is not altered.

The retina is the inner layer in the eyeball. In short, it is an extension of the cerebral cortex of the brain that contains the visual receptors that are found in the posterior part of the large interior cavity of the eyeball. The retina contains nerve cells and synapses with well defined layers. Polyak (1941) states that there are ten distinguishable layers of nerve fibres in the retina. The retina is a light sensitive area at the back of the eyeball. Light must pass through several layers of nerve cells to react the receptors. The receptors of light rays are called rods and cones. The receptors lie inverted facing the choroid coat and do not receive light directly, but through outer surface of the retina. These *receptors (rods and cones) form the first layer* which is very distinctive in the retina. The *second distinctive layer of the retina is the bipolar cell layer* which make synaptic connections with rods and cones and the *third is the ganglion cell layer,* the fibres of which form the optic nerve.

Thus, rods and cones are stimulated by the light and get excitation and pass on this to the bipolar cells. In other words the rods and cones convert the light energy into nerve impulses and pass them on to the bipolar cells. The bipolar cells in turn pass on the excitation or impulses to the ganglion cells. The axons in the ganglion cells which form the optic nerve that carry the impulses from the eye to the visual centres of the brain. Since we are concerned with perception of colour and the rods and cones are the receptors of light let us discuss this in detail. Geldard (1953) has made extensive study of the colour vision.

Functions of Rods and Cones

The fovea region falls in the retina area just opposite to the lens. It is a small pit in the retina in line with pupil of the eye. Fovea is thickly packed with receptors and therefore, it is the point of clearest vision in the eye. The fovea area is the colour zone of the eye. In the colour zone there are two kinds of sensitive cells called cones and rods. They are densely packed together and the cones *look like bulbs* whereas the rods *look like cylinders.* Light reaches the cones in the fovea region directly and since they are so numerous that the vision is more clear than the vision in the peripheral area. Light rays from the object are focused by the lens on the fovea region of the visual point. The cones are the colour-sensitive receptor cells of the retina. The rods are concerned with colour vision only in a small degree. The rods are connected in groups and each group has a neuron, going to the optic nerve. The cones are grouped in the peripheral region into units along with rods. Each cone in the fovea region has a separate nerve to the brain. It is because of this that when light rays strike the fovea region our vision is very clear and acute. The excitation and impulses are straightaway taken to the brain through the private nerve without any missing of signals. Sometimes we turn our head directly to look at the object as we want to have a clear view.

But under dull lighting situation the cones are not functioning properly and we can find a dull or a faint object. If we do not directly look at the object the image falls just outside of fovea region where the rods are closely packed together and object is seen with a dull look. The rods may respond to much dull object than the cones. But the image will not be very clear. In the night we can see the object, but with unclear outlines and without much details about the object not like as we see the object in day light.

The incoming light on the retina produces chemical and electrical changes which stimulate the tips of the cones and rods. Each cone is connected to a bipolar cell. The bipolar cells are connected to axons. The axons through optic nerve cells carry the stimulation to interbrain. A bipolar cell may also stimulate several rods and some cells may stimulate both rods and cones. The cones are more highly developed cells than the rods. Cones are primarily concerned with colour vision. The rods are concerned with light and concerned with colour only to a smaller level.

In the retina area straight back to the pupil there is a small depression. This depression area is the fovea region (Fig. 13.2). Since the cones are thickly packed in this area this becomes the centre of the colour vision. If we want to see a small object distinctly we turn our eyes to the object straight so that light from that object falls on the fovea region and we see

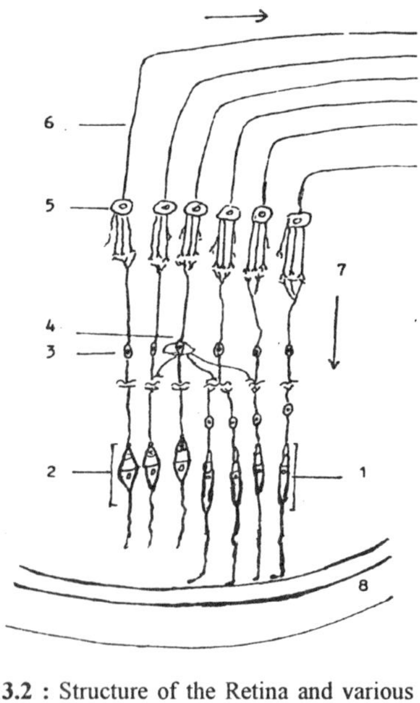

Fig. 13.2 : Structure of the Retina and various parts

1. Rods
2. Cones
3. Bipolar Cells
4. Horizontal cells connecting Rods and Cones
5. Optic Nerve Cells (Ganglion)
6. Axons leading to optic Nerve and Interbrain
7. Light
8. Choriod coat

the colour of the object clearly. Outside of this small fovea region cones and rods are found intermingled and on moving from this region through periphery towards the lens there are fewer and fewer cones and more and more rods. This result gives the idea that the form and the colour vision depend mostly upon the cones. Cones can be differentiated from rods, but some of the studies made on this show that many photo-receptors of rods and cones are anatomically look similar.

It is observed from some studies that we can differentiate rods and cones from the effects. That is, the more the image of the object moves from the fovea region to the periphery region and towards the lens the more we are derived of the colour vision. In one of the studies made by Chamanis (1949) it has been estimated that the number of cones in the fovea region alone is 17,000 and on either side of the fovea the number of cones are constant, but the number of rods are reduced. But the estimation of cones and rods varies from study to study. According to Geldard's (1953) study there are about 6.5 million cones and about hundred million rods in the retina area of the human eye. Geldard states that in each square millimetre there are about fourteen to sixteen lakhs of photo-receptors on the average in the human eye. According to Delov, a Russian Physiologist, there are about seven million cones and several hundred million rods in the human eye. They are unevenly distributed over the retina.

The rods and cones vary in size. Each rod is of about 0.07 mm long. The cones look wider than the rods but shorter (Fig. 13.3). The external limbs of the rods contain visual purple or *rhodopsin.* This is a photochemical visual pigment of the rods which fades under the action of light. The cones contain *iodopsin.* Iodopsin is a substance sensitive to light. While moving on to the periphery (towards the lens) the number of cones and

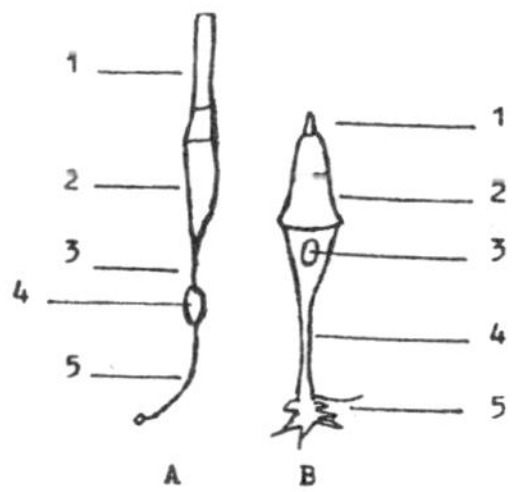

Fig. 13.3 : Rod and Cone

A — Rod.
1. Outer Limb
2. Inner Limb
3. Fibre
4. Nucleus
5. End Bottom

B — Cone.
1. Outer Limb
2. Inner Limb
3. Nucleus
4. Fibre
5. Stalk

rods are reduced. But, except in the fovea region the rods predominate the cones in the whole of retina area. In the posterior part of the retina where the optic nerve emerges from the eyeball from the point of optic disc (see Fig. 13.3) there are no sensitive elements to light. This point is called the *blind spot*. But the blank space in the field of vision (due to the blind spot) is not usually felt as it is compensated by the activity of the cells of the neighbouring regions of the retina.

How do we see Colours ?

The visual stimulus is generally broken down into three aspects, such as *hue* or wavelenth, *brightness* or radiant energy, *saturation,* or homogeneity of the wavelength. There are also other measures in use. Various terms are used to indicate the aspects of light. Therefore, the nomenclature system in the physiology of vision and other senses is not yet clearly brought out by experts in this field.

The study of psychophysics and the physiology of vision needs some elementary knowledge of the physics of the light energy which causes excitation in the retina area of the eye. Light is a complex phenomenon and studies of different types and controversies are going on regarding the functions of rods and cones.

Light, as we know, is an electromagnetic energy of wave like character and hence we speak of it in terms of wavelength (Woodworth, 1952). If the light is made to pass through a spectrum, different wavelengths may be brought out and separated. The electromagnetic energy travels through a vacuum at the rate of 186,272 miles per second, much faster than sound (Leukal, 1968). Light is a vibrating energy and it forms a part of electromagnetic spectrum of wavelengths. The wavelengths include radio waves, infr-ared waves and X-rays and cosmic rays. The light from the sun which reaches the eye is a mixture of all the visible wavelengths. The beam of light which passes through a prism glass is bent or refracted. The longer wavelengths are bending less and the shorter wavelengths are bending more. In the spectrum the different degrees of bending can be seen. The shortest wavelength is for violet and the longest wavelength is for red. At the extremes there are infra-red and ultra-violet. The infra-red waves are longer than the red and the ultra-violet waves are shorter than the violet. The infra-red gives heat sensation and the ultra-violet gives no sensation (Fig. 13.4). The rays for the hues, violet, indigo, blue, green, yellow, orange and red are slowly decreasing in the level. This is a natural phenomenon, can be seen in the rainbow. Therefore, the visual experience of colour is classified into three components such as *brightness, hue and saturation.*

1. *Brightness :* All colours may be divided into two groups as *achromatic* or colourless and *chromatic* having definite colours. All shades of grey, white and black are classified as achromatic group. The colours differ only in number of rays reflected, i.e. the brightness. The more rays of light reflected from a body the brighter the object is. An object absorbing fully all the rays falling upon it is obsolutely black. All the achromatic colours can be arranged on the basis of their brightness into a gray scale, i.e. from pure white through various shades of gray upto black. Thus, brightness may be defined as having more or less proximity to white colour. It is the intensity of visual experience. It may vary on very wider range.

2. *Hues :* The eye perceives light waves of different length of so called chromatic colours. The hue or the quality of colour depends upon the wavelength. There are seven basic colours distinguished in the spectrum.

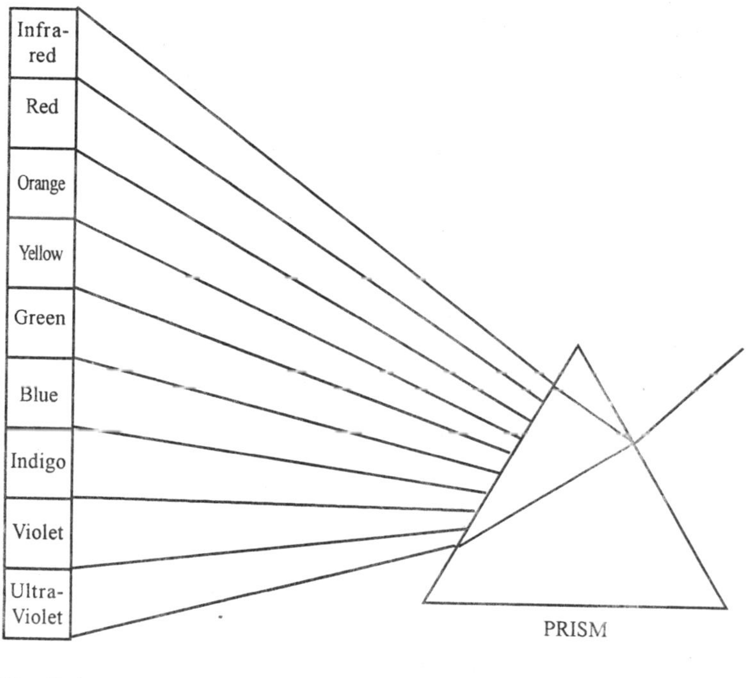

Fig. 13.4 : Composite beam of light for Prism. Red with long wave. Violet with short wave. The Infra-red heat wave longer than Red. The Ultra-violet wave longer than Violet.

They are red, orange, yellow, green, blue, indigo and violet. These colours have different levels of light wavelengths. The red has the longest wavelength 760-602 mu (millimicrons), orange 620-690 mu, yellow 590-560 mu, Green 530-500 mu, blue 500-430 mu, indigo 470-430 mu and violet 430-390 mu (Delov). Some of the chromatic colours are bright and some are dark. In the spectrum the yellow-green colours are the brightest, while the red, blue and violet are the darkest. These chromatic colours are distinguished by their brightness and also by their colour tones.

3. *Saturation :* Saturation refers to the intensity or richness of colour present in the hue. Saturation means the degree of colour response of the eye to a colour. It is black or grey in colour. The blue colour may be deep navy blue. In this, there is much saturation. On the other end it may be a faded sky blue with little saturation. If there is more mixing of colours there is little saturation. A full, pure, bright red colour is saturated, but a pale and dull red colour unsaturated. For example, pink and reddish-brown are unsaturated red. It means, these colours are mixed with other colours. These are the general relations between physical light and visual sensation. For example, when colour tone changes its saturation and brightness also change. Therefore, the psychological characteristics of colour are hue, brightness and saturation. These are known as physical properties of light.

Colour Mixture

In the study of colour, psychologists consider four colours as primary colours such as red, green, yellow and blue. The artists think that green is a mixture of yellow and blue colours. He mixes all colours together and get black. But we see green as a single colour. The seven colours we see in the spectrum are only arbitrarily designated. It is also true and clear that red, green, yellow and blue can be mixed and evolved quite number of shades like orange, yellow, green, green-blue and purple. But the four unique colours red, green, yellow and blue can be used any two at a time to produce any colour. The unique red and green or unique yellow and blue may produce grey colour. All four colours red, green, yellow and blue on mixing results in grey. When mixing black with any colour the brilliance of that colour is lowered.

In colour mixing clear view has not been arrived at so far. For example in the case of complementary colours, we do not get correct answer for the question, which are the complementary colours? What happens if we add yellow and blue? Woodworth (1952) discusses that those who mix paints will say blue and yellow will give green colour. But mixing of two paints is not adding lights, because each paint either assimiliate or take away part of the light. This process of taking away the part of light in both colours is different from adding blue and yellow colours. If we add blue and yellow we get white or gray colour. When two colour wavelengths are acting on the retina simultaneously the resulting sensation is grey or white. Thus, blue and yellow are said to be complementary colours. Woodworth says that red and green are not complementary colours, like blue and yellow. Red and green may be called disappearing colour pair. When we mix blue and yellow, both colours disappear and there is white or grey. There is yellow or blue colour resemblances. But when we mix red and green both colours disappear and the resulting sensation is yellow. Therefore, Woodworth says that red and green are not complementary. But Leukel (1968) says that just like yellow and blue colours, unique red and green when we mix, it gives grey colour and therefore red and green are complementary colours. The general principle in defining complementary colours is that any two colours when mixed together in right proportion should yeild a grey or white sensation. Garrett (1961) states that red and blue-green colours, when blend, yield grey colour and therefore they (red and blue-green) are complementary colours.

What are the colours which are not complementary? When we mix two colours if the resulting sensation is an intermediate colour then they are not called complementary colours. For example, red and yellow when mixed give orange colour, blue and green yield a blue-green colour. There are two kinds of colour mixing. One is substractive colour mixing and the other is additive colour mixing.

In substractive colour mixing the result is always in diminishing brightness. When the three primary colours red, green and blue are mixed together by substraction a dark grey or black colour is usually seen. All the three colours have lost their brightness. The wavelengths of these three colours are absorbed and the resultant colour is the reminder. Substractive colour mixing is made in mixing of paints. It is also very much uselul for artists, painters and dyers. Artist mixes blue and yellow to get green. Generally, the laws of colour mixing is applied to lights. But the artist, the painter and the dyer use different laws for their purpose.

In additive colour mixing the brightness is increased by addition. When two complementary colours, blue and yellow are mixed with right proportion and made to fall on the retina region the resulting sensation is not green. It is only grey. In additive colour mixing, by mixing of all colours white colour is produced and not grey. The principle in additive colour mixing is that if the original wavelengths are added it results in a diffferent colour. If a spotlight from a red spotlight were made to fall on a white reflecting surface of the screen a red circle is seen. If a yellow spot of light were on the screen yellow wavelengths is reflected. But if both spots of light, red and yellow were shown on the reflecting surface of the screen for overlapping, this overlapping area would look orange — it is a mixture of red and yellow colours. In addition the orange area would be brighter than red and yellow areas as it is reflecting the light from both spotlights to the eye. By increasing the brightness of the wavelengths of red and yellow a different set of colour follows.

In our everyday life we observe that some colours are more prominent than others. For example, white and black. In colour mixing the white and black are the extreme of series of greys. Actually there is no colour called grey. Psychologically there are four primary colours, red, green, blue and yellow. It is reasonably inferred that the salient colours, red, green, blue and yellow are also primary colours and all other colours are derived from these colours by mixing them in different combinations. It is also reasonable to assume that the retina has certain primary activities in varying degrees to provide numerous effects in our perception of colour vision.

As the result of colour mixture we come to know that all the shades of colours including white and black can be obtained by mixing the wavelengths of three colours, red, green and blue in different proportions. Since yellow can be produced by mixing red and green, it is also not needed. This is the basis upon which theory of colour vision was proposed by Young Helmholtz. According to this theory there are three primary responses to light from the retina area, red, green and blue and therefore, we get the sensation of red, green and blue.

Colour Deficiencies in Vision

Colour deficiency refers to the inability to distinguish colours. Human beings do not possess normal visual ability to distinguish colours or hues. They are deficient in colour vision. It is also stated in various names as colour-blindness, colour-deficient, colour-defect, colour-weakness. In the earlier text books it is stated as colour-blindness, but in recent books it is stated as colour deficiency or colour defect. In whatever name it is called it is discussed in many practical situations. Colour deficient individuals differ from normal individuals in the perception of both colour and brightness. Colour deficiency is causing several disadvantages in children and in those who are to make discrimination of colours in printing and dying industries where the employees have to make accurate colour discrimination for evolving different shades in printing and dying. There are persons with minor deficiencies may discriminate colours as a function of brightness or saturation. Some colour deficients escape unnoticed. Therefore, unless a test of colour deficiency is conducted it will not be possible to identify the colour deficients. The Ishihara test (1920) is one most commonly used for this at present. But the first colour deficiency test was designed by Rayleigh in 1881. Various other methods have been developed for testing the colour deficiency. Colour deficient persons will not be able to match hues. This is tested by the test designed by Holmgren's wool test. Later on Edridge-green beat test (1891, 1920) and Nagel's card test were designed. Certain tests require the persons to distinguish hues instead of matching them. In these type of tests coloured spots are arranged in such a way that a person of normal vision is able to distinguish a number or a letter. A person with colour deficiency neither sees a letter or number, or sees a different letter or number. Apart from these tests Pickford (1951) has designed a *four corner test* based upon the psychophysical principles and Rayleigh equation. In this test red, green, yellow and blue filters are used. The test procedure is to present the participant with two separate colour spots, red and green. The participant is asked to adjust and make them to appear equal in brightness. When both the red and green spots are seen equal then he is asked whether he sees any difference in colours. He is asked to adjust the spots till he sees no difference by using the psychophysical method of minimal changes. The same procedure can be used for blue and yellow colours.

The Ishihara test consists of several pages of coloured dots with numbers and letters in a booklet form. The dots are arranged in such a way that they differ in colour and brightness in two patterns which will form two different numbers. One number is seen by a person of normal colour vision and the other is seen by a person who is a colour deficient. The changes are in relatiwe brightness of the coloured dots. The normal eye discriminates three system of colours like light-dark, blue-yellow and red-green. On the basis of the results of such tests the deficiencies of colour vision are classified in three categories such as monochromatism, dichromatism and trichromatism.

Monochromatism

Monochromatism is total colour deficiency. The person will see all colours as gray and he cannot distinguish between any colour and a grey with equal brightness. He sees only light and dark. He can see only the difference in brightness and not in colour and saturation. This kind of colour deficiency is rare. There are two types of monochromatism, one is functioning without cones and seeing all colours as one, the other is without functioning of rods and seeing all wavelengths as grey. According to the studies made by Geldard (1933) it is observed that in a monochromat the cones are not functioning totally or the cones are not existing and therefore he has to function only on rod vision.

Dichromatism

This is partial colour deficiency. The person is not able to distinguish red and green. The person can discriminate between light-dark and blue and yellow. Dichromat has normal vision of illumination (light-dark). The rods do not affect colour blindness. This type of colour deficiency takes place in four different forms. They are protanopes, denteranopes, tritanopes and tetertanopes. The first two forms lack red-green vision, but blue and yellow vision is clear. The last two forms lack blue yellow vision, but has red-green vision.

Trichromatism

The trichromatism is of two types as normal trichromatism which is also called dischromatism. It is three colour perception or normal vision. The other type of trichromatism is anomalous trichromatism which is mostly normal vision. The trichromatic vision, which is anomalous needs different amount of the primary colours to match than the normal trichromatic vision (dichromatism). The term relates to a number of colours which a person needs to mix for matching the colours. The person with trichromatic vision can match all the colours of the spectrum with three colours, red, green and blue. The trichromatic person can also match white. In the functioning of the anomalous trichromatic vision *three forms* colour deficiencies *out of the four* shown above take place. In *protanomaly* form the eyes are weak for red, in *denteranomaly* form the eyes are weak for green and in *tritanomaly* form the eyes are weak for yellow-blue.

Colour deficiency or blindness occurs from the lack of certain retinal cells or cones or from the lack of light-sensitive cells in the retinal area. The bee and other insects can see only two colours, yellow and blue. But birds and all mammals evidently can see all colours. Colour deficiency or blindness occurs in men 6 to 7 percent, but in women the percentage is higher. Colour deficiency is an occupational risk or danger for railway pilots, engineers, car and bus, lorry drivers and also it is a handicap for dyers, textile salesmen, printers and to persons who deal with colour. Visual deficiency arises due to vitamin deficiency. Vitamin A in food may relieve night blindness.

Theories of Colour Vision

The theory of colour vision tries to explain how the visual system is able to function in such a way that all the observable facts that are associated with colour vision can be stated in advance. On this issue there are speculations centred on the role of photo-receptors of the retina with regard to the number and nature of functions assumed for the photo-receptors or the cells of the retina. There are several theories of colour vision. One of the theories, aimed to explain the colour vision is called *trichromatic theory.* This theory is the most substantiated one. The fundamental ideas of this theory were first expressed by Lomonosov (1756) in the eighteenth century. Lomonosov, a brilliant Russian scientist, has stated that: "nature is all the more amazing, since.... from a small number of causes it creates countless forms of properties, changes and phenomena". He has developed the idea that various colours can be produced by the fusion of the three primary colours, red, yellow and light blue. In confirmity with them the eye contains at the bottom three colour sensitive substances. These basic principles become the essence of trichromatic theory. Lomonosov has established his three primary colours from the results of the mixture of paints.

Later on in the beginning of nineteenth century Young advanced a similar trichromatic theory of colour vision. In continuation of this in the middle of the nineteenth century this theory advanced by Young was thoroughly elaborated by Helmholtz. Young's proposition of the primary colours was very close to that made by Lomonosov. The primary colours were red, yellow and blue and later on Young correctly defined the three primary colours as red, yellow and blue. Thus according to the trichromatic theory of Lomonosov-Young-Helmholtz the retina area of the human eye consists of three sets of colour sensitive elements corresponding to the three primary colours, red, green and blue. Each one of these elements is stimulated by one of the primary colours, but also reacts to other colour rays to a lesser extent. Therefore, the action of red ray stimulates the red component and also stimulates the green component to a much lesser degree and also stimulates the blue component to a very slight degree. When one set of senstive elements are excited that particular set of sensitive elements evokes the sensation of a saturated colour which is related to one of the primary colours. But when all the three colour sensitive elements are equally excited the resulting sensation is white.

Further, trichromatic theory of colour vision tries to explain the problem of colour blindness satisfactorily. But it has not succeeded fully. The problem lelt unanswered by the trichromatic theory is that if the functioning red-green receptors can produce yellow colour, how is that a person with red-green colour blindness is able to see yellow colour without any difficulty? The defect of any one component of colour vision may cause colour blindness. The protanopia, a partial colour blindness, occurs due to the loss of the red components, similarly denteranopia occurs due to any defect in green components and so also the tritanopia occurs due to the defect in blue components. Granit (1947) has verified and substantiated this theory by electrophysiological studies. According to his study it seems that some receptors in the retina area possess maximum sensitivity in the region of red-orange colours, some in the region of green colour and some in the region of blue colour. But this theory disregards the important role played by the cortical area in the processes of analysis and synthesis of colour influences. But it is also found that colour sensitivity may be modified by administering substances which stimulate or depress the cortical region. The clinical observations state that cerebral lesions (injuries) cause total or partial derangement of colour vision with regard to separate colours.

A theory of colour vision has been formulated by Karl Ewald Hering (1834 –1918) in 1870. This theory is able to solve the problem left out by the trichromatic theory. Hering ascertained that yellow is also a primary colour. He based his theory on psychological primaries, whereas the trichromatic theory is based upon mixing of colours. Hering states that there are three types of receptors, one type is responding to degrees of brightness, the black-white continuum. The other two types are colour receptors, one type provides the basis for red-green colour vision and the other blue-yellow colour vision. It is assumed that each of these pairs function in two ways. Either differentiated or made similar by some physiological and chemical process. One colour of the pair is produced when the receptor is in a building up the place (anabolic-energy input) and the other appeared when the receptor is in a dismantling phase (Catabolic-energy release). The first is also called assimilation and the second is called dissimilation. The two functions cannot occur at the same time in a receptor. If red-green receptor is stimulated either red or green is perceived and not both. Each of the primary colours may be produced in this way. It is because of this, according to this theory that we never see red-green or blue-yellow. Rather we see reddish blue or greenish yellow. But when stimulation is withdrawn the contrasting colour appears. This is the reversed function of the anabolic-catabolic reaction of the photo-receptors. For example, if we look at a *red circle* steadily for 20 seconds and shift our *look to a white or grey* sheet of paper a green circle will appear. This theory is called opponent-process theory. A recent finding is that the opponent-process is not taking place in the receptors but in the mechanism of the optic region of the brain.

Disorders of Colour Vision

Colour vision disorder occurs in the inability to perceive colours. It may be partial colour or total colour blindness. Total colour blindness is rare among human beings. Individuals suffer fiom disorder of colour vision. These individuals distinguish various colours of external environment only by the brightness of the colours. It is by different shades of grey colour. Partial colour disorder occurs very often in many people. Partial colour blindness is more common in men than women. According to Delov there are *three kinds* of partial colour disorder commonly occurring. They are protanopia, denteranopia and tritanopia. We have already made mention about these three components of colour vision elsewhere. But here we are stating them in different context.

Protanopia

This disorder is also stated as daltonism or protanomaly. We have stated this disorder of colour vision as protanomaly elsewhere. Protanopia signifies blindness for red and green. Persons with this disorder are unable to differentiate between red and green shades. These people see the whole spectrum as colourless neutral portion divided into two parts. One portion is having yellow background and the other a light blue. They do not see rcd and grccn colours.

Denteranopia

This disorder also signifies blindness for red and green, mostly for green colour. The point of maximum brightness for denteranopia is situated in the orange part of the spectrum (600 mu wavelength). The point is shifted from normal to the red end of the spectrum.

Tritanopia

This is characterised by blindness for blue and violet which occurs very seldom. The tritanopia is said to be shortening of the blue-violet end of the visual spectrum. Since the wavelength of these two colours are shortened, the blindness for these two colours occurs.

Persons with disorders of colour vision are not aware of their disorders. It is estimated that about four percent of all men suffer from abnormalities of colour vision. Studies on disorders of colour vision are very few and the existing studies do not provide us with clear cut idea about this. There is some difference between the systems of nomenclature which are often causing confusion.

Measuring the Field of Vision and the Colour Zone (Perimeter)

In all psychophysical studies of sensory experiences the measurement of threshold and its proper determination and the specifications are made. These are available in large number of measures. For example in the case of wavelength and hue the absolute threshold for human is determined as 400 mu for violet and 750 mu for red (Leukel, 1968). The thresholds will vary when there is change in the illumination and saturation.

In the study of psychophysics of illumination and brightness factors such as the amount and radiant energy, location and size of the area of retina under stimulation, intensity and duration of the stimulus all should be considered in the determination of the threshold. If the wavelength is of homogeneous in nature the human subjects can discriminate the difference in the amount of white light added to a wavelength. For example, if a yellow and blue colour of the same brilliance are presented many human beings may judge that the blue is more saturated than the yellow. It is because the blue wavelength is more saturated than the yellow wavelength.

In measuring saturation thresholds two fields are generally used. Both can have equal luminiance. One is designed in such a way that the amount of white light may be altered. In measuring the difference in purity of a given wavelength, the standard psychophysical procedure, the method of minimal changes may be used by varying the amount of white light in one field and asking the person to judge when the two fields are different or equal in saturation. In this case the luminous should be kept constant as the person judges the field on the basis of saturation. It may be found that the thresholds may be increased with the increase of wavelength. The experiments conducted by Jones and Lowry (1926) illustrate this phenomenon.

There are also other studies of threshold for different hues as the function of the area of retina on which hue was presented. The eyes are not capable of seeing the colours of the objects wherever they are presented. If the objects are on the edge of retina area then it will not be possible for us to see the colour in the object. The object would appear to us as grey. It is because, the image of the object falls away from the fovea region of the retina. We can see the colour of the object if only the image falls in the fovea region. This can be illustrated by a single example. Hold an object in your right hand and stretch it on the right. Keep your hand horizontally, parallel to the ground. See the object without turning your head. The object appears to you like grey. Slowly move your hand from right side to your front and you can see slowly the colour of the object. When the object is moved to your front you see the colour. It is because, the image of the object falls in the fovea region of the retina.

The eye perceives a certain space in a fixed position. All points of the space is seen simultaneously. This space which is simultaneously visible to the eye, is limited by the insensitivity part of the eye --- the extreme retinal peripheral area. The extreme peripheral area of the retina is not sensitive to light stimulations. Therefore, the area between the points of simultaneously visible and the point of insensitivity to light stimulation is called the field of vision. The perimeter is the instrument used to measure this *field of vision.* It is also stated that the retinal area which is sensitive to light stimulation has a limitation in its reaction to the light stimulation (Fig. 13.5).

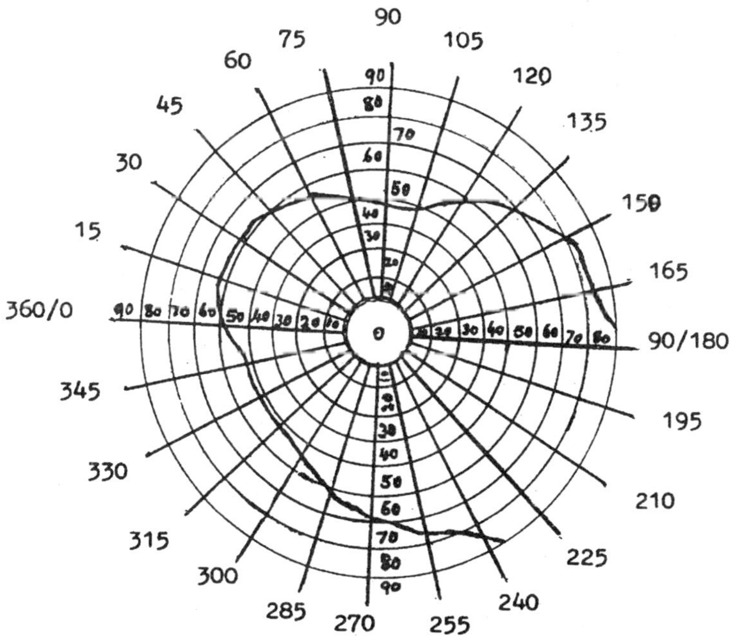

Fig. 13.5 : Visual Field Chart. Maping the colour zone of the right eye (for white colour).

The sensitivity of the human eye varies to different spectral colour stimulations. The yellow spot of the retinal area whose central part contains only cones which are the most sensitive cells to light or colour stimulations. The farther from the yellow spot the lower the colour sensitivity of the retina. The curve of the spectral sensitivity for the average eye in pure cone vision shows that the cones are most sensitive for the yellow colour (565 mu wavelength). Sensitivity to colour diminishes on both sides from this point towards red and violet ends of the spectrum.

The spectral sensitivity curve is also called the visibility curve. The visibility curve varies with intensity of illumination. At a low illumination, for example at twilight, the colour tones are not perceived and the maximum sensitivity shifts towards the short waves, to the region of bluish-green rays. The shift of maximum visibility towards short wave region during the period of transition from day light vision to twilight vision is called the *Purkinje phenomenon.* It was Purkinje, a Czechoslovakian scientist who first discovered this phenomenon in 1923. As the illumination diminishes the red colours are the first to become indistinguishable and the blue colours are the last. But at the same time at a very high intensity of illumination the colours loose their saturation and become white or yellow. The violet colour changes the most and the red colour the least.

The differential sensitivity to colour vision shows variation in different regions of the spectrum. It is observed that closer to the end of the spectrum the sensitivity is very low and finally the ability to discriminate between colour tones disappears entirely, i.e. in the violet part of the spectrum. It is estimated that there are 128 hues generally perceived in the spectrum.

We have discussed above that the central part of the retina is the yellow spot, which contains only cone cells which are the most sensitive to colours. The peripheral part of the retina which consists of mostly rods, are most sensitive to weak light (twilight) stimuli. The cones serve for daylight and colour vision and the rods are generally adapted to low intensities of illumination, particularly to colourless vision, the twilight. Thus the cones are for the central vision and the rods are for the peripheral vision. This is stated as the *duplicity theory* of the visual apparatus.

Experiments have been designed to trace the areas of the retina which are sensitive to colour vision. The plotting of the areas of the retina which are sensitive to colour called *perimetry.* The apparatus designed to assess the area is called *perimeter.* The original perimeter consists of one semi- circular rim, a chin rest in front of it and at the back of rim is a disc, angle from 0° to 360° with pointers. But the original perimeter has been modified and improved model has been brought at present. Certain disadvantages found in the original apparatus were eliminated in the improved model.

On the semi-circular rim a small coloured square bit (patch) may be moved along the rim in which it rests. The participant in the experimental situation should focus his attention held constant in front of him on a point by resting his chin on a chin rest. Different colour bits (patches) are moved from extreme left or right (periphery) towards the fovea region slowly, step by step until the participant is able to identify the colour of the bit. It should be recorded at which point the participant is able to identify the colour in the bit partially and also fully. The method of minimal changes may be used to determine the colour zone. Whatever method is used it is important that the trials should be conducted from only one direction. The colour bits should be moved on the rim only from extreme left or extreme right on the semi-circular rim, that is from the peripheral region towards fovea region.

The experimental assumption would be defeated if the counterbalanced procedure is followed by having the stimulus (colour bit) moving from fovea region to the peripheral region. By this procedure the participant is fully aware of the colour of the bit that is moved to the peripheral area. Since he has seen and known the colour even if the colour becomes grey he would say that there is colour. But Candland (1968) suggests that if the experimenter wants to find out when a colour becomes grey, then it would be correct to move the stimulus from the fovea region to the peripheral area. But this is more a counterbalancing the trials and the participant is much influenced by his experience and he would not tell the correct place where the colour is changed into grey.

In the perimeter experiments interesting results were obtained. It was found that some colours like blue and yellow are perceived and identified more quickly than red and green. It is also found that though the participants are more influenced by the intensity of the colour rather than the hue the peripheral area of the retina is more sensitive for the hues of blue and yellow than for other colours. Experimental subjects in the perimeter experiment are able to identify the hues of blue, yellow, red and green correctly. They were able to say when these colour change from grey to the respective colours. *The perimatric studies* of Teuber, Battersby and Bender (1960) revealed the *damage of vision in the parts of central nervous system* and also the *damage in the visual cortex region.*

The human eye is a very complex apparatus. It consists of very sensitive parts. How we are able to see and distinguish various colours in the outside world? It is very difficult to explain without any controversal view. Studies on colour vision were going on for more than 200 years from 1756. Since the sensitivity of the human sensory apparatus varies from person to person, now and then additional facts from the studies are added to the existing knowledge and hence various views are expressed. Therefore, whatever information is available without much controversy may be taken as valid. In the case of colour vision we are able to plot the areas of retina which are sensitive to colour. We have discussed this in detail in the preceding section.

EXPERIMENT-11 : Tracing the Field of Vision and the Colour Zone by Modern Psychophysical Scaling Method

Problem : The three retinal zones that we have discussed in the preceding section, are sensitive to the specific pairs of colours. The field of vision for each colour zone varies. The field of vision for brightness or for *black-white* is much larger than for the other two fields of vision. The field of vision for *blue-yellow* is larger than the field of *red-green.* This type of distribution is not rigid. There may be overlapping of one field into the other, depending upon the function of anabolic-catabolic reactions of the photo-receptors.

The eye in a fixed position perceives a certain space, all points of which are seen simultaneously. This space which is simultaneously visible to the eye is limited by the insensitivity of the extreme retinal periphery to light stimulations. This space is called the *field of vision.*

Aim : Therefore, the aim of the present experiment is to trace out the field of vision and the colour zones in the left and right eyes of a person by using the instrument, the perimeter (The aim may be also stated in another way). The aim of this experiment is to plot the areas of the retinal colour zones of the left and right eyes of a person using a perimeter.

2. METHOD

Participant : Choose a person who has no knowledge about this experiment and state his/her personal characteristics like, his age, sex, qualification, occupation, whether he/she wears spects and so on.

Materials : 1. Perimeter instrument with adjustable chin rest, 2. blindfold,

3. square colour strips of white, red, green, blue and yellow colours, 4. Stick for moving the colour strips or patches, 5. Perimeter charts.

Description of the Material : The perimeter is made of steel and wood. There is a wooden base of about 4" width and one foot long. At one end an adjustable chin rest is fitted to the wooden base. At the other end a steel bar is fixed vertically. The height of which is about one foot. In the steel rod at three-fourth of its height a steel semi-circular arm or rim is fixed horizontally. There is half opening in between the two ends of the semi-circular arm. The arm is of one inch width. A scale showing the angular distance is marked in the arm. This semi-circular arm is called perimeter arm. It is also called perimeter arc. It is movable and adjustable. A rider is attached to the arms of the perimeter and the (stimulus) colour strip or colour patch is fixed in the rider. The rider is movable forward and backward. At the centre of the perimeter arm, two round discs, one big and one small are attached on the horizontal bar. On the back of the disc angles from 0 degree to 360 degrees are marked. There is also an indicating iron rod used as the pointer. The smaller disc is attached with the perimeter arm in such a way that when the perimeter arm is rotated in an angular way, the disc also is moved. The pointer is to be kept parallel to the axis 0° (zero degree). At the centre of the perimeter arm just in front of the iron bar on the big disc there is a black 'fixation point' in line with the participant's eye. The perimeter arm or arc may be placed in four meridians with two points fixed at the opposite ends of each meridian. The meridians may fall on the angles of 45, 135, 225 and 315. There are nine steps in the perimeter chart starting from 10, 20, 30, 40, 50, 60, 70, 80 and 90. The colour strip should be moved on all nine steps.

Procedure : The participant should be seated comfortably in front of the perimeter apparatus in a well illuminated room. The light should be at his back side. His/her right eye should be blind folded and his/her left eye should not have any interference or disturbance. The participant's chin should be made to rest on the chin rest. The height of the chin rest is to be adjusted in such a way that the eye of the participant should be in line with the 'fixation point' on the bigger disc.

The perimeter arm should be adjusted in a horizontal position that the angle of 180° should be on the left of the participant. The rider should be on the extreme left of the perimeter at the 9th step (90). The same procedure may be followed also for the right eye. The experimenter should select the four colours, red, green, blue and yellow for his experiment, and these should not be shown to the participant.

The following instructions should be given to the participant:

"Please fix your left eye on the 'black point' in front of you. On the left of the metal arm (pointing out the perimeter arm) I will be putting something and you please tell me whether you are able to see it and how it looks like. You should not move your head or eye from the 'fixation point' and do not see the object directly."

The experimenter, after having given this instruction, should keep the rider to the extreme left of the perimeter arm at 90th the 9th last step and fix first a red colour strip in the rider without the knowledge of the participant. Then he/she should move the rider with the stick slowly step by step from 90, the left peripheral end towards the centre (fovea region) of the perimeter arm where there is the black point until the participant is able to identify the colour of the strip. Suppose at certain point if participant says that he sees grey colour the point should be noted down. He/she should watch when the participant identifies the object with red colour and note down the place (the degree). He should continue moving the colour strip step by step (i.e. 90, 80, 70, 60, 50, 40, etc.) and note down the colour at every step. The object of the given colour appears to change when the hue approaches the fovea region. Persons do not always perceive the hue of an object correctly when they first detect it. Four colours should be correctly identified. Red, green, blue and yellow are perceived to change from grey to appropriate colour. The experimenter should note down the point at which the grey colour changes to appropriate colour and also should note down the place (the degree) where a second change, if any, in hue takes place, i.e. from red to something else.

The experimenter should follow the same procedure on the opposite side, i.e. on the right of the perimeter arm on the same horizontal position. It is the (0 or 360) zero or 360 degree position. He should move step by step from 90, 80, 70, 60, 50, 40, 30, 20 and so on all nine steps. He should note down the point at which the stimulus colour strip is noticed as grey and also perceived as red and should continue further moving step by step towards the 'fixation point' and note down in how many steps he sees red colour. He should move further whether there is any second change in the colour. As soon as it is over the experimenter should remove the colour strip from the rider.

Then the experimenter should change the position of the perimeter arm to the upper and lower quadrants of the visual fields, 90° and 270°. He can start from the upper quadrant (90°) and insert the same red colour strip in the rider at the end of the upper most part of the arm. He/she should give the following instructions:

"Now, the position of the perimeter arms are in the upper and lower levels. You will have to fix your eye on the same 'black point' and see whether you could see anything on the upper arm and say what do you see and how it looks like."

Then the experimenter should move the red strip step by step from 90 with the same speed towards the centre (fovea region) till the participant reports that he sees the red colour strip. At once the experimenter should note down the point, the degree at which red colour is perceived and should continue to see in how many steps he sees red colour and note down. He should move it further to see whether there is any second change in the colour. The same procedure should be followed at the lower quadrant of the visual field (270°). The red colour strip with the rider should be fixed at the extreme end of the lower arm at 90 and ask the participant to do the same thing as he did previously and note down the points, the degrees at which red colour is perceived and also should continue moving the strip to see whether there is any second change in the colour.

After maping the field of vision for the red colour other colours such as green, blue and yellow also should be used and the same procedure should be followed. The same procedure may be repeated also for the right eye of the participant. But the experimenter should make it a point that the participant should not see the colour strip while inserting it in the rider. He/she should not be aware of the colour next appearing in the perimeter arm. Otherwise the purpose of the experiment would be lost. To have a correct area of the colour zone, the experiment may be extended also to other angles of 45, 135, 225 and 315 and the colour zone may be investigated. As soon as everything is over the experimenter should get the introspective report from the participant and allow him/her to go away.

3. RESULTS

The experimental results should be presented in a Table. The point at which change of colour perceived and the various steps at which the colour was perceived by the participant for each colour at both the ends should be tabulated and presented in Table 13.1.

Table 13.1 : Showing the field of vision and the colour zone of the left eye and right eye of the participant in the perimeter experiment. The figures in the Table are the degrees of the various steps.

1	2	3	4	5	6	7
Sl. No.	Stimulus colour	Arm	Degree at which object perceived colour of it	Degree at which the correct colour perceived succes-sively	Degree at which 2nd change if any taken place	Remarks Any disorder or colour blindness
1.	Red	Left				
		Right				
2.	Green	Left				
		Right				
3.	Blue	Left				
		Right				
4.	Yellow	Left				
		Right				

There are 9 steps ranging from the centre like, 10, 20, 30, 40, 50, 60, 70, 80 and last 90. The moving of colour strip should begin at 90 and move to the next step 80 and then to 70 and so on. If the participant sees grey at a point note it down at once. Move the colour strip further. At another step if he sees red, note it down at once and move to the next step, if he says red, note it down. Like this in how many steps successively he sees red colour should be noted down. In column 5 it is important that these results should be entered. While moving the strip to the end if there is any second change, i.e. from red to grey or any other colour the step should be noted down in column 6. The second change is the indication of colour blindness. Note down whether it takes place in the left eye or in the right eye.

Plot the experimental results in the perimeter chart, the reports of the participant for all four colours for left and right eyes separately. State the average extension of each colour. Use the respective colours for plotting the colour zones. Indicate the blind spot for left and right eyes by a black dot at the centre of the perimeter chart.

4. DISCUSSION

Compare the points at which the first change of colour has taken place for all four colours. At how many points the same colour was seen by the participant. Discuss whether there was any second change of the colour, if so, in which colour it has taken place. State which colour in your experiment has wider field of colour vision. Is it in line with the theories of colour vision or varies. State whether there is any difference between the left and right eyes in the field of colour vision. Has your participant colour blindness? Or did you observe any other disorder in your participant in his/her colour perception. Discuss your results with those of other earlier studies.

14

VISUAL ACUITY : Spatial and Temporal Resolution

Brightness Discrimination : An Introduction

Man's successful performance of his activities in the world to a large extent depends upon his sense of sight. His adjustment in space, discrimination and manipulation of colours, forms and objects, all these and many other activities depend upon the proper functioning of the visual system. Our responses to visual stimuli are closely integrated and coordinated with other response mechanisms like the auditory, static and motor systems of the organism. An analysis of the functions of the varied visual experiences is very much essential for proper understanding of the visual functions, the properties of visual stimuli and their measurements. Human visual experiences mainly depend upon the stimulation of the sensitive receptors of the eye by the radiant energy. The radiant energy refers to the wave motion with two basic dimensions, the wavelength and the intensity.

Here, we are going to deal with one of the characteristics of the visual function, the visual acuity. This function mainly deals with the resolution of power of space.

The resolution of power of space according to Postman and Egan (1949) means the capacity to discriminate different parts of visual field from each other. This power of discrimination provides us the ability to see the differences even in very small objects and to respond also to very small separations among the objects in the visual field. Visual acuity is mainly concerned with the spatial problems when two stimuli in the visual field appeared differently or in the same manner. When we look at a point at a distance, it is not the object alone, but the total visual areas become the stimuli which may be called the visual field. Visual acuity may be also defined as the reciprocal of the visual angle delimited by the smallest object or gap whose presence can be detected (Boring, 1942). Visual acuity can be also stated as the visual capacity or power with which the smallest separation between two objects can be detected. According to Postman and Egan it is measured in terms of minutes of arc. This measure has one advantage. It is independent of the distance of the stimulus from the organism's eye. According to Kimble *et el.* (1985) visual acuity is the ability of the eye to distinguish small details.

Visual acuity is tested by using many objects. Small objects such as small dots and hairlines, separation between two dots, two thin lines, minimum discriminable opening in a circle, letters e, c, f, framework of bars consisting of alternate light and dark bars etc. Visual acuity is a function of the conditions under which judgments are made. Under some best possible conditions a thin hairline can be detected in as small as 0.5 seconds. A characteristic measure of minimum detectable separation between two lines has been 30 seconds. This is stated as the maximum acuity under favourable conditions. The normal visual acuity in medical eye examinations is an angle of 60 seconds.

In our everyday experience it is found that visual acuity is low in dim lighting arrangement. This means that acuity mainly depends upon brightness or intensity of light. At twilight even big objects cannot be correctly seen. Also distance between objects cannot be accurately discriminated. If the intensity of light is increased from very low level then visual acuity is increased. But in low intensity of light the visual acuity is also low. Therefore, we may state that visual acuity is a form of *brightness discrimination.* Mueller (1969) states that determining visual acuity is the same as the deterrnination of threshold in psychophysical experiments. In determining visual acuity the threshold width should be large for, very dim illumination and small for high level of illumination. In a clear day light bright background a line can be resolved subtending in a half second of visual angle. This is equivalent to a fine wire .1 inch diameter seen at hundred yards. To achieve this resolution the line must be very long. If the length is shorten we must widen the wire to see it. To determine the threshold of a long wire in a twilight sky the wire should be thicker many times. Therefore, there is always a definite quantitative relation between the thinness of a line that is to be detected and the illumination of the background. Therefore, this also becomes one of the important psychophysical experiments.

Visual acuity also highly depends upon retinal area. The retinal area in the human eye consists of receptor elements. These are connected to nerve cells. Many receptors are connected to one nerve cell. Visual acuity mainly depends upon the stimulation of visual receptors. These visual receptors also known as rods and cones. These are responsible in determining the visual acuity. These rods and cones are very thickly packed in the fovea region of the retina area and they are very sensitive to light and colour. Therefore, the physiology of the eye is also to be known to understand the visual acuity. The physiology of the eye is described in some other experiment.

One of the important functions of the visual sensation is to determine the spatial relations of the visual objects, their size, dimensions, forms and distance. The simplest form of spatial vision is the determination of small objects and the details of the same. This process is called visual acuity. It is generally measured by the shortest distance between two sources of light which the eye is able to see it as separate. The higher this discrimination ability the greater the visual acuity is.

The perception of two objects separately in the external world depends on the size of the image focused on the retina. If the distance between the images on the retina is shorter than certain limit and if the images fall on two adjacent cones or rods the two objects perceived get merged and as result of it, it becomes impossible to make any discrimination between two objects. The size of the image focused on the retina area depends on the visual angle.

Visual Angle

The visual angle is formed by rays which proceed from two visual points and cross at the nodal point of the eye which is situated at a distance of 7 mm from the top of the cornea of the eye towards the direction of the retina. This visual angle is an important component in the visual acuity. The visual angle is formed at the eye near above cornea by the light rays coming from an object outside. At the nodal point the light rays are subtended. What we measure as the visual acuity is, the angle subtended or the limit set by the light rays which go into the eye from the objects. The smaller the visual angle at which the eye is able to perceive two objects separately the higher the visual acuity is. Leukel (1968) states that a larger object at a greater distance may form the same visual angle at the cornea of the eye that the smaller object from a shorter distance could form.

Researchers like Dalov has ascertained that the normal eye can perceive two objects separately if the angle is formed by rays coming from two separate points of an object equals one minute. An angle of one minute is supposed to be normal visual acuity according to physicians' norm. The sensitivity of the eye to see two objects separately depends upon several factors. It depends upon the brightness of the visual objects, on the degree of contrast between objects, the background of the object, the region of the retina, where the image is focused for the formation of the angle and the adaptation of the eye. It has been experimentally verified that if the pupil is 3 mm in diameter the visual acuity is the highest.

Measurement of Visual Angle

Visual angle is measured in two ways. One is measuring the minimum visual angle and the other is measuring minimum separable angle. The factors stated above are the determining the degree of acuity. If the degree of contrast between objects is greater and if the background is strikingly different then the visual acuity is greater. This principle is applied in designing the tests to measure visual acuity. There will be maximum visual contrast, having white background and black material or black background against white material.

The minimum visual angle is the smallest angle. This is delimited by the light rays that is coming from two points of a visual object which is in a contrasting bright background. The minimum visual angle can be tested with a black wire against a white background. The diameter of a black wire in a white background should be seen at a standard distance. The diameter is the thickness of the black wire and the black wire can be used in any design.

The other measure of visual angle is the minimum separable angle. This is quite similar to the classical *psychophysical experimental method,* the method of minimal changes. The minimum separable angle is a spatial problem, whether two stimuli appear as one or as two, separately. The minimum separable angle is formed by the smallest distance between two objects that can be seen in a contrasting bright background from a standard distance. In the test two black wires in a white background are moved closer together till the person just see the space between the wires. *The minimum separable angle is always greater and it is one minute. The minimum visible angle is usually smaller, and it is one second.*

Measurement of Visual Acuity

Visual acuity is usually measured by special charts, called optotypes which contain symbols of different sizes, for example, letters, figures, rings and hooks. The letter charts have letters of different sizes, from largest to smallest. The ring charts have rings of different sizes from largest to smallest with breaks somewhere in the rings. The width or the thickness of the letters or rings are drawn so as to make the width or the thickness of the lines or the breaks visible at angles of 1', 2', 5', 10' and more.

The most commonly used visual acuity test is the Snellen chart. Since letters are used in this test it is also called Snellen letter chart. The Snellen letter chart consists of rows of letters of diminishing size. Usually, this chart is made to hang at 20 feet away from the person. The person to be tested should name every letter. The person's performance is compared with the performance of an average individual. For example, the largest 'E' at the top of the Snellen chart forms a separate angle. If a person could see an object which is subtended by one minute of the visual angle from a standard distance then he is said to have the normal vision, 20/20. But if the same object could be seen by the person only when it is subtended by two minutes of the visual angle then he is said to have his vision as 20/40. In the case of a third person who could see the same object only when it is subtended by three minutes he is said to have his vision as 20/60. In the Snellen letter chart the letters are correlated in height with the distance. The largest letter in the chart can be discriminated by a person with normal vision from a distance of 200 feet. The next row of letters are half as high as the first row. This can be discriminated by a person of norrnal vision for a distance of 100 feet. In the same way the height or size of the letters can be correlated with the distance.

The scoring method in Snellen chart is called 'Notation System'. This system gives the visual acuity in fraction. The distance at which the normal eye can see a given row of letters is used as denominator of the fraction. The distance at which the person stands and could see the given row of letters is used as numerator. Thus, the standard distance is 20 feet which forms the numerator and denominator for the normal eye. But for the person with eye defect the numerator 20 remains constant and the denominator goes on increasing as 40, 60, 80, 100 and so on. The Snellen letter chart is a best test for testing visual acuity.

Studies on Visual Acuity

The visual acuity has certain similarity with the CFF (Critical Flicker Fusion). The difference between these two is that the CFF is concerned with temporal (time) problem, while visual acuity is concerned with spatial problem. But both problems are influenced by certain variables such as intensity, illumination, wavelength and the retinal area. Assessing visual acuity is important for many kinds of activities and for personal selection to various kinds of occupations. Hence lots of data have been collected on this area.

Regarding visual acuity there is no one technique which can provide us with complete information. Because of this Rabideau (1955) a psychophysicist attempted to assess the visual acuity by using several measures. Candland (1968) states that there is one difficulty in using Snellen Letter Chart for assessing the visual acuity. He states that the shapes of the letters provide sufficient information for making discrimination. In visual acuity there are two kinds of tests. One is to assess whether the person is able to see the object and identify it. This is called *minimum visible.* The other is assessing whether the person is able to indicate when the two objects presented are separated. For this two drawn lines, circles, stars can be used. This is called *minimum separable* test. In Snellen letter chart there is no chance for the second test. Therefore Landolt ring chart is suggested for assessing the two aspects of the visual acuity.

The Landolt Ring Chart consists of circles unclosed similar to the letter C. This test may be used for minimal separable test. In this test, the person is required to indicate where the circle is closed and where it is not. The person is further asked to say where the gap appears on the circle. Unless the person's visual acuity is normal he may find it difficult to indicate the gap on the circle from a standard distance. Osgood (1953) strongly protests the idea expressed by some investigators that illumination affects the visual acuity as there is no experimental evidence for this. With regard to the operation of visual system huge amount of experiments and researches on the psychophysics of vision and related areas have been brought out. Knowledge for various areas of vision like perception of colour vision, perceptual organization, perception of space in depth and so on are available for answering even some difficult questions.

Visual Acuity in Children

Observing where a baby is looking, has become an important study of visual perceptual development. Fantz (1961) has designed an apparatus for observing the visual preferences of the infants. In his study the infant is placed on his back in a small rack which can be slided inside the enclosed test space. The baby is made to look up at two panels. The experimenter watches closely through a small hole in the roof of the chamber and he was able to see a small reflection of the object the baby looks at on the pupil of the eye. The experimenter fixed the timing as soon as the reflection appears on one or both eyes. Stopped when the baby turned away or closed his eyes. This study revealed that the infants as young as one week old looked longer at complex patterns such as the bull's eye design checker board than at the simple figures such as the cross or circle etc. To test the visual acuity the experimenter has presented a *solid grey square* together with a *striped square* to the babies of different ages. The stripes became finer trial by trial. At the age of two weeks the babies, fixated on a square with stripes and could distinguish it from the grey square (Fig.14.1). Visual acuity in early infancy was found to be very poor. The babies could

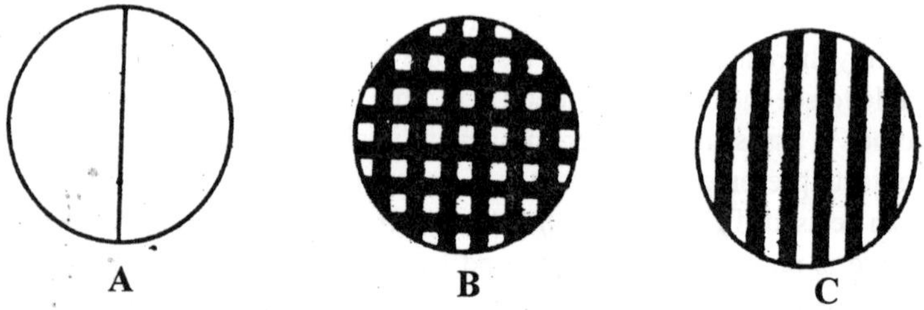

Fig. 14.1 : Types of Visual Acuity Figures. A Minimum Visible. B and C Minimum Separable.

accommodate to focus on the objects at the age of one month. Their eyes had a fixed focus of about 19 centimetres. The objects that are nearer or far away looked blurred. This made the visual acuity in the babies impossible. But there was rapid change, improvement took place in the visual acuity of the infants at the age of six months.

EXPERIMENT-12 : Estimation of Visual Acuity of the Right and Left eyes and both eyes

Problem : The problem to be investigated in this experiment is the estimation of visual acuity of right and left eye and of both eyes of a person by applying the modern psychophysical scaling method.

2. METHOD

Participant : Find out a person for this experiment, who has no knowledge about the task involved in this and the materials. Collect the required personal information such as age, gender, qualifications, whether wearing eye glass and any physical deformities etc.

Materials : Snellen's Letter Chart, Blind-fold, Landolt Ring Chart, and Metre Scale.

Description of the Materials : The Snellen Letter Chart is mostly seen in the familiar sight on the walls of the Eye Physician's clinics or rooms. It is a chart in rectangular shape. (Now they use electronic boxes in different patterns). The letters are printed in rows, in black on a white background. The letters range from the biggest at the top and going down diminishing to the smallest letters. There are eleven rows of letters. In the first row there is only one biggest letter. In the second row there are two letters little smaller. In the third row there are three letters still smaller. Thus the size of the letters are going reducing in size row to row and the number of Ietters are increasing. In the eleventh row, which is the last row there are eleven letters.

Procedure : The Snellen's Letter Chart should be fixed at a height on bar with the participant's eyes. Measure 20 feet with the metre scale from the chart. Make the participant to sit or to stand at 20 feet away from the Chart. Check that, that the testing area is properly illuminated. The participant's right eye and left eye should be tested separately. While testing one eye the other eye should be blind folded. After setting the experimental situation correctly the experimenter should blind-fold the participant's left eye and should give the following instructions :

"Now your left eye is blind folded. You see with your right eye the chart in front of you at a distance. There are letters in eleven rows from largest to smallest. Read the letters first at the top, then the next row, then the third row and so on. In the same manner you will have to read the letters from largest letters to smallest letters at the bottom row. When you complete this task with your right eye I shall blind fold your right eye and you will have to do the same with your left eye. Then you will have to do the same thing with both the eyes. "Now, ready, you can go".

As and when the participant reads out the letters the experimenter should watch carefully and note down the errors committed by the participant in each row in all the three conditions, right eye, left eye and both the eyes. The participant should go on reading the letters in the chart till he is able to see and read the smallest possible letters correctly.

In the case of illiterate participant Landolt ring chart should be used. Here the subject is required to indicate the direction in which he sees the gap in the ring. It is to be done from the biggest ring to the smallest ring row by row. While the test is conducted the participant should not wear eye glasses.

The smaller the letters the participant can read, the greater the visual acuity he has. The scoring method is called *Notation System.* The Snellen notation acuity scores is in the form of a fraction. The smaller the fraction the poorer the vision is. In this fraction the numerator is constant and it represents the distance of the test. In this way the visual acuity score 20/20 is standard. For example a score of 20/40 means that a person can read at twenty feet distance only a letter twice as large as the standard, that is a letter that a 'standard eye' can read it from a distance of forty feet. A score of 20/60 means that a person can read at twenty feet distance only a letter thrice as large as the standard, a letter that the standard eye can read it from a distance of sixty feet. Thus, the distance at which the test is conducted can be used as the denominator.

The American Medical Association (MaCormick and Tiffin, 1979), has simplified the scoring system, and also the method of interpretation of visual acuity scores. It is a percentage system of acuity notation with the title of 'Visual efficiency'. The loss of vision in percentage is determined. The conversion scale shows both the scores (Appendix II).

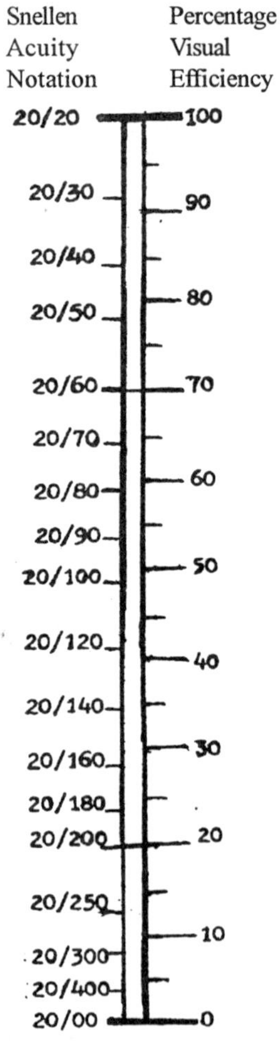

Fig. 14.2 : Snellen Scores and the corresponding percentage scores.

RESULTS

Enter the visual acuity of right and left eye and for both eyes of the participant in Table-14.1.

Collect the group data of the visual acuity from other experimenters and enter them in Table 14.2.

Table 14.1 : Showing the visual acuity of the subject for left and right eyes and for both the eyes

S. No. of the Row	Distance	Right eye Errors	Left eye Errors	Both eyes
1.				
2.				
3.				
4.				
5.				
6.				
7.				
8.				
9.				
10.				
11.				
Visual acuity				

Table 14.2 : Showing the visual acuity of the group for right and left and both the eyes

S. No.	Name	Right eye Visual Acuity	Left eye Visual Acuity	Both eyes
1.	R.V.			
2.	P.K.			
3.	K.V.			
4.	M.S.			
5.	T.C.			
6.	A.L.			
7.	R.M.			
8.	M.T.			
9.	S.S.			
10.	G.G			
	Mean			

State in what condition your participant has committed more errors? Whether it is with right eye or left eye or with both the eyes. Which eye is normal and which is defective? Has he committed more errors with both eyes or with single eye? Which is the smallest letter row he/she can read out without errors? From the position work out the corresponding distance and find out the visual acuity of the participant for each eye and for both eyes. Work out the mean visual acuity for the group. How many above the mean and how many below the mean? Whose acuity is very poor and whose acuity is very good?

Draw the picture of the Snellen Letter Chart (Fig.14.1.)

Draw the picture of the Landolt Ring Chart (Fig.14.2.)

4. DISCUSSION

Discuss the individual scores of right and left and both the eyes of the participant. With which eye more errors are committed. State the reason. What is the letter row he/she can read without error? State your participant's visual acuity. Discuss the group data. What is the group mean visual acuity? How many above group mean and how many below group mean? State who has committed more errors. Discuss your subject's place in the light of the group data. What are the factors influencing visual acuity in this experiment. Do you find any difference between males and females in visual acuity. Is there any difference in the visual acuity among the group members. Who are those having normal acuity and who are those having subnormal acuity? Did you find anything new in your experiment?

5. CONCLUSIONS

State the total errors of your subject with his right and left eyes and both the eyes. What is his/her visual acuity?

State who has made more errors and who no errors? State the reason. How many in the group had normal visual acuity and how many had poor visual acuity?

15

THE PSYCHOPHYSICS OF AUDITION OR SENSE OF HEARING

Sense of Hearing : An Introduction

The sense of hearing in humans, just like all other sensory systems is an important sensory area which needs to be understood psychophysically. All living organisms, including humans, differ in their sense of hearing. All living creatures do not respond to a sound in the same manner. Some respond at once, some take little more time to respond and some do not respond. In this respect humans are far behind some animals and birds. Hearing is a response made to some sound or sound intensities. The individual differences in humans depend upon several factors. The difference in hearing may occur due to stimulating factors that are caused in sound and the transmitting factors and also due to the response mechanism in the sensory apparatus of the human ear. In the case of physical stimulus the frequency of the stimulus and its amplitude cause the difference in hearing. Frequency refers to the number of cycles the sound waves move per second or the rate at which the vibrations are made. Amplitude refers to the extensity of frequency. The other aspect is the characteristics of sound produced from the vibrating body. These are pitch, loudness and timbre from the response side.

We hear sounds in our everyday life from various sources and ways. These sounds may be classified into two kinds as tones and noises. Tones are smooth and harmonious, whereas noises are discordant or harsh and irregular sounds. Sounds are moving in wavelike manner in increasing circle from the body they are produced. When a metal body is struck sound waves are vibrating from it in circle forms, going on widening the circles from the body. For example, a bell or a radio produce sounds and these sounds move in a wavelike manner from these bodies in circle forms widening in all directions. This is just like when a stone is thrown into a pond of still water.

Thus the pitch, loudness and timber are psychological aspects as they are the characteristics of sound. But these aspects depend upon the nature of physical stimulus. The pitch, loudness and timbre are with regard to the sensation of sound, the frequency and amplitude are with regard to the physical stimulus. These two aspects, the physical stimulus and the corresponding psychological reaction, the sensation are having certain relationship proportionately, and also vary proportionately. These relationships and variations were estimated by devising psychophysical scales. While we want to know more about the estimation or a relationship between the stimulus dimensions and the corresponding psychological responses, it is important that we must know something about the various aspects associated with the sensory systems. The more important aspect in this connection is the physiological mechanism in audition, the structure, more specifically the anatomy or the structure of the ear and the auditory threshold.

The Anatomy of Auditory Mechanism

Therefore we shall first discuss the physiological mechanism of audition and then go for the auditory threshold and its measurement. The ear is the specialized sensory apparatus in hearing, not only for human beings, but also for all living creatures, except few living creatures which may use other parts also for hearing the sound. Though the human ear is very much sensitive to sounds, he is falling back to certain animals in the sensitivity of hearing. The human ear is divided into three important parts, such as the external ear, the middle ear, and the inner ear.

The External Ear

The external ear is the outer part of the ear. It has two important structures, one is the pinna which appears outside. The other is the external auditory meatus which is the path of sound waves. The outer ear pinna catches the sound waves and sends them through the path and the path ends at the ear drum, which is a thin membrane of .01 mm thickness and it is also called tympanic membrane. But the role of this ear drum is very little in the auditory function of the ear. The structure of pinna and the function of it is such that it serves as a sound reflector. The pinna serves the purpose of locating the sounds and it could discriminate whether the sounds are from back side or front side. But the pinna is not a good reflector of sound waves in human auditory function. The reason is that the wavelength of sound frequencies in air is 3000(cps) cycle per second and below are larger than the pinna. As result of it the pinna throws the sound waves here and there and not accurately reflecting the sound waves by turning and adjusting the outer part, the pinna, to the direction of the sound waves just like what the animals like the dogs, cats and the stags do.

The other structure of the outer ear is the auditory meatus. This is more important in human auditory functions than the pinna. This is like a cylindrical hallow space having about one inch in length. The size of the cylindrical space is about 3/10 of an inch. The cylindrical cavity is always open and ends at the eardrum from where the middle ear begins. The eardrum is made to vibrate when the sound waves pass through the cylindrical passage and the waves give pressure on it. The eardrum plays an important role in the auditory sensation. The eardrum on receiving the pressure of the sound waves reacts to it by means of vibration. The top portion of the eardrum is so sensitive that it vibrates even to a single blow of the sound wave. The eardrum has one special characteric of getting the wound healed when it is damaged or torn in certain circumstances. But any injury to the membrane is the most painful incidence for the human body. Heavy damage may result in deafness as it fails to regenerate the membrane. The tympanic membrane or the eardrum which is the inner part of the outer ear is connected to the malleus.

The Middle Ear

When there is the pressure of sound waves in the tympanic membrane or the ear drum it vibrates and the malleus attached with the eardrum also vibrates in harmony with it. The middle ear consists of three ossicles known as malleus (hammer), incus (anvil) and stapes (stirrup). These three are small bones connected to each other and function in a chainlike manner. The middle ear is an air filled cavity. These three bones (ossicles) are going from the eardrum to the oval window of the inner ear. The third part of the middle ear the stapes (stirrup) is attached to the first part of the inner ear, the oval window. This oval window is connected with the round window. The middle ear with its three parts plays an important role in the auditory perception. In the transmission of the vibrations from the tympanic membrane to the oval window of the inner ear through the stapes the chain system of the three bones of the middle ear cause certain mechanical advantage. That is, even if there is some loss of strenth in the vibration of the tympanic membrane (eardrum) to the stapes the system functions in such a way that the stapes transmit the same to the oval window. Geldard (1953) who made extensive studies on human ears has stated that the pressure on the oval window by the stapes is much greater to the extend of 20 to 30 times to that of the original pressure on the tympanic membrane (eardrum). This is possible because the area of the tympanic membrane is much larger than the area of the oval window. Therefore, this increases the pressure through the auditory canal from tympanic membrane to the oval window and from there to the fluids of the inner ear. This mechanical process makes the middle ear to protect the inner ear from any louder sounds. The eustachian tube connects the middle ear with the throat. This tube maintains balance between the middle ear and the inner ear.

Further, it is also observed that sometimes the steady pressures and very low changmg pressures do not serve as effective auditory stimuli. But the steady differences in pressure between the middle ear and the external ear make changes in human sensitivity to the hearing of varied frequencies of the sound waves. The fluid filled inner ear is sealed by a membrane at the place where the stapes is fitted to the oval window. The smaller area of the oval window and the stapes provide a good balanced resistance to the air pressure from the tympanic membrane. The air pressure which is distributed over the large area of the eardrum is focused on the smaller area of the oval window which vibrates the fluid of the inner ear.

The middle ear as a chamber is sealed from outside for atmosphere pressure. But eustachian tube is opened at times to balance the pressure with outside air by voluntary act of swallowing or yawning. The pressure felt in the ear is equalized by this function. The middle ear cannot make any change in the air pressure which was taken in by the eardrum unless the eustachian tube is opened. Every human being might have experienced this sometimes by opening the jaw widely and might have observed the passing of air into the mouth from the ear.

The Inner Ear

We have discussed above that the third ossicles of the middle ear, the tapes (stirrup) continues the chainlike action and extends the pressure to the oval window. The oval window vibrates and disturbs the fluid in the cochlea of the inner ear. The inner ear is spread right back into the skull (brain). The inner ear is made of three important parts such as the semi-circular canals, vestibule and the cochlea. The semicircular canals are three membraneous structures responsible for maintaining the sense of balance or equilibrium and it is a part of auditory structure called the labyrinth. The vestibule is a structure with two parts such as utricle and saccule, but collectively they are called vestibule, that mainly responds to head position and movements. It also maintains the upright posture, which is a non-auditory function in nature. The cochlea is the real organ of hearing and it is the main part of the inner ear. Since it is an important part of hearing, it is protected both by the tympanic membrane (eardrum) and the three ossicles of the middle ear. These parts protect the cochlea by reducing the strong vibrations of high amplitude of sound waves.

The cochlea contains three chambers known as scala vestibuli, the scala tympanic and the scala media or cochlear duct. The cochlea is a snail shapped organ which contains a bony canal coiled spirally around a conic bony pillar (modiolus). The basilar membrane is another important part of the inner ear which runs parallel to the structure of cochlea and completes the division of cochlea into upper scala media and lower scala tympanic chambers. It consists of thousands of fibres, vibrating like the piano strings.

The scala vestibule in cochlea is the upper chamber and the scala tympanic is the lower chamber. When there is pressure in the oval window it bulges, by which it sends communication to the lower chamber and the communication is transmitted through the opening called helicotrema, at the high point of cochlea. These two chambers are filled with the fluid called perilymph. The third chamber, the cochlear duct is filled with the fluid called endolymph.

The external ear is a sound collecting apparatus, the middle ear a sound transmitting apparatus and the inner ear, the cochlea with the organ of corti is a sound receiving apparatus. Thus, sound waves, gathered by the external ear, pass through the auditory canal. These waves strike the tympanic membrane (eardrum) which vibrates and the vibrations make the three bones, the ossicles of the middle ear to react in a chainlike manner and the vibrations reach the oval window of the inner ear. The small movements of the eardrum to the air vibrations are converted into strong movements by the oval window. The oval window increases the pressure because it is very difficult to set in motion the fluid compared to the air. The oval window by bulging stimulates the upper chamber of the cochlea, the scala vestibule, which in turn sends the communication to the lower chamber the scala tympani. The true auditory receptors are in the cochlear duct. They are tiny hair cells located in the organ of corti. The receptor cells rest on the basilar membrane. The highest points of these cells are fixed in the basilar membrane within the cochlear duct. The vibrations of the fluid produce movements in the basilar membrane. These movements make the highest points of the hair cells to bend and twist. This sort of twisting and distortion in the hair cells is converted into nerve impulses in the fibres of the cochlear branch of the auditory nerves.

The nerve fibres that lie at the bottom of the basilar membrane are about 25,000 hair cells and they join together and form the auditory nerves and these auditory nerves send their impulses to the temporal lobe of the brain and these impulses are converted into the sensation of sound. When a few impulses are generated in the nerve fibres, they are sensed as weak sounds at every vibration. Only high vibrations with greater amplitude may cause more impulses which are sensed as louder sounds.

Thus, the original air vibrations at the tympanic membrane are transformed into liquid vibrations at the oval window and the liquid vibrations are transformed into impulses in the basilar membrane and the impulses are transformed into the sensation of sound.

Sounds and the Characteristics of Sound

Sound is a physical environmental component. The existence of saund is realized in various ways. All living organisms, humans, animals, birds and other creatures react to sounds and also produce sounds. Though it is a physical environmental component it is heard with our ears and we perceive the sound when we hear the incident of a sound, it means that we perceive it with our ears and thus it is a sensation. The sensation is provided by the vibration or pulsation of a material body when that vibration is transmitted to the basilar membrane of the inner ear and perceived by the brain. The vibrations that are pulsating from the material body are also called sounds. When vibrations occur regularly, at a definite rate of frequency, pure tones are heard. Most of the sounds we hear are the results of the mixture of vibrations of several different frequencies. When the vibrations with several frequency rates are mixed together and if they are not with regular sequence, the resulting incidence is noise.

When a tuning fork is struck with a metal stick there are regular movements or vibrations from the tuning fork. These vibrations have the characteristic of frequency rate and also the characteristic of amplitude or extensity. The motions of the tines of the tuning fork strike the molecules of the air and the air molecules collide with each other and transmit the energy among the molecules. The energy radiates in all directions from the vibrating body. Since the vibrating body produces the frequencies and amplitude consistantly, the air molecules also react in the same manner. Air molecules move and collide with one another and going away from the source in a regular fashion. There is change in the waves of air pressure which constitute the sound. The intensity of sound decreases with increasing distance from the sense of the sound.

The characteristics of sound may differ qualitatively when it is produced in different mediums. The transmission also varies from medium to medium. The transmission of sound is faster in solid materials and in water than in the air. Sound has two types of characteristics, one is physical and other is psychological. The physical characteristics are concerned with sound wave and the psychological characteristics are concerned with sense of hearing. The physical characteristics are frequency, amplitude and harmonic factors. The psychological characteristics are pitch, loudness and timbre.

The important characteristics of sound are the sound waves. Sound waves may be stated as pure sine wave and impure waves. The simple sine wave is caused by the air pressure change. A simple vibrating body produces the simple sine wave. If the air pressure change is simple and regular, it may result in producing a simple tone. The sine wave is not subjected to measurement as there is no distortions in it. The other type of wave is the impure or distorted sine wave. There are two types of impure sine waves. They may be stated as complex periodic wave. It is constituted of various sine waves, different phases, different frequencies and different amplitudes. The wave pattern is repeated. The other is a periodic complex wave. If the vibrating body is starting and ending at different times, the complex wave is not repeating itself and hence it results in noise.

Condensation and Rarefaction

When a tuning fork is struck, it puts pressure upon the surrounding air. It blows the air, squeezes the air molecules. The air has the quality of moving forth and back, after a push returns to the original position. This movement is evenly distributed. Hence the air is put into series of pushes and pulls. When you forcibly move your hand or loudly shout you push the air. The push or the beat successively increases and decreases in intensity of the air molecules. These movements are called vibrations of the sound causing object. In the pushes and pulls of the air there are areas of condensation and rarefaction of the air. In the condensation the air molecules are densely packed and move fast at the rate of 1000 feet per second. Behind this there is the region of rarefaction where the air molecules are less densely packed, then again there is another region of condensation and also rarefaction. But the speed of sound in the air is constant. The frequency vibrations or the cycles in the form of condensation and rarefaction per second determine the pitch of the tone. Thus, the wave compression takes place with condensation and rarefaction in a cyclic manner.

Resonance

The basilar membrane of the inner ear plays an important role in hearing of pitch. The fibres of basilar membrane vary in length. This is quite similar to a piano string. Just the short strings produce high pitches and the long strings produce low pitches, the basilar membrane reacts to the nature of sound waves by spreading out the coiled fibres and function like the piano strings. The response that takes place in basilar membrane seems to be sympathetic to the sound waves reached the basilar membrane from the eardrum. This sympathetic vibration is called resonance. Resonance means the sound produced by a body, vibrating in sympathy with the neighbouring source of sound.

Beats

When two tones of different frequencies with smaller difference are produced, a new type of the tone in between the two is heard. The ear is not perfectly transmitting the sound waves to the basilar membrane of the inner ear and analyse the complex waves as the hearing sensations are not related to the properties of sound. There is a small amount of distortion in the transmission. This distortion produces combination of tones. If two pure tones are produced, for example, 500 CPS and 1000 CPS, both reach the ear at the same time and we hear two different tones. We may also hear two new tones, one relating to the frequency of 500 CPS, the difference between the two original tones (1000 – 500) and the other relating to the frequency of 1500 CPS, the sum of the two original tones (1000+500). These two tones, (1000 – 500 and 1000+500) the difference tone and the summation tone are the results of the distortions caused in the transmission of the sound vibration through the middle ear. In transmitting the complex tones there is also certain amount of imperfect analysis of the complex sound waves. This is stated as beats. When two pure tones of different frequencies transmitted with the frequencies of 1000 CPS and 1030 CPS, having a difference between them less than 200 CPS we may hear only a single tone, increasing and decreasing in loudness at regular intervals. The frequency of the sound will be in between the two pure tones as 1015 vibrating at the rate of 30 beats per second and it will be varying in amplitude. This characteristic of the sound is known as beats.

Auditory Threshold — An Introduction

The study of auditory sensation involves two important aspects, one is with regard to the characteristics of sound, and the other is with regard to the sensation of hearing. The first is dealing with the physics of sound and the second is dealing with the psychology of hearing. But in any study of the sensation of hearing or sound both the aspects are interrelated. The sensation of sound or how do we hear or perceive the sound, cannot be studied intelligibly without studying the characteristics of sound. Thus, the auditory thresholds are important for any psychological study for several reasons. A few of the reasons may be, how an organism responds to a threshold or how a threshold arouses response in an organism. Why some levels of thresholds fail to arouse response in all organisms, why different thresholds are required for different organisms to arouse response? Is it true that the upper auditory threshold reduces with age of humans? Apart from these it is important to determine the auditory threshold for many practical purposes.

The school psychologists and modern industrial and organisational psychologists should know how to measure the auditory thresholds. Because if the student lacks sense of hearing in the class room, he misses many things which may affect his future prospectus. Similarly, an industrial worker, foreman, the engineer, and the executive should have acute sense of hearing in the industrial and organisational situations. Any loss of hearing on the part of any of the categories may cause accidents which may result in heavy loss of property. Therefore, the measurement of auditory threshold becomes one of the important physical necessities for the managements in selection, recruitment and placement, and training of the employees. In signals, military and communication departments one's sense of auditory acuity needs to be tested and measured with suitable instruments and methods.

The auditory threshold is based upon several attributes, the physical characteristics of sound such as frequency, amplitude, phase, type of sound wave, resonance and beats, and other aspects like duration of the stimulus and age. In determining the auditory threshold the psychological characteristics such as pitch, loudness, volume, density, fatigue and masking also should be taken into consideration. Because of these the measurement of auditory threshold is very difficult, unless certain variables are controlled. Frequency is measured in terms of cycle per second (CPS) or hertz while phase is measured in terms of degrees. Any increase or decrease in amplitude may have effect on pitch and loudness. It has been observed in some studies that variables like fatigue and masking of the tones are affecting the thresholds.

Thresholds and Auditory Defects

Thresholds are affected by physical aspects of sound and also by psychological aspects and other characteristics. But one important characteristic that may affect the threshold is the auditory aspect. The ear is the specialized sensory apparatus for hearing. Any defect in any part of the auditory mechanism starting from the outer ear to the end, the cerebral cortex may impair the sense of hearing and the threshold may be affected. The parts of the ear are so delicate that it is very difficult to detect the place of impairment by judging the responses to sound stimuli in the everyday life events. Persons who are partially deaf may not be aware of it, since the type of defect is not interferring in their life events. Such persons are not able to compare any two sounds heard with variations as their sense of hearing is not normal like that of others. This type of defects are determined only by audiometry devices. The auditory threshold is tested over a range of frequencies.

Any defect in the part of the outer ear may also affect the frequencies. The auditory passage, the meatus may be blocked with wax which may prevent the sound waves reaching the eardrum. There may be also holes in the eardrum which may result in poor vibrations to the sound waves. There may be also defects in the middle ear, the ossicles which may result in greater loss of sensitivity to lower frequencies. The transmission of sound waves to the oval window is very much affected by the middle ear. Mostly in old age period the transmission deafness occurs. The defects in the middle ear is often set right by using two types of hearing aids. One type of hearing aid is to strengthen the sound waves. The loud speaker of the aid is placed in the auditory path way (meatus) for conducting the sound waves to the eardrum. The other type of aid placed behind the pinna on the temporal bone (mastoid bone) for transmitting the sound vibrations to the cochlea of the inner ear. This hearing aid bypasses the external and middle ear parts.

Any defect in the inner ear affects the threshold very much. The defect mainly is due to damage in the basilar membrane, specifically damage in the hair cells. This is called nerve defectness and it mostly affects the high frequencies. If the basilar membrane is exposed to the louder or high intensity of sounds for longer period of time then the hair cells get damaged in certain areas. These defects are called **nerve defects or exposure defects.**

The nerve and exposure defects are more common in old age. The nerve defects may be for some specific frequencies which may be called tonal gaps, which refers to an area where there is loss of sense of hearing. The tonal gaps cause tonal island. The tonal island refers to the normal sensitive area in the basilar membrane surrounded by the tonal gaps.

Therefore, there is always some difficulty in determining the auditory threshold as the tonal frequencies are not distinguishable clearly even by the persons who have normal sensitivity for hearing. The threshold to certain frequencies may vary from person to person. Therefore, psychologists who studied auditory thresholds differentiate the thresholds as **feeling thresholds and auditory thresholds.** The feeling thresholds are to sensations which are arising from the stimuli and they are heard, but they are not clearly heard and identified, whereas auditory thresholds are the sensations arising from the stimuli which are heard and identified clearly.

Thus, the study of auditory thresholds, compared to other sensory thresholds, are very complicated which involves several variables in the experimental situations to be controlled. Therefore **an auditory threshold may be defined as the minimum sound intensity required to cause vibrations in the tympanic membrane (eardrum) and transmit the vibration to the ossicles of the middle ear and exerting pressure on the oval window of the inner ear and stimulate the hair cells of the basilar membrane and makes it to transmit impulses to the temporal lobe of the brain and convert the impulses into the sensation of sound in the organism.** Though the definition appears to be little lengthy, it involves all the parts of the ear in causing the sensation of hearing. **A threshold may be also defined as the smallest amount of sound energy which can vibrate the tympanic membrane, the ossicles and the basilar membrane and arouse to response of hearing the sound in an organism.** The auditory threshold can be determined by using an audiometer. The auditory threshold is an absolute threshold. This may be determined for pure tones of various frequencies. The minimum frequencies to which the normal humans may be sensitive varies from 15 to 25 CPS and the maximum frequencies are 15,000 to 25,000 CPS. This range from 15 CPS to 25,000 CPS is only an arbitrary. The upper limit of the scale depends upon the age of the subject to be tested. It appears that frequencies around 100 CPS not affected by age differences. Frequencies from 1000 CPS to 4000 CPS seem to be a good range for normal persons.

In determining absolute limens or thresholds for sounds (ALS) in humans the psychophysical methods are employed. The person tested is to indicate his sensation of hearing by verbal reports. The verbal reports provide the immediate response of the person. The psychophysical method can be applied for several purposes in the case of auditory sensation such as determination threshold, (ALS) determination difference threshold (DL), threshold for audition as a function of age, relationship between frequency and the perception of pitch, absolute auditory thresholds as different frequencies and amplitude, relationship between physical intensity and frequency of the stimulus and perceived loudness and so on.

EXPERIMENT-13 : Measurement of Auditory Threshold

Problem : The problem of auditory sensation is a common occurrence among the people who are working in noisy environmental situations like the metal industry, textile industry, power generation industries, and also among the people living close to railway stations and aerodromes. These people do not maintain normal auditory sensation and they need higher thresholds for responding to any auditory stimulus. The sensory acuity of such people can be tested and the amount of loss of hearing can be assessed by audiometry devices and the defects in hearing may be diagnosed and suitable treatments can be provided.

Aim : The aim of this experiment is to assess the sensitivity of an individual to tones of given frequencies and assess the loss of hearing and comparing it with the normal adult person's sensitivity.

2. METHOD

Participant : Choose a person who has no knowledge about this experiment and collect the personal information such as age, gender, class etc. The person should be free from physical defects like eye defect and sense of hearing.

Apparatus : The suitable instrument is the (1) audiometer for this experiment. This instrument should produce tone of different intensities and frequencies, (2) Earphone, (3) A push button switch and (4) a signal light.

Description of Audiometer : This is an instrument intended to assess the response of each ear to the tones produced by the audiometer with different frequencies and intensities. A single ear phone is used. One end of the ear phone is used by the participant and the other end is connected to the audiometer. Normal hearing range is included in the audiometer. The extensity of the scale may be divided into required levels before using the audiometer in the experiment in such a manner that for every frequency the setting of zero will be in agreement with the absolute threshold for the persons of normal hearing. The positive numbers are set above zero. This will facilitate to know the loss of hearing in db. How many times the db were above the average threshold, the tones should be for the participant to hear.

Procedure : The person who serves as a participant should be free from physical defects like eye defects and hard of hearing, the experimenter should choose a quite room where there is no disturbance of any type. The experimenter should test each ear separately. The experimenter should operate the audiometer. He/she should make all the preparations to conduct the experiment by sitting close to the audiometer on the dial side. The experimenter should choose eleven frequencies ranging from 100 to 5000 CPS. The comparative threshold should be as far as possible the middle of the range between 100 and 5000 CPS. It is better to keep the participant at a distance not less than 20 feet and the experimenter should test first whether the earphone is normally functioning at a distance of 20 feet away from the audiometer and the signal light is burning when the switch is pressed.

When he/she is fully satisfied with functioning of the instrument, the experiment may be started. Then the participant should be provided with earphone and he/she should be asked to hold it close to the ear and attach it to the left ear first. The participant should be given the following instructions:

"Please hold the earphone at your left ear. There is a switch push button in front of you. When you hear some sound through the earphone at once press the push button of the switch. If you are not hearing any sound you need not press it."

The experimenter first turn the frequency dial of the audiometer to a given frequency. It is better to turn the middle frequency first at 1000 CPS. Then the sound intensity should be adjusted to the level that the participant can hear it. The turning of the frequency dial should be stepped down in slow steps. At each step the P's response should be recorded. This should be continued until the 'P' says that he/she is not hearing the sound any more. It is better that the experimenter should continue 2 or 3 steps more even if the 'P' reported that he is not hearing the sound to check whether there is any tonal gaps.

Then the experimenter should continue the same procedure for different intensities. It is better to have half of the trial in decreasing order and half of the trials in increasing order. While starting the procedure in the decreasing order the frequencies should be of the highest point and the sound intensity also should be correspondingly higher. The experimenter at each step should note down the frequency levels and sound intensities. The turning of the frequency dial should be continued until the 'P' reports 'not hearing'. In the increasing order the 'P' may be reporting not hearing at the lower intensities level. But the turning of the dial should be continued in smaller steps until the 'P' reports that he is hearing the sound at least in 2 or 3 steps. It is better to have five trials above the middle frequency position and five trials below the middle frequency position.

3. RESULTS

The experimenter, then should work out from the observations recorded, the intensity levels to which the 'P' has responded and the levels below which the 'P' reported that he did not hear the sounds. The thresholds for all the trials should be estimated and the loss of hearing should be determined and presented in the Table 15.1.

Table 15.1 : Showing the Frequency levels (CPS) sound intensity, the auditory threshold and the loss of hearing in a person on the threshold determination experiment [Normal 20 CPS (Hz)]

S. No.	Frequencies (CPS)	Intensity of sound in (db) Range 0 to 120 db	Type of Response	Hearing loss in db
1.	20			
2.	40			
3.	60			
4.	100			
5.	500			
6.	1000			
7.	2000			
8.	3000			
9.	4000			
10.	5000			
11.	6000			

The experimenter after having entered all the reports and completed the Table 15.1, can interpret the data taking into consideration the frequency levels, the sound intensity levels and the loss of hearing in the participant. It should be stated where the P's responses are below the normal (20 CPS) and where the P's response is above the normal level. If the experimenter had noticed any tonal gap, it should be stated, at what frequency levels it has occurred.

A graph should be drawn having the sound intensity on the ordinate and the frequencies on the abssissa and the threshold can be indicated.

4. DISCUSSION

The experimenter may discuss how the participant has performed in the experiment in responding to the auditory stimuli of various intensities. It should be discussed whether the P is on the normal hearing or varies at each level. If varies the levels of variation and the loss of hearing may be stated. Was there any tonal gap in the auditory response of the participant? If so, state the frequency levels they occurred. State also whether the person possesses normal sensitivity in hearing, whether normal or has defects. If he has defects what sort of defects they are. Is it possible to overcome the defects or not.

The experimenter may relate his results with the results of some earlier studies and state whether the results are in agreement with them or not. The experimenter may also discuss the theory through which he can explain his results.

5. CONCLUSIONS

1. What is the auditory threshold of the person as revealed by this study. State whether the threshold is above normal or below normal, if so how much.
2. State whether the participant is having normal sensitivity in hearing or having any defect. State the nature of defect.

PART - IV

Modern Psychophysical Scaling Methods - II

An Introduction to Part IV

The scaling methods are mainly referring to the methods of measuring the variables on various levels such as nominal scale, ordinal scale, interval scale and ratio scale, rating, ranking, pair comparisons, first choice, factor analysis and so on. Thus, from the beginning to this level we come across three types of methods, namely, the psychophysical methods, the psychophysical scaling methods and (psychological) scaling methods. Among these methods generally the procedures are almost the same, but the end results or the measurements vary. In the first, the end results are on the physical continuum, whereas in the other two the end results are on the psychological continuum. Guilford (1954) states that the scaling method is a common meeting place of psychophysical and psychophysical scaling methods.

In the scaling methods the stimuli are not evaluated on the physical energy level. The aim of the scaling methods is to assess the affective values, beliefs and attitudes, quality of performance like paintings, writings, and drawings, assessing personality traits, social distance, prejudices and so on. Though some psychometricians treat this simply as scaling methods or psychological scaling methods, these methods find their origin only in the classical psychophysical methods. Psychophysics is always used as the scaling technique. In all psychophysical experiments, the experimenter is trying to convert the sensory experiences which resulted from the perception of the physical stimuli into numerical values. This is one way of correlating the physical values of the stimuli with the psychological values. Therefore, what all these indicate is, that how from the classical psychophysical methods the psychophysical and the modern or contemporary scaling methods are evolved.

16

SCALING METHODS AND MEASUREMENT OF VARIABLES

Levels of Measurement and Psychophysics

Psychophysics had its birth when the scientists began to think seriously about the possibility of measuring sensations and also the psychological reactions systematically. Many of them wondered at the varied sensory experiences and had described how sensations differ in quality. Seeing and hearing are not the same, taste is different from smell, pain is not the same as the touch. Each of these sensations vary in degree or intensity. A sensation of sound may be said to be strong or weak. But how strong it is or how weak it is? Is it possible to measure the strength or weakness (magnitude) of a sensation? Or can we say that sensation is too personal that we can only feel the presence of it and cannot measure it quantitatively?

Many of them felt for a long time that sensation is subjective in nature and therefore, an objective assessment of it cannot be made directly. Some of the scientists came to a conclusion that some kind of indirect measurement is possible and any direct attempt is absurd and cannot be accurate. Psychophysicists for about hundred years have tried to solve the central problem, the measurement of sensation by indirect methods. But, however, later on some kind of simple and direct method of measurement was evolved and put to use.

The concept of 'measurement' refers to setting up of an estimated value of something. An estimated value can be given through an instrument or tool or a scale. Therefore, a sacle is to be invented for the measurement. Since this scale is to be used for the main problem in the measurement of sensations the scale has to be invented psychophysically. Fechner, the founder of psychophysics has defined long ago that psychophysics is the science that enquires into the quantitative relationship between physical events and the corresponding psychological events.

Therefore, psychophysical scaling is referring to the construction of scales relating to the magnitude of sensory response to the magnitude of physical stimulus. But Guilford (1954) differs from other psychophysicists in designating these scaling methods as psychophysical scaling methods. According to him these scaling methods may be called as psychological scaling methods and not psychophysical scaling methods. Because these scaling methods differ from the traditional psychophysical methods. The reason is that in the scaling methods the end results are not obtained as values on the physical scales. The results are obtained on the psychological scales. Then, how they can be called as psychophysical scaling methods? This shows that psychophysical laws are not rigidly followed. In many cases psychophysicists often deviate from psychophysical laws to some extent. Therefore, they are called psychophysical scaling methods.

It is very clear that all the physical values are determined only from the psychological functions and yet we call them as psychophysical functions. Therefore, there is no clear line of demarcation between psychophysical and psychological scaling methods. Till the psychophysicists come to a definite conclusion and make a final decision with regard to the boundary lines of these two methods, we may treat these methods as psychophysical scaling methods. But calling these methods as psychological scaling methods is also need not be ruled out because of the rational arguments put forth by some psychometricians.

Since psychological knowledge depends upon understanding the relationship between the stimulus and response and this understanding we acquire from experiments conducted on sensory areas, experiments on sensory areas become the basis for psychological knowledge. Therefore, as Guilford said, in a broader sense much of psychology is psychophysics.

Generally, we use scales when we differentiate objects or events. When a person points out three of his friends by saying Ram is short, Nathan is taller and Mohan is tallest, he is using a scale. He can also state them in another way as 1st, 2nd and 3rd or 1, 2 and 3. Here numbers are assigned to persons. Therefore a scale results from the assignment of numbers to persons or objects or events or mental phenomena. A ruler is used to measure the length of objects, a calendar is used to measure the days, months and year, similarly a thermometer is used as a temperature scale. In the same way psychophysics is stated as the scaling technique. In psychophysics the experimenter is trying to convert the behavioural phenomena into numbers. That is, he is recording the relationship between the physical stimulus and the corresponding mental phenomena or response in an organism. The psychophysicist is trying to relate the effect of physical stimulus on the organism, the psychological value. If the physical stimulus of certain value is exercised in an organism what is the amount of value elicited in the organism and if certain number is assigned to the stimulus value, certain number is also assigned to the response value. This is the fundamental basis upon which the psychophysical scaling method is developed. This principle had long history on the phenomenon, has been paffling psychophysicists for a long time. They tried to apply the principle to measure all areas of sensations like the hearing, seeing, tasting, smelling and touching. Psychophysicists, in the beginning, were trying to determine thresholds. This is the construction of scale relating to magnitude of sensory responses for the magnitude of the use of physical stimulus. Suppose, for example an experimenter wants to determine among the two tones, how much one is louder than the other. Here the experimenter is concerned with one aspect of the stimulus. In the case of testing the tone the subject is asked to judge the nature of loudness. Here only one aspect, the decibel (unit of measuring relative loudness of sound) alone is varied and the other aspects such as auditory stimulus, the hertz (the international unit of frequency) are held constant. If the experimenter wants to know among a group of many tones, which one is more sweet, he has to go to the other aspects such as loudness, pitch, volume and experience for determining the sweetness of the tone. Therefore, a scaling method is used to determine all these aspects and it is a more complex phenomenon much better than the psychophysical methods.

Arithmetic was invented to serve the purpose of measurement in terms of number. Philosophers, mathematicians and scientists have studied in detail the theory of mearsurement and analysed the various classes of measurement. The theory of measurement has special significance in psychology. Many of the psychological variables are not measurable in the same way as the natural sciences are measuring. Therefore, the same principle as applied to physical or natural sciences cannot be applied in psychological measurements. In the psychological measurements properties are assigned to numbers. Numbers as such stand fixed. Therefore, the stimuli to which the numbers are related determine the scale. Stevens (1951) states that scales are possible in the first place only, because there exists an isomorphism between the properties of the numeral series and the empirical operations that we can perform with the aspects of the objects. That is, the properties of numbers are assigned to the scale corresponding to the properties of the objects (stimuli) themselves and therefore Stevens (1974), further states that the isomorphism, between and counting is tight and coherent, like the fit of a sood glove.

Therefore it is now recognized that measurement is stretched to wherever systematic rules are invented for fixing numbers on things. The number system becomes a schematic model and it is used in whatever manner we want. It is a rich model that one expects of its structure, can be made to describe one of the properties of the objects or events that we want to measure. It is because of this that we define measurement as the assigning of numbers to objects or events according to a systematic rule. Since there are different kinds of rules there are different kinds of measurements also. Stevens (1974) states that for every kind of measurement there is some degree of isomorphism between the two domains, the objects and the numbers. The relations among the objects and the relations among the numbers become the function of isomorphism. The numbers serve in four useful ways as schematic model for the empirical properties. They are 1. Identity, 2. Order, 3. Intervals and 4. Ratios. The first is identity, which means that numbers serve to identity items or classes or objects. The second is the order. According to this numbers fix the place or the rank of the items or objects. The third, intervals indicates the distance or differences between items or objects. The ratios indicate the fixed nature of relation between two similar items or objects either in fraction or multiple.

In all the four uses the numbers, the classes or items of similar nature are identified, ordered, differentiated and relations between them are fixed. On the basis of the four uses of the numbers four main scale types have been developed. They are called nominal scale, ordinal scale, interval scale and ratio scale. These are the four levels of measurement clearly stated by Stevens (1946, 1975). These scales are distinguished in terms of certain rules. On the basis of this, these four scales are arranged from lower level to higher levels.

The Nominal Scale

In the nominal scale measurement, only the number is used as a label to identify a class or item. This is used with qualitative variables and is the lowest of the four scales. This scale mainly is referring to naming. Objects belonging to the same category of qualitative variable receive the same numeral and objects that are belonging to different categories are assigned different numerals. In other words numerals serve as names for the separate categories and may be having any symbols. For example, religion is a qualitative and it may be indicated with the numerals H (Hindu), M (Muslim), C (Christian). The three categories of qualitative variables may have numerals H, M and C assigned to them or 1, 2 and 3, or X, Y and Z and discriminatory symbols can be used. The requirement is that all the Hindus be designated by one of the symbols H, and the Muslims by M and so on.

The number is used here to distinguish one religious person from another and the purpose is only to name the objects or persons that they are somewhat different from the other and no other magnitude of difference is possible in this scale. This is a more primitive scale. Torgerson (1951) omits this scale in his analysis on the ground that it is not a scale in the proper sense. Though Stevens (1951) and others used this in their early works, later on dismissed this scale on the ground that it is included in the ratio scale.

The Ordinal Scale

This is little better than the nominal scale. This scale indicates that objects are different and it provides one more information about them. It can state the direction in which one object is different from the other, that is, whether, one is greater or less than the other and nothing more than that in its magnitude. Except the nominal scale all other three scales, the ordinal, interval and ratio make quantitative measurement. Among the three, the ordinal is the lowest of all, because the ordinal measurement may reveal that the object X possesses the quantitative variable more than the object Y. This scale is mostly used in lifted weights or comparing one stimulus with another. If the weights are more than 2 or 4 then the weights are measured with respect to order. In the ordinal scale measured objects are numbered as first, second, third and so on. They are ranked in order and the order does not indicate the distance between the ranks of the objects.

If X and Y are not equal then they may differ in some direction. The direction may be some one aspect of the objects like, weight, height or loudness. The basis of classification of the objects into categories may be a composite, because there may be three or more variables. For example, if individuals are to be ranked on the basis of socio-economic-status level, then more than two variables like, education, occupation and income are involved. Two or three individuals might be in the same rank order for education and in the reverse in income. In such cases we must use relative weighting system for the indices to make a composite of the variables so as to provide one ranking. This type of ranking is common in psychological studies. In complete discrimination only one object in each category is to be placed like the method of rank order, one frequency in each category. Spearman's rank-order coefficient of correlation method solves the problem of times in the ranks by presupposing a complete ranking using consecutive numbers.

The Interval Scale

The nominal and the ordinal scales differentiate objects as events from one another. The nominal scale could be used only to name the objects while the ordinal scale states which object or event has more or less of the quality than the other one. However, the ordinal scale does not indicate the magnitude of the difference between the items judged. But an interval scale provides the magnitude of difference. For example, if the temperature is 30°C on Friday, 35°C on Saturday and 40°C on Sunday it is possible to say the magnitude of the differences among the temperatures. These numbers indicating equal difference between days may be referred to as interval scale. The interval scale differentiates the items or events. The interval scale has got all the characteristics of the nominal and the ordinal scales. It has also an additional characteristic that it could tell us the magnitude of the difference between items or events. In the stated example of the interval scale one can easily state that the temperature on Saturday was 5 degrees warmer than on Monday and 5 degrees cooler than on Wednesday. Thus the interval scale indicated the magnitude of difference between items or events. Guilford (1954) states that interval scales are also called equal unit scales. The numerically equal distances stand for empirically equal distances in some characteristic of the objects. Examples of interval scales are temperature scale — either Farrenheit or Centigrade, the thermometer, calendar (which shows the time interval in days and months), clock (which shows the minutes interval).

In the case of interval scales all the common statistical procedures such as the mean, standard deviation, Pearson product-moment correlation coefficient and other statistics may be applied.

The Ratio Scale

This is supposed to be the highest form of scale among the four scales. It has all the characteristics of the other three scales (nominal, ordinal and interval) and in addition the ratio scale implies the presence of a true zero point. In the technique of constructing a ratio scale we must begin with a zero point and go on plotting equal units. These units must be equal and if each value is multiplied by a constant it should also yield equal ratios. For example, in a yardstick there are marks indicating 1 cm, 2 cm, 3 cm, 4 cm, etc. In the same yardstick if we take 4 cm and 8 cm we have a ratio of 4:8 (1:2). If these two numbers are multiplied by a constant 3 the ratio between the numbers is 12:24 or 4:8 or 1:2. In all these the equality of ratios has been maintained. Therefore the yardstick as a form of measure becomes a ratio scale. In the ratio scale the relation between two similar events or objects is always fixed.

Scaling Methods based on Interval and Ratio Judgments

There are several diverse scaling methods in usage and most of them are having interval and ratio judgments as the basis. According to D'Amato (1970) psychophysical scaling experiments can be brought under two general classes of response procedures. They may be termed as experiments of response procedures, because the experimenter depends upon the participant's responses. The participant's responses may be of verbal type or some other type. These response procedures are stated as estimation procedures and production procedures.

In the case of the first one, the experimenter presents one or a group of stimuli to the participant and the participant (P), is expected to give his/her estimation of the stimulus or stimuli either by verbal means or otherwise as required by the experimenter. The P estimates the magnitude of the sensation evoked by the stimulus. In this procedure the experimenter manipulates the stimulus. In the scaling method the stimulus presented to the P is kept constant till the experiment is over.

The other response procedure is the production procedure, in which the P himself/herself manipulates the stimulus according to the direction of experimenter. The P moves or adjusts the stimulus to produce a sensation to the requirements of the experimenter. The P produces or changes the magnitude of the sensation as required and therefore, the procedure is called production procedure. Generally, the stimulus in this procedure is varied on the physical dimension as required. In the psychophysical scaling procedures the important characteristic is the type of judgment made by the participant. The P is expected to make three types of judgments. The P is to judge the difference between the sensations, judging the absolute magnitude of the stimuli and the relative magnitude of the stimuli. The psychophysical scaling methods yield judgments on the sensory scales on the basis of the properties of the stimuli serially, that is, in an expressed order and therefore, they are stated as the ordinal scales of sensation.

Therefore, the interval scale is based upon the report or judgment of the P. The P should equate the intervals or distances between the stimuli or events. That is, the observed differences between stimuli are equal. The other scaling methods are based upon the participant's power to judge that one stimulus appears to be fraction of another or appears to be multiple of another.

Scaling Methods from Interval Judgments

The psychophysical scaling methods are mainly based upon the judgments of the characteristics of sensations emited by the stimuli. The scaling of interval judgment is a direct method. The sensory scales are produced with the interval properties which are obtained by pairing the stimulus properties. Interval judgments are the judgments on the magnitude of the intervals separating two or more sensations. In an interval judgment the P places a sensation in two or more categories as directed by the experimenter. Therefore, the important procedure involved in this method is to equate two intervals at a time and also equating several intervals at a time.

There are two important methods according to this procedure. One is the method of equal sense distance and the other is the method of equal appearing intervals. We shall first discuss these two methods of interval judgments and then go for the other methods of scaling, the Ratio judgments.

Method of Equal Sense Distance

The method of equal sense distance involves the presentation of two standard stimuli and the participant's task is to bisect the distance between the two stimuli. D'Amato (1970) calls this method as the procedure of interval production. Interval production is a procedure in which the P is asked to separate a set of variable stimuli into intervals as directed by the experimenter. Generally, in place of equal intervals the terms equisection or bisection is often used where only two intervals are to be produced by the P. The stimuli used in this experiment for bisection can be anything that can be visually seen or sounds heard.

The bisection is made on a psychological continuum. The P has to judge the point at which certain psychological continuum is bisected. For example, the experimenter may present two sound intensities S_1 and S_3, the S_3 being greater in magnitude. Now the P's task is to find out the sound stimulus S_2 in such a way that $S_3 - S_2 = S_2 - S_1$. The location of S_2 bisects the psychological continuum between S_1 and S_3. The participant is required to bisect the two standard stimuli S_1 and S_3. Therefore, this method is also called the method of bisection.

The experimenter can also use taste in this experiment, by using two substances with different taste intensities and also the P may be asked to select a substance in taste in between these two tastes. The taste can be sweetness or sourness or bitterness. In this type of experiments not only sounds and tastes, but also smells and brightness of light can be used as stimuli. But it should be noted that whatever type of stimuli are used the participant should equate the intervals between the standard stimuli on the psychological continuum. The experimenter should see that the P is not having any physical deformities like deafness or eye defect.

EXPERIMENT - 14 : Determination of Point of Subjective Equality by the Method of Equal Sense Distance

Aim : The aim of this experiment is to determine the point of subjective equality by the method of equal sense distance, by the process of bisection using, any sensory stimuli like the brightness of light or loudness of sound or different intensities of taste.

2. METHOD

Participant : Find out any person who is not aware of this experiment and collect relevant personal information from him/her such as age, gender, qualifications, socio-economic status, whether has any physical deformities like the eye defect or short of hearing etc.

Material : This experiment requires the brightness of light which can be varied from 20 FCP (Foot Candle Power) to 40 FCP. Three such lights are required, two to serve as standards and one as comparative stimulus.

Procedure : The experiment may be conducted with brightness of Lights. The instruments are three lights and the brightness of these lights may be altered, each one independently. The brightness may be varied from 20 Foot Candle Power to 40 Foot Candle Power. The middle light serves as the comparative stimulus and the lights on either side serve as standard stimuli. One standard stimulus is set at 40 FCP and the other is set at 20 FCP. The experimenter can increase and decrease the brightness of the comparative stimulus.

The participant may be seated comfortably in a room where there is no disturbance of any type, at a distance of eight feet away from the lights in the front. The P should be given sufficient instructions as to what he/she should do. The P is expected to estimate the brightness of light which should be on the halfway between the two standard stimuli. The P's task is to judge the level of the intensity of light and indicate whether the comparative stimulus which is at the centre is brighter than the estimated halfway position to the standards or equal in brightness or less in brightness. This, the P is to judge In every trail when the brightness of the comparative light is changed. The experimenter can vary the brightness magnitude of the standard stimulus in random order from right to left and left to right to counterbalance the constant errors of expectation and habituation.

There are three response categories in this experiment and the P is expected to judge and indicate whether the comparative light is more brighter than half or less brighter than the half or equal or the same in the bisection process. Therefore, in the measure of discrimination the PSE falls in between the upper (more bright) and the lower (less brighter) judgments. The experimenter can carry out several trails five or seven on either side of the comparative stimulus, so that the P can judge the level of brightness of the comparative stimulus having the standard of 40 FCP half of the times on the right and half of the times on the left. Thus, a number of such bisections in the same manner can be made and for each bisection one PSE (Point of Subjective Equality) is derived. The experimenter can make entries in his/her tabular columns.

3. RESULTS

The experimenter may treat the results and workout the mean for every trail. The mean of every trail is a PSE. The mean of all PSEs is the PSE in this experiment. This is the bisecting stimulus value which divides the psychological interval into two equal units. In the determination of Point of Subjective Equality by the process of bisection, all steps followed in the method of minimal changes for determining the difference limen should be followed. The data obtained in one of the experiments conducted by using the method of equal sense distance are presented in Table 16.1.

4. DISCUSSION

The experimenter may write the discussion taking into account the above mentioned estimations made by the Participant. The PSE is given for each trial and also for the whole experiment. How accurately the P has made the estimation of the distance, can be discussed. If group data are available this can be compared with the group mean (PSE).

Table 16.1 : Showing the estimations made by the Participant for determining the Point of Subjective Equality in the Brightness discrimination Experiment by the Method of Equal Sense Distance.

Order of the Stimulus Values	1 SR D	2 SR I	3 SR D	4 SR I	5 SR D	6 SL I	7 SL D	8 SL I	9 SL D	10 SL I	Total	Mean PSE
St. 40 FCP	+		+		+		+		+			
38 "	+	+	+		+		+		+			
36 "	+	+	+	+	+	+	+	+	+	+		
34 "	+	+	+	+	+	+	+	+	+	+		
32 "	=	=	+	+	=	+	+	=	=	+		
Comp30 FCP	=	=	=	=	–	=	=	=	–	=		
28 "	–	–	–	=	–	=	–	–	–	=		
26 "	–	–	–	–	–	–	–	–	–	=		
24 "	–	–	–	–	–	–	–	–	–	–		
22 "	–	–	–	–	–	–	–	–	–	–		
St. 20 FCP	–	–	–	–	–	–	–	–	–	–		
(Upper Threshold) T+	34	34	30	32	32	32	30	34	32	30	320	32.0
(Lower Threshold T–	28	30	28	28	30	28	28	30	30	26	286	28.6
PSE	31	32	29	30	31	30	29	32	31	28	303	30.3

SR = Standard Stimulus on the Right
SL = Standard Stimulus on the Left
T+ = Threshold above the standard Stimulus
T– = Threshold below the standard Stimulus.
FCP = Foot Candle Power.

Method of Equal Appearing Intervals

The method of equal appearing intervals is one of the psychophysical methods used for scaling sensory stimuli. The method is also used in scaling statements as a psychological scaling method when the statements are in large number. The method of equal appearing intervals is used extensively for determining the scale values of the statements in the development of attitude scales. This method was originally used by Thurstone and Chave (1929). They first called this method as psycho-physical method of equal appearing intervals.

The important characteristic of this method is that the P is given all the stimuli at the same time and is asked to sort out them into a fixed number of categories. The number of categories is fixed by the experimenter and number normally may range from 5 to 9 or even 11 and the stimuli should be judged and sorted out and put in the category to which a stimulus should go on the basis of its value. For example, in an experiment of this type, the experimenter may use brightness of light with varied intensities or whiteness of colour with different shades of whiteness or spots pattern with different intensities. Whatever type of stimuli is used in the experiment the number of stimuli should be many with different values of the same characteristic. But, there should be some difference among the stimuli in value. For example, if brightness is used there should be different levels of magnitude of brightness. There can be any number of stimuli and each stimulus should be presented more than once.

Guilford (1954) has explained the method of equal-apperaing interval by designing an experiment on the perception of the density of spot patterns. He used 4 sets of cards, 25 cards in each set and each card was 5 x 5 inch in square. A square of 2.5 x 2.5 inch was drawn on each card and within this area there were spots ranging from 15 to 74 in number, but not in a systematic serial order. The Participant was asked to sort out the cards into 9 piles on the basis of the density of the spots in cards. The card which contains the lowest number of spots should go into the category one and the other cards should go into the piles keeping equal intervals between them psychologically on the basis of the intensity of the spots. The observer was asked to sort out the deck cards into 9 piles 10 times. This was done in order to increase the frequencies in the piles. The statistics applied were the median and the semi-interquartile range, Q. The spots in the cards were the stimulus values. The mean values and the standard deviation also can be determined. But Guilford's perception of density spot patterns experiment for equal-appearing interval may not be that much of accurate in the interval judgment as the experiments with brightness of light or shades of whiteness as stimulus values. The density of spots in a card has got very wide range from 15 to 74 and to sort out them into 9 piles 10 times may cause confusion to the observer in judging the intervals equally. Probably, because of this Guilford, himself has compressed the number of stimulus values in the process of determining the scale values of the stimuli. There are certain amount of difference of opinion with regard to the trust of this method. Hevner (1930) has observed that intervals among greater stimuli were under estimated when compared with those of lesser stimuli. Thorndike (1910) has stated that the scale values of this method vary very much from the scale values obtained by the method of pair comparisons. In analysing the data the mean category judgment is taken as the primary measure although the category judgment median and the standard deviation also could have been used.

EXPERIMENT - 15 : Determination of Scale Values by the Method of Equal Appearing Interval

Aim : The aim of this experiment is to determine the scale values of lifted weights by the method of equal appearing interval.

2. METHOD

Participant : Choose a person who is not aware of this experiment and collect certain personal information relevant to the experiment, such as age, gender, qualifications, occupation, socio-economic status, whether the person has any physical deformities etc.

Materials: The materials for this experiment are nine lifted weights, each one varies from the other by 2 grams.

Procedure : Keep the participant seated comfortably in a well illuminated room where there is no disturbance of any type. The P in this method is given all the stimuli that are used in the experiment at the same time.The P's task is to divide the stimuli into categories and this is left entirely to the decision of the P. In the example shown here, the P was presented with 9 lifted weights. Each weight differed from the other by 2 grams. Then the following instructions were given to the P:

"Please look at this. There are 9 weights. Each one varies from the other in weight to some degree. Your task is to lift first all the weights one at a time and make judgment of its intensity. Having got some idea by this means, you will have to put them into five categories. The lowest weight should go into the category of 1, the heaviest should go into the category of 5. All the others should go into the categories in between these two on the basis of the characteristic of each weight. The categories are 1, 2, 3, 4, and 5. You will have to judge each weight six times. Each time you will have to put each weight into one category to which the weight should go. You can take your own time and your own convenient method of judging. But each one should be lifted and judged and put into category.

The distribution of stimuli in each trail into the categories is left entirely with the P in this experiment. The experimenter sets only the number of categories into which the stimuli should go. In this experiment the P is scaling the lifted weights which differ from each other by 2 grams. Since the P puts the stimuli into 5 categories six times the experimenter should note down each distribution. When all the six trails are over the P may be allowed to go away.

3. RESULTS

The experimenter on collecting the distributions made by the P, should work out the frequency distribution of each stimulus and present them in Table. In this illustrating example, the data are presented in Table 16.2.

Table 16.2 : Showing the distribution of the 9 stimuli into 5 categories by the P in the method of equal appearing interval

S.No.	Stimulus weights in grams	Categories					Mean
		1	2	3	4	5	
1.	90 grams	4	1	1	—	—	1.5
2.	92 "	1	4	1	—	—	2.0
3.	94 "	1	2	3	—	—	2.3
4.	96 "	—	1	4	1	—	3.0
5.	98 "	—	1	3	2	—	3.2
6.	100 "	—	1	2	3	—	3.3
7.	102 "	—	1	1	4	—	3.5
8.	104 "	—	—	1	4	—	4.0
9.	106 "	—	—	1	1	4	4.5

The data presented in Table 16.2 are the results of the judgments made by the participant by the method of equal appearing interval. The 9 stimuli of lifted weights are put into five categories six times. On the whole the P has made 54 judgments, of which 6 were gone into the first category, 11 into the second category, 17 into the third category, 15 into the fourth category and 5 were gone into the fifth category. The frquency distribution seems to be symetrical. Therefore, there is no abnormal distribution of the stimuli. The participant has judged the 9 stimuli in a most nornal manner.

The last column provides the mean category placement for the stimuli. This is obtained by computing the mean of the categories to which each stimulus was assigned. The placement of each stimulus into the categories are multiplied and added for each stimulus and then divided by the total number of times the stimulus was judged. For example, in the case of 90 grams stimulus, it has gone into 3 categories, which are 1, 2, and 3. The Stimulus 90 grams is placed 4 times in category 1, one time in category 2, and one time in category 3. Now the number of judgments into each category are multiplied by the respective category value and summed up. While summing up these values, we have (4 x 1) + (1 x 2) + (1 x 3) = 9. This value is divided by the number of (trails) placements. The number of placements are 6. Thus, the mean category placement for 90 grams weight stimulus is $\frac{9}{6}$ = 1.5. In the case of 90 grams the stimulus value for each of the 5 categories are 4, 2, 3, 0, 0. In the same manner the stimulus values for each of the five categories were worked out and by dividing this value by 6 (the number of trails in placement) the mean category judgments for all the stimuli were determined. This is the primary measure in this experiment (Table 16.2).

These results, the mean category judgments, may be plotted in a curve to see how the participant has distributed the 9 stimuli into five categories.

Scaling Methods from Ratio Judgments

The scaling method of ratio judgment is always discussed in association with interval judgments. Though these two methods are discussed together, these two are treated differently. There are different types of scaling techniques designed and used by the psychometricians. Because they often face many special problems and they are to be solved. They also devised different kinds of discriminations. Since the existing scaling methods did not meet the requirements they will have devise various scaling methods. Stevens *et al.* (1957) have developed **three scaling methods based upon ratio judgments. They are, ratio estimation, ratio production, and magnitude estimation.** In these methods, unlike other scaling methods, the P is asked to give the estimation ratio not in fraction or in multiple, but by evaluating the value directly. In the ratio production method the observer (P) is asked to produce a fraction of the original stimulus and it is the experimenter who specifies the fraction needed. In the magnitude estimation method, the experimenter provides the continuum of physical stimulus to the P randomly and the P is to assess each continuum or dimension. But these methods do not make much difference from the existing scaling methods. Candland (1968) states that these methods do not estimate the real sensory experiences but estimating the P's error in judgments.

But, however, the ratio judgments could be differentiated from the interval judgments. Guilford (1954) had differentiated the ratio judgments from the interval judgments. But this distinction was not intended to identify and classify into the groups, but to show that different type of tasks are involved on the part of the P in the methods.

Therefore, the scaling methods evolved from ratio judgments need the P to make the judgments to produce a stimulus that should be of some ratio to the standard stimulus. There is also another way of conducting the procedure. The participant is given two or more stimuli and he is asked to state the ratio that could exist among them. If the variable stimulus is judged as having some ratio of the standard stimulus, the variable stimulus is **supposed to be smaller than the standard to some degree.** Therefore, **this method is called fractionation.** In the other case the variable stimulus is supposed to be **greater than the standard stimulus to some degree. Hence, it is called method of multiple stimuli.** We shall discuss these two methods in detail.

1. *Method of Fractionation*

In this method the observer selects a stimulus that should have the ratio of 1/2, 1/3, 1/5 or 1/10 to the standard stimulus. **The comparative stimulus is always smaller than the standard to certain times.** The observer is presented with all comparative stimuli at once. He is also presented with a standard. The observer's task is to select a comparative stimulus which is a given fraction of the standard stimulus. He may be asked to select a comparative stimulus half of the size or quarter the size of the standard. The experimenter can decide any fraction that the observer is required to do. This method is similar to the method of equal sense distance, but differs from the method of equal sense distance. In the method of fractionation one or more standards at a time may be presented whereas in the method of equal sense distance two standard stimuli are presented.

In the method of fractionation the observer's task is to select a comparative stimulus which should be a given fraction of the standard. The experimenter can use any fraction. The method can be explained through an experiment.

Method of Fractionation — Psychophysical Scaling

EXPERIMENT - 16 : Determining the Given Fraction of the Standard Stimulus by the Method of Fractionation

Aim : The aim of this experiment is to judge the comparative stimulus to the given fraction of the standard stimulus by the method of fractionation and to determine the mean weight judged.

2. METHOD

Participant : Choose a person who has no knowledge about this experiment to serve as a participant and collect his/her personal information such as age, gender, qualifications, and find out and state whether the person has any physical defects.

Materials : Lifted weights. Four of these weights should be used as standard stimulus weights. They should be 68 grams, 72, 76, and 80 grams differing from each other by 4 grams. There should be 33 weights; used as comparative stimulus weights, ranging from 40 to 80 grams, each one differing from the other by one gram.

Procedure : The experiment is to be conducted with lifted weights. The comparative weights 33 in number range from 48 to 80 grams with one gram step difference. The standard stimulus weights which are being tested are 4 in number, as 68, 72, 76, and 80 grams with 4 grams step difference and they are tested one at a time. The participant must judge which of the comparative stimuli is three-quarters of weight of the standard stimulus. The P is given 5 trials for each of the 4 standard weights. The correct three-quarters of the standard weights are 51, 54, 57, and 60 grams. The experimenter should keep secretly the values of the standard and comparative weights. The P should not know what each weight weighs on any account.

The person who serves as a P should be free from physical defect. The P should be seated comfortably in a well illuminated room and there should not be any disturbance. The experimenter on making all arrangements with the test materials for the experiment should give the following instructions to the P as to what he/she should do.

"Please look at these weights. There are two sets of weights. In one set there are 4 weights and they are called standard stimulus weights and the other set consists of 33 weights and they are called comparative stimulus weights. Your task is to lift one of these four weights (showing the 4 weights) and judge its weight in your own way and then find out a weight which is three-quarters of the standard stimulus weight from these (showing them) 33 comparative stimulus weights. You can lift the comparative stimulus weights one by one and find out that which weighs three-fourths of the standard weight. You can use all the comparative weights for this. In the same manner you will have to find out weights of three-fourths for every standard weight. You will have to make five judgments and find out five three-fourths of weights for every standard weight. You can have your own time for this. Now, ready go."

When the P started performing the task, the experimenter should enter the judgments in a tabular column which he/she has already prepared. The experimenter should note down the weights of the standard stimulus, the weights of the comparative stimulus and the weights judged by the P as three-fourths of the standard stimulus weights. The P has to perform twenty trials (4 x 5) to complete the experiment. On completing 20 trials the P may be allowed to go away.

3. RESULTS

The judgments made by the P are presented in Table 16.3. The weight of each judgment of the comparative stimulus as three-fourths of the standard in all the five trials are shown in the Table and mean weight judged as three-fourths for all the four standard stimulus weights are worked out and given in the last but, one column.

Table 16.3 provides a measure of the mean weights judged to be three-quarters of each standard stimulus. These figures are obtained by summing up of the weights judged by the P as three-quarters of the standard weights and dividing them by five, the number of trials. The data in Table 16.3 would tell us whether the P has underestimated or over estimated the 3/4th value of the standard stimulus by using the comparative weights. In the case of all four standard weights there are underestimations and not even in one case there is overestimation. The trials were carried out in random order to avoid the errors of expectation and the errors of habituation. The standards were tried in the order of 72, 76, 68, and 80 grams. The orders were prearranged. The first trial started with 72 grams standard stimulus and the P's five judgments are 53, 52, 52, 52, and 53 grams and the mean judgment is 52.4, but the correct 3/4th of the standard weight is 54 grams. The difference is very small. It is underestimation. The P's judgments for the second standard stimulus 76 grams, are 54, 55, 56, 54, and 57 grams. The mean judgment is 55.2 grams, but the correct weight is 57 grams. In this case also the P has underestimated the standard weight 76. The third standard stimulus judged is 68 grams and the P's judgments are 52, 51, 49, 48, and 50 grams and the mean judgment is 50 grams. But the correct weight is 51 grams. The P has underestimated the standard by one gram. The last stimulus judged is 80 grams. The P's judgments are 57, 58, 57, 59, and 58 grams and the mean judgment is 57.8 grams. The correct 3/4th of the standard is 60 grams. The P has underestimated the standard stimulus by 2.2 grams. This is also a small difference. On the whole there is no abnormal deviation from the correct weights.

Table 16.3 : Showing the judgments made by the participant as three-quarters of the standard stimulus by the method of Fractionation

S. No.	Comparative Stimuli	Standard Stimuli	Trials 1	2	3	4	5	Mean weight judged as 3/4	Correct 3/4 of the Standard Wt.
1	48								
2	49								
3	50								
4	51								
5	52								
6	53								
7	54								
8	55								
9	56								
10	57								
11	58								
12	59								
13	60								
14	61								
15	62								
16	63								
17	64								
18	65								
19	66								
20	67								
21	68	68	52	51	49	48	50	50.0	51.0
22	69								
23	70								
24	71								
25	72	72	53	52	52	52	53	52.4	54.0
26	73								
27	74								
28	75								
29	76	76	54	55	56	54	57	55.2	57.0
30	77								
31	78								
32	79								
33	80	80	57	58	57	59	58	57.8	60.0

The Ps judged mean weights as three-fourths of the standards in all the four cases as far as the number of comparative weights are concerned, the differences between the standard and the comparative weights are very small. This much of difference in fractionation is possible, because of the selection of size of weights and the difference among the weights. If the step difference is less, then the judgment errors may increase. A small difference of 0.5 gram among the comparative stimuli will cause greater amount of error unless the P is professionally experienced in weighing and judging things. Therefore, some preliminary trials were conducted before selecting these weights.

It was observed in the trials that the P was able to judge and differentiate the comparative weights in comparison with the standard weights only 3 to 4 grams steps differences. The difference between 68 grams and 67 and 66 was not easily felt. Similarly, the difference between 68 grams and 69 and 70 was not felt. But the P was able to differentiate between 68 and 65 and 64, and between 72 and 74 and 76 and between 72 and 71 and 70. Therefore, a 4 step difference in grams was choosen for this experiment.

But some experimenters use the comparative stimuli weights ranging from 5 grams to 15 grams with .5 gram step difference. The differnence of .5 gram was not felt by many observers as difference is very small. Therefore, in this illustrative experiment the comparative stimuli were made to range from 48 grams to 80 grams each with one gram difference and the standard stimuli with 4 grams step difference. The function shows that the P tends to estimate the values of the comparative stimuli to the level of 3/4ths of the standard stimuli with very small negligible difference. The important measure obtained in this experiment is the mean weight judged as three-quarters. The mean values of the stimuli judged are the fractions of the standard stimuli (Table 16.3). A graph can be drawn plotting the actual physical stimulus values of three-quarters of each stimulus (standard) and the corresponding psychological judgments obtained from the P.

Method of Multiple Stimuli

The method of multiple stimuli is another method of scaling from ratio judgments of sensations. The method of fractionation and the method of multiple stimuli are both based upon the ratio judgments. D'Amato calls the method fractionation as the partition method, and the method of multiple stimuli as the method of magnitude. He calls both the methods of ratio judgments as the proportionality method. This name seems to be quite appropriate as the purpose of these methods are constructing scales with numerical values which are proportional to the levels of sensations experienced. The method of multiple stimuli seems to be simple and easy in application compared to the method of fractionation.

These two methods are used as checks upon each other. In the method of fractionation the comparative stimulus is judged as half or one-fourth, or three-quarters of the standard stimulus, whereas in the method of multiple stimuli a stimulus is judged to be as two times or three times or four times of the standard stimulus. Therefore, the method of multiple stimuli is also stated as an extension or an inversion of the method of fractionation.

The important characteristic of the method of multiple stimuli is that the P is to select a stimulus which is a multiple of the standard stimulus by two times or three times or four times greater. Geiger and Firestone (1933) have conducted some experimental studies comparing these two methods using sound intensities. They found that there were too much discrepancies in the scaling drived from these two methods. The greatest discrepancies they observed were with the ratios. But the discrepancies in the scale values depend upon the nature of stimulus we use in the experiment. We could avoid or reduce them in scale values with the stimuli like lifted weights, judging lengths, and brightness of light.

Psychophysical Scaling — Method of Multiple Stimuli

EXPERIMENT-17: Determining the given multiple values of the Standard Stimuli

Aim : The aim of this experiment is to judge the standard stimulus to the given multiple values by using the comparative stimuli.

2. METHOD

Participant : Find out a person who is willing to serve as the participant in this experiment and collect relevant information from him/her such as age, gender, qualifications, occupation and also find out whether the person has any physical defects etc.

Materials : The suitable material for this experiment is the lifted weights. Four standard stimulus weights of 20, 22, 24, and 26 grams. Twenty-seven comparative weights, ranging from 56 grams to 82 grams, with one gram step difference.

Procedure : This experiment also can be conducted with lifted weights. There are standard weights and also comparative weights as in the case of fractionation method. In this experiment we are reversing the procedure. The experimenter on any account should not reveal the values of the stimuli. Having made the materials ready for the experiment, the participant should be seated comfortably in a well illuminated room where there is no source of disturbance of any type. Then the following instructions should be given to the P.

"Please look at these weights. There are two types of weights, these four weights (showing them) are called standard weights and these weights (showing them) are called comparative weights. Your task is to lift one of these four weights and judge its value and then to find out which of the weights among these comparative weights is three times as much as the standard weight. You can use all these 27 weights for this purpose. You will have to judge all the four standard weights and find out the weight 3 times greater than the standard weight. You will have to judge each one 5 times and get the weight five times which must be three times of the standard stimulus. You must lift every weight and judge it. Now, ready go."

While the P is making judgments the experimenter should make a note of it and enter in a tabular column which he/she has already prepared. The experimenter should note down the values of the standard weights, against the judged weights. When all the 20 trials are over the P may be allowed to go away.

3. RESULTS

The experimenter should sum up the five judgments and find out the mean values by dividing them by five and present them in the column last but one in the Table 16.4. In the last column the correct weight, three times of the standard weight, should be given. The judged weights should be stated. In this illustrative experiment the results are given in Table 16.4. The correct three times bigger weights are 60 grams, 66, 72, and 78 grams. But the judged weights are 61.4 grams, 68.2, 73.8, and 80.0 grams.

The standard stimulus 20 grams was judged by the P as three times greater five times. The correct comparative stimulus is 60 grams. But the P judged it correctly only once as 60 grams. On all the other four trials the judgments were 62,61, 62, and 62 grams, and the mean judged weight is

61.4. This means, the P has overestimated the standard stimulus (20g) while judging the comparative weight three times as much as the standard. Table 16.4 provides the measures of mean weights judged as three times. In the case of the standard weight 22g only once there is correct judgment as 66. The other judgments are 70 grams, 68, 70, and 68 grams. The judged mean value is 68.2 grams. This is little higher than the correct value (66g). The standard weight 24 is judged three times bigger, and the values are 74 grams, 72, 74, 75, and 75 grams and the mean judgment value is 73.8 grams.

Table 16.4 : Showing judgments made by the participant judging the comparative stimuli three times of the standard stimuli, by the method Multiple Stimuli

S. No.	Comparative Stimuli	Standard Stimulus	Trials 1	2	3	4	5	Mean weight judged 3 times	Correct weight 3 times
1	56								
2	57								
3	58								
4	59								
5	60	20	60	62	61	62	62	61.4	60
6	61								
7	62								
8	63								
9	64								
10	65								
11	66	22	70	66	68	70	68	68.2	66
12	67								
13	68								
14	69								
15	70								
16	71								
17	72	24	74	72	74	75	75	73.8	72
18	73								
19	74								
20	75								
21	76								
22	77								
23	78	26	78	79	82	81	80	80.0	78
24	79								
25	80								
26	81								
27	82								

The correct three times value of 24 grams is 72 grams. The P has made only once the correct judgment as 72. There are overestimations in all four judgments. The standard weight 26 has been judged by the P five times as 78 grams, 79, 82, 81, and 80 grams. But there is one correct judgment. The mean judged value is 80.0 grams. Here also there is little higher overestimation of the standard stimulus. In the case of the first two standard stimuli, 20 and 22 grams the discrepancies are very small. But in the cases of the last two, 24 and 26 grams the differences are greater. On the whole the judgment of the four standard stimuli seem to be overestimation.

A graph may be drawn plotting the correct values and the judged values to see how far the P's judgment goes away from the correct value.

4. DISCUSSION

The results may be discussed taking into account the varied judgments made by the P in valuating the comparative weights as three times of the standard weights. It appears from model experimental results that as and when the weights increased the judged values also increased considerably. For example, in the case of the standard weight 20 grams the overestimation is 1.4 gram, in the case of 22 grams the increase is 2.2 grams. For the standard weight 24 the difference between the correct weight and the judged weight is 1.8 grams and for the standard weight 26 the difference becomes 2.0 grams. This shows that as and when the standard weights increased the judged values also are increasing correspondingly. We saw earlier, in the method of fractionation that there was underestimation of the standard stimulus weights in the judgments made by the P. But in the method of multiple stimuli there is consistently overestimation of the standard weights by the P.

There is a contrasting effect in these two methods. This sort of contrasting effect in the P's judgments is possible, because the process of judgment in the fractionation is to find out a weight which must be smaller than the standard weight. While searching for the smaller weight the P goes below the weight of the standard stmulus weight. But in the method of multiple stimuli the reverse is the case. The P goes in search of a weight which must be three times greater than the standard weight. In this type of effort, the P goes beyond the weight of the standard stimulus weight and therefore, there is overestimation in the P's judgment. In the method of fractionation the P goes in search of smaller weight and goes below the limit. In the method of multiple stimuli the P goes in search of bigger weight and goes beyond the limit. This kind of psychological effect is a common occurrence. This type of error in the ratio judgments may be called as anxiety error. Because the P out of anxiety to find out the correct weight goes below the limit and beyond the limit.

In their earlier studies, Geiger and Firestone (1933), while using both the methods of ratio judgments on sound stimuli, have observed too much of discrepancies in the scaling, derived from these two methods. The greater discrepancies in scaling between these two methods quite but, nature, because of the anxiety errors on the part of the P.

The method of fractionation and the method of multiple stimuli are evolved from the scaling of ratio judgments. Since the judgments made by the P are psychophysical in nature, it is very difficult to conduct experiments using these two methods unless the type of stimuli selected for this experiment provide us with complete cognizable results. For example, variables like sound, heat, smell, light and taste can never help us to arrive at a correct conclusion in the judgments however sophisticated instruments are used in these experiments. We would be only evolving the results from the uncertain judgments made by the P. But the only variable which can provide us with somewhat correct conclusions is the lifted weights. The lifted weights of varied steps with one gram would be best for this type of experiment in the laboratory situations.

Other Ratio Judgment Techniques

There are several other ratio techniques evolved from the scaling from ratio judgments. They are used in solving certain special problem as now and then the psychometricians encounter in judging the sensory experiences. In these methods the P is asked to make different kinds of discriminations. The leading psychophysicists who worked hard on these problems were Stevens and his co-workers (1957). They devised a method by which the P is forced to make ratio judgments directly. The methods they used are ratio estimation, ratio production and magnitude estimation. In these methods the P is provided with certain clues to make judgments as desired.

The variations brought out by Stevens and others in scaling methods seem to be not only easy, but also simple. The experimenter straightaway gets his/her data without giving any treatment to the results. Barker and Dudek (1955) have used this variation method of ratio estimation and found to be satisfactory. In the case of the ratio estimation the P is presented with two stimuli of different values and he/she is asked to estimate the ratio that is existing between them and he/she is asked to state them. This sort of experiment is limited to only variables like light or anything that is visible or felt by hands, like weights. In an experiment, two lights with different brightness are presented to the observer and he is asked to say directly the ratio existed between them. He has to state what value he gives to light X and what value he gives to light Y. If light X is equivalent to 20, then the light Y is equivalent to 100. This must be his judgment and he is not asked to say that light Y is five times brighter than light X. Here the observer himself is giving the ratio judgment. This procedure is completely different from the classical psychophysical methods. The observer's ability to judge the ratio is also evaluated. Further, the statistical procedure is also eliminated.

In the method of ratio production, unlike in the method of fractionation, the observer is straightaway asked to state the fraction of the standard stimulus. He is not asked to produce fraction but to state what fraction exists between the two stimuli. This is approximate to the ratio.

In the method of magnitude estimation, the observer is provided with a dimension of physical stimulus. The experimenter presents various values of physical stimulus randomly. The observer is to judge each stimulus in terms of the continuum. In the case of light, the judgment should be on light continuum. If weight, it should be on the weight continuum. For example, if a light presented is valued as 20 in brightness then what the other lights are to be valued. He is expected to give in the form of values like 40 or 60, or 80 and so on. The judgments directly provide the ratio between the stimuli. These three methods have certain advantages over the other methods.

17

MODERN PSYCHOPHYSICAL SCALING METHODS - III

Method of Successive Categories

The method of successive categories is also one of the Psychophysical Scaling Methods, very widely applied in psychological measurements. The judgments are obtained in this method mostly by experimental operations. The basic assumption involved in scaling by the method of successive categories is that the categories into which the stimuli are rated or sorted are equal. Therefore, this method is also called method of successive intervals. The experimental operation is judging each of several stimuli to one of the several categories which are differing quantitatively from one another on certain continuum.

It appears that what is applicable to the method of equal intervals is also applicable to the method of successive intervals or successive categories. The sorting of stimuli into intervals or categories does not make any difference in these methods. The judge or the participant in the process of categorization does not discriminate stimuli placed within the same category, for example, if a stimulus is placed in an extremely favourable or unfavourable category earlier, and he/she has placed similar stimulus in the same category. But after few seconds, he/she finds another stimulus more extreme than the one placed already in an extreme category. Since the categories are already specified the P does not find a category beyond the extreme that he/she has already placed a stimulus. In such situation the P is not given the chance to make his/her own judgment and the P is forced not to make any such discriminations among the stimuli. This is normally taking place in the method of paired comparisons and in methods having similar procedure. But here the only thing that can be done is that the P can put the first stimulus in a lesser extreme category to find a place for the more extreme stimuli. But generally in sorting the stimuli on the basis of the qualities of the stimuli the Ps or the judges do not resort to this kind of adjustment.

Therefore, it is possible that if some stimuli are sorted out closely in terms of their qualities at one or the other extremes in an equal appearing interval scale, the scale values of these stimuli may show wider spreading when judged by the scaling method by allowing the judges or the Ps to make discrimination between the extremes. This sort of inconsistencies were observed by psychometricians like Hevner (1930) and Kelley *et al.* (1955). Because of this they have also suggested various other procedures. The method of successive categories or intervals like the method of equal appearing interval should have a single judgments by the judges or the Ps for sorting the stimuli.

But, however in the method of successive categories, the assumption is that the categories are in correct ranking position and the boundaries of the categories are well defined and supposed to be permanent. The problem is scaling the categories. It is done by estimating the value of each category or the limit of each category on the psychological scale. The method of successive categories is often related to several similar techniques. The most commonly used scaling techniques or methods are rating or successive categories, ranking and paired comparison. These three methods are very popular in the experimental operations for several reasons. They are very easy to apply to a variety of scaling problems. The operation is simple and easy for the participants to manipulate the stimuli. Further, the experimenter also can find it relatively easy to apply, collect data, compute the data and to interpret them. Another important advantage of this method is that it is not necessary to know the physical value of each stimulus in the experimental situation in order to scale it psychologically. Thus, this method has several advantages over other scaling methods. The experiment also can be performed without taking much time. In all the three methods mentioned above, we have stated that the important experimental process is that the judge or the P is to arrange the stimuli into certain specified groups, ranks or categories.

The procedure, whether, it is rating or ranking or categorising the participant decides which person or stimulus deserves to be in the first rank, which are the persons or stimuli to receive the 2nd and 3rd ranks and so on. Here the P is expected to sort out the quality of the stimulus or a person's performance into ranks or categories. Let us briefly state each of these three methods.

Rating Method

Rating means appraising or evaluation of some objects, persons, or performance and placing them in certain ranks or grades or class. In psychological measurements for evaluating scale values for stimuli this rating procedure is used. A person who acts as a judge or subject; or a participant is asked to judge and grade or rank the persons or objects in an order according to the value. Rating also means classifying the stimuli according to some order.

The rating method is very widely used in a variety of situations and most frequently used in the field of applied psychology. Apart from basic research of many types, the rating method is also used in the evaluation of individual's behaviour. People in various walks of life use this method for their purpose in their own ways. The method is applied in several forms and each form is given a name. All of them are alike and they seek for assigning some order. But they may differ in operation and placement. Guilford (1954) states five forms of rating method. They are numerical scaling method, graphic scaling method, standard scaling method, cumulated scaling method and forced choice scaling method. According to him the type of classification is very loose as the types are alike and there is no much difference in the procedures. The P has to sort out the stimuli into categories.

EXPERIMENT - 18 : Determination of Scale Values of the Stimuli by the Method of Rating

Aim : The purpose of this experiment is to determine the scale values of the given stimuli by sorting out them into categories on the basis of the qualities of the stimuli.

2. METHOD

Participant : Find out ten persons who have no knowledge about this experiment and collect their personal information such as age, gender, qualifications, occupation, income, whether any of them is having any physical defects etc.

Material : The materials required for this experiment are colour disk as stimuli. The colour disks are five in number in five colours, such as Red, Green, Blue, Yellow, and Orange. A placing sheet with five categories like, More Pleasant, Pleasant, Neither Pleasant nor Sad, Sad and More Sad should be prepared by the experimenter.

Procedure : This is an individual test and may be also conducted as a group test. But if the experimenter is required to watch the performance of the P then it should be conducted individually. If ten sets of the colour disks are available and the experimenter can go through the seats of all ten persons and watch, then all ten Ps may be allowed to perform the task and they should be seated separately, independent of each other so that each one is not encroaching into another person's performance. Whether there are ten persons or one person all the five stimuli should be given to the P(s) at the same time for rating them. The stimuli should be five colour disks. The P's task is to sort out the five colour disks into five categories. The name of five categories are More Pleasant, Pleasant, Neither Pleasant nor Sad, Sad and More Sad. The experimenter is not expected to mention anything about the magnitude of the categories and nothing about the values of the stimuli. The P is expected to give his/her reaction to all the five stimuli in terms of five categories. The P is to rate the stimuli and the rating is to be expressed in an order of the stimuli.

The experimenter on making arragements for conducting the experiment, should make the P seated comfortably in a well illuminated room where there is no disturbance of any type. Then the following instruction should be given.

"Please look at these disks. There are five colour disks with the colours of Red, Green, Blue, Yellow, and Orange. See in front of you there is 'Placing Sheet' with five categories such as, More Pleasant, Pleasant, Neither Pleasant nor Sad, Sad, More Sad. Your task is to judge each of these disks and place them into any one of these five categories. You can express your reaction to these colours by placing the colour disks in these categories. You will have to place one colour disk in one category only. All the five disks should go into these five categories shown here (showing the placing sheet). Now, ready go."

When the P or Ps finished the task, he/she or they may be allowed to go away. If the experiment is conducted one by one then, another P may be called and the same procedure should be followed.

3. RESULTS AND DISCUSSION

The experimenter should collect all the placing sheets and enter the P's judgments in a Tabular column. An individual person's rating of the five Stimuli into the five categories should be entered in a Table. The Table should have all the five categories.

Table 17.1 : Showing an individual's rating of the five stimuli into five categories.

S.No.	Stimulus	Categories				
		More Pleasant	Pleasant	Neither Pleasant nor sad	Sad	More Sad
1.	Red	0	1	0	0	0
2.	Green	1	0	0	0	0
3.	Blue	0	0	1	0	0
4.	Yellow	0	0	0	0	1
5.	Orange	0	0	0	1	0
	Total	1	1	1	1	1

The ratings made by 10 persons of the five colours into five categories according to their evaluation of the qualities of the five colours are summed up and given in Table 17.2. The expressed reactions of the 10 Ps were distributed in all five categories.

Table 17.2 : Showing the ratings made by 10 persons of the five colours into five categories.

S. No.	Stimulus (Colours)	Categories					Total
		More Pleasant	Pleasant	Neither Pleasant nor Sad	Sad	More Sad	
1.	Red	5	4	1	0	0	10
2.	Green	4	3	2	1	0	10
3.	Blue	4	2	2	1	1	10
4.	Yellow	1	2	2	2	3	10
5.	Orange	3	2	3	1	1	10

The results presented in Table 17.2 shows how the 10 persons have perceived the five colours on the basis of the qualities. The ratings reveal that 5 persons judged that Red as more pleasant, 4 judged it as pleasant and one judged it as neither pleasant nor sad, and none judged the Red colour as sad or more sad. The Green colour seemed to be preferred next to Red colour. Four persons judged as more pleasant for them, three stated by rating as pleasant, two rated that Green was neither pleasant nor sad for them, one judged it as sad and none rated as more sad. Blue colour was rated as more pleasant by 4 persons, two rated as pleasant, two rated as neither pleasant nor sad, one rated as sad and one rated as more sad. This showed that blue was rated into all five categories. Yellow was rated by one as more pleasant, two as pleasant, two as neither pleasant nor sad, two as sad and three as more sad. Orange was rated as pleasant by three persons, two as pleasant, three as neither pleasant nor sad, one as sad and one as more sad. Blue, Yellow and Orange were rated into all five categories.

The data given in Table 17.2 are only the number of preferences of the Ps to different colours. In the next step these data are to be converted into proportions. The proportions are obtained by multiplying the number of preferences given in the columns of Table 17.2 by 10 and dividing them by 100. Thus, the number of preferences are converted into decimals. The decimal values are presented in Table 17.3.

Table 17.3 : Showing the proportions of the ratings made by 10 persons of the five colours into five categories.

S. No.	Stimulus	Categories					
		More Pleasant	Pleasant	Neither Pleasant nor Sad	Sad	More Sad	Total
1.	Red	0.50	0.40	0.10	0.00	0.00	1.00
2.	Green	0.40	0.30	0.20	0.10	0.00	1.00
3.	Blue	0.40	0.20	0.20	0.10	0.10	1.00
4.	Yellow	0.10	0.20	0.20	0.20	0.30	1.00
5.	Orange	0.30	0.20	0.30	0.10	0.10	1.00

The data in Table 17.3 were obtained by multiplying the number of placements (5) by 10 and dividing it by 100. In column one the proportion for Red is 0.50. The number of placement 5 for Red in the first category is multiplied by 10, the number of persons. This figure is then divided by 100 (5 x 10 = 50 ÷ 100) = 0.50. The figure in category 2 (Pleasant) for Red is 4 and this is multiplied by 10 and divided by 100 and the (decimal) proportion is 0.40. In the same manner all the ratings are multiplied by 10 and divided by 100 to get the proportions. The rating figure is multiplied by 10 because the number of participants are 10. The multiplied figure is divided by 100, because the figure must be converted into proportions. The same procedure was followed in converting the numbers in columns into proportions, in all the columns for all the colours.

Suppose, for example if the participants in the experiment were more than 10, *i.e.*, 20 or 25, then the judgments in columns should be multiplied by 5 and 4 and divided by 100. Since we are converting the number of judgments into proportions (decimals) the multiplied number must be less than 100. This can be stated in another way. We will have to divide 100 by the number of participants (100 ÷ 20 = 5 or 100 ÷ 25 = 4). The obtained figure 5 or 4 should be used to multiply the number judgments and then it should be divided by 100 (5 x 5 ÷ 100 = 0.25 or 0.20), in the case of the number of participants 20 and 25.

The next final step is to convert the proportions into cumulative proportions and presenting them in Table 17.4. The cumulative proportions have been worked out and presented in Table 17.4. This is very simple, once we have obtained the proportions in the categories. The proportions in the categories are added from left to right and entered in columns of Table 17.4.

Table 17.4 : Showing the cumulative proportions of the ratings made by ten participants of the five colours into five categories.

S. No.	Stimulus	Categories					
		More Pleasant	Pleasant	Neither Pleasant nor Sad	Sad	More Sad	Total
1.	Red	0.50	0.90	1.00	1.00	1.00	1.00
2.	Green	0.40	0.70	0.90	1.00	1.00	1.00
3.	Blue	0.40	0.60	0.80	0.90	1.00	1.00
4.	Yellow	0.10	0.30	0.50	0.70	1.00	1.00
5.	Orange	0.30	0.50	0.80	0.90	1.00	1.00

The proportion figures presented in Table 17.3 are added from left right and presented in Table 17.4. In the case of Red colour, in the first column there is 0.50, which is added to 0.40 in the next column and 0.10 in the third column is added to the sum which makes the total 1.00 and the same total is carried out in the next two columns as there is nothing to add. The same procedure was carried out for all the five colours. Thus, the cumulative proportions reached the highest point 1.00, in all the rows. A curve can be drawn plotting the figures. The cumulative proportions may be plotted against the categories. The placements of each colour in different categories may reveal the picture of the dispersion. If there was proper dispersion in placements then the graph would be in a straight line. The proportion of 1.00 must be achieved at the last category for each stimulus. This indicates the maximum dispersion in the placements of this experiment.

Method of Ranking

The method of ranking is another successive category method of psychophysical scaling. Ranking means assigning a position or place to a person or an object on the basis of quality. The P is required to place the stimuli into categories like the method of rating, but in the method of ranking only one stimulus is to be placed in each category. In the method of rating there can be more than one stimuli in category. The P must place the stimuli along the category continuum or in series of ranks, so that one stimulus is given first place, one is given second place and another is given a third place and so on. The experimenter provides the category continuum or series of ranking files on which the Ps are to rank the given stimuli. The P's task is to judge which stimulus has more or less of the quality of being judged as the first or second or third or last.

In the method of ranking, like the method of rating, all the stimuli are presented to the P simultaneously. The participant has no chance of assigning or placing the same stimulus in two ranks or assigning the same value to more than one stimulus. The P is not asked to indicate the quality or quantity of difference between the stimuli but only to assign in some ranks.

EXPERIMENT - 19 : Determination of Scale Values of the given number of Poets by the Method of Ranking

Aim : The aim of this experiment is to determine the scale values of the given stimuli by judging and placing them in the order of preference by the method of ranking.

2. METHOD

Participants : Choose ten persons who have known something about the famous English Poets and collect their personal information, such as age, gender, qualifications, professional experiences, socio-economic status etc.

Material : The material for this experiment is a group of seven famous English Poets. The names are: (1) Shakespeare, (2) Milton, (3) Wordsworth, (4) Coleridge, (5) Keats, (6) Shelley, and (7) Byron.

Preparation of Test Materials : The experimenter should prepare ten sets of test materials. The name of every poet should be written in a small slip.

There should be only one name of the poet in one slip. The 7 names should be in 7 slips. There should be ten sets of the same type. Any list of names 1 to 7 in any order may create an impression in the minds of the Ps that the experimenter prefers that order and the Ps may react on this. Therefore, in order to avoid such misconception each name should be in a separate slip.

Procedure : The ranking method is used in this experiment. The ten participants are asked to rank the 7 famous English Poets in terms of their preference for each poet. The preference is the continuum or a series of ranking on which the Ps make the ranks of the poets. The Ps are to assign number one to the poet whom the Ps prefer most and assign number 2 to the next preferred poet and to assign number 3 to the third preferred poet and so on till all the 7 rankings are completed. But the number 7 should be assigned to the last preferred poet. In this experiment of the method of ranking each poet is ranked along a continuum or a series of ranks of preference and that only one poet is placed in each rank or category. This **type of ranking generates the ordinal scale.** This means that the preference is expressed in the serial order.

Having made all the arrangements with the test materials to conduct the experiment, the experimenter should keep all the ten participants seated comfortably in a well illuminated room where there is no disturbance of any type. In the seating arrangement, each P should maintain certain distance from the other P to avoid some encroachment. Then the following instructions should be given to the Ps.

"Please look at these slips. In each slip the name of one famous English poet is written. There are 7 slips in this bundle and you will find 7 names of the poets. Your task is to go through all the 7 names once, and then arrange them in the order of preference. Assign number one to the poet whom you preferred most. Assign number 2 to the next preferred poet, give number 3 to the third preferred poet. Carry out the same procedure till you complete the ranking of all 7 poets. But the rank number 7 should be given to the last preferred poet. Place only one poet in each rank. Arrange these slips according to the ranks you assigned to the poets and return them to me. You can take your own time."

After giving these instructions the experimenter should hand over the slips to all the ten persons. Then the experimenter can give the order, "Now, ready go".

When the Ps completed the task, the experimenter on collecting the slips may allow them to go away. The experimenter should check the slips, whether all the 7 slips are there and then enter the judgments made by the Ps in a Table which the experimenter prepared already.

3. RESULTS

The rankings made by the 10 participants through the slips of the seven poets are to be entered in Table 17.5, from 1 to 7 under the respective name of the poet.

Table 17.5 : Showing the Rankings of the 7 famous English Poets made by 10 Participants by the Method of Ranking

Respon-dents	Shakes-peare	Milton	Words-worth	Coleridge	Keats	Shelley	Byron
1	3	5	4	6	1	7	2
2	4	5	3	2	1	6	7
3	3	5	7	1	4	6	2
4	1	4	5	7	3	2	6
5	1	2	3	5	7	6	4
6	2	1	3	4	7	6	5
7	4	3	5	1	2	6	7
8	6	4	2	3	7	5	1
9.	2	3	1	7	6	5	4
10	3	4	5	6	7	1	2
Mean	2.9	3.6	3.8	4.2	4.5	5.0	4.0
Rank	1	2	3	5	6	7	4

In this experiment by the method of ranking each poet is ranked along a continuum of preference and only one poet is placed in each rank or category. The first P, for example has given the first rank to Keats, second rank to Byron and third rank to Shakespeare and so on. The P has given the rank of 7 to Shelley. This shows that Keats is the most preferred poet for this person and Shelley is the last preferred poet. The second person also preferred Keats as the most liked poet and placed him in the first rank, Coleridge as the second preferred, Wordsworth thirdly, Shakespeare fourthly and Byron as the last preferred poet. The third P preferred Coleridge mostly, Byron secondly, Shakespeare thirdly and Wordsworth lastly. The fourth P's most preferred poet is Shakespeare, the second preferred is Shelley, the third preferred is Keats and the last preferred is Coleridge. The fifth P's most preferred poet is Shakespeare, the second preferred is Milton, the third preferred is Wordsworth and placed Shelley and Keats in the sixth and last places. The sixth P assigned first place to Milton, second place to Shakspeare, third place to Wordsworth and sixth and seventh places to Shelley and Keats like the 5th P. The 7th P's most preferred poet is Coleridge, the second preferred is Keats the third preferred is Milton and the last preferred is Byron. Byron is the most preferred poet for the 8th P, the second preferred is Wordsworth, the third preferred is Coleridge and the last preferred is Keats. The 9th P's most preferred poet is Wordsworth, second preferred is Shakespeare, the third is Milton and the last preferred is Coleridge. The 10th person preferred Shelley as the most preferred, Byron as the second, Shakespeare as the third and Keats as the last preferred.

The mean rank is worked out by adding all of the given ranks to each poet and dividing the total by the number of participants, 10. The mean rank for Shakespeare is 2.9, for Milton 3.6, for Wordsworth 3.8, for Coleridge 4.2, for Keats 4.5, for Shelley 5.0 and for Byron 4.0. According to the mean ranks Shakespeare received the lowest mean (2.9) and Shelley received the highest mean (5.0) along the preference continuum (Table 17.5).

4. DISCUSSION

The results of the experiment presented above indicate that the lowest mean score 2.9 received the first rank and the highest mean score 5.0 received the last rank. The mean rank scores range from 2.9 to 5.0. According to the mean rank scores Shakespeare was given first rank, though only two out of ten assigned the first rank and two have assigned the second rank to Shakespeare. Only one person assigned sixth rank and none had assigned the last (7th) rank to Shakespeare. The ten participants have given second rank to Milton with a mean rank score of 3.6. Of the ten persons one P placed him in the first rank, one placed him in the second rank, two placed him in the third rank, three Ps placed him in the fourth rank and three placed him in fifth rank none placed him in sixth and 7th ranks.

In the case of Wordsworth, who was placed in the third rank, one placed him in the first rank, one placed him in the second rank, three placed him in third rank, one placed him in fourth rank, three placed him in 5th rank and one placed him in the last (7th) rank. It can be seen that two persons preferred Coleridge most and two preferred him the last and he was placed in 5th rank. Poet Keats was most preferred by two persons, but four persons preferred him last, because of this he was placed 6th rank. One person most preferred Byron two placed him in the second rank, two placed him in the last rank and he was placed in the fourth rank. One person most preferred Shelley one placed him in the second rank, two placed him in 5th rank, four persons placed him in sixth rank and one placed him in 7th rank and the whole group in this experiment placed him in the last (7th) rank. The order of preference expressed by ten persons about the 7 poets in the continuum is (1) Shakespeare, (2) Milton, (3) Wordswoth, (4) Byron, (5) Coleridge, (6) Keats, (7) Shelley.

In the method of ranking, if one participant ranked the stimuli and only one stimulus is placed in each rank, then each stimulus is having equal distance from the other stimulus. But if more participants take part in ranking the stimuli, then equal distance relationship suffers. The distance between stimulus vary considerably because every P may have his own preference and the order of preference of the stimuli varies person to person. In such cases the mean of the preferences is computed which may reveal the correct position of each stimulus.

In the method of ranking one procedure is that one person may be asked to rank the same stimuli several times. It is quite but natural that however he/she may be reliable, he/she may give the same rank to the stimuli on retesting. The person's previous judgments may have influence upon the succeeding judgments.

There is another alternative method in ranking. It is ranking several stimuli by the same person on different occasions. In this method there will be more dispersions. The P will make judgments around the mean and the judgments are normally distributed since every time he/she may find different stimulus for the particular rank or category. Experiments have been conducted using the method of ranking very widely on different types of stimuli. Peryam and Haynes (1957) used the method of ranking on food preferences. Singh and Wherry (1963) used this method on job factors. They all found that the method was very much successful.

There is another method of rank order, discussed elsewhere in this book in connection with determining the rank values by psychometric procedures. The operational procedure in both the methods is the same almost, but the treatment of the data in both the methods vary considerably. In both the methods the results are obtained on psychological continuum unlike the psychophysical methods, where the results are obtained on physical continuum.

But the ranking method we have discussed here is more simple and easy for the experimenter and also for the participants. Therefore, this method is more preferred to the other methods.

Method of Pair Comparison

The method of pair comparison is one of the scaling methods very widely applied in psychological measurements. This has been classified one among the psychophysical scaling methods. But now, some of the psychometricians like Edwards (1969) call this as one of the psychological scaling methods. The reason they state is that the scale values of the stimuli are not related to the physical continuum, but they are on the psychological continuum and the values are in psychological scale. The important characteristic of the method of pair comparison is that the participant is presented with two stimuli at a time and he/she must judge which one of the two has greater amount of quality or quantity than the other. There are only two categories of judgments. Therefore the P has to guess to decide the one. The response in this method is a comparative judgment. The method of pair comparison is fully based upon the law of comparative judgment developed by Thurstone (1927a, 1927b) in 1920s.

In the method of pair comparison a single participant may judge a given pair of stimuli on several occasions or several participants may judge the same stimuli at a time. In either case the method of pair comparison provides measures of dispersion. There is an additional information obtained in this method. The information is with regard to the attributes of the stimuli. The same stimuli are judged by the same person differently on different occasions. The same stimuli are judged by different persons differently. Because of this we get additional information, the measures of dispersion.

The method of pair comparison has certain advantages and certain disadvantages. In this method the stimuli are always presented in pairs. Candland (1968) states that the method has some built-in controls which are not found in other methods. Further, this method is very widely applied in psychological measurements.

The method can be applied in experiments where the stimuli are presented in pairs successively or simultaneously. It is mostly used in judging affective values and in the measurement of opinions and attitudes. Among the rating scale methods, the method of pair comparison is considered to be more accurate. The chief disadvantage of this method is that it takes too much of time to complete an experiment and also it is very tedious and cumbersome for the person who serves as a judge, if the number of stimuli are more than 20. Since every stimulus is paired with every stimulus, with 20 stimuli there are 190 pairs. The computation of scale value also is very much laborious on the part of the experimenter. In this method there is every chance for the relevant variable to have influence in the data.

In the method of pair comparison since every stimulus is paired with every other stimulus, it serves the purpose of counterbalancing and the time and space errors are removed. Further, the same stimulus is presented several times to the P in pairing with other stimuli the P gets more chance to judge the stimuli accurately even if the P misses the chance in the first time.

But there are procedures to reduce the number of pairs in the experimental situations and also to reduce the labour involved in computation of the scale values. These procedures are considered as variations in this method. Guildford (1931) has suggested one method to reduce the number of pairs, if the stimuli are too many, and another method (1928) to reduce the computational labour. According to him 7 stimuli of lifted weights can be reduced to three or five without affecting the accuracy of the results. The procedures suggested by Uhrbroch and Richardson (1933) to reduce the pairs appear to be more relaxing for the experimenter. According to them 990 pairs can be reduced to 390 pairs. McGarmick and Bachus (1952) have suggested another procedure to reduce the number of pairs in this method.

EXPERIMENT - 20 : Determination of Scale Values for the Given Stimuli by the Method of Pair Comparison

Aim : The aim of this experiment is to judge the stimulus which is having greater value in a pair by the method of pair comparison and estimating the scale value of each stimulus.

2. METHOD

Participant : Find out a person who is not aware of this experiment to serve as a participant and collect his/her personal information like, age, gender, qualifications, socio-economic status, whether there is any physical defects, like eye defects etc.

Materials : Seven colour disks with seven different colours, like Red, Green, Blue, Yellow, Orange, Rose, and Purple.

Procedure : The method of pair comparison is applied in this experiment. It is for determining the scale values of seven colours which are used as stimuli. Every stimulus in this experiment is presented to the P in pair with another stimulus and the P has to state which of the two he/she prefers most. One important procedure in this experiment is that every stimulus is placed in the first place in a pair and also placed in the second place in another pair. In both the cases the P's preference is recorded. The P should indicate the preference by placing the forefinger on the stimulus. If the first one is preferred then 1 is marked in the scoring sheet. If the P did not prefer the first, but preferred the second, then a zero (0) is marked.

In pairing the 7 colours, every colour stimulus is in the first place and also in the second place after few trials. Thus, every colour is paired with every other colour, both in the first place and in the second place. Therefore, there should be 21 pairs for the 7 stimuli. The experimenter should prepare a Table in which all 7 colours should be written on the left in a column, vertically and against which in the columns in the same order all the 7 colours should be written in a row (Table 17.6). The experimenter personally should present each pair to the P and the P has to indicate the preference.

The experimenter should make the participant seated comfortably in a well illuminated room in front of a Table against him/her. Then the following instructions should be given.

"I shall place before you two colour disks every time in pair. Your task is to see them and decide and indicate which of the two colours you prefer mostly. I shall first present red and green and you will have to indicate by putting your forefinger on the colour you prefer. Then, secondly, I shall present red and blue, thirdly red and yellow, and so on. Every time you will have to do the same thing, by indicating your preference in all the pairs. I think, you have understood the point. Now, get ready to start."

Having given these instructions, the experimenter may start presenting the pairs he/she has already arranged. As and when the P indicates his/her preference, the experimenter can make markings, 1 for preferring the first placed stimulus and 0 for not preferring it. This procedure should be continued till all the 21 pairs are completed.

3. RESULTS

In the experimental procedure, the red colour was presented with green colour first, secondly red was presented with blue, thirdly red with yellow, fourthly red with orange, fifthly red with rose and lastly red with purple.

Thus, red was presented in pair with every other colour. In the same manner green in pair was presented with red blue and with other colours. Then blue, yellow, orange, rose and purple were presented in pair with other colours. Thus, 21 pairs were presented successively. The participant's task was to judge the colour in terms of liking between the two colours.

In determining the number of pairs for the 7 colour stimuli, the formula applied is : $\frac{N(N-1)}{2} = \frac{7(7-6)}{2} = \frac{7 \times 6}{2} = \frac{42}{2} = 21$, where N stands for number of stimuli being tested in the experiment. In the present experiment the 7 different stimuli were to be tested, were in 21 pairs, and they were tested. The meaning of the formula $\frac{N(N-1)}{2}$ is to give chance to each stimulus to be paired atleast once with every other stimulus. This is to be known that in arranging the pairs, each stimulus should appear first in half of the pairs and appear in the last in half of the pairs. This is called the process of counterbalancing the position of the stimulus variables which may eliminate the error of position preference.

In Table 17.6, there are rows and columns and the name of the colours are given (1 to 7), are from red to purple in the first column. The rows are going from red to purple. In this order, the red on the left is compared with green, blue, yellow and so on and the P has given his/her choice which is indicated by 1. In Table 17.6, in the first row against red under green 0 is given which meant that the participant between red and green, has not preferred red, hence it is 0. Between red and blue colours the P preferred red, therefore, 1 is given against red. Between red and yellow the P has preferred red, hence 1 is given against red. In the third row, blue is on the row and red is on the column and between these two the P has not preferred blue and hence 0 is given against blue. This was how all the 7 colours tested in pairs. The important point in this procedure is that, whether the P has preferred the first colour given on the left in comparison with the second colour given above in the row. If the P has preferred any colour on the left in column, then 1 is marked, otherwise 0 is marked. In this experiment the total number of pairs tested were 21 and therefore, there are 21 ones, and 21 zeroes (0) not preferred.

Table 17.6 : Showing an individual's choices on scaling seven colours by the method of Pair Comparison

S. No.	Colours	Red	Green	Blue	Yellow	Orange	Rose	Purple	C Score	Percentage	C' Score	P'
1.	Red	x	0	1	1	1	1	1	5	83.3	5.5	79
2.	Green	1	x	1	1	1	1	1	6	100.0	6.5	93
3.	Blue	0	0	x	1	0	1	1	3	50.0	3.5	50
4.	Yellow	0	0	0	x	0	0	0	0	0.0	0.5	7
5.	Orange	0	0	1	1	x	1	1	4	66.3	4.5	64
6.	Rose	0	0	1	1	0	x	0	2	33.3	2.5	36
7.	Purple	0	0	0	0	0	1	x	1	16.6	1.5	21

We can understand from the results as given in Table 17.6, that the first colour red was preferred by the individual over blue, yellow, orange, rose and purple. Green colour was preferred over all other six colours. Blue was preferred over yellow, rose, and purple. The colour orange was preferred over blue, yellow, rose and purple colours. Rose colour was preferred over blue, yellow, while purple was preferred by the P over only rose. But, the colour yellow was not preferred by the P. The C (choice) score for green is the highest, 6, for red 5, for orange 4, for blue 3, for rose 2, for purple 1 and for yellow 0. The C score was obtained by adding all the choices made by the P for each colour. The next step is to work out the percentages for the colours preferred by the P. This is worked out for each colour. The formula used to work out the percentages of cases is :

$$\frac{C}{N-1} \times 100$$

where C = the number of times the stimulus was chosen.

N = the number of stimuli.

We can use this formula and work out the percentage red colour. It is

$$= \frac{5}{(7-1)} \times 100 = \frac{5 \times 100}{6} = 83.3$$

Red colour was preferred in 83.3 percentage of cases. The percentage values for all colours are given in the column under percentage.

We can observe that in this type of pair comparison there is always a tie within the stimulus. Each stimulus faces a tie as it has to be compared with itself. In this experiment, for example, red is compared with all other colours, but not with itself. This is the case with all other colours. Red is compared with green and green is compared with red, but red is not compared with red and green with green. Therefore, a correction is suggested for the comparison of each stimulus and the value of it is 0.5. This value 0.5 is added to each C value to justify the tie. The score of this is stated as C'. Hence the C' scores for the respective stimuli are 5.5, 6.6, 3.5, 0.5, 4.5, 2.5 and 1.5. The P' scores for all the stimuli were worked out from the C' scores in the same way as the percentage scores were obtained making a small change in the formula. The formula for P' score is = $\frac{C'}{N}$x100, where the C' is the C' score, N number of stimuli. The P' scores were computed for all the 7 stimuli and presented in the last column of the Table 17.6. The value are 79, 93, 50, 7, 64, 36 and 21 percentages. **Since the values provide an order of the preferences it may be called an ordinal scale.**

The following is an alternative method of treating the same data, we are providing, which is also simple and easy.

Table 17.7 : Showing the Results of the choices made by an individual and the scaling of 7 colour stimuli and the order of the Scale Values from highest to lowest by the Method of Pair Comparison.

S. No.	Colours	Red	Green	Blue	Yellow	Orange	Rose	Purple	Choices	P'	Z Value	Rank
1.	Red	x	0	1	1	1	1	1	5	0.83	+0.95	2
2.	Green	1	x	1	1	1	1	1	6	1.00	+2.58	1
3.	Blue	0	0	x	1	0	1	1	3	0.50	+0.50	4
4.	Yellow	0	0	0	x	0	0	0	0	0.00	-2.33	7
5.	Orange	0	0	1	1	x	1	1	4	0.67	+0.44	3
6.	Rose	0	0	1	1	0	x	0	2	0.33	-0.44	5
7.	Purple	0	0	0	0	0	1	x	1	0.17	-0.95	6

The preferences treated by the alternative method bring out almost the same results. The rank order given to the stimuli in both the treatments is the same. The rank given by the individual by means of preference is (1) green, (2) red, (3) orange, (4) blue, (5) rose, (6) purple, (7) yellow. The P's first preference is for green and last preference is for yellow. The proportion values of the saven colour stimuli are also the same in both the treatments. The values are, for green 1.00 (100.0), for red 0.83 (83.3), for orange 0.67 (66.5), for blue 0.50 (50.0), for rose 0.33(33.3), for purple 0.17 (16.6), and yellow 0.00 (0.0). The z values range from +2.58 to —2.33, with blue zero (0.0) value.

The p' (proportion) values for the preferences were obtained for the 7 colour stimuli in the second method by using the formula $\frac{C}{(N-1)}$, where C is the number of choices for a stimulus, N is the number of stimuli used in this experiment. One example in computing the p' value for a stimulus red is : $\frac{5}{(7-1)} = \frac{5}{6} = 0.83$. The same procedure was follow in computing the p' value for all the colour stimulti. The corresponding z values were obtained through the p' values from the conversion Table.

4. DISCUSSION

The individual mostly preferred the primary colours like red, green and blue but did not give the third preference to blue colour and gave third preference to organge. The primary colours red, green, blue and yellow are psychologically classified from visual experience. All other colours are complementary colours. The complementary colours can be obtained by mixing the primary colours in certain proportions. But the artists do not agree with the psychologists. The artist thinks that green colour is a mixture of yellow and blue colours. But from visual experience green is a unitary, pure colour. We can readily perceive orange, and also we see it more or less reddish or yellowish. Similarly, we can see in purple colour both red and blue colours. But we can see green as a single colour as we see red and blue colours. The primary colours red, green, yellow and blue may yield different colours. They may shade into various blends like organge, yellow-green, green-blue, and purple. Generally, red and yellow produce orange colour. The normal human beings who are not having eye defects or colour blindness can see the primary colours and prefer them.

The participant in this experiment had expressed his/her preference for the colours in the order of green, red, orange, blue, rose, purple and yellow. Though yellow is one of the primary colours the P in this experiment placed it in the seventh place. The P had given third place to orange colour. People may have certain personal experiences in preferring colours in their life. The artist frequently mixes blue and yellow pigments to get green. The reason is that when yellow and blue pigments are mixed the yellow pigment assimilates all wave lengths that are thrown back by the blue pigment. Though yellow colour has certain inherent characteristics, somehow it is not attractive for many people. Orange seems to be taking its place as it has the characteristic of yellow colour. In this experiment the P was more attracted by orange colour than yellow colour. The P has given 5th and 6th places to rose and purple colour as these two are not very much in normal usages.

Multi-dimensional Scaling Methods — Current Problem in Psychophysical Scaling

We have discussed various psychophysical scaling method in the preceding pages. One of the scaling problems that is becoming more important in these days is multidimensional psychophysics. This has yielded multidimensional scaling methods. This scaling method raises several issues which were not considered in other scaling methods. The basic scaling methods yielded several variations as in the case of psychophysical methods. One psychophysical scaling method in combination with other scaling methods give birth to several scaling methods.

In psychophysical methods and in scaling methods we have been using one dimension or attribute of the stimulus in the judgments. But a stimulus may have more than one dimension or attribute. In all the scaling methods we have been dealing with one psychological continuum or dimension at a time. Only one of the many attributes of the stimulus is judged. The respondent is made to isolate only one dimension of the stimulus as the experimenter is interested in it, though he can judge more than one dimension or attribute. It is also difficult for the respondent to react to more than one attribute and make accurate judgment on the physical characteristics of the stimulus. For example in the case of sound stimuli there are variations in the wave frequency. This causes variations in pitch and loudness. In an experiment the respondent may be asked to respond to either pitch or loudness and not to both as the experimenter is interested in only one dimension of the stimulus.

There may be some physical stimuli which are more intricate and whose physical dimensions are not well defined and it will not be possible for the respondent to make judgments on the psychological continuum. Certain quality cannot be explained with corresponding physical characteristics. Here arises the dimensional problem. The psychological continuum may be very unusual, because it does not yield any scope for clear judgment. It is not consisted of one single dimension, but more than two or three attributes. This cannot be studies by ordinary methods. Therefore, it becomes a problem. Stevens (1975) say that a one to one correspondence between sensation attribute and stimulus dimension occurs only rarely even in the case of very simple stimuli or objects. Guilford (1954) says that this problem arises mainly in affective judgments. According to him in a pleasant-unpleasant continuum the scale values obtained represent actually the variations of a composite continuum. Stevens (1975) says that this problem arises even with a very simple stimulus with certain geometric features such as the length of a straight line. A straight line may be perceived and judged apparently equal to stimulus length. The length of the line is one dimension. But the line has also other dimensions like, the thickness, colour, slanting and so on. These dimensions of the straight line may not evoke any responses or attributes, unless and until a specific instruction is given to the respondent. Not only in the case of affective values but all sensations invariably exhibit a multiplicity of dimensions, or attributes or aspects. This means that all stimuli themselves are multi-dimensional in nature. There may be variations in the dimensions, some being closely associated with stimulus. But, nature, in general has not decided and assigned between a stimulus dimension and attribute a correct one to one relationship. Therefore, we face the multidimensional problems in scaling. The basic problem underlying the scaling is that any object has many properties and hence separate scales should be devised for each property.

In all the scaling methods we have been measuring only one aspect of the stimulus at a time, because the attributes of the objects were mostly unidimensional. Since every object has more than one dimension or attribute it is important that specific dimension should be stated in the measurement. For example a sound, a patch of light, a straight line are multidimensional attributes. In sound, according to Stevens (1975) there are four unidimensional attributes such as density, volume, pitch and loudness. In the pitch of light there are several unidimensional attributes such as brightness, hue and saturation, duration, shape and location. Saturation refers to depth or strength of a colour in the light stimulus. A straight line, apart from its length, has attributes like thickness, colour and slop. Thus, every stimulus object is a multidimensional. There is no such thing as one dimensional stimulus object. All objects or stimuli are multidimensional.

The multidimensional scaling problem is also important in the assessment of opinions and attitudes. In the definable social attitudes the multidimensional potentiality is very much. In the measurement of social attitudes the multidimensional problem can be approached from the point of scale development and also determining the individual differences through the scales. Klingberg (1941) has applied a method called multidimensional rank order as one of his experimental procedures. In his method each stimulus in turn becomes a standard stimulus and other stimuli (n – 1) are compared with the standard in similarity and placed in rank order. Attneave (1950) for judging the interstimulus distances has used the method of multidimensional successive categories. The judgment was with regard to the degree of similarity. In his study he found that the inter-relationship in terms of distances among the stimuli did not yield any consistency in his results. Torgerson's (1951) experiment on colour was found to be successful. He used the multidimensional scaling method keeping hue as the constant and making changes in brightness and in chroma. This is a two dimensional situation. In another experiment he tried with a series of grey colour in different shades in one dimensional situation. In these experiments of multidimensional scaling method Torgerson was able to identify the correct number of dimensions.

Since the method was tried on many of the dimension of sensations of various types it was facing severe criticisms and the results that were arrived at also were dubious for a long time. However, the method was found useful mostly in the field of perception even though some objections were raised in the affecting fields. The basic problem of the multidimensional scaling method is that an attribute or a dimension is having a value. What is the corresponding value of a second attribute or dimension to the value of the first by keeping one constant and making changes in the other attributes in the experimental situation. The basic multidimensional problem was in existence for a long time and was arousing the attention of the experimental psychologists. The continuous efforts taken by Richardson (1938), Klingbery (1941), Attneave (1950), Torgerson (1951) and Stevens (1975) gave prominence to be multidimensional scaling method and how it has become relatively a new technique in the development of scaling procedures. In determining the common factors in the individual differences and in groups by the process of factor analysis it is in no way much different from the multidimensional scaling method.

PART - V

Psychological Experimentation and Research

Modern experimental psychology finds its foundation on the psychophysics and psychophysical methods founded by Gustav Fechner. The experimental procedures devised according to the psychophysical law are strictly followed in conducting the psychophysical experiments for obtaining the accurate absolute limen and the difference limen. The same procedures are followed with some modifications and improvements in psychological experiments and researches. The research and experimental methods evolved in this manner from the psychophysical methods are very much utilised in applied areas and in social situations.

The experimental designs, formulations of hypothesis, determining the effects of variables, selection of population, the sampling techniques, the procedure of collecting the data, the application of statistical methods to the psychological data are all formulated more scientifically for obtaining accurate results in the studies of behavioural phenomena. Modern psychological experiments and researches are put forth for solving individual and group problems and also aimed at solving certain crucial national and international problems.

18

AIM AND SCOPE OF PSYCHOLOGICAL EXPERIMENTATION

I. EXPERIMENTAL PSYCHOLOGY : NATURE AND SCOPE

Introduction

Knowledge comes to us from various sources and by various means. Any natural event may be pleasant or unpleasant to us. We may like some and dislike some. Some may perplex us and may arouse our curiosity. Why it occurs? Even though our sense organs are said to be the gateways of our knowledge it does not occur spontaneously without any effort. In knowledge getting activity man must strive, thrive and act and keep himself alert to events around him. Therefore, man, right from the very beginning of his intellectual and sensory awareness, has been very curious to know the complexities of the world and also the phenomena which he could not comprehend with his inadequate methods and procedures. But he has been fighting relentlessly with his ignorance and marching towards the horizon where he can see the dawn of wisdom and progress. In his efforts he has never failed to make use of science and technology. He also observed that the progress and maturity of a science are resting on the extensity and the utility of mathematics. Mathematics is not an empirical science, but a universal language that any science can make use of it with great accuracy. Scientists will have to make use of it with great accuracy. Scientists will have to make use of this language either for proving a hypothesis or disproving it. Psychologists like all other scientists have never hesitated to make use of mathematical approach for their own purpose. This has facilitated the student of Psychology of the present times to make his knowledge more accurate and objective. Experimental Psychology is one of the fields which has made rapid progress by the application of mathematical knowledge. Otherwise experimental psychology itself would be meaningless if the results were not stated in terms of postulates and theorems.

Experimental psychology has its origin when Gustav Theodor Fechner (1801–1887) began to study the relationship between the organism and the external world. In other words it is the outcome of the study of sensory process. The other topics added later on in this are, reaction time, attention, perception, emotion, learning and thinking. Traditionally experimental psychology was defined in terms of the study of sensory processes and psychophysical methods were used for this purpose.

Psychology has emerged as an independent branch of science about 1860. Around this time Fechner, Helmholtz (1821–1894) Wilhelm Wundt (1832–1920) followed scientific methods in their studies and explained the psychological events. Though there was scientific spirit, widely prevalent everywhere and experiments were conducted at smaller levels, it was only after the establishment of a Psychological laboratory by Wilhelm Wundt in 1879 at Leipzig that psychological experimentation at loboratory level received recognition. Sensory experiences were studied quantitatively by psychophysical methods. Weber's law was studied and modified by Fechner and this modification later on came to be known as Fechner's law. But the change of time also changed the concept of experimental psychology. So, the present trend is to define experimental psychology in terms of a study of scientific methodology in general and not in terms of specific area.

Nature of Experimental Psychology

At present experimental psychology is considered simply as a branch of psychology in which the experimental methods are mostly used. It has become a very broad discipline and thus it is a specialized way of getting information about psychological phenomena. The specialised way is having certain advantages by revealing the actual factors which are influencing psychological reactions. Experimental psychologists by using experimental methods can answer any question raised on cognitive, conative and affective process. For example, a question raised on memory, attention perception, likes and dislikes, prejudices can be answered. Therefore, we may state that whenever experimental method is applied on psychological events it is called experimental psychology. Experimental psychology may be also defined as the scientific methods applied for psychological phenomena. It is a scientific approach to verify a hypothesis set up on behavioural event, which may cause some problems. Therefore, a psychological experiment always starts on the formulation of a problem which is stated in the form a question.

What is An Experiment?

An experiment can be performed in any physical, biological behavioural or social sciences. Whenever we face a problem or an event which is beyond our understanding by ordinary means we try to understand it by inventing some procedure which can throw some new light on it. Therefore, we state that an experiment is a planned activity to get some new information. We cause some event to occur. The event may yield some new information. But how man has inferred this idea for experimentalism? It is a long history. Man inferred this idea only from the natural events. You can regress into the scientific inventions and discoveries of the modern world. It is an accidental observation of the natural events and attributing cause and effect theory. History of science would tell you hundreds of stories . How the steam engine was invented, the Automobile, the Aeroplane, your famous Computer, Television, the gravitational power of the earth etc.? Man is always shrewd and selfish and so he never failed to make use of it for his comforts and therefore experimentation cause existence. An experiment may be defined as the planned manipulation of variables for observational purposes in which one of the variables either independent or dependent variable is altered in a predetermined condition during the experiment. This definition may be applied to all the sciences. An experiment may be also defined as an event performed by manipulating more than one variable in a controlled situation with a purpose of verifying a hypothesis set on a problem.

A definition may also be stated in terms of method. While defining in terms of method, it is an application of the experimental method in which there is purposive manipulation of the independent variable.

At present experimental psychology is not representing the narrow old definition, confining itself into the laboratory. Psychologists do not want to miss the great advantage of applying experimental method for complex and socially meaningful subject matters.

Objectives of Experimental Psychology

Human behaviour is highly complex and mysterious. His words and actions do not go together. Every one thinks, feels and acts in his own way. There are no two people think alike and feel alike.

A uniform pattern of act cannot be expected in man and therefore we cannot predict it accurately. But by the way of manipulation, human behaviour psychologists hope that they can predict the behaviour.

Therefore, experimental psychology functions on three main objectives.

The main objective is to measure behaviour on psychological events. The second is to limit or control and predict the behaviour. The second objective would tell us the condition under which behaviour occurs. The third objective is to produce the desired behaviour at will.

Human behaviour is controlled in a variety of ways everyday. For example, you are all in a controlled situation waiting for the instruction from the teacher to carry out something which you have not done previously. After a few days you gain some experience. You carry out the work with little gesture from the teacher and you can also imagine the assignment your teacher is going to give you. The classical example we can quote is the well known experiments performed by Pavlov on dogs to study the phenomena of conditioning.

Modern life is becoming more and more highly conditioned. We, the University people are conditioned to the ringing of the University bell. The bell is the stimulus and the students' fast movement in the campus and entering the class room is the response. This is a conditioned behaviour. This means, we can predict what the teachers and the students are going to do on hearing the University bell. They do not respond to the Temple bells or Railway bells in the same manner. Therefore, human behaviour every where is controlled and predicted in the same manner.

Pychological Experimentation

Any scientific investigation can be started only after collecting certain amount of information and when the information do not provide us with right knowledge, then the knowledge existed previously is not sufficient to fulfil the needs. Therefore, fresh enquiry or experimentation should be started. Here, there is a problem and the formulation of a problem is important. This is going to guide us throughout the experiment or research. If the experiment is to be useful for the society we must put forth great amount of imagination and creative ability in this task. Therefore, we must be aware of the problems that exist and secondly, select and formulate a specific problem in which we are interested and the problem must be solvable. A problem is a question that is raised and should be answered with the tools available for us. There may be also unsolvable problems. They are concerned with supernatural matters.

All psychological experiments can be classified into certain types. Underwood (1957) classified them into two types as 'I-wonder-what-would happen' type and 'I-will-bed-this-would happen' type. In the case of first, Underwood meant whether the particular stimulus variable is capable of producing any response in an organism or in the experimental situation. This is to be verified by an experiment. The other type is for testing a hypothesis. The experimenter knows already the related factors of the problem and has also reviewed the relevant literature and also knows the possible effects of the independent variable and therefore asserts that this would happen.

Authors like McGuigan (1978) classify the experiments into three types as exploratory experiment, confirmatory experiment and crucial experiment. In the case of the first type the experimenter is having very little knowledge about the problem and he could not fulfil his curiosity by formulating a hypothesis of his own and verify it. At this stage the experimenter resorts to exploratory experiment. Here, he proceeds with the idea, "if I do this what would happen". In the second type the experimenter is able to formulate hypothesis and able to predict the events going to take place. The experimenter is able to predict the effects of independent variable upon the dependent variable. The crucial experiment is for testing the existing hypothesis to accept or to reject it.

Therefore, the aim of psychological experimentation is to formulate a theory or to verify the existing various hypotheses of the theories. The experimenter is motivated with the aim of finding out some answer for some basic problems, or to formulating any new theory or for verification of some existing theories.

Experimental psychology in recent times is applied to various areas like clinical, educational, counselling, industrial situations and to the study of various types of maladjustments and personality development.

The experiment has to be started to verify a hypothesis based upon a problem. Therefore, a problem is to be known. What a problem is? An experiment is to find out a solution to a problem. It is a question proposed for solution. The general meaning of problem is that any thing or a matter, that is difficult to deal with, solve or overcome. For example a problem child, a puzzle, a question etc. set for solution. Therefore, there is a problem and it is difficult to solve it with our limited knowledge and we will have to find out ways and means of solving it. This means, we will have to search for the solution. Having got the problem, the next step is the statement or formulation of the problem. The problem should be clear for scientific study. It should be explicit and concrete, solvable, limited in size and length.

Ideas for research come to you by reading scientific literature. Once if you have any basic idea for research, take the advantage of the valuable resources in literature, research experts, teachers or other faculty members. These people have deep knowledge of the area of your interest and provide information for you in the respective area. In this way you may become more specific about the topic of your study by the association of the experts.

There are several sources which may be giving lots of information to your topic. One easily available sources are the textbooks. The library card catalogue under the topic of the area of your interest, then the psychological abstracts, a journal that provides you with brief summaries of most of the articles published in psychological journals are some of the sources.

There are also other sources like the psychological review, psychological bulletin, annual review of psychology etc. The references given for the articles of your topic may provide further references. It is also better to ask for reprints of the articles published in scientific journals. To understand articles published in scientific journals is very difficult unless you have some background in reading such articles. It is better to gain some experience in reading and understanding articles published in the scientific journals.

Formulating of Hypothesis

While attempting to solve the problem the experimenter should generally state a tentative solution to the specific problem he has selected. This tentative solution is generally called a hypothesis. There are several definitions of hypothesis. Time to time, it is seen that psychologists define and redefine hypothesis. The hypothesis should be formulated on the basis of the problem before the experimentation commences. Therefore, a hypothesis is a testable statement of the relationship between the independent and the dependent variables. There can be more than two variables. A hypothesis may be also stated as the suggested explanation for a group of facts or phenomena either accepted as a basis for further verification or accepted as likely to be true. It is an assumption used in an argument. According to *Oxford Dictionary* : It is a particular case of a general proposition. A proposition or principle put forth or stated merely as a basis for reasoning or argument or as a premise, from which drawn a conclusion. It is also stated as the supposition or conjuncture put forth to account for known facts. It is a provisional supposition which accounts for known facts, and serves as a starting point for further investigation by which it may be proved or disproved. It is something assumed to be true without proof. Hence a hypothesis is a mere assumption or a guess.

There can be even more than one hypothesis. The hypothesis is a potential solution. It may yield a positive solution or negative solution. The solution is going to be only a guess and it need not be correct. This is an empirical hypothesis. On the basis of the hypothesis the experimenter tries to verify whether the hypothesis is having the probability of being true or false. So the next step is to collect data. Data can be collected by using several methods, but, here we are using the experimental method. This method is supposed to be very powerful one because of its technique.

A hypothesis looks forward for something new and states the same. It is a proposition which can be put forth to a test to ascertain its real position or validity. It may prove whether it is correct or not. Whatever the result we may get, the outcome is an answer of some kind to a question put forth in the form of a hypothesis. Thus a hypothesis leads to an empirical test in a systematic manner.

A hypothesis is not only looking forward for an empirical testing and determining its validity but also for constituting a theory. On the basis of the experimental findings or facts obtained from the empirical study the theory is built. Therefore the relationship between the hypothesis and the theory is very close. A theory brings out logical relationship between facts. A theory may permit for the formulation of additional hypothesis.

A hypothesis should have two aspects. They are referred to an antecedent condition and consequent condition. This may, in other words, be stated as cause and effect. This means a hypothesis should propose a relationship between two variables. It should have a potential empirical relation between two variables. These two may be independent and dependent variables. It means that if 'X' is present then 'Y' also is present or if 'X' occurs in a situation then 'Y' also occurs in the situation.

Types of Hypotheses

Hypotheses are classified in several ways. According to McGuigan (1978) there are two types of hypotheses. They are universal hypotheses and existential hypotheses.

According to universal hypothesis the relationship that is in discussion, is held common for all the variables stated at all the time and at all the places. The time and place do not affect the relationship.

The existential hypothesis refers to specific case. According to this, it is asserted that the relationship stated in the hypothesis is true at least in the case of one particular case or subject.

There is another way of classifying the hypothesis, as positive hypothesis and negative hypothesis. Kerlinger (1965) who classified the hyposthesis in this way state that a hypothesis may be stated in a positive way. That is, the relationship between two variables in the experimental situation is positive. For example, more number of trials in a learning situation increase the efficiency in learning. Similarly, the negative hypothesis, the relationship between two experimental variables is stated in a negative way. For example, students who are taking part in extra curricular activities are not progressing well in their studies like students who are not taking part in it. These hypotheses may be stated as empirical hypothesis. Empirical hypothesis states that there is difference between two groups. It states that there is empirical relationship between tow variables without distinguishing anything. A hypothesis is empirical means that it directly refers to the result that we can obtain from the experiment. An experiment is conducted to test the empirical relationship between variables.

Null Hypothesis

A hypothesis that is more useful in experimental situation is the null hypothesis. The hypothesis is also stated as two tail test. Many of the experimenters use null hypothesis for designing and conducting experiments. A null hypothesis predicts that no difference between subjects will exist. For example, students who do not take part in extra curricular activities are not in any way more efficient in their studies than the students who spend more time in extra curricular activities. The null hypothesis predicts no difference between these two groups of students in their academic performances. Accordingly, the hypothesis may be rejected if either group of students differ significantly in their efficiency from the other group. Sometimes, the prediction of no difference or difference may be superfluous. Therefore, it has to be established statistically. The difference between the two groups should be established significantly. A statistics used to test this is the 't' test or critical ratio in which the mean scores of the two groups are very important. The 't' test is to decide whether the difference between the two groups is the result of random fluctuation or sampling error or whether the difference is really existing.

If a hypothesis is carefully verified then it becomes a law or theory. If a hypothesis is rejected or accepted and if the results of other investigators confirm the earlier results then the hypothesis becomes a law. If a hypothesis is rejected once that does not mean that a hypothesis cannot become a law. The rejection is only a suggestion for the revision or reformulation of the hypothesis.

The null hypothesis is generally used in most of the Psychological experiments. The term null hypothesis was first used by Sir Ronald Fisher. This was first used by physicists in their experiments. The null hypothesis states that there is no difference between the mean scores of the two groups ($M1 - M2 = 0$, $X1 - X2 = 0$) on the dependent variables. The important point involved in this is, comparing the two groups' mean scores of the dependent variable. The null hypothesis is also called a 'statistical hypothesis' and it is set up for the purpose of disproving it.

Experimental and Control Groups

An experiment involves two groups of people. The people who cooperate with the experimenter and allow themselves for studying their behaviour and to collect data are called participants. Traditionally, they are called subjects. The term participants is more apt as it is socially more desirable. While using the term 'subjects' there is a status difference between the experimenter and the subject (like master and servant). Therefore, the American Psychological Association has suggested the word participants. The participants should be put into two groups, one as the experimental group and the other as the control group. Any number of persons can be in a group, but it should be done randomly. The experimental group receives experimental treatment, that is, what the value the experimenter wishes to study in a group while the control group receives normal treatment or used as a standard. This requires certain explanation.

Suppose, for example, the experimenter wants to study the effect of salt pills on fatigue. The problem is whether salt pills could reduce the fatigue on industrial employees? This is in the form of a question. A hypothesis is formulated like this. 'Salt pills can reduce fatigue effect on industrial employees'. To verify this hypothesis and to answer the problem, two groups of people were chosen, one as the experimental group and the other as the control group. The experimental group is administered with salt pills when the employees were engaged in work. They were asked to swallow some salt pills, whereas the people in the control groups were not given the salt pills. But both the groups are engaged in the same type of industrial work. After some hours of work the efficiency of the performance of the two groups was tested. If there is any difference in the efficiency or in the production between the experimental group and the control group it is due to the effect of the salt pills. The assumption or hypothesis is that the experimental group which has taken salt pills is supposed to have increased the production. If there is any increase in production then the salt pills had effect on fatigue of the industrial employees. The salt pills have made some physiological changes in the body and thereby change in the behaviour of the employees. But there was no change of any type in the case of the contract group which has not taken the salt pills.

The terms experimental group and control group are generally employed in psychology, in some of the social sciences and in related sciences. They are applicable to separate groups of an experiment, designed with a single independent variable. In such experiments one group of subjects is treated without the influence of the independent variable which is called the control group. The other group which is put under the influence of the independent variable is known as the experimental group. In this way an experiment involving the administration of a drug to a group and non-administration of the same drug to another group may be designed, in which the former group is called the experimental group and the latter is called the control group. If the experimental groups and the control groups are treated in the same way except with regard to the independent variable (drug), then any difference between the two groups on the dependent variable (effect) is ascribed to the independent variable (drug).

One important point the experimenter should bear in mind is that the assignment of participants to the groups should be made in such a way that the groups should be almost equivalent at the start of the experiment. This can be done by randomization. In the next step, the experimenter should administer an experimental treatment to one of the groups. What the experimenter wishes to evaluate is called the experimental treatment and it is administered to the experimental group and the other group is the control group. The control group is free from the experimental treatment and receives normal or standard treatment.

Variables

In the earlier section we made mention about variables, particularly independent variable and dependent variable—the two important components of an experiment. Variable is an adjectival term, the general meaning of which is "liable or capable of change". Liable or capable of change of what? It is capable of change of behaviour, opinions, attitudes, reactions, emotions etc. The term is also applied in other areas like mathematics, electricity, astronomy and in other sciences. Therefore, the concept variable is defined with reference to psychological experimentation. The term variable refers to a characteristic or property or measurement that is likely to change. According to McGuigan (1978): "a variable is anything that can change in value. It is a quality that can exhibit differences in value, usually in magnitude or strength". Thorndike (1970) says that anything that exists in some quantity is a variable. Postman and Egan (1949) state: "a variable is a characteristic or attribute that can take on a number of values". Accordingly to D'Amato (1970): "What is meant by the term variables, namely, any measurable, attribute of objects, things or beings". Therefore, we may state that a variable is a characteristic or quality that may be stated in quantitative terms. It may be also defined as any aspect of an event or function that by its nature or pressure changes some other event or function which the experimenter wishes to study.

Types of variables

Variables are classified in a number of ways. The general classification of the variables are independent variables, dependent variables and relevant variables. But according to D'Amato both the independent and dependent variables are interdependent and neither of them can identify positively in the absence of the other.

All variables are not having measurable attributes. Such variables are called qualitative variables. For example, the inclusion of the variables such as race, religion, sex, community etc., in the experiment do not yield quantitative measures. Therefore, they are qualitative variables.

While classifying the variable in quantitative and qualitative, D'Amato (1970) states that the quantitative variables can be separated into continuous variables and discrete variables.

Thus, we have the independent variables, dependent variables, relevant variables, quantitative variables, qualitative variables, continuous variables and discrete variables.

Authors like McGuigan (1978) classify the variables into two categories, the first being the independent variables which include response variables, stimulus variables and organismic and mediating variables and the other dependent variables.

Hull and Spence have stated the existence of intervening variables in their theory of instrumental conditioning. They determine performance in instrumental conditioning.

But the most commonly discussed variables in psychological experimentations or researches are the independent variables and the dependent variables. All other variables are taken into consideration in certain specific experiments if the influence of such variables are realized.

Independent Variables

An independent variable may be defined as some object or event that an experimenter can introduce or administer in the experimental situation and vary it as he wishes. It may be also stated as an aspect of the environment that is experimentally investigated for the purpose of varying the hypothesis.

A dependent variable is an event or an aspect of behaviour that the experimenter observes with a purpose of noting the changes if any, that might have occurred as a result of the introduction of the independent variable. The dependent variable is the variable whose value is determined by the value of independent variable.

A variable is a quality that can show some differences in values generally, in magnitude. The difference is stated always in terms of numerical values. But psychological variables may change from time to time and from organism to organism. This change is due to environmental conditions. If the independent variable made any change in the dependent variable, then the experimenter usually will try to find out the nature of relationship between the two variables. This relationship is generally called functional relationship. This shows that there is predictive relationship between the two variables. One is independent variable which is also called predictive variable or predictor and the other variable is dependent variable which is also called the predicted variable. Factor is another term used to indicate the independent variable. The independent variable in its simplest sense may be called as stimulus variable.

Dependent Variable

A dependent variable is an aspect of behaviour. In its simplest form it is the response of the organism which the experimenter measures in an experiment. In an experiment one of the two variables is controlled. This controlled variable is dependent variable. The response may be anything. It may be the amout of time the participant has taken to memorise a passage or number of times he has repeated the passage for memorising or number of items he answered correctly. It is to be noted that whether the independent variable is exerting any effect or not, it is a value for the dependent variable. It is assumed that the value of the dependent variable is depending upon the value of the independent variable. Therefore, while conducting an experiment the experimenter should carefully watch whether the independent variable elicit any change in the dependent variable. But it should also be noted that there may be some change in the dependent variable even without any change in the independent variable. This is due to some extraneous variable. The experimenter should have only one interest. That is to find out the relationship between the independent variable and the dependent variable. If the experimenter allows other variables to have influence in the experiment then his experiment is going to be corrupt or impure. These variables are called extraneous variables. Particularly in psychological experiments, the experimenter should see that at the time of conducting experiment, no other variable from the experimental situation is interfering into his results. For example, even the movements of some persons or animals (visual stimulus) and voices (auditory stimuli) of other people in the situation may affect the responses of the participants of the experimental group.

Relevant Variables

In an experimental situation there are certain variables other than independent variable have influence upon the dependent variable. Such variables are called relevant variables. These variables have clear recognizable effect upon the dependent variables. The variables that have no recognizable effect upon the independent variable are called irrelevant variables. Mention has been made about the relevant variables earlier.

There are three kinds of relevant variables which are to be controlled in every psychological experimentation. They are :

1. *Subject relevant variables :* These variables are from the subject's characteristics of the experiment. The subject's motivation or interest may interfere in the experiment.

2. *Situational relevant variables :* These variables refer to all environmental variables interfering in the experimental situation. They are mainly concerned with the experimental tasks in which the subject is involved. The variable include all physical aspects of the experimental situation, for example light, noise, temperature, humidity and the time of the day, that is, whether it is forenoon or afternoon or night.

3. *The sequence relevant variables :* These variables refer to the situation in which the subject is tested under two or more conditions. For example the practice effect may be very little in the beginning, but will have more effect in the end. So also the fatigue effect is not experienced by the subject during first few trials but after some trials the effect may be severe.

Control of Variables

These relevant variables are to be controlled in the experimental situation. Otherwise the experimental results may become dubious. In psychological experimentation rarely the relevant variables are held constant. Therefore, the variables that affect the dependent variables should be controlled. The methods applied, generally are three. They are (1) matching techniques, (2) randomization, and (3) counter-balancing.

By applying the matching techniques the experimenter is able to have full control of the relevant variable in a particular experiment conducted by him. In the randomizing technique the relevant variable might not be well equated in an experiment. Because there are chance fluctuations if the number of subjects involved in the experiment is small. But if the subjects are many then there is good equalization. The third one, counter-balancing technique can provide control in either way. In psychophysical experiments the counter balancing technique is generally employed to avoid the constant errors. The independent variables are presented always in counterbalancing manner. This becomes one of the experimental procedures.

The simplest method of controlling the influence of variables which affect the dependent variables is to remove them from experimental situation. For example, if light and sound affect the dependent variable, then the experimenter can have a dark room and sound proof for eliminating light and sound.

Experimental Design

The experimental design is explained in various ways. The simplest way of explaining an experimental design is that it is a plan for research, assigning subjects and manipulating one or two independent variables. Planning involves also controlling the influence of relevant or extraneous variables in the dependent variable. The aim of the experimental design is to test a hypothesis formulated by the experimenter and to reveal the relationship between the variables. If we know the relationship between variables we can predict the events and we can also improve our prediction in future events. In short, experimental design has two important objectives: (1) it provides answer to experimental questions, (2) it controls the variances. According to Kerlinger (1965) experimental designs tell us, what observations are to be made. How to make them and how to make quantitative analyses.

Experimental psychologists classify experimental designs in a variety ways or types. These different types depend on such variables as what the experimenter considers as logically sound and what dimensions of design he thinks as very important and what can be communicated easily.

McGuigan (1978) has stated that even though a number of designs are available for the experimenter the "two-groups" design is basic in psychology which forms a sound foundation for the more complex and difficult designs. Therefore, according to him the "two groups" design may be referred to as the "two-randomized-group-design". This design requires that the participants are to be assigned to each group in a random fashion. The assumption in the case of two-randomized-groups design is that the chance of assigning the participants will result in two equal groups. But the basic logic of all experimental designs is the same. That is to start with groups that are essentially equal in all characteristics, than giving the experimental treatment to one group only and not to the other and noting down the changes on the dependent variable. If the two groups yielded equal mean scores on the dependent variable before the experimental treatment and if the two groups yielded a significant difference in the mean scores on the dependent variable after the experimental treatment and if the extraneous variables were properly controlled, then the difference between the means is due to the experimental treatment. Thus McGuigan classified the types of designs as between-groups design and within-groups design. The between-groups design are:

1. Two-randomized group design.
2. Two-matched-group design.
3. More than two-randomized-groups-design.
4. Factorial design.

In between-groups designs, we are computing the mean difference between groups and then assess the effect of varying the independent variable. McGuigan (1978) also suggests an alternative type of design which he called as within groups design. In within groups design two or more values of the independent variables are used in turn on the same participants. For each independent variable the participant's dependent variable value (response) is obtained under each value of independent variable. Then comparisons of the values of dependent variable, under different experimental treatments of the effects of varying indepentent variable, are made and assessed. In the case of between groups design, since they have been treated differently the values of dependent variable are compared between groups. But in the case of within-groups design, since the same participants are treated differently in the experimental situations at different times, their different scores are treated differently as the function of different experimental treatments. Most of the psychophysical experiments and memory experiments are good examples for within-groups design experiments.

According to Kerlinger (1965) experimental designs can be classified into two categories. He calls them as poor designs and good designs. The poor experimental designs are :

a. Simple group design.
b. Single group design-pre-post-test.
c. Stimulated pre-post test.
d. Two groups design-without control.

The good designs are :

i. Explicit, group control : group randomized subject.
ii. Multi-group randomized subjects.
iii. Multivariate designs.
iv. Randomized matched designs.
v. Matched pre-post-control group designs.
vi. Pre-post different experimental group, control group designs.
vii. Three group experimental group : control group designs.

There are several experimental psychologists who have classified the experimental designs into various types. D'Amato brought the experimental designs into two categories. They are :

1. Single group or within subjects designs.
2. Separate groups or between subjects designs.

Matheson (1971) and others have classified the experimental designs under two types as naturalistic research designs and experimental research designs. Under the type of naturalistic research designs there are four designs. They are :

1. Case studies.
2. Natural environmental studies or field studies.
3. Contrived natural environmental studies.
4. Correlational studies.

Under the type of experimental research designs there are three designs. They are :

1. One-group designs.
2. Two–group design.
3. Multiple treatment designs.

Thus there are number of designs available to the experimenter. It is better to discuss a few important designs which may be very much useful for the experimentation. The two-groups design is basic and widely used in psychological experimentation. The two-groups design is also referred to as two randomized groups design. The experimenter uses one independent variable which can be varied in two ways so as to have two conditions. Thus, he gets two kind of data and can be treated in two different ways. The experimenter expects that the two conditions should yield significant effect upon the dependent variable. The experimenters will have to verify his hypothesis or find out answer for his experimental question only in a population. Therefore he has to define a population and make a statement.

Sample and Sampling Techniques

From the population he has to select a random sample of participants for his experiment. The population may be the student population or the general population. It will not be possible for experimenter to study or to conduct an experiment on the whole student population or on the whole general population. Therefore, he will have to select a sample from the particular population in which he is conducting the study. A sample is a part taken as representative of a whole thing or group or population. A sample is also stated as a subset of observation from a population. Sample generally means 'specimen' from a product or population. Statistically, it is also called sampling which means a set of individuals or items selected at random from a population and analysed to yield estimates of, and to test the hypothesis about the parameters of the population. Experimentally, sampling means the process of selecting sample. It is the technique used for selecting participants for the study. Sampling is an elaborate process and the sample is chosen or selected in advance which may be consists of a few hundred or a few thousand people who are representative of a very large population. The sample may be proportionally based upon certain factors like age, sex, education, occupation, income etc., the same as in the large population.

There are several sampling techniques. We can discuss here two kinds of sampling techniques. They are : (1) random and systematic sampling and (2) stratified sampling.

(i) *Random Sampling*

Random means having any definite plan or having no pre-arranged order. Random sampling is a process of sampling carried out so that each member of the population has an equal probability of being selected. Therefore, when random sampling is used, all members of the population under consideration have an equal chance of being chosen.

Random sampling is made either without replacement or with replacement. In random sampling without replacement a participant cannot be chosen twice. Most of the psychological experiments are done without replacement. Once if a person is chosen and used there is no use of making use of him again. Because after the first choice there may be some changes in him. For example, he might have acquired some knowledge about the test. Therefore, he should not be used again. But in this sampling method the chance of a particular person's being selected varies with the number of persons already chosen. For example, if the experimenter starts with 30 persons and selects one, then the chance of any of the remaining persons being chosen next is 1 to 29 and not 1 in 30.

In random sampling with replacement once a participant is chosen he is replaced in the total population again and he is having the probability of being selected as any other persons for future sampling. Because one's selection at a given time has influence on future selections. Therefore, he is considered as 1 in 30 and not 1 in 29. Thus a random sample of the population of a town would be made if the town had a population of one lakh and the chance of any one person's being selected is 1 in 1 lakh.

If an investigator wants to test as a random sample of a college population he must bear in mind that each student must have an equal opportunity of being selected. He cannot do this by standing in front of the college library as most of the students go to library everyday. But all the students of the college do not pass through library equally often. In such case if the sampling is collected it would be biased sample. The sample would be in favour of those students who pass by the college library. Therefore, there are several selection procedures of selecting a random sample. One is the use of telephone directory or the list of college students. However, the use of telephone directory becomes a biased sample as it would be in favour of persons who have telephones unless the target population itself is telephone holders. Therefore, to avoid such bias in sampling the systematic sampling is preferred.

(ii) *Systematic Sampling*

This sampling procedure is having little variation from the random sampling. An investigator wants to use 20 percent of the students of a college having 4000 students on the roll for his study. In this case, it is better that he should use a table of random numbers. The first step is to use the formula $\frac{N}{n} = K$, where N is the total number of population , n is the number of students to be selected and K is the sampling interval.

In the case of the example stated here, N = 4000, 20 percent of the population or the number to be selected is n = 800 and the sampling interval is K = 5. Applying the formula on the data 4000 ÷ 800 = 5, is the sample interval. The next step is to choose an arbitrary point, a number between 1 and 800 . For example, the number is 15 (X) . Then the fifteenth person on the list is to be chosen. The sample interval is 5. Then the next step is to add 5 to 15 to determine the next participant. That is, (X + K) 15+5 = 20, the student number 20 is chosen from the total population. Then the next student to be chosen is 15 + 2K = 15 + 10 = 25. The third is 15 + 3K = 15 + 15 = 30. Thus from the total population list the students having the numbers 20, 25, and 30 are selected. This procedure should be continued till all the 800 students for the sample are selected. It is always better to have the names arranged in an alphabetical order.

(iii) *Stratified Sampling*

It is felt by some experimenters that the process of randomization is not making sure that they get a representative sample of the whole population. They wish to have their sample, a correct composition of the population. They wanted to make sure that various parts of the country, political opinions are also represented in their sample in a proportion. This is like doing the same thing with age, sex, race and political affiliation etc. Generally, randomization is used within these imposed limits. Therefore, these samples are placing constraints on randomness. If one wishes to have his samples to assure that it is representative, he should use a rational procedure in the sample selection. That rational procedure is called stratified sampling. In stratified sampling procedure care is taken to see that certain important elements are proportionally present in the sample as those in the population. For example, in selecting a sample from a human population for an experiment the experimenter should see to it that the proportion of male and female subjects are the same as the proportion of them found in the whole population. If the population consists of different ethnic groups the experimenter should assure that his sample also consists of the same proportion of different ethnic groups as in the whole population.

Further, if the experimenter's target group is student population then he should see to it that his sample consists of the same proportion of students studying in various courses in the college population as a whole. A stratified sample uses several random samples, representing some characteristics within the total sample. If the experimenter wishes to have his sub-samples on the basis of sex, class, age, religion then he should plan to have his sub-samples the same proportion as the total college population in every category or sub-population. If the sub-sample categories have been selected by choosing participants in this way then every category is selected in accordance with its true proportion within the total population. This may be also stated as proportionate stratified sample. But it is not always possible to have proportionate stratified sampling as certain categories are very difficult to use in proportionate selection. Then the disproportionate sample may occur in such cases. If the stratified sampling is collected carefully with the small number of participants, then the result of which may be quite similar to the result of the total population. The result of a small group may be used for generalization. The stratified sample is having certain advantages over the random sampling. Attention may be given in this to reduce errors by using unbiased questionnaires. It also guards against the biasing that occurs normally under random sampling.

Two Randomized-groups Design

This experimental design needs two groups. In our example stated earlier 800 participants were selected randomly from a college population of 4000. Those 800 participants should go into two groups. Let us assume that we will study two conditions in one experiment. Since each group is to be assigned to a condition, the group should be separated into two. Therefore, the 800 students form into two groups, each having 400 students. This may be done by a random method. A table of random numbers may be used again here. But we may use a different method. Let us write the name of each student on a separate slip of paper and place all 800 slips of paper in a card board box. Then, we may decide that the first name drawn is assigned to first group, the second name drawn to the second group, the third name to the first group, the fourth to second, so on.

In this way we have two groups, each with 400 participants. Among the two, one will be the experimental group and the other will be the control group. This may be decided by flipping of a coin assigning one side for each group. Now the participants are randomly assigned to two groups and therefore it is called *two-randomized-groups design.*

Now, there is every reason to believe that these two groups are essentially equal in all respects as the process of randomization is properly carried out in selecting the samples and dividing them into two groups. An important basic assumption is made in any type of experimental design. It is that the mean scores of the groups do not show any significant variation in the beginning of the experiment. These two groups in a two group design are equal in all respects.

In an experiment of a two groups design, the independent variables with two values may be administered on the two groups. The experimental group is administered with some positive value of the independent variable while the control group with zero value in the independent variable. Then the scores of all the participants as observed in the dependent variables treated statistically and the mean scores are compared. If the mean scores difference between the two groups were found to be statistically significant then it may be stated that the difference is due to the variation of the independent variable. In other words, the positive value of the independent variable had effect upon the dependent variable more than the effect the zero value of the independent value had upon the dependent variable. Therefore, it may be conclude that the two different (experimental and control) independent variables had different effects upon the dependent variable in such a way that the difference produced by the variables is very much significant.

Analysis of the Data and Testing the Hypothesis

The experiment was conducted on a two-randomized group and the data were collected from both the groups on the dependent variable or on the respondent variable. Now the next step is to verify the hypothesis. The assumption is that the experimental group had better effect upon the dependent variable than the control group and thus the experimental group should have scored higher than the control group in a test. This can be tested by computing the mean scores for both the groups. Suppose, for example in an experiment the mean score of the experimental group is 65 and that of the control group is 50. This shows that the experimental group had scored higher than the control group in the test. The difference in the mean score between the two groups is 15. Can we say whether it is a real difference or the difference is due to the testing error or it is a fluctuation? It is not possible to say unless it is tested with a statistical treatment called the 't' test. The primary data required for this test is the mean scores of the two groups and the number of participants.

One important point the experimenter should bear in mind is that the 't' test is applied only when the experimental and the control participants were below 30. If the participants were more than 30 then the statistical treatment to test the hypothesis is the 'critical ratio' (C-ratio). Therefore, the 't' test is applied to the data obtained from small groups. The equation is :

$$t = \frac{X_1 - X_2}{\sqrt{\left[\frac{SS_1 + SS_2}{(n_1 - 1) + (n_2 - 1)}\right]\left[\frac{1}{n_1} + \frac{1}{n_2}\right]}}$$

Here X_1 is the mean scores of the experimental group (first).
X_2 is the mean score of the control group (second).
SS_1 is the sum of squares of the first group.
SS_2 is the sum of squares of the second group.
n_1 is the number of participants in the first group.
n_2 is the number of participants in the second group.

The formula to compute a mean is $\overline{X} = \frac{\Sigma X}{n}$

The sum of the scores of the participants is divided by n.

The formula to compute the SS is : $SS = \Sigma X^2 - \frac{(\Sigma X)^2}{n}$

Let us apply this equation to an experimental data and verify a hypothesis. Suppose, for example in a small class there were 12 students. They were the students of 6th standard and they were randomly divided into two groups and in each group there were 6 students. A few days before the commencement of examination, the first group, supposed to be the experimental group was given two model tests in arithmetics. The model tests were quite similar to the actual examination. The other group, the control group was not given any model test. The experimental and control groups were decided by flipping of a coin. The examination was conducted after a few days. The hypothesis was that there is no difference in the mean scores between the two groups of students in the examination. The marks of the two groups were released :

Students : Group 1 : Experimental			**Students : Group 2 : Control**		
1	X_1	X_1^2		X_2	X_2^2
1	62	3844	7	50	2500
2	64	4096	8	44	1936
3	64	4096	9	46	2116
4	60	3600	10	48	2304
5	66	4356	11	42	1764
6	68	4624	12	40	1600
ΣX_1 384		ΣX^2_1 24616		ΣX_1 270	ΣX^2_2 12220

The mean of the first group is : $60 + 62 + 64 + 60 + 66 + 68 = \frac{384}{6} : 64.00$

The mean of the second group is : $50 + 44 + 56 + 48 + 42 + 40 = \frac{270}{6} : 45.00$

$$\overline{X}_1 = 64.00, \quad \overline{X}_2 = 45.00$$

$$SS_1 = \Sigma X_1^2 - \frac{(\Sigma X)^2}{N_1} = 24616 - \frac{(384)^2}{6} = \frac{14756}{6} = 24576$$

$$= 24616 - 24576 = 40$$

$$SS_2 = \Sigma X_2^2 - \frac{(\Sigma X)^2}{N_2} = 12220 - \frac{(270)^2}{6} = \frac{72900}{6} = 12150$$

$$= 12220 - 12150 = 70$$

$$\bar{X}_1 = 64, \quad \bar{X}_2 = 45$$

$$N_1 = 6, \quad N_2 = 6$$

$$SS_1 = 40, \quad SS_2 = 70$$

Applying the formula to the data :

$$t = \frac{64-45}{\sqrt{\left[\frac{40+70}{(6-1)+(6-1)}\right]\left[\frac{1}{6}+\frac{1}{6}\right]}}$$

Let us go through the steps to obtain the 't' value :

1. The mean difference betwen the groups 1 and 2 : $64-45=19$
2. The sum of squares of group 1 and 2 : $SS_1 + SS_2 = 40 + 70 = 110$
3. Work out the n_1 : $n-1=6-1=5$
4. Work out the n_2 : $n-1=6-1=5$
5. Sum up : $\frac{1}{n_1}+\frac{1}{n_2}=\frac{1}{5}+\frac{1}{5}=\frac{5}{25}+\frac{5}{25}=\frac{10}{25}$

The next step is : $t=\dfrac{19}{\sqrt{\left(\frac{110}{5+5}\right)\left(\frac{10}{25}\right)}}$

The next Stage is : $t=\dfrac{19}{\sqrt{(11)(.4)}}=\dfrac{19}{\sqrt{4.4}}=\dfrac{19}{2.097}$

Therefore $t=\dfrac{19}{2.097}=9.06$

The computation of the 't' is very simple. But mistakes may likely take place if careful attention is not paid in the computation. Now, we must see whether the mean score difference between the two groups is real or spurious. The 't' test is a criterion to judge this assumption. The 't' may be small or very small or large. Whether it is small or large it may determine the level of differernce between the means of the two groups. To test this one must make use of the Table IV of Fisher. This table may be found in every statistic book under the heading of 'Table of t'. The Degrees of freedom (df) is found vertically (column) and the P horizontally (row).

Here the N is $n_1 + n_2 = 12 = 6 + 6$
The df is : $12 - 2 = 10$.

In our example the t value is 9.06, and the df is 10. Now from the table we will have to find out the P value associated with the df(10) and the t value (9.06). Keeping the finger on 10 go across the P values on the right. On the table the P values run like this against the df 10, 0.129,0.260, 0.397, 0.542, 0.700, 0.879, 1.093, 1.372, 1.812, 2.228 etc. We will have to go across this line reading the values until the value comes close to our t value 9.06. But the largest value in the row of the table is 3.169 only and this we must take as the nearest value. The P is associated with 0.01. This means the t value 9.06 is greater than the table value 3.169 and therefore is significant with 0.01 level. The mean difference between the two groups is not spurious, or due to sampling error, but real difference. In other words, if this experiment is conducted for 100 times there is only one chance of being no difference between the two groups. On all other times (99 times) difference between the two groups in the mean scores occurs. Therefore, the null hypothesis is rejected in this case. This shows that the independent variable has effected some influence on the dependent variable and the two groups have received different values from the independent variable. Therefore, the empirical hypothesis is confirmed.

The null hypothesis for this experiment is : There is no difference in the arithmetic examination marks between the students who have taken the model tests and those who have not taken the model tests.

The empirical hypothesis for this experiment is : While testing the arithmetic examination marks of the students who have taken the model tests and those who have not taken the model test, the students who have taken the model test get high marks in the examination.

A scientific study should have report. It is also called evidence report which is the summary of the results of the investigation. In other words, it is the statement concisely stated what was found in the investigation. It is intended to verify the hypothesis, whether it is true or false. It should be also noted that every experimental study in the laboratory situation is to find solution to a problem, and to verify a hypothesis. Therefore, every experimental data may be taken as the new data and an evidence report can be prepared. But the method, the experimenter has used to collect data might have been any method. Since, we are dealing with experimental psychology it is important to stress in experimental methods. The reason for stating this is that there are also non-experimental methods to collect data. For example the case history method or life history method or clinical method is traditionally used to deal with the client's emotional, educational and vocational problem.

There are certain social sciences, for example, sociology and anthropology have little chance for experimental methods. Since they deal with cultural development and social institutions they mainly depend upon non-experimental methods. Psychological experimentation does not depend upon natural events to occur as they are not adequate and necessary for observation. Further the experimenter cannot manipulate the independent variable in non-experimental methods and also cannot control the extraneous variable — unlike the experimental methods. The data in the experimental methods are more reliable than the data of non-experimental method. But there are also criticisms on the experimental method. Experiments conducted in the laboratory do not always yield events naturally. Events are made to occur. Therefore, some are of the view that experiments in laboratories also have certain limitations.

However, the experimental results are subjected to verification, is even if the experiment repeated on the same situation any number of times. Whatever the individual's reaction might be in an experiment, in the laboratory situation many of the extraneous variables which might be having influence in the dependent variable or result can be controlled. Therefore, an experiment should be planned whether the type of experiment is of exploratory or confirmatory. This depends upon the state of knowledge and the problem to be dealt with.

If the knowledge or information on the particular problem is inadequate or insufficient then exploratory experiment may be planned. Here it will not be possible to formulate an explicit hypothesis that such and such event or result is going to occur. It is just a curiousity to see what is going to happen. The data, the experimenter collects, are not based upon any guess. He just collects whatever occurs. But still a hypothesis can be formulated and it will not be a formal or systematic hypothesis. One advantage in the exploratory experiment is that we can discover the variables having influence in the experiment.

Instead, the confirmatory experiment can be designed with well defined and clear cut hypothesis and data may be collected quite relevant to the problem. The confirmatory experiment will prove whether the given independent variable is having any effect in the dependent variable or not. The effect of the variable can be also assessed quantitatively.

Social scientists or psychologists find sometimes that their experimental results were yielding more than what they have expected or planned and also failing to yield what they have planned and expected. This may take place in both exploratory experiments and also in confirmatory experiments.

A group of school students in a class were not performing their examinations constantly, even though they were also receiving the coaching from the same teacher. An intelligence test was conducted for all the students of the class and a survey of socio-econoic-status was also conducted on all of them. It was found that there was no difference in the 1.Q between the students who performed well in all the examinations and who have not performed well. Further, both the category of students belonged to the same socio-economic status. This means that intelligence and socio-economic status were not the real cause of one section of students' poor performance in the examination. They were found equal with other students in all other respects. Therefore, there must be some other variable interfering with their performance. An on the spot study was made on all the students and it was found that the boys who were making poor performance in the examinations were living in the Railway Quarters which were very close to a big Railway junction. There were quite number of trains going and coming with horrible noise, night and day and the boys were put to constant disturbances and because of this they were not able to study their lessons properly. Those boys who were doing well were away from the Railway station and they were living in a city suburb area. When the boys were asked the reason they at once stated that because of the horrible and irritating noise, they were not able to concentrate on their studies and do well in the examinations. Therefore, the irritating noise is found to be a new independent variable interfering in the dependent variable on the performance. This new independent variable is traced by an exploratory experiment.

The same new independent variable later on can be used in a confirmatory experiment as an independent variable and a hypothesis can be formulated and the influence of it can be tested and verified and quantitative relationship between the two variable (the irritating noisy situation and the students' performance) can be determined. To put it in Underwood's (1957) style it should be surprise or wonder. "I am highly anxious to know what would happen if I did this matter in this way". This refers to exploratory type of experiment, because this arouses one's curiosity about the result as it was not existed earlier. Therefore, something new is going to emerge from this. But in the case of confirmatory type of experiment some consequent is ascertained. "I promise that this is the result going to take place if I dealt with this problem in this way." Here the result is tested whether it is true or false.

II. PLAN OF THE EXPERIMENT

Therefore, in view of the aforesaid discussions, while planning an experiment several points should be borne in mind. First of all we must state that there is a problem to be solved. Towards the solution of the problem we must see a tentative solution to the problem — that is the hypothesis. One hypothesis or more than one hypothesis should be formulated. It should be in the form of an answer to the problem and it should determine whether the tentative solution is true or false. While designing an experiment the experimenter should bear in mind that he can obtain the data which will be helpful to verify the hypothesis.

Having chosen the problem and formulated the hypothesis the experimenter then should think of the instrument or the test material to be used for collecting data. In this context it is also important to see how best he can manipulate the instrument or administer the test. He should also observe the circumstances under which the experiment is conducted, the circumstances in which the extraneous variables may have effect in the dependent variable and if so, how to control them. How best the results cab be observed, obtained and recorded. If the conditions are not satisfactory the results may not be relevant to verify the hypothesis. Some authors are of the view that if the antecedent conditions were not satisfactory the experiment may fail to fulfil the requirements or our aims. The past conditions might have been like that, but at present the conditions may be very favourable for collecting reliable data and our aims can be fulfilled. For example the climatic conditions in winter may be different from that of summer. If the winter season was found to be unfit to conduct a particular experiment it can be conducted in summer and we need not stop the enquiry. There may be some unfavorable conditions prevailing at one time and any experiment or survey might have been very difficult to conduct. But if certain condition is a must for an experiment and such condition does not prevail there, then it is not advisable to have any study there. In such cases the antecedent conditions should be taken into account. If such conditions do not prevail the consequent conditions also will be absent. Then the experiment will become futile.

The experimenter should make out the plan of the experiment fully on paper and should give it to more persons who are well versed in designing experiments and ask their opinions and comments on every aspect. This is one way of reducing the errors in the experimental designs. But however carefully an experiment is planned it can be criticized by some reviewers. Hence much care should be paid on planning an experiment and it should be also borne in mind that each aspect should be mentioned under separate sub-heading.

The Title of the Experiment

We must know that every day thousands of experiments in Psychology are conducted all over the world. There is every chance of repeating the same experiment in different places. Therefore, in order to avoid repetition and confusion, the experimental write up should provide certain information with regard to the specific title and problem, time and place of the experiment and also the name of the country.

Introduction

Under this sub-heading the definitions and explanation and the historical development of the problem and the important concepts should be stated. The theoretical aspect involving the important authors and the importance, the problem has received in the past and present should be described fully.

Review of Literature

The experimenter is expected to be thorough with all the studies conducted earlier in relation to his experiment. There might have been some studies partially related to the present experiment and some studies might have been mostly related. The survey of such studies may serve several purposes. First of all it is helpful in finalizing the problem and to formulate the hypothesis. The experimenter by this means can ascertain that this particular problem was not studied previously. Further the experimenter can also make certain correction or modifications in his problem either by making some change in the title or in the design of the experiment or in the choice of population or in selecting sample or in using the type of instrument and thereby making the experiment more important and it is to be conducted in view of its value. Further the experimenter can get certain ideas from the previous studies with regard to the elimination of errors and also the ways and means of controlling the extraneous variables that might have effect in the dependent variables. It is also necessary that the previous studies should be summarised and given in this section. The *Psychological Abstracts,* a professional journal published by the American Psychological Association every month provides the abstracts of hundreds of studies conducted all over the world. The *Journal of Indian Psychological Abstracts* also provides the abstracts of Psychological researches conducted in India. The experimenter should make use of all these for this purpose.

Problem

The problem should be stated in a precise manner without any ambiguity. It is always better to state it in one sentence. The statement of the problem should also express the shortage of knowledge in this problem area. This experiment is conducted because of the shortage of sufficient knowledge.

Hypothesis

The hypothesis should be stated in a sentence involving the variables mentioned in the problem stated. The hypothesis, since, tentative solution to the problem may be stated empirically or statistically. It may be in a single sentence in the form of answering a question positively or negatively. Or, it may be also in the form of relationship between independent variable and dependent variable. For example, "if 'a' exists then 'b' also exists". It is also just like relating to cause and effect in an activity.

Variables

While making the statement of the problem the independent and dependent variables should be involved. The hypothesis should relate these two variables. The independent and dependent variables must be defined without any ambiguity. In some experiments there may be more independent and dependent variables. Therefore, it will not be possible to mention all the independent and dependent variables in the title as in the statement of the problem. In such cases it is better to state here what are the independent variables and what are the dependent variables in this experiment. If there were any extraneous variables that might affect the dependent variables they also should be mentioned even though they are to be controlled.

Test Materials

In a laboratory situation the experimenter might be manipulating the instrument by himself or he might have asked the participant to manipulate in a particular fashion by giving him suitable directions. Whatever the case might be, the experimenter should record two things. One is the strength of manipulating independent variable and the other is the effect observed in the dependent variable. The former, in other words may be called stimulus and the later response. The independent variable is manipulated and the resulting value is seen in the dependent variable. Many of the present psychological apparatus are electrically operated or having some mechnical devices. But some apparatus are manually operated.

For example, the Muller-Lyer Illusion Board, Depth perception apparatus, Aubert Diaphargm are operated manually without electrical assistance. The first two are manipulated by the participant in the experimental situation and the experimenter records the responses in the dependent variable. In the case of the third apparatus, the Aubert Diaphargm the experimenter manipulates the independent variable and records the responses as revealed by the participant. But in the case of Flicker Fusion Apparatus the experimenter operates the control switch for increasing or decreasing the percentage of illumination on the basis of responses the participant makes by looking through the viewing chamber. This apparatus is operated with the assistance of electricity. All these apparatuses and instruments were used for the experimental treatment. In other words, they are devised to present the stimulus to the participant for obtaining the response as desired. There are also instruments designed and developed to record the reactions of one bodily features such as the pulse rate, the blood pressure, brainwaves, skin response and so forth.

The instruments and apparatuses are not foolproof. They have certain limitations. The instruments have certain defects which the experimenter might not have noticed. As result of it the recording of the responses may be wrong and the data become inaccurate. These are considered as disadvantages of the instruments.

Control of Variables

The control of variables in the experimentation is extremely important if we want to elicit reliable data. While reviewing the previous studies we might have noticed certain variables in some researches interfering with, having influence in the dependent variables and certain variables which were not having influence were ignored. Whatever the previous researchers have observed it is important to observe from time to time in the experimentation whether there were any variables having effect upon the dependent variables. First of all it is better to evaluate whether there are any extraneous variables affecting the dependent variables. If there were any such thing they might invalidate the experiment or the data might be unreliable and will not fit into any type of treatment. Therefore, measures must be taken to control such extraneous variables.

There will be also other, such as intervening variables in the experimental situation. Some will exert influence and some will not. Since they exert equal influence on all conditions they may be ignored. But if the influence of these variables were serious, it is better not to carry out the experiment. Suppose for example the experimenter wants to conduct an experiment involving hearing and which may range from very feable sound to loud noise. But in the nearby place there is a metal factory causing abnormally loud noise. In this condition it will not be possible to carry out any experiment on hearing. The participant will not be responding to the experimenter's stimuli however stronger they were.

Selection of the Design

There are various types of designs of experiments. They are the case of two randomized groups design, case of more than two randomized groups design, case of two matched groups design, within-groups design and the factorial design which are very much used in most of the psychological studies. We have elsewhere described the case of two randomized group design as it has certain advantages. It is considered to be basic for Psychological studies. A sound knowledge in this may help us to proceed to more complex and difficult designs. If the independent variable is varied in two ways this design can be used. The other more advantageous design is the multiple group design or the factorial design. If the independent variable is varied in more than two ways then the factorial design is used. And also if two or more than two independent variables are used in one single experiment then the factorial design is used. There are several types of factorial designs. The factorial designs with two independent variables are 2 x 2 factorial design, the 3 x 2 factorial design, the 3 x 3 factorial design, the 4 x 2 factorial design, the 5 x 2 factorial design and 6 x 2 factorial design.

In 2 x 2 factorial design there are two independent variables and each one can be varied in two ways. The numbers 2 x 2 at once indicate that there are two independent variables and each one has two values. Therefore, this experimental design has four (2 multiplied by 2) experimental conditions.

The 3 x 2 factorial design has two independent variables. These are the two conditions under which the participants should respond to the stimulus presentation in three different ways. Thus there are six experimental conditions (3 x 2 = 6) to which the participants are exposed to. That is, one independent variable has two conditions and the other has three conditions.

The 3 x 3 factorial design is also having two independent variable and each one is varied in three different ways. Thus the participant is exposed to (3 x 3 = 9) nine experimental conditions.

There is a 4 x 2 factorial design in which there are two independent variables, of which one independent variable is varied in four ways and the other in two ways. Thus we have (4 x 2 = 8) eight experimental conditions.

In a 5 x 3 factorial design there are two independent variables. One independent variable is varied in five different ways and the other assumes three ways. Thus there are (5 x 3 = 15) fifteen experimental conditions.

It is also possible to have a 6 x 2 factorial design with two independent variables. In this design one independent variable is varied in six different ways and another independent variable is varied in two different ways and thus there are twelve (6 x 2 = 12) experimental conditions.

A second type of factorial design is with more than two independent variables. The simplest is 2 x 2 x 2 factorial design in which three independent variables can be studied. In this design each of the three variables is varied in two ways. This design has eight (2 x 2 x 2 = 8) experimental conditions.

The three independent variables may be varied in three ways if they assume three values. Then the resultant conditions are (3 x 3 x 3 = 27) twenty-seven. Every independent variable may be varied in any number of ways. Therefore, in an experimental design with three independent variables, the first independent variable may be varied in two ways, the second in three ways, and the third in four ways. Then this experimental design has (2 x 3 x 4 = 24) twenty-four conditions. Similarly, in the factorial design with three independent variables any one independent variable may be varied in any number of ways. Therefore, a factorial design with three independent variables may assume more values like this : 4 x 3 x 3 = 36 conditions, 5 x 4 x 3 = 60 conditions and so on. Any factorial design may be selected, either the two independent variable type or the three independent variable type and among the varied ways any one of them may be selected according to the facilities available to the experimenter.

Selection of population and sample and assigning participants

Though in many of the psychological experiments the populations might have been, various animal species like rats, cats, dogs and monkeys, the ultimate aim is to study human behaviour by conducting experiments. Towards this, the experimenter must select some participants from some group. The problem here is the group. Having conducted some experiments on a small sample the experimenter wants to generalize his findings to the larger group or population. Therefore the group from which the participants are to be selected becomes very important. The sample refers to the participants included in the study. What we call population, need not be only animated beings like human beings or animals, birds, creatures living in water like fishes, crabs, octopus etc. It may be also some learning activities like learning to throw a ball, learning to hit a ball, learning to run the maze, learning to operate a puzzle box and so on. While choosing the human beings as the population we may come across several types of groups like the children groups, adolescent groups, adult groups, old age groups, men groups, women groups, various age groups, employed groups, unemployed groups, various socio-economic status groups, white collar groups, blue collar groups, school student groups, college student groups and so on and so forth. Therefore, in designing an experiment we must specify the population and the group more precisely and relevant to the purpose. In other words, the participants selected from the chosen group for the experiment, should fulfil the needs by providing relevant data in the experimental situation and help the experimenter to generalize the results to the whole population. The size of the sample or number or participants should depend upon the size of the group or population. If the group is very big, more number of participants must be selected. Then only the data would be reliable to generalize the results to the population. The technique, the experimenter should follow is the random selection. The advantage of using this technique is that every member of the population has an equal chance of being represented in the sample. The method of random sampling technique and the method of assigning a participant to a group are discussed elsewhere in this chapter.

When a sample is selected from a population according to the random sampling technique it can be taken for granted that a representative sample has been selected. But it is also better to check up whether the sample really a representative or random sampling or some error has occurred in it. It can be tested with a normal probability curve. If the experimenter is satisfied with his sampling of the specified population and if the experimental design is finalized then he can divide the sample into number of groups according to his plan.

Conducting an Experiment

We have explained all the essential features of the experimental psychology in the preceding sections. Now we shall see how an experiment is conducted. An experiment whether it is conducted in a laboratory situation or in a social situation the experimenter is likely to make errors as he/she is dealing with such situation for the first time. However, the experimenter is conversant with the theoretical aspects, while performing something new, there is every chance of committing errors and he/she can also understand the mistakes and can correct it later on. Therefore, every act of experiment is contributing to new knowledge. The student of psychology by conducting several experiments in the laboratory situation understands how and where mistakes or errors, that affect the results, are possible and how to avoid them. In the subsequent experiments he/she should be very careful that such errors do not creep into the experiments. The experimenter in a laboratory is conducting some experiments everyday with a view of verifying several hypotheses and finds out solution to every problem. This sort of experience he/she gains in some small experiments qualifies him for further elaborate and complicated experiments and finally may utilize the training and knowledge to conduct some research work.

Suppose, for example the experiment is to assess the level of aspiration of the participant. It is to see how far human drives an incentives and function in a given task. If the result is known to the participant for every trial of performance what effect it is having? Whether the performance on knowing the result of the task improves or not? It can be also tested in the other way, whether the participant's level of aspiration increases or decreases on knowing the result of his performance on the previous trial. Therefore, the hypothesis is : If the knowledge of results is provided to the participant then the participant's performance will be improved. The experiment can be performed with Rotter's Level of Aspiration Board and the hypothesis can be verified.

The apparatus is a wooden board of one metre long with a long groove in the centre and the groove is divided into ten parts, numbered from 1 to 10 from bottom to top of the board. It is held slightly in slanting position. A ball is placed at the bottom, just few inches below the lowest division, one. A wooden stick is used to push the ball through the groove. If the ball is made to move to the top division which is the 10th division then the score is 10. If the ball reached 5 then the score is only 5. If the ball reached 0 division then the score is 0. A sheet of paper for recording the participant's aspiration is to be provided to him/her.

The task the participant performs, is to push the ball through the groove to the number he aspired to reach. Before the participant starts the task he/she should call a number he/she aspired to reach. The experimenter should note down the number. It is the level of aspiration. If the ball is pushed, it might reach 8 then the participant attained the score of 8 only. Then he/she is informed that the attainment score is 8. The first hit is over. When the second hit is started he/she should be asked to call a number he/she aspired to reach and the experimenter should note down. The participant should be made to know that in the first hit he/she aspired 10, but attained only 8. Thus, the participant is provided with the knowledge of the result of the performance and this knowledge is supposed to have some effect in the performance of the next hit. Five hits constitute one trial. The participant will have to perform 20 trials which means 100 hits in all. The experimenter should demonstrate one trial or 5 hits and then he/she can ask the participant to start. The task is explained to the participant as follows: "Now hold the stick" (The experimenter hands over the stick to the participant "you have seen what I was doing. You will have to do in the same manner. You will have to call out a number (pointing out the board) to which you aspire to reach. Then push the ball with this stick along the groove, so that the ball moves along the groove and stops against a number. If the ball stopped at 10, your score is 10. This is the highest possible score for a hit. If the ball stopped against any other number that number is your score. If the ball bounced off or stopped where there is no number your score is zero. Now you can have some practice hits." Twenty practice hits may be permitted.

When the participant was fully satisfied with the practice hits, the experimenter can start the experiment by giving the following instructions: "Now we are starting the test. I shall give you twenty trials. Each trial has five hits of the ball. If you push the ball at ten in all hits your score will be 10 x 5 = 50. Instead, if you push the ball to a place where there was no number your score is zero. In every hit if the ball stopped on different numbers then your score is the total of the five numbers. I shall tell you the score you attained for every trial at the time when you start the next trial. Now you can write down the 5 numbers you are going to reach in the first trial in the sheet. When the first trial was over, similarly, write down the 5 numbers you are going to reach in the next trial. Remember, I shall be telling you the score you have attained in the previous trial before you start the next trial. When I say ready go, you must start hitting the ball, Ready go".

Before starting every trial the experimenter should be quite sure that the participant has made entry of the 5 numbers, that is the aspirations score in the sheet. The experimenter should note down the score for each hit and add the scores of five hits and inform the participant.

While conducting this experiment the experimenter should take some precautionary measures. The scores of each trial (5 hits) attained by the participant should be announced to him/her before he/she makes entry of the next trial's (5 hits) aspiration score in the sheet. The experimenter should not make any comments or remarks on the aspiration on the performance of the task or on the scores of the participant.

This experiment has two types of scores. One is Goal Discrepancy Score (GDS) and the other is Attainment Discrepancy Score (ADS). The Goal Discrepancy Score is the difference between the aspiration for a trial (5 hits) and the performance in the previous trial. If the aspiration score is higher than the performance score on the previous trial, then the GDS is positive (+) (GDS = AN – NP). If the aspiration score is lower than the performance score on the previous trial then the GDS is negative (—). The Attainment Discrepancy Score is the difference between aspiration score for a given trial and performance score in that trial (ADS = AN – PN). For 20 trials there are 19 Goal Discrepancy Scores and 20 Attainment Discrepancy Scores. The average for both the scores should be worked out to get the mean GDS and the mean ADS for each participant. It can be tested whether the knowledge of the results had any effect in aspiration scores or in the attainment scores.

The independent variable in this experiment is the knowledge of results provided to the participant. It might have varied from the lowest score (zero) to the highest score (ten). Two groups are required to conduct this experiment, one is the experimental group and the other is the control group. The experimental group should be provided with the knowledge of the results while the control group is not. The population is defined as the college students. From a list of students of a class 40 participants may be randomly selected for the study. The 40 participants may be randomly divided into two groups, 20 in each group. (The method is described elsewhere in this chapter). The groups, then are randomly decided that one of the groups is experimental group and the other as the control group.

The next step is, controlling the extraneous variables that might have influence upon the dependent variable. In this experiment there are two dependent variables. While determining the GD Score, the aspiration score becomes the dependent variable as it is fixed by the participant after knowing the result of the previous trial. The result of the previous trial is the independent variable. While determining the AD Score, the aspiration score become the independent variable and the attainment score is the dependent variable.

It should be observed that both the groups should be treated in the same manner in all respects, except in the case of independent variable is concerned. The independent variable of knowledge of the results of the performance must be provided only to the experimental group and not to the control group. The experimental group after every trial would receive the knowledge of the result of the previous trial while the control group will not, but should carry out the performance after writing down the aspiration score for the trial. The instruction should be the same for both the groups except providing the knowledge of result to the experimental group. The experimenter should not show any sign of the feeling of gay to some and frowning at some other persons.

The participant in this experiment is going to perform 20 trials at the rate of 5 hits for each trial. He/she has to perform 100 hits. Therefore, it may take more than one hour to complete all the trials. In such case, it is necessary to have time between the trials. Generally, experimenters suggest little time between the trials. Therefore, in this experiment this time variable must be held as constant for all the participants of both groups. Each participant should wait for ten seconds after every trial. He/she should start the next trial after waiting for ten seconds.

What time of the day is more convenient for the participants to perform the task? Whether it is in the morning or forenoon, or in the evening, the person could perform better. Whatever is the convenient time, it should be for both the groups. The days also sometime become important. Researchers are of the view that some people perform certain tasks better on Mondays but differently, the same task on Saturdays. It is because of the strain accumulated in them due to six days work. Those who do better on Mondays start the task fresh as they had rest for a day. The date on which the experiment is conducted should also be mentioned. It may be hot summer or biting cold winter.

The other extraneous variables may be the temperature of the room, illumination, ventilation and humidity. Since the psychological experiments are conducted on human beings all those factors that might cause inconveniences to human beings, might have influence in the performance of the participants. Therefore, all these variables should be controlled as far as possible. The findings of the experiment sometimes may contribute to the formulation of empirical laws and they may be also inducted into the frameworks of theoretical aspects of experimental psychology.

III. WRITING THE REPORT OF AN EXPERIMENT

In the preceding sections we have been discussing about the salient features of psychological experiments and the conduction of an experiment. Once an experiment is planned and executed well the remaining task for the experimenter is to report accurately his findings and draw conclusions on the meaning of the data. The data should be presented always in the tabular columns after giving suitable statistical analysis. Then the experiment should be written up according to the format laid down. In order to facilitate the report writing, psychologists like all other scientists have evolved certain conventions that have become standard for many professional journals. Therefore, the format should be used for writing up the experiment whether the report is sent for publication in a scientific journal or whether the experiment is conducted in the class room as a part of curriculum for learning by a student of experimental psychology in the degree course.

The student, by writing the report of his/her findings of the experiment he/she gains more and more knowledge in this area and this knowledge can be correspondingly transferred for preparing a scientific paper for publication in some technical journal or may carry out some research programme on some important problem as a professional psychologist. Further, while writing up a report on an experiment the student may learn many things and can eliminate the possible errors that the student makes. It is true that the writing up of the experimental findings according to the format is a very difficult job and students sometimes become nervous to write a report on their experimental findings and they take unusually longer time for it. This shows that they have not become familiar with the format and report writing.

The report writing is a way of communicating the results of the experiment, conducted to study a problem, to the scientific world. Any research work whether it is conducted in the laboratory situation in the form of an experiment or in the form of a field survey or investigation should be reported to the scientific world by publishing it in a professional journal or in the form of a monograph. It is better to publish it within a year or two. Otherwise the lapse of time may outmode the results or some one may take up the same study and publish it. One, who is interested in conducting an experiment or a research, should have in mind that the scientific report, written on the basis of the results, is the most essential subject matter for the scientific world and for the further research work. Therefore, care must be taken to write the report in such a way that it should communicate everything clearly with accuracy of data and it should be easily understood by the reader. It is not easy unless one has attained proficiency in preparing the report. The proficiency can be achieved only by practice and by reading scientific reports or articles thoroughly in some professional journals. Any Journal of Experimental psychology published by the British Psychological Society or American Psychological Association or an Indian Journal would serve the purpose. While going through the article in a Journal it is important to observe very carefully that how the author of the article handled each section and the manner of dealing with every point. The writer of the report should handle the language carefully. It is not the test of one's proficiency in a language. This is for communicating the findings to others. Therefore, the report should be written in a simple style clearly, so that anybody who reads the article in a journal should be able to understand it without any ambiguity and able to repeat the same experiment. A working knowledge of these principles of report writing will help the students or researchers to describe more clearly and accurately their own experimental findings and equip them with basic standard of knowledge to review the experimental reports of other psychologists.

Generally, the report of psychological experiments should include a title and the following sub-divisions :

1. **Introduction**
   (a) Problem

2. **Method**
   (a) Participants/Sample
   (b) Apparatus and Description of the Apparatus
   (c) Experimental design
   (d) Procedure
   (e) Method of Scoring

3. **Results**
4. **Discussion**
5. **Conclusion**
6. **References**

1. THE TITLE

The title should be short, but it should include a brief description of the experiment and should include the independent and dependent variables. The title should also answer an important question : "By what name can this experiment best be known?" The title should express clearly the nature of the experiment. Its length is not important. But the length of the title should be within 12 words. *There should not be any abbreviations in the title.* For example, "Effect of Frequency of KR and nAch on the Performance of Line Drawing". Here the author of this article has used KR for 'Knowledge of Results' and nAch for 'need Achievement'. Such abbreviations should be avoided. The title should not begin with : "A Study of ...." Or "A Survey of ...." or "An Investigation into ...." as it is known like that. Therefore, the title should begin with: "Development of Need/Antonomy.........", "Effect of Imposing Time Limit on.......", "Causes of Infanticide and Child Murder......." The title should appear on the first page of the report. For example, the title should be like this : "Public Perception of the Social Status of the Elderly Persons" or "Intelligence and Creativity as Determinants of Anxiety", "Villagers' Aspiration Level and Change Proneness".

The title may be in *capital letters fully* or the *first letter of every important word* may be in capital letters. Just below the title of the article at the centre the author's name should be written in capital letters or the first letter may be in capital letters and the rest in small letters. Below the author's name the Institution to which he/she is affiliated should be written. The name of the Department need not be there. In case of multiple authors of different Institutions, the Institution's name will go below the respective authors. This is the format the report writer should follow while giving the title, author's name and the name of Institution to which he/she belongs to.

Abstract

The author of the article should prepare the abstract of article and put it below the title in a distinctive manner. The length of the abstract mostly depends upon the size or length of the article. But the abstract should carry all the relevant information of the article and it should be a short summary of the article in all respects. But the abstract should not carry the title and author's name and should be typed in a separate sheet. The abstract should be within 150 to 200 words in length and should give the reader of the article the full substance of the report. In the abstract there should be statement of the problem giving the independent and dependent variables, the population chosen for the study, the size of the sample or participants' number, sex, age, the socio-economic status, the research design and the instruments used in the study. What the experimenter did to collect the data and what results he/she got should be listed down. Since the results are the most important part of the study the abstract should also carry the levels of significance and the logical conclusions drawn from them.

There are journals publishing research abstracts and organizations collect abstract of relevant researches. The abstract that accompany the article for publication should provide complete information and the reader of the abstract should not have vague idea about the experiment. The abstract should not carry references, for example, author's name or his/her study, the year of publication and citing the results of the earlier studies. The experimenter should prepare the abstract only at the end when he/she has completed the writing of the article. Then only it will be easy for him/her to give the essence of the article in few lines. At the end of the abstract, in a separate line the experimenter should list the key words of the abstract.

1. INTRODUCTION

The introductory section is the first part of the article in which the experimenter should state the general background to the problem area and a logical explanation of why he/she is undertaking this study. The problem should be logically stated giving most relevant earlier studies. The historical development of the problem, the various theories and principles developed by the scholars in the problem area may be also briefly summarised. It should also include a general statement of the phenomenon under experimentation or investigation followed by the reviewers of relevant studies from psychological literature. At the end of this section the problem should be stated in precise form. The problem is the statement of the purpose of the experiment or the working hypothesis that is to be tested. Having reviewed the available earlier studies made in this problem area the experimenter then should state that this particular problem was not studied previously. Therefore, the problem may be stated thus: "Do salt pills have effect upon continuous physical work?" *This will help us to set up a hypothesis logically.* The logical presentation of the hypothesis should be short, in one sentence.

"The industrial workers who have taken genuine salt pills have shown much higher proficiency in the work than those who have taken sugar coated pills". *This empirical hypothesis* may be also stated with 'if and then'. *"If the industrial workers were given genuine salt pills then they show much higher proficiency than the workers who were given sugar coated pills"* .

Therefore if you are testing some hypotheses state it clearly and indicate the theoretical consequences of the positive or negative results. The statement of the problem, the hypothesis and the definition of the independent and dependent variables may provide the reader of the article to understand what you have wanted to do and what you have done to get the expected results and for what purpose. For example a problem may be stated like this:

Problem

The purpose of this experiment is to test the effect of genuine salt pills on the performance of industrial workers. *If we state a problem in this way the independent and the dependent variables are indicated. Here the independent* variable is the genuine salt pills and the dependent variable is the peformance. The type of participant is industrial worker. The population chosen for this study is industrial worker.

2. METHOD

This section, 'Method' may also be stated as 'Methodology' and it severs the purpose of describing the method of collecting data pertaining to the hypothesis and the data may serve the purpose of testing the hypothesis. This section is intended to state that how the experiment was conducted to collect data. The report writer should state here all the possible advantages and disadvantages in conducting this experiment and also the inconveniences he/she has experienced in it. There are four or five sub-sections under this heading, Method. They are (a) Participant (Subject or Sample), (b) Apparatus, (c) Design of the Experiment (if necessary, the Design of the Experiment may be added to it), (d) Procedure, and (e) Method of Scoring.

Participants (Subjects or Sample)

The participants are those persons who serve as subjects in the experiment.

The experimenter should choose a population and state it in detail as to why he/she chooses it. Then the sample size and the method of selection should be specified. It is also better to state the factors that affect the randomness of the sample. The participants should be described in such a way that each one may serve as an independent variable. The total number of participants and the number of participants assigned to the experimental group and to the control group should be specified. Other particulars such as sex, mean-age, socio-economic status, location, race, religion etc. should be stated. The experimenter should also state whether the participants have volunteered themselves or they were promised of something for participating in the experiment. Further, the participants should be sufficiently informed about what is required of them in the experimental situation.

Apparatus

The main apparatus and other auxiliary parts required to conduct the experiment should be stated and they must be described. If the apparatus was manufactured by a renowned company then it need not be described as it might have been used in every psychological laboratory. Therefore, it is important to mention the model of the apparatus, the name of the inventor and the company manufactured it. For example, if the name of the apparatus is stated as O'Connor Finger Dexterity Test, we are associating the inventor's name with the apparatus. In order to establish the familiarity with the apparatus the experimenter or the student who conducts the experiment must draw the diagram of the apparatus, pointing out the names of the parts of the apparatus. If the experiment is conducted with paper-pencil test material it is necessary to describe the test material stating the name of the person who has designed and developed it and its reliability and validity, number of items, method of administering, method of scoring and what it measures etc., also should be stated.

Design of the Experiment

In one of the preceding sections we have stated about the types of designs of experiments and the selection of designs. But where the design or experiment should be incorporated in the report? It is after describing the apparatus the type of design is stated. The important characteristics of design of the experiment are (1) method of assigning participants to experimental group and to control group (This is already described elsewhere) and labeling them, (2) stating the independent and dependent variables and giving operational definitions, (3) controlling of experimental variables.

The experimental variables should be carefully manipulated. Otherwise there may be errors which may spoil the accuracy of the results. These errors are called constant errors. When a participant responds repeatedly several times to the same stimulus his/her judgments may not be the same every time to the stimulus. Therefore, there are several probable sources of this type of variability. The participant's sensitivity may vary from moment to moment and at some instance the condition of the organism may be more or less favourable for a fine discriminating performance. There may be unavoidable changes in the physical characteristics of the stimulus however carefully the instrument is manipulated. This leads to certain marginal fluctuation which cannot be eliminated. In addition, factors such as the participant's interest and attitude also may interfere in the judgments. Therefore, the judgments differ from trial to trial providing an index of the amount of variable error. For example, when two equal stimuli 'P' and 'q' are presented to a participant, he/she does not always judge them as equal. Even though they are equal the participant judges the stimulus 'p' sometime as larger, sometimes as smaller and sometimes as equal. This is because of the manifestation of variable errors. Sometimes the stimulus 'p' is overestimated and sometimes understimated. There is a systematic tendency on the part of the participant to over estimate or to under estimate. This tendency is known as constant errors and this cannot be eliminated. But the experimenter by using the methods of randomization and counter balancing the experimental variable, the constant error can be cancelled out.

Procedure

This section requires to describe exactly how the experimenter has conducted the experiment to collect data. The procedure should be described in the same order in which he/she performed the task. The instruction given to the participants should be given in the same form. What sort of experimental treatment was given to the experimental group and how the control group was kept ignorant of the treatment given to the experimental group. The experimenter should state how he/she administered the independent variable and how the results were recorded. The important purpose of describing the procedure is to demonstrate the experimental design in sufficient detail and make another experimenter to understand

and to replicate the same experiment if he/she wished. The report is written after conducting the experiment. Therefore, the procedure should be always written in past tense.

Method of Scoring

The procedure involved in the Method of scoring vary considerably from test to test. The method of scoring the individual score in the performance tests vary from paper-pencil test. In the performance test also the procedure of scoring is not uniform. For example, the intelligence tests of performance vary from the test of reaction time, perception test, attention test, concept formation test, creativity tests and so on. Similarly, with regard paper-pencil tests the scoring procedures vary. All the intelligence tests of paper-pencil type are speed tests. Time is an important factor. All other tests, like the aptitude, attitude, interest, personality, temperament are not speed tests. The nature of response or answer is important. Therefore, in scoring a test we must go through the test manual and find out how the test is to be scored.

The test designers have their own way of formulating the scoring methods. Some test are easily scored and some take longer time. For example some of the intelligence tests, aptitude tests and personality inventories need more time and some minor calculation in finding out the individual score. In some tests the raw score is converted into percentile score or standard score according to the procedure. In some aptitude tests and personality inventories templates are used. In some personality inventories the number of rights and wrongs are counted and the score is assigned to the right and wrongs. In attitude scales the responses are assigned scores. The type of responses may vary from 3 to 5 or 7 or 9 to 11. The Thurstone's psychophysical method of equal appearing interval there are 11 types of responses. In Likert type of scaling technique there are 5 types of responses whereas in Guttman's scalogram there are only three type of responses. Therefore, the experimenter should find out the method of scoring the responses by going through the respective manual.

The responses of the participants are assigned with a score of 1 to 5 or 5 to1 depending upon the nature of the item and the scoring technique. Every test or scale may have a maximum score and a minimum score and the individual score may fall in between these two scores. Therefore, a test or a scale or an inventory should be scored according to the procedure as given in the manual. The manual should be strictly followed.

The scores obtained for the individuals according to the scoring procedure are only raw scores. The raw scores as they come to the experimenter do not reveal the correct meaning of the performance of the individual. They must be meaningfully converted by using certain statistical methods. Since we are comparing the individuals or groups in our analysis or discussion the raw scores should be converted into mean scores, or standard scores or percentile scores or whatever the score the author of the test has shown in his/her test manual. While working out the mean score it is also important to find out the dispersion scores like the standard deviation and the standard error of the mean. The dispersion scores would tell us the nature of responses given by the subjects or whether the individuals have taken the test in a real sense or given fake answers. If there were more fake answers in the testing it would be dubious and the answers should be discarded.

3. RESULTS

Having obtained the data by conducting an experiment, the experimenter should treat the data statistically and analyse the results. This is the most difficult section for the student of experimental psychology and to the researcher who writer the report for the first time. But if the student in the experimental psychology class was having much curiosity and developed much interest in it and conducted the experiment with all seriousness and written the experimental procedures and dealt with results of the experiment in his/her record notebook as directed by his/her Professor the student would not find any difficulty in writing the report of an experiment independently. In a course of study many experiments are conducted and the reports are written and every experiment in psychology is a piece of research work. Therefore, if a student was paying special attention to all such matters he/she had to facc no problem in writing a research report.

This section is to provide sufficient information to the reader to know how the experimenter has gone through the procedures to obtain such conclusions. Here the author of the report presents the data systematically in tables and explains what they meant. The author finds out meanings and reasons for such results of the data presented in the tables and analyses them in relation to the hypothesis. While interpreting the data, the report writer or student may directly go into the conclusions without making any reference to the data in the table. He/she must state first how the data were arrived at and what treatments were given to them. It has been observed that some researchers who prepare research paper for publication in scientific journals not only give little importannce to the format but also simply give the mean scores and the 't' values and state that the 't' value is not significant. This is not the correct way of presenting the data. It is important that all the values right from the mean scores to the 't' test values and other in between values such as SDs, SEMs, and the mean difference etc., also must be presented in the table systematically. The author of the report (research paper) should bear in mind that he/she is presenting the data to a reader who may carry out similar research or experiment using the same apparatus or test material and therefore, he/she must understand it fully without raising any doubt in his mind.

Apart from the knowledge and experience the report writer (student) has gained in the experimental psychology class, it is also important that he/she should develop the habit of going to the library and establish good familiarity with research journals and select some well written articles from good scientific journal and go through every step very carefully and understand how each section is dealt with by the author of the article and must pay special attention to the various components of the results section. He/she can make even a note of such components, presentation of the data, interpretation and analyses of the data and the way in which the author associates them to the hypotheses and how he arrives at the conclusion and makes the matter suitable for discussion. If the report writer finds his/her data are in accordance with the empirical hypothesis then he/she can conclude that the hypothesis is accepted. Instead if the data are not in agreement with the hypothesis or not the same as what the hypothesis has predicted then it is rejected.

In the results section the important component is the presentation of the data in tables and figures. The tables and figures are the summaries of the data after giving suitable statistical treatment. The raw data should never be presented in the table in the results section. The raw data may be very lengthy and unwieldy and may not yield for any meaningful presentations. For example, in psychophysical experiments the same stimulus is presented even hundred times and hundred responses are recorded. Some might have the same value and the rest might have fluctuated up and down. Such data can never be meaningfully explained. Therefore, the mean values are worked out and other statistical treatments are given to the data to present them in a table. A table, as we look at for a moment, we find that it consists of numbers. These numbers are the presentation of the results recorded in the experiment. The presentation of the results in the form of numbers is not made in the original form. The data are cultured by statistical treatment, shortened and only the quintessences are presented in the table. The same experimental data may be presented in figures of various forms using suitable statistical procedures. Thus, the data may be presented in the form of chart or graph. The chart may be drawn as pie chart or bar chart and the graph may be polygon or whatever the shape the data get.

The main aim of the experiment is to assess the relationship between the independent variables and the dependent variables and the data given in the tables show whether such relationship exists or not. The data given in the tables also show the level of relationship that existed between variables.

Illustrative example with an Experiment

It is better to illustrate this matter by citing some experimental data in tables with mean scores and all the measures of variability and with statistics of inferences. Let us cite an example with some experimental data in tables and illustrate the treatment of the data statistically and test the hypotheses with a simple example of a small group sample. A memory test was conducted among the students of four schools to test the level of their performance and also the difference between the students who come from semi-urban and rural areas. The first and the last groups were drawn from semi-urban areas and the groups 2 and 3 were drawn from rural areas. The following null hypothesis and the empirical hypotheses were formulated.

The Null Hypotheses were : (1) There is no difference between the mean scores of the memory test of the students who are drawn from different schools situations, (2) There is no difference between the mean scores of the memory test of the students who are drawn from semi-urban and rural areas.

The Empirical Hypotheses were : (1) If the students were drawn from different schools, then they differ in their memory test scores, (2) There is difference between the students of semi-urban areas and the students of rural areas in their memory test scores

Let us test the null and empirical hypotheses with this experimental data and show first how the F-ratio was obtained by using the formula stated earlier. We can test the hypotheses with F-test to see whether the groups differ among themselves and if the difference is significant then we shall work out the t-test to find out the differences between groups. Here is the data obtained from four students group in memory test. There were 44 students on the whole from 4 different schools who have taken the memory test. In the first group there were 8 students, in the second group 10 students, in the third group 12 students and in the fourth group there were 14 students. The scores of these students are given in Table 18.1.

Table 18.1 : Showing the scores of 4 groups of students in memory test

S. No.	Group-1 (N – 8) Semi-urban		Group-2 (N – 10) rural		Group-3 (N – 12) rural		Group-4 (N – 14) Semi-urban	
	X	X^2	X	X^2	X	X^2	X	X^2
1.	14	186	8	64	13	169	18	324
2.	13	169	6	36	12	144	17	289
3.	16	259	10	100	14	196	18	361
4.	14	196	9	81	16	256	20	400
5.	15	225	7	49	13	169	16	256
6.	16	256	12	144	11	121	15	225
7.	17	289	11	121	9	81	14	196
8.	18	324	10	100	10	100	15	225
9.	—	—	8	64	8	64	16	256
10.	—	—	7	49	10	100	17	289
11.	—	—	—	—	9	81	18	324
12.	—	—	—	—	10	100	16	256
13.	—	—	—	—	—	—	14	196
14.	—	—	—	—	—	—	15	225
Σ	123	1911	88	808	135	1581	230	3822
Σ X	123		88		135		230	
ΣX^2	1911		808		1581		3822	
n	8		10		12		14	
X	15.34		8.8		11.25		16.43	

Now, let us find out first, the basic measures of this study such as mean scores, standard deviations and the standard errors of the means. The mean scores of all the four groups are already there as 15.34, 8.8, 11.25 and 16.43. The other two measures S.D. and SEM, we will have to find out. Since the sample is very small 8,10,12 and 14, the standard deviation can be worked out from the original measurements, that is from the raw scores straightaway. In this case we need not go through frequency distribution. Hence we can use the formula :

$$SD = \frac{1}{N}\sqrt{N(\Sigma X^2) - (\Sigma X)^2}$$

We have all the three data above, ΣX^2, ΣX and the N for all the four groups. Let us apply the formula systematically on the data of each group separately.

Group 1 : $SD = \frac{1}{N}\sqrt{N(\Sigma X^2) - (\Sigma X)^2} = \frac{1}{8}\sqrt{8(1911) - (123)^2}$

$$= \frac{1}{8}\sqrt{15288 - 15129} = \frac{1}{8}\sqrt{159}$$

$$= \frac{12.61}{8} = 1.58$$

Group 2 : $SD = \frac{1}{N}\sqrt{N(\Sigma X^2) - (\Sigma X)^2} = \frac{1}{10}\sqrt{10(808) - (88)^2}$

$$= \frac{1}{10}\sqrt{8080 - 7744} = \frac{1}{10}\sqrt{336}$$

$$= \frac{18.33}{10} = 1.83$$

Group 3 : $SD = \frac{1}{N}\sqrt{N(\Sigma X^2) - (\Sigma X)^2} = \frac{1}{12}\sqrt{12(1581) - (135)^2}$

$$= \frac{1}{12}\sqrt{18972 - 18225} = \frac{1}{12}\sqrt{742}$$

$$= \frac{27.33}{12} = 2.28$$

Group 4 : $SD = \frac{1}{N}\sqrt{N(\Sigma X^2) - (\Sigma X)^2} = \frac{1}{14}\sqrt{14(3822) - (230)^2}$

$$= \frac{1}{14}\sqrt{53508 - 52900} = \frac{1}{14}\sqrt{608}$$

$$= \frac{24.66}{14} = 1.76$$

Now, we have the SDs for all the four groups as 1.58, 1.83, 2.28 and 1.76. These SDs shows that there was some fluctuation in group C as the SD is higher.

Let us go to the next step to find out the standard error of the mean (SEM). The simple formula is : SD√N. The standard deviation should be divided by the respective root of N.

Thus we have :

$$\text{SEM for group-1}: \frac{SD}{\sqrt{N}} = \frac{1.58}{\sqrt{8}} = \frac{1.58}{2.83} = 0.56.$$

$$\text{SEM for group-2}: \frac{SD}{\sqrt{N}} = \frac{1.58}{\sqrt{10}} = \frac{1.83}{3.16} = 0.58.$$

$$\text{SEM for group-3}: \frac{SD}{\sqrt{N}} = \frac{2.28}{\sqrt{12}} = \frac{2.28}{3.46} = 0.66.$$

$$\text{SEM for group-4}: \frac{SD}{\sqrt{N}} = \frac{1.76}{\sqrt{14}} = \frac{1.76}{3.74} = 0.47.$$

Let us present all these four measures in a table

Table 18.2 : Showing the scores of the four students groups on the memory test.

Group	Code	N	Mean	S.D.	SEM
Group-1	A	8	15.34	1.58	0.56
Group-2	B	10	8.8	1.83	0.58
Group-3	C	12	11.25	2.28	0.66
Group-4	D	14	16.43	1.76	0.47

All the four groups differ considerably in their mean scores. But we must know whether the differences among the four groups are real differences or spurious. This can be tested by a 't' test if there were only two groups. For testing the existing real differences if there were more than two groups, it is better to test them with a F-test by working out an analysis of variance. If the F-ratio is significant then we can go for 't' test, otherwise it is better to stop with analysis of variance.

I. Therefore we can first work out the analysis of variance to find out the F-ratio for the groups. We will have to compute the (1) total sum of squares and the (2) sum of squares for among the groups. The formula for *total sum of squares (SS)* for this experiment is :

$$= \Sigma X^2_1 + \Sigma X^2_2 + \Sigma X^2_3 + \Sigma X^2_4 - \frac{(\Sigma X_1 + \Sigma X_2 + \Sigma X_3 + \Sigma X_4)^2}{N}$$

$$= 1911 + 808 + 1581 + 3822 - \frac{(123_1 + 88_2 + 135_3 + 236_4)^2}{44}$$

$$= 8122 - 7698.27 = 423.73.$$

II. The next step is to compute the *sum of squares for among groups.*

The formula is :

$$\frac{(\Sigma X_1)^2}{n_1} + \frac{(\Sigma X_2)^2}{n_2} + \frac{(\Sigma X_3)^2}{n_3} + \frac{(\Sigma X_4)^2}{n_4} - \frac{(\Sigma X_1 + \Sigma X_2 + \Sigma X_3 + \Sigma X_4)^2}{N}$$

$$\frac{(123_1)^2}{8} + \frac{(88_2)^2}{10} + \frac{(135_2)^2}{12} + \frac{(230_4)^2}{14} - \frac{(123_1 + 88_2 + 135_3 + 230_4)^2}{44}$$

$$= 1891.13 + 774.4 + 1518.75 + 3778.57 - 7698.27$$

$$= 7962.85 - 7698.27 = 264.58.$$

III. The third step is to find out sum of squares for within groups. It is by subtracting the second result from the first. In other words, subtracting the sum of squares for among groups from the total sum of squares. Thus we have :

Total sum of squares is = 423.73
Sum of squares of among groups is = 264.58
Therefore the sum of squares for within groups is = 159.15

IV. The fourth step is to find out the mean squares, for among groups and the within groups. The mean squares are the sample values or population values. The mean squares are obtained by dividing the sum of squares by the corresponding degrees of freedom. We need here three degrees of freedom as there are three sum of squares, the total SS, among group SS and the within groups SS. The total SS is divided into two as among groups and within groups. Therefore, we follow similar procedure to determine the degrees of freedom.

The degrees of freedom is used in several places in the statistical application to psychological analysis. Even in the determination of standard deviation we use the degree of freedom. For example for a good estimation of standard deviation of the population mean we use the formula : $SD=\frac{\sqrt{\Sigma X^2}}{N-1}$ when the sample is large. The X^2 stands for sum of squares of deviations in the sample. The N stands for the number of cases or size of the sample. But in determining the standard deviation from the original measurements we use a different formula for determining the SD. Therefore, the SD is $\frac{1}{N}\sqrt{(N\Sigma X^2)-(\Sigma X^2)}$. This formula is used when the sample is very small. This formula does not involve N−1. The degrees of freedom is always indicated by two letters (df). In any measurement, if the sample is small this becomes very important. We do not always use N−1 for the degrees of freedom. This varies depending upon the statistics we use. The N−1 indicates the size of degrees of freedom. It may be a big sample, or small sample, or a big sample may be broken into several sub-groups or sample. For example a big sample 44, is broken into 4 sub-samples or groups, in the first group there are 8 students, in the second 10, in the 3rd 12, and in the 4th 14 students. In this case for the big sample or for the total sample, the degrees of freedom is N−1, i.e. 44 − 1 = 43. The degrees of freedom for among the groups is n − 1 or 4 − 1 = 3 and the degrees of within groups is N − r = 43 − 3 = 40. Here r stands for small groups. The degrees of freedom among groups (3) plus the degrees of freedom within groups (40) becomes the degrees of freedom for the total = 3+40 = 43. All these can be presented in Table 18.3.

Table 18.3 : Showing the summary of the Analysis of Variance for the data obtained in memory test among four groups

Source of variance or components	Sum of Squares	df	Mean Squares	F-ratio	Level of sig
Among groups	264.58	3	88.19	22.16	.01
Within groups	159.15	40	3.98		
Total	423.73	43			

Now, we could see that the obtained F-ratio is 22.16. In our example, we have 3 as the degrees of freedom for among groups. The sum of squares for among the groups is 264.58. This is to be divided by the corresponding degree of freedom (df) 3 and we get the value as (264.58 ÷ 3) 88.19. This is the numerator of the F-ratio fraction. The sum of squares for within groups is 159.15. This is to be divided by the corresponding degrees of freedom (df) 40 and we get the value as (159.15 ÷ 40) 3.98. This is the denominator of the F-ratio fraction. Then divide the mean squares of the among groups 88.19 by the mean squares of within groups 3.98 and we get the (88.19 ÷ 3.98) F-ratio 22.16. Now we will have to find out the P value for 3 and 40 degrees of freedom.

Let us refers to *Fisher and Yates Table* to find out at what level the F-ratio 22.16 is significant. This Table is found in every book on psychological statistics, and in Guilford's (1987) book on 'Fundamental statistics in psychology and education', and in his Psychomatric Methods (1954). In the Table at top we find 'df'. This 'df' is combined with both the numerator, the numbers going on a parallel line, left to right and the denominator going from up and down. Our degrees of freedom are 3 and 40. Let us see in the column mentioned 3 and going down where the number 40 is. Against 40 on the row below the column 3 we find two F values, one the light type 2.84 for .05 level and a bold type value 4.31 for .01 level. The probability value 2.84 is significant at 5 percent level and the 'P' values 4.31 is significant at one percent level. Since our F-value is 22.16 which is higher than the 'P' value 2.84 and 4.31, it is significant more than at one percent level. Therefore, we may state that the four groups of students differ in their memory test scores at a highly significant level (0.01). Hence our null hypothesis is rejected on the ground that the mean scores of the four groups of students in the memory test differ significantly.

The empirical hypothesis that, if the students were drawn from different schools then they differ in their memory test scores, is accepted on the ground that the four groups of students drawn from four different schools differ in their memory test scores significantly at (.01) one percent level. Thus the both types of hypotheses are tested and verified. But, how far each group differ from the other? The highest mean score (16.43) was obtained by the fourth group and the lowest score (8.8) by the second group. Let us now test the level of difference between groups. To know this we must test the second hypothesis. The data required for this, are the mean scores of all the four groups. The standard deviations, the standard errors of mean scores, mean scores differences, the standard errors of the mean score differences and the size of each samples (N) or the number of cases in every group. Let us present the data in Table 18.4. Before this, we must combine each group with every other group to test the hypothesis. There are four groups in our experiment. The formula to find at the number of combination is $\frac{N(N-1)}{2}$.

Therefore, we get $\frac{4(4-1)}{2} = \frac{4 \times 3}{2} = \frac{12}{2} = 6$. There are six combinations among four groups. The following Table 18.4 is a continuation of the Table 18.2.

Table 18. 4 : Showing the mean score difference and the 't' ratios between the four groups on the memory test

S. No.	Groups	N	Mean	Mean Diff. $(M_1 - M_2)$	SEM Diff.	(t-ratio) $\frac{M_1 - M_2}{\text{SEM Diff.}}$	df	Level of sig. P value
1	Group-1	8	15.34	6.54	0.81	8.06	16	.01
	Group-2	10	8.80					
2.	Group-1	8	15.34	4.15	0.85	4.88	18	.01
	Group-3	12	11.25					
3.	Group-1	8	15.34	1.09	0.73	1.49	20	NS
	Group-4	14	16.43					
4.	Group-2	10	8.80	2.45	0.86	2.97	20	.01
	Group-3	12	11.25					
5.	Group-2	10	8.80	7.63	0.75	10.17	22	.01
	Group-4	14	16.43					
6.	Group-3	12	11.25	5.18	0.79	6.56	24	.01
	Group-4	14	16.43					

We have already obtained the standard error of the mean for all four groups (Table 18.2). The standard error of the mean difference is worked out from the SEMs of any two groups. The formula to work out the

SEM_{Diff} is : $SEM_{Diff} = \sqrt{SEM^2_{\ 1} + SEM^2_{\ 2}}$

We are using the SEMs here from Table 18.2.

---

1) $SEM_1 = 0.56$, $SEM_2 = 0.58$

$$= \sqrt{.56_1^2 + .58_1^2} = \sqrt{.3136 + .3364}$$

SEM_{Diff}

$$= \sqrt{.6500} = .806$$

---

2) $SEM_1 = 0.56$, $SEM_3 = 0.66$

$$= \sqrt{.56_1^2 + .66_3^2} = \sqrt{.3136 + .4096}$$

SEM_{Diff}

$$= \sqrt{.7232} = .85$$

---

3) $SEM_1 = 0.56$, $SEM_4 = 0.47$

$$= \sqrt{.56_1^2 + .47_4^2} = \sqrt{.3136 + .2209}$$

SEM_{Diff}

$$= \sqrt{.5345} = 0.73$$

---

4) $SEM_2 = .58$, $SEM_3 = .66$

$$= \sqrt{.58_2^2 + .66_3^2} = \sqrt{.3364 + .4096}$$

SEM_{Diff}

$$= \sqrt{.7460} = 0.86$$

---

5) $SEM_2 = .58$, $SEM_4 = .47$

$$= \sqrt{.58_2^2 + .47_4^2} = \sqrt{.3364 + .2209}$$

SEM_{Diff}

$$= \sqrt{.5573} = .75$$

---

6) $SEM_3 = .66$, $SEM_4 = .47$

$$= \sqrt{.66_3^2 + .47_4^2} = \sqrt{.4096 + .2209}$$

SEM_{Diff}

$$= \sqrt{.6305} = .79$$

The next step is to determine the t-ratios for the six combinations, 1 to 6 given above. What is the 't'? The 't' is actually the ratio of the deviations between two mean scores differences of a sample distribution. This is mostly applied for testing small samples.

The formula for determining the 't' ratio is :

$$t = \frac{M_1 - M_2}{SEM_{Diff}} \quad \text{or} \quad \frac{M_1 - M_2}{\sqrt{\left(\frac{X_1^2 + X_2^2}{(N_1 + N_2) - 2}\right)\left(\frac{N_1 + N_2}{N_1 N_2}\right)}}$$

1) The t-ratio of groups 1 and 2 =

$$\frac{M_1 - M_2}{SEM_{Diff}} = \frac{15.34 - 8.80}{0.806} = \frac{6.54}{0.806} = 8.01$$

---

2) The t-ratio of groups 1 and 3 =

$$\frac{M_1 - M_3}{SEM_{Diff}} = \frac{15.34 - 11.25}{0.85} = \frac{4.15}{0.85} = 4.88$$

---

3) The t-ratio of groups 1 and 4 =

$$\frac{M_1 - M_4}{SEM_{Diff}} = \frac{15.34 - 16.43}{0.73} = \frac{1.09}{0.73} = 1.49$$

---

4) The t-ratio of groups 2 and 3 =

$$\frac{M_2 - M_3}{SEM_{Diff}} = \frac{8.80 - 11.25}{0.86} = \frac{2.45}{0.86} = 2.97$$

---

5) The t-ratio of groups 2 and 4 =

$$\frac{M_2 - M_4}{SEM_{Diff}} = \frac{8.80 - 16.43}{0.75} = \frac{7.63}{0.75} = 10.17$$

---

6) The t-ratio of groups 3 and 4 =

$$\frac{M_3 - M_4}{SEM_{Diff}} = \frac{11.25 - 16.43}{0.79} = \frac{5.18}{0.79} = 6.56$$

The mean score difference can be elicited either from $M_1 - M_2$ or from $M_2 - M_1$. Similarly, it may be from $M_2 - M_4$ or from $M_4 - M_2$. Any mean score can be deducted from any mean score. The point is, the difference between two mean scores. Therefore, the difference can be between any two mean scores of the study. The smaller mean is always deducted from the larger mean. We need only the difference whether it is plus value or minus value.

Having elicited the t-ratio between the mean scores of any two groups of the four experimental groups, we must know at what level the t-ratios are significant. For which the Fisher's Table of 't' should be referred to. In using the Fisher's Table of 't' the degrees of freedom must be made available. How many subjects have functioned in this experiment? Since there were two groups involved in this, the degrees of freedom should be N–2. This capital N is referring to the total number of subjects in both groups. This capital N is constituted by adding the number of subjects (n_1) of group 1 with the number of subjects (n_2) in group 2. Hence the formula is : $N = (n_1 + n_2)$; N–2.

Applying this formula to find out the degrees of freedom for all six combinations we will have to use the respective two ns ($n_1 + n_2$). Thus by adding the n_1 and n_2 we get 8 + 10 = 18. N–2 = 18–2 = 16. Therefore :

(1) The df for groups 1 and 2 is : 8 + 10 = 18; N–2 = 18 – 2 = 16 df
(2) The df for groups 1 and 3 is : 8 + 12 = 20; N–2 = 20 – 2 = 18 df
(3) The df for groups 1 and 4 is : 8 + 14 = 22; N–2 = 22 – 2 = 20 df
(4) The df for groups 2 and 3 is : 10 + 12 = 22; N–2 = 22 – 2 = 20 df
(5) The df for groups 2 and 4 is : 10 + 14 = 24; N–2 = 24 – 2 = 22 df
(6) The df for groups 3 and 4 is : 12 + 14 = 26; N–2 = 26 – 2 = 24 df

The next step is to find out whether our t-ratios are significant or not, if significant at what level. As stated above the Fisher's 't' Table should be referred to. We must have two values. In the case of the first combination between groups 1 and 2 the degrees of freedom is 16 and the t-ratio is 8.01. The t-ratio Table needs only two values unlike the F-ratio Table which needs 3 values. In the t-ratio Table the P values are given in row, from left to right and the degrees of freedom are given vertically in column on the extreme left. The Table is full of the numbers of 't' values. We will have to find out the probability value associated with the degrees of freedom and the 't' value.

Since we are testing a hypothesis, it is to be stated whether it is true or false. But we cannot say that it is true or false unless it is tested. Therefore, we may only state approximately, the probability of being true. Probability is a statistical term, which means an event or other thing is likely to occur. Or a measure of value is likely to occur, or there is a likelihood of occurrence of an event. It is probable that a value can be between zero (0), which is false or impossibility and one (1.0), which is true or certainty. This is the probable result that can occur in any experiment. Thus, a hypothesis or proposition is testable if only a degree or probability for it is determined, possibly. Therefore, let us find out the P value for each degree of freedom and the N.

In the case of first df 16 (Table 18.4), let us go down from 1 down to 16 on the column of the 't' Table. The P values begin with a 't' value 0.128, 0.392, 0.525 and go on till 4.015. But we must read the values in this row until the value is the same as our 't' value or to the nearest or very close to our specific 't' value. In this case the obtained 't' value is 8.01. In the 't' Table the highest value against the df 16 is 4.015. This is the highest 't' value in the Table closest to our obtained value 8.01. Therefore, we read the Table up to the number closest to the obtained value 8.01 and the P value associated with the obtained value. In this particular case the level of significance is 0.001, which is very highly significant. Since the 't' value 8.01 is more than the Table value 4.015, ($P<0.001$) it is highly significant at .001 level. If our 't' value is less than 4.015, than the P value be either .01 or .05, depending upon the obtained 't' value.

Let us also assume that our obtained 't' value in two of our cases for 16 df are 2.25 and 2.95. In these cases, the former (2.25) 't' value is having the P value as .05 and in the later case (2.95) the P value is .01. Generally, we are satisfied, if the obtained t value has the P value of .05 or .01. From this we can infer one fact that if the 't' value goes higher, then the P value becomes smaller and the significance also is becoming more accurate. For example, with 16 degrees of freedom if the 't' value is 1.28 or 1.75 then the P value is 0.90 and 0.10. In other word a greater difference between two mean scores and lower standard deviations among the groups or of the sub-samples, the higher will be the 't' values and, the smaller will be the P values, we would obtain.

Therefore, the result may be stated that a 't' value of 8.01 has an associated P value smaller than 0.01 ($P<0.01$). This means that the obtained 't' value 8.01 is greater than the 't' value of 2.92 associated with the P value 0.01. Hence, we may interpret the first 't' value and the associated P in this manner. The difference between the mean scores of the groups 1 and 2 that was obtained has a probability, smaller than 0.01. In other words, a difference between the mean scores of this size (8+10) we may expect the P value may be less than this obtained value only once if the experiment is repeated for one hundred times. Therefore, there is no chance of accepting the null hypothesis when the difference between the two mean scores is so high and hence it is rejected. The empirical hypothesis is accepted as the difference between the two mean scores (19.34 – 8.80 = 10.54) in this case has yeilded a t ratio of 8.01 with a probability of .01 (Table 18.4).

Since the difference between the two means is significant at one percent level there is no chance of attributing the result to chance or any other reason as the experiment was conducted with sufficient protection. The difference is real difference, because the independent variable had produced different effects in both the groups. This is what expected in this experiment. The same procedure should be followed to determine the probability and the result should be interpreted in the same manner in all other cases.

The mean score difference between groups 1 and 3 is 4.15 which has yeilded a t-ratio of 4.88. With 18 df, the obtained P value is higher than any of the t-ratios given in the Table. The obtained 't' value is nearest to 2.88 which has the probability of 0.01. Since the obtained 't' value 4.88 is higher than the Table 't' value (2.88) the P is less than 0.01 (P<.01). In other words, even if the experiment is conducted one hundred times the same result would be obtained for ninety nine times. Since the obtained 't' value is too high (4.18) the probability is too small to the extent of 0.001 (P< 0.001). The Table 't' value is only 3.92 for a P of 0.001, but the obtained 't' value in this case is 4.88. Therefore, we may also state even if the experiment is repeated for one thousand times the same result would be obtained and only once there will be a chance for variation from this result.

The third comparison is between groups 1 and 4. With 20 df the 't' value is only 1.49, since the difference between the two mean scores is very small (1.09). Therefore, the difference is not significant at any level. The null hypothesis in this case is accepted and the empirical hypothesis is rejected.

The fourth comparison is between the groups 2 and 3. The mean score difference 2.55 has yielded a t-value of 2.97. With 20 df, the probability is less than 0.01 (P< 0.01). The t-value associated with the P value of 0.01 is 2.85 which is smaller than the obtained t-value (2.97). Therefore, the difference between these two groups is a real difference. Hence the null hypothesis is rejected and the empirical hypothesis is accepted.

The fifth comparison in this test is between groups 2 and 4. The mean score difference 7.63 has yielded a t-value of 10.17. With 22 df, the t-value has a probability of less than 0.01 (P< 0.01). The result shows that a difference between the means of these two groups of this size (10+14 = 24 – 2 = 22) has a probability, smaller than 0.01. A result different from this may occur only once out of one hundred times if the experiment is repeated. Therefore, the difference between groups 2 and 4 is highly significant. The null hypothesis is rejected and the empirical hypothesis is accepted. The difference between these two groups is a real difference and no other variable can be attributed to this result. The independent variable seems to have had different influence in these two groups. The independent variable had the expected influence in the scores of the dependent variable in these two (2 and 4) groups. The mean score difference is so high as to yield a high t-value on a highly significant smaller probability value of 0.001. The t-value for the probability of 0.001 is only 3.79 whereas the obtained 't' value is 10.17. Therefore the obtained 't' value 10.17 has still smaller probability (P<0.001) than the P of 0.01 (P<0.01). This means that a variation from this result may occur only once out of one thousand times, if this experiment is repeated.

The sixth comparison is between the groups 3 and 4. The mean score difference between these two groups is 5.19 and the obtained 't' value is 6.56. With 24 df (12+14=26−2=24) the probability value for the 't' value of 6.56 is smaller than 0.01 (P<0.01). The mean score difference between two groups of this size may occur only once out of one hundred times. Therefore, the difference between these two groups is a real difference. Since the experiment was conducted in a protected manner the influence of no other variable can be attributed to this result. The independent variable had exerted different effects on the two groups or the two groups had different effects from the independent variable so as to have influence in the test scores. This is the effect expected in this experiment. Therefore, the null hypothesis is rejected and the empirical hypothesis is accepted. The Table value for the probability of 0.01 is 2.80, whereas the obtained t-value is 6.56. Therefore, the P value for the obtained t-value may be still smaller. To what extent it is smaller? The Fisher's Table indicates that the 't' (6.56) has a P of less than 0.001 (P<0.001) since the Table t-value is only 3.75. This may be interpreted that the mean score difference between these two groups may be obtained for 999 times out of one thousand times if the experiment is repeated. Only once there is a likelihood of different result.

Let us interpret the result. The results of this experiment reveal that there is definite difference in scores between the semi-urban and rural students in their memory test. The semi-urban students scored higher than the rural students and the differences between semi-urban and rural students are highly significant. Groups 1 and 4 consisted of semi-urban students and groups 2 and 3 rural students. There is no significant difference between groups 1 and 4 who were from semi-urban area. But there is significant difference between groups 2 and 3 who were the students of rural areas. The reasons for having no difference between the two semi-urban groups might be that the semi-urban areas are almost the same. The influence the students receive from home and other environmental areas also might be the same type. Therefore, there is no difference between the scores of the two semi-urban groups in the memory test. But in the case of rural students, there might have been varied reasons, such as home situation, parents' occupation, income, education, facilities for going to school, the distance between home and the school, how they spend the holidays, all might have contributed to the difference in the scores of the memory test of the rural students.

In the preceding section we have described an experiment conducted on a small sample and the data were treated systematically by statistical methods of analysis of variance and a 't' test. It was also explained how a different formula was used for determining the standard deviations of small groups. The formula for determining the standard deviation of a larger group is by using the frequency distribution method. Therefore, the scores of the four small groups were treated statistically and the mean scores, the dispersion scores, like the standard deviations (SDs), the standard errors of the mean scores (SEMs) were determined.

To test whether there is any significant difference between the four groups, the F-test based upon analysis of variance was worked out.

Since we have to find out whether there is significant difference between group means, and the sample of four groups involve $\left[\frac{N(N-1)}{2} = \frac{4(4-1)}{2} = \frac{12}{2} = 6\right]$ 6 pairs, in order to reduce the labour required in this calculation, first of all we can have a overall test of the four groups simultaneously to see whether the differences between the group means are significant. It is a single composite test. Therefore, the analysis of variance was worked out to find out the F-ratio.

In this test the obtained F-ratio is 22.16, which is significant at ($P<.01$) one percent level. The Table value for one percent level is only 4.31, whereas the obtained value is 22.16. Therefore, the differences between the means of the groups are highly significant and therefore, we can test the six pairs by a 't' test to find out the level differences between the groups. Another important component required for determining the 't' ratio is the standard errors of the mean scores differences. Hence we worked out the Standard Errors of the Mean scores Differences (SEM_{Diff}) for determining the 't' ratios and to find out the level differences between the groups.

This example, to illustrate the treatment of the scores and the analysis of the results presented in the Tables for discussion, is only for small groups with limited hypotheses. Therefore, in order to have some comprehensive idea about the treatment of the data and discuss the results, an example of larger sample is needed. This larger group example is taken from one of the studies conducted on an earlier occasion by Rajamanickam and Mercy Arunmozhi (1992).

The problem of this illustrated larger group study, is to assess the influence of adjustment problem of adolescent girl students on their psychosomatic problems. The population chosen for the study was the adolescent girl students studying in higher secondary schools, in 11th and 12th standards. Their age ranged from 15 to 19 years. From six schools, out of 1200 girls student a sample of 25 percent of students was randomly drawn, which constituted 300 students. Three test materials were administered to them. They were (1) Adjustment Inventory of School student, (2) Cornell Index, (3) Personal Information Questionnaire. The collected materials were scored according to the procedure and the individuals scores were obtained.

The scores were treated statistically and presented in tables for analyses and discussion of the results. The statistical treatments applied to the data to verify the hypotheses were coefficient of correlation, means, standard deviations, standard errors of the mean scores, Analysis of variance, Standard errors of the mean score differences and the critical ratios. Since the sample size in each sub-group was above 30 in number, the critical ratios were worked out and not 't' test as this applied to small groups below 30. Every treatment is systematically presented step by step as given in the sample of the small groups test. The following hypotheses were formulated and tested in this study.

1. There is a positive association between adolescent girls adjustment problems and their psychosomatic disorders.
2. The well adjusted adolescent girls are emotionally stable and have less emotional stress.
3. The well adjusted adolescent girls are less prone to psychosomatic disorders than the maladjusted and the moderately adjusted adolescent girls.
4. Students from high income families are free from Psychosomatic problems and students from low income families are more prone to Psychosomatic problems.

To test the first hypothesis the correlation coefficient between the scores of adjustment Inventory and scores of Cornell Index test was worked out and given in the Table 18.1 with the test of significance and level of significance.

Table 18.5 : Coefficient of correlation between the scores of Adjustment and Cornell Index test (N-300)

	Tests	No. of Subjects	Correlation	Test of significance	Level of significance
1.	Adjustment Inventory				
2.	Cornell Index	300	0.42	7.58	0.01

This Table provides all the relevant information about the experiment. The population, sample size, tests used, the correlation coefficient, the test of significance and the level of significance are given in the Table 18.5. The subjects were 300 adolescent girls studying in schools. The result can be analysed and explained clearly if only all the information as given in the Table are provided.

The experimenter should not begin this section with the results of the statistical analysis. But, for example, he/she should begin with something like this : The result of the present experiment, as given in Table 18.5, indicates clearly that the students' adjustment problems as revealed by the Adjustment Inventory are having positive association with the students' psychosomatic disorders as revealed by the Cornell Index test.

If the students' adjustment problems increased then their psychosomatic disorders also increased. The correlation coefficient, (0.42) which indicates the level of association between adjustment problems and psychosomatic disorders, is low which means that most of the students were not having serious adjustment problems and psychosomatic disorders in this sample. But the correlation coefficient is significant. This shows that those students, the adolescent girls, who have adjustment problems have psychosomatic disorders and those who have no adjustment problems are free from psychosomatic disorders. The correlation coefficient is significant at 0.01 level, which shows the consistency between the two variables and the interaction between them. Since the adjustment problems and psychosomatic disorders go together hand in hand in the case of adolescent girl students the hypothesis one is confirmed.

With regard to the second hypothesis, if the girls were well adjusted then their emotional stress should be low and their psychosomatic disorders also should be low. This is tested by arranging their adjustment scores from lowest to highest. The top 25 percent of the scores are considered as upper group, the bottom 25 percent, the lower group and the middle 50 percent, the middle group. The mean scores, the S.Ds and S.E.Ms of these three groups in the emotional scale and in the Cornell Index test were worked out. Thus there are three groups, the upper group well adjusted (scored low) the lower group maladjusted (scored high) and the middle group moderately adjusted (scored in between).

Table 18.6 : Distribution of Mean scores, SDs and SEMs for three groups of adolescent girl students in the Emotional and Cornell Index tests

S. No.	Groups	Code	N	Type of scores	Emotional scores	Psychosomatic scores) Cornell test)
1.	Well adjusted	A	75	Mean	5.13	25.29
				SD	3.23	12.60
				SEM	0.38	1.47
2.	Moderately adjusted	B	150	Mean	6.91	33.32
				SD	4.01	13.32
				SEM	0.33	1.10
3	Maladjusted	C	75	Mean	7.75	39.31
				SD	3.17	15.73
				SEM	0.37	1.83

Table 18.6, is another example for providing relevant information for analysis and interpretation. It is important that the mean scores should be followed by dispersion scores, the SDs and the SEMs. Most of the Indian researchers never take cognizance of the dispersion scores. The report writer should know the difference between smaller SDs and the larger or wider SDs. If the dispersion score is smaller the subjects have answered the questionnaire very well or in case of experiment reacted or responded accurately. It may also reveal the interest with which the subjects have taken the test. Therefore, the SDs and SEMs of the mean scores are more relevant data in the table for analysis and also for further treatment of the data to find out the 't' ratio or critical ratio. (The important uses of SDs and SEMs are explained elsewhere).

The results of the present experiment (Table 18.6) indicate clearly that the well adjusted adolescent girls are emotionally stable without much emotional stress and are least prone to psychosomatic disorders. The maladjusted girl students are found to be more emotionally unstable or prone to more emotional stress and have developed more psychosomatic disorders. The middle group girls who are moderately adjusted show moderate emotional stress and also have developed moderate psychosomatic disorders. The results show that about 25 percent of the adolescent girl students are very much maladjusted, have more emotional stress and more prone to psychosomatic disorders while the same percentage of adolescent girls are well adjusted, emotionally stable and least prone to psychosomatic disorders. But, about 50 percent of the adolescent girls who fall in the middle are moderate in all respects. Therefore, the results confirm the second hypothesis.

The tabular form is the summary of the data in which the raw data are avoided. The summary of the data is expressed in the form of means, standard deviations (SDs) and standard errors of the means (SEMs). It can be seen that the well adjusted group obtained the lowest mean (5.13) with an SD of 3.23 in the emotional scale and obtained a mean of 25.29 with an SD of 12.60 in the Cornell Index test. In the case of the maladjusted group the dispersion score in the emotional scale is little smaller in comparison to the well adjusted group. In the case of moderately adjusted group the dispersion score in the emotional scale is little higher. This shows that in the emotional scale the maladjusted group girls answered the items little more consistantly than the moderately adjusted group. The narrower the dispersion score, the SD, the greater the consistency in answering the items. In the case of Cornell Index test the well adjusted and moderately adjusted groups answered the items much better than the maladjusted group. The dispersion is wider (15.73) for the maladjusted group which means the maladjusted adolescent girls were very much inconsistent in answering items in Cornell Index test. The standard deviation in any measurement is an important variance of the population mean.

Another important or best estimate of variance is the standard error of the population mean. The standard error is a measure of the influence of some extraneous variable or it may be also due to instrument or chance. The errors inherent in the instrument or test can be stated as systematic and unsystematic errors or random errors. However carefully an instrument or test is designed and developed the influence of random errors will be there in the measurement. Therefore, these errors will cancel out each other when sufficient measures are made and averaged in a study. But, however, in a small sample studies random errors may be accumulated significantly. The other errors like constant errors or systematic errors can be eliminated or reduced to a minimum by applying various methods in the experimental situation or by calibrating the instrument. But in the case of random errors, however precise instruments we use, and whatever steps we take to control the circumstances in the experimental situation, the random errors may be inherent in all our measurements. In an experiment the standard error may be due to noise or visibility or heat. The level of the influence of this variable can be measured in the population. This we call the standard error of the population or population mean. Many of the researchers in psychological studies and those who wish to publish papers in scientific journal do not understand the importance of the standard error of mean and often omit or neglect it. It is important that this should be included in the tabular column of their studies and interpreted.

Some are of the view that the standard deviation is sufficient to indicate the error variance of the population. But the standard deviation sometimes will exaggerate the influence of variables. Therefore, the standard error of the population mean should be given in the tables. The standard error, therefore, is the corrected form of the standard deviation of the population for the influence of the sample size. The formula to work out the SEM is : SEM $\frac{SD}{\sqrt{N}}$. The standard deviation when devided by the root of the number of observations or the sample or the size of the sample we get the standard error of the mean.

Let us interpret the data given in Table 18.6. The standard errors of the mean (SEM) on the emotional scale for all the three groups are almost same. But the middle group (moderately adjusted) is having little smaller (0.33) SEM compared to the other two groups. This is because of the sample size (N-150). For the smaller samples the SEM may go higher and higher and for the bigger samples it may go lower and lower. This is in accordance with the statistical principle. This is also true in the case of Cornell Index test scores.

In this study of adjustment problems and psychosomatic disorders among adolescent girls, the adjustment problem is the independent variable and the psychosomatic disorder is the dependent variable. The other minor dependent variable in this study has been the emotional states. The maladjusted girls (N = 75) scored high on both dependent variables. They have more psychosomatic disorders and their variance score (SD) is higher indicating greater dispersion of scores. The individual scores seem to be fluctuating between too high and too low. Because of this the standard error of the population mean also is higher (1.83). The maladjusted girls, therefore, had not answered the items of the Cornell Index test consistently. They seem to have struggled whether to answer the items with 'yes' answer or 'no' answer.

It has been observed in this study that the adjustment problem as an independent variable classify the 300 adolescent girl students into three groups, as well adjusted, moderately adjusted and maladjusted and these three groups differ considerably in the major dependent variable, the psychosomatic disorders (Table 18.6). In the analysis of the result and in the interpretation of scores it has been observed that these three groups showed marked differences in their mean scores on psychosomatic disorders. Now, we will have to test whether these differences are real or spurious, keeping in mind the third hypothesis. The classical statistical procedure applied to this type of multi-group design is the analysis of variance. The analysis of variance permits us to assess simultaneously whether something other than error is responsible for the differences observed in the multi-group experiment.

According to McGuigan (1978) analysis of variance is a method of analysing the total variance present in an experiment into components and computing ratios between those components. By means of these, various empirical questions can be answered such as testing whether two or more groups in an experiment are reliably differing. The logical sequence of analysis of variance is almost as the 't' test. McGuigan says that the simplest application of analysis of variance would be in testing the mean differences between the randomized groups. On a two-groups design the result of the analysis of variance would be equivalent to that of a 't' test. Therefore, the analysis of two-groups design can be done either by using a 't' test or analysis of variance (F-test) and can obtain almost the same conclusions. But if we use more than two groups we cannot use 't' test for testing the means simultaneously. Therefore, we must use analysis of variance if we want to test more than two groups simultaneously.

While testing more than two groups there are several means (one mean for each group) to be compared in analysis of variance and since the simple method of analysis of variance (that t test) is not feasible, the F statistics is normally used. The formula is :

$$F = \frac{\text{Between or Among groups variance}}{\text{Within group variance}}$$

The F statistics has two different degrees of freedom, one for the numerator, i.e. among groups and the other for the denominator, i.e. within groups. Since the numerator is referring to the number of groups (minus one), it is always smaller depending upon the number of groups involved in the study. But since the denominator is referring to the number of subjects in the groups (minus number of groups), it is always greater. Therefore, while calculating the degrees of freedom for the variance between or among groups we must subtract one (1) from the number of groups and while calculating the degrees of freedom for the variance within groups we must substract one (1) for each group. For example, in our study there are 3 degrees of freedom. The number of freedom for variance between or among groups is 3 — 1 = 2. The number of degrees of freedom for within groups is 300 — 3 = 297. For the total variance the degrees of freedom is 300 — 1 = 299.

The F ratio is the mean square (MS) between or among groups over the mean square within groups. This may be stated as :

$$F = \frac{\text{Mean square between or among groups}}{\text{Mean squares within groups}}$$

The mean square is the sum of squares divided by its respective number of degrees of freedom. Therefore, we must first determine the total sum of squares. The total sum of squares is worked out from the dependent variable values or the scores of all the participants irrespective of experimental conditions. What we are doing here essentially is that the total sum of squares are analysed into two major components, as (1) the sum of squares between or among groups and (2) the sum of squares within groups.

The equation for computing total sum of squares is this:

Total sum of squares

$$= (\Sigma X_1^2 + \Sigma X_2^2 + \Sigma X_3^2 \ldots\ldots \Sigma X_r^2) - \frac{(\Sigma X_1 + \Sigma X_2 + \Sigma X_3 \ldots\ldots \Sigma X_r)^2}{N}$$

This equation needs some explanation. The values within the bracket such as $\Sigma X_1^2 + \Sigma X_2^2 + \ldots\ldots\ldots\ldots$ refer to the sum (Σ) of squares of the individual scores $X_1^2 + X_2^2$ etc. In other words, every individual score is squared, and all the scores squared are summed up.

The second portion of equation refers to the sum of the individual scores in each group squared and divided by the total participant of all the groups. For example, in the equation the value $\Sigma X_1 + \Sigma X_2 + \Sigma X_3 \ldots\ldots\ldots\ldots$ all refer to the total scores of all the participants in every group. The next step is to sum up all the group scores and the sum should be squared. The third step in this equation is to divide the squared value into the number of total participants of all the groups (N). The subscript 'r' in the equation in two places refers to the number. It may be denoting any number of values (groups).

The second important step in the application of analysis of variance is to analyse the total sum of squares (SS) into two major components.

They are (1) the sum of squares among the groups and (2) the sum of squares within groups. The equation is stated in this way :

Sum of squares among the groups

$$= \frac{(\Sigma X_1)^2}{n_1} + \frac{(\Sigma X_2)^2}{n_2} + \frac{(\Sigma X_3)^2}{n_3} + \ldots \frac{(\Sigma X_r)^2}{n_r} - \frac{(\Sigma X_1 + \Sigma X_2 + \Sigma X_3 + \ldots\ldots \Sigma X_r)^2}{N}$$

This equation also needs a simplified explanation. The first part of the equation $\frac{(\Sigma X_1)^2}{n_1}$ etc., refers to the total score of n_1 participants in group 1 squared and divided by the number of participants of that group. Since in groups the scores of participants and the number of participants vary, each group's score is treated separately and summed up.

The second part of this equation is the same as the second part of the first equation. That is, the sum of individual scores in each group squared and divided by the total number of participants of all the groups.

By using the above quoted two equations to our experimental data, we need to compute two mean squares. One mean square for the among groups and the other for within groups.

Table 18.7 : Summary of the Analysis of variance for the scores of three types of adjustment groups of students in the Psychosomatic disorders (Cornell Index)

Source of variation	Sum of Squares	df	Mean Squares	F-Ratio	Level of significance
Among Groups	7410.69	2	3705.29	19.42	0.01
Within Groups	57049.47	297	190.80		
Total	64460.85	299			

The first one is computed by dividing the sum of squares (7410.58) by the corresponding degrees of freedom (2) and for the later by dividing the sum of squares (57049.47) by the corresponding degree of freedom (297). Thus the mean square for the among groups is (7410.58 ÷ 2) 3705.29 and for the within groups (57049.47 ÷ 297) is 190.80. The summary of the data of analysis of variance is given in Table 18.7. Now we must see whether the mean square variance among the groups is greater or smaller in proportion to the mean square variance within groups. If it is proportionately greater, then we may state that the value of the dependent variable of the experiment for the groups are varying considerably and the dependent variable had some effect upon the dependent variable. To what extent the independent variable had effect upon the dependent variable? To test this phenomenon we must use Fisher's statistical Test called the F-test. The answer obtained by this test is called F-ratio. This is obtained by dividing the mean square among groups by the mean square within groups (3705.29 ÷ 190.80) and the F-ratio is 19.42. This means that the mean square variance among groups is 19.42 times greater than the mean square variance within groups.

The F-ratio indicates that the three groups in this experiment certainly vary among themselves on the basis of the influence of independent variable upon the dependent variable. This is in relation to the hypothesis. The hypothesis is: The well adjusted students are less prone to psychosomatic disorders than the maladjusted and moderately adjusted students.

The F-ratio 19.42 shows that these three groups differ among themselves in the level of psychosomatic disorders. The next step is to determine the P value associated with this F-ratio. Let us assume that the P value is 0.01. That is P = 0.01. If the F value is less than P value then the hypothesis is rejected. If the P value associated with the F-ratio is greater, then the hypothesis is accepted. Then we may conclude that there is significant difference among the group means.

In our example, illustrated here with data in Table 18.7, let us ascertain the P value associated with the F value. The F value as given in Table 18.7 is 19.42. From the Table of F (Fisher and Yates table) we can ascertain the P value with the help of the degrees of freedom, 2 (numerator) and 297 (denominator) given in the table in the column under df. Let us search for the value. The numerator values are going from left to right in the table and denominator values are going from top to bottom. For the degrees of freedom 2 and 297, go down from top 2 (numerator) till you find the denominator 297. In the F Table after the denominator 120 there is only infinite. The denominator df is gone into the infinite numbers. Therefore we find in the F table, the highest P value is 4.60 for 2 and 297 degrees of freedom. If the F value is 4.60 then the P value is 0.01. But in our example the F value is 19.42 and it is very much higher than the table value 4.60. Therefore, we may conclude that the groups differ from one another at a high significant level. This means, the variation of independent variable had definite influence upon the dependent variable. The dependent variable measure is the psychosomatic disorder which is highly varying from group to group. The groups are divided on the basis of the level of adjustment problems. The well adjusted group is definitely different from the maladjusted and the moderately adjusted groups.

While analysing the results as given in Table 18.7, we have ascertained that the F value is too high and it is overall reliable. Therefore, we must make comparisons between pairs or any two groups to see which are the groups differ significantly. To ascertain this we must use the t-tests. Suppose, for example in this study if the F value is not having overall significant difference then we must state that there are no reliable differences among the groups and therefore the difference between groups does not exist significantly. If this condition exists in a multigroup experiment then we need not go for the next statistical treatment, the t-test. But in our example, the difference among groups is highly significant (F-19.42) and therefore, we are going for the t-tests. Since there are three sub-groups in this experiment, there should be three t-tests. The t-tests are worked between groups and we get three pairs, using the formula $\frac{N(N-1)}{2} = \frac{3(3-1)}{2} = 3$, between groups 1 and 2, between groups 1 and 3 and between groups 2 and 3.

Since the F-test value is too high (F-ratio = 19.42) we can assume the t-values between groups 1 and 2, between group 1 and 3 and between groups 2 and 3 are significant at 0.01 level. If the t-test value is reliable at 0.01 level then we can accept hypothesis. One statistical theory is that if the sample size is below 30(N=30) then the t-test is used. But if the sample size is above 30 then the appropriate statistical test is critical ratio (C.R.). In our example the sample size is 300 (75+150+75=300). In Table 18.6 all the other statistics like the mean, SD, and SEM are given for the 3 groups. In Table 18.7 the summary of the results is given. The SE of the mean difference, the CR were computed using the data as given in Table 18.6. The Standard Errors for the mean difference (SEM_D), and the Critical Ratios were worked out and presented in Table 18.8, with the level of significance.

The purpose of ascertaining the t-value and the critical ratio in multi-group experiment is the same. Both the statistics indicate the level of difference between any two groups. Table 18.8 shows the critical ratios between the groups A and B, Groups A and C and Groups B and C and the critical ratios are significant at 0.01 level. Fisher's Table IV is used for both the t-ratio and for the critical ratio for ascertaining the probability value. The degrees of freedom for t-test and for critical ratio is N-1. We will have to search for the P value by going from top to bottom and find out where the t-ratio or the critical ratio value falls in the table against the degrees of freedom (N−1).

Table 18.8: Mean Differences, critical ratios and the level of significances for the three types of adjustment groups on the level of psychosomatic disorders

S. No.	Groups	Code	Mean scores	Mean difference	S.E. of Mean difference	C.R.	Level of significance
1.	Well adjusted	A	25.29	8.03	1.82	4.42	0.01
	Moderately adjusted	B	33.32				
2.	Well adjusted	A	25.29	14.02	2.33	6.02	0.01
	Maladjusted	C	39.31				
3.	Moderately adjusted	B	33.32	5.99	3.13	2.94	0.01
	Maladjusted	C	39.31				

Since all the three critical ratios are significant at 0.01 level or one percent level, each group is different from every other group. The psychosomatic disorders of the maladjusted girls seem to be too high among the three groups of adolescent girls and even the moderately adjusted girls differ from the well adjusted girls at one percent level in their psychosomatic disorders. The well adjusted adolescent girls scored the lowest (25.29) indicating that they were the least prone to psychosomatic disorders. These results further support the hypothesis. Therefore, we may conclude that the well adjusted adolescent girl students do not seen to suffer from much of psychosomatic disorders as revealed by this enquiry, whereas the maladjusted adolescent girl students seem to suffer from too much of psychosomatic disorders. The moderately adjusted girls also seem to suffer from the psychosomatic disorders to some extent. Further enquiries also may be pursued to see who are those well adjusted girls and who are those maladjusted girls. What are the other independent variables that determine the psychosomatic disorders? We may state tentatively, income of the parents of the students seem to have influence in the psychosomatic disorders.

Therefore, the hypothesis, that if the students are from high income groups then they are free from psychosomatic problems and if the students from low income groups then they are prone to psychosomatic disorders, is tested in this studey and the results are presented in Table 18.9. Family income position is not without any effect upon the children's life. The poor income of the parents may cause maladjustments which may also lead to the development of psychosomatic disorders.

Table 18.9 : Showing the critical ratios and the levels of significance for different income groups on the Psychosomatic disorders as revealed by Cornell Index test

S. No.	Group	Code	N	Mean	SD	SEM	Mean difference between	SE of Mean Difference	CR	Level of sig.
1.	Below Rs.500	A	110	34.44	14.24	1.36	AB: 2.07	1.77	1.18	NS
2.	501 to 1000	B	117	32.37	12.28	1.14	AC: 6.66	2.15	3.09	.01
3.	1001 to 2000	C	49	27.78	11.64	1.68	AD: 9.63	2.55	3.79	.01
							BC: 4.59	2.01	2.28	.05
4.	2001 and above	D	23	24.78	10.38	2.21	BD: 7.59	2.44	3.11	.01
							CD: 3.00	2.76	1.09	NS

Table 18.9 shows the scores of the adolescent girl students who were drawn from various income groups. It is found that the highest score (34.44) on the Cornell Index test was obtained by the lowest income groups girls. This group also scored high (20.11) in adjustment inventory. This means that the girls who come from the lowest income group had more adjustment problems and psychosomatic disorders than in other groups. The scores on Cornell Index test are in a systematic order from highest to lowest (34.44, 32.37, 27.78 and 24.48) in accordance with the income order *i.e.* from lowest to highest income. The four income groups on the Cornell Index test have scored with considerable variation. The groups A and C, A and D and B and D differ from each at 0.01 levels and groups B and C differ at 0.05 level. Groups A and B, C and D did not show much difference between them. The first two low income groups and the last two high income groups have small difference between them. The two low income groups scored high in the Cornell Index test as to show much difference with the two high income groups who have scored low. Therefore it may be stated that girl students who come from high income groups are free from psychosomatic problems and the girls students who come from low income groups are prone to more psychosomatic problems. Therefore, the results support the hypothesis (Table 18.9).

The statistics we have been applying to treat the experimental data is the conventional approach that has been in vogue for a long time. This approach involves the application of analysis of variance, the F-test, the t-test and the critical ratio. Of late some of the statisticians are not fully satisfied with this approach, as this is not fulfilling all the requirements. Therefore other statistical procedures have been designed for comparing the mean scores of the multiple groups in an experiment. One such approach now widely prevalent is the Duncan's Range Test (For details see Chapter 2, Psychological Statistics).

Use of Tables and Figures

We have already stated in the earlier section that the results of an enquiry should be presented in the tabular columns or in the form of figures. The table is a summary of the data. The writer can present the data in tabular colums or in figures depends upon the nature of the data and the aims of the writer. Whether the data are presented in tables or in figures an order should be maintained. While presenting the data in whatever form it is important that the mean scores of the study should be given in a table. The other important variations are the SDs and the SEMs. Straight-away going for the analysis of variance or t-test or critical ratio is not advisable. What you are ascertaining is the level of difference between groups, for which the basic data required is the mean scores the SDs and SEMs. The reader of your paper should not be put into confused state in understanding the meaning of your results. It is often observed that some of the Indian researchers who published papers in scientific journals straightaway go to the final data and start analysing them. The researchers should know that this is an incorrect way of presenting the data. It is for the readers that the paper is published and he/she must be in a position of repeating the same experiment if he/she wished. If the important data like the means and other variations or dispersions scores are not given in one of the tables the reader will not be in a state of understanding the paper and he/she may skip over to another paper which provides all relevant information in the tables. Thus, such writer's research paper is neglected by the readers and the paper looses its importance however valuable the problem might be. Therefore, paper writers should pay more attention to these aspects.

The paper writer, if he/she wishes to present the data of his/her investigation in the form of figures he/she should bear in mind that the relationship between independent and the dependent variables should be clearly stated. The dependent variable should be plotted on the vertical axis (y) and the independent variable on the horizontal axis (x) and the analyses should be made. The type of scores the writer uses on the vertical axis and on the horizontal axis depends upon the writer's motivation. It requires to label clearly the x and y axes and should specify the unit of measure for the independent and dependent variables. Colour pencil should not be used to indicated different functions. The writer should use continuous or broken lines or different geometrical symbols for each separate function.

The Table, which summaries the data, whether it is big or small should be given in a separate page and the Table heading should be always at the top of the Table. The Table heading should indicate the independent and dependent variables. The Tables' numbers should be always given in arabic numbers, *i.e.* 1, 2, 3, 4, 5, etc. in the order of their appearance. The figures, if any for presenting the data should also be given in a separate page and the heading of the figure should be always at the bottom of the figure. The heading of the figure also should indicate the independent and dependent variables. It is also important that the author of the paper should indicated the place where the table or figure should be put in the text of the paper. For example it should be indicated like this :

Insert Table 1 or Figure 1 here

The writer of the paper should pay more attention and care in preparing the tables and figures for publication in the scientific journals. Specifications for preparing the paper as given in Journal Wrapper pages should be read thoroughly and the format should be followed meticulously. The data presented in the Table and Figures should be sufficient enough for the readers to understand the substance of the paper correctly. All graphs and pictures should be labelled as "figures" and not as graphs or charts. The number of Figures should be serially indicated with arabic numerals, i.e. 1, 2, 3, 4, 5 etc.

The Tables and figures should have explanatory titles so that the reader can study the data and he/she should form his/her own conclusions. If the results are clearly titled it would be possible for any reader to know what was found out about the problem within reading the rest of the report. The writer of the paper should bear in mind that tables and figures are supplementary materials which are used to provide clarity to the data and therefore he/she should not substitute graphic materials in place of verbal description of the findings.

4. DISCUSSION

The discussion section, in general, should not contain any tables and graphs. Here the experimenter or the writer interprets and evaluates the empirical findings in relation to the specific problem or hypothesis. The experimenter should also write his/her results relating to the issues, theoretical controversies and other empirical findings described in the introductory section.

The experiment might have been conducted to verify some hypotheses formulated by the experimenter on the basis of review of earlier studies. Since the experimenter has observed that there was a gap of knowledge in the area in which he/she is interested the experimenter had the curiosity to explore that area and evolve some new information through the experiment. Or, the experimenter wished to verify the existing knowledge in certain area whether he/she could get the same result by repeating the same experiment. Whatever the reason might have been for conducting the experiment the writer should state this while interpreting the data. He/she can explain a theory and can state that the results of his/her study are in line with the results of the particular earlier study or run contrary to it. The discussion of the results of the present study may lead to confirm the hypothesis of the author or may reject it. If it is confirmed then the writer should relate it to a similar earlier studies. But, instead, if it is rejected the author should find out reason for the contrary results. The writer may formulate even new hypotheses which may be the reverse to the hypotheses already formulated and tested.

It is also important to related the results to other studies reviewed already in the introductory section. It is possible to evolve certain new ideas by relating the present results to the previous studies. If the experimenter finds any steep raise or fall in the result he/she should state it and also should explain why it is caused. The author of the paper or the experimenter should carefully observe whether any new problems seem to have interfered in the experimental situation and had influence in the result. If such thing was discovered the experimenter should state, why and how it has taken place. There might have been certain limitations in an experiment conducted in a situation. Or, certain variables such as situational or critical might have been beyond the control of the experimenter. All these instances should be stated by the experimenter in this section as suggestions for further studies. The experimenter can also suggest the population for further studies of this type and the instrument suitable for administering on the population. Suggestions to save time, avoid trouble, improvements in the techniques and any problems that may arise in the experiment can also be stated here. The experimenter should finally state whether his/her results can be generalized, if so to what extent. Instead, if the results could not be generalized, the experimenter should suggest the lines on which his/her experiment can be carried out further to verify his/her results and also the population suitable for this.

One strange incidence the experimenter may experience rarely is getting the negative results in his/her experiment. In such cases the experimenter need not feel sorry or wonder. The experimenter can accept the negative result as the experimental result. In a population where there were no studies earlier, results reverse to the hypothesis may occur. Therefore, there is nothing wrong to accept the negative result if any. The negative result itself is a result obtained in an experiment. The experimental result need not always confirm the hypothesis. But authors do not support this idea as research papers with such negative results are not accepted for publication in scientific journals.

The experimenter, therefore, should begin with a short introduction and should give the summary of the important results citing the studies that support his/her findings and the studies that do not support. But the experimenter should also state here all the new results of his/her study and should state what additional knowledge he/she has contributed to this particular field of study.

Let us illustrate the discussion section by giving 'a model discussion' for the data presented in Tables 18.5, 18.6, 18.7 and 18.8 in the result section of the study shown in the example.

The higher secondary education is an intermediate stage in between the high school education and the college education in our country. The students who go to the higher secondary schools are normally between 15 and 17 years of age. In this investigation the age of the students ranged from 15 to 19 years. This shows that some of the students either might have started their school life late by 2 or 4 years or might have failed in 2 or 3 classes once. The higher secondary school period is the period of prime adolescence and often subjected to the emergence of problems. Particularly, the girls who are studying in higher secondary schools often express all types feelings and emotions, show different levels of reactions to situations and develop different kinds of problems. They also complain some kinds of pains and illness and parents have anxieties as to how to deal with them. The adolescent girls students often face adjustment problems and also become highly emotional without expressing it overtly. There are instances that four or five adolescent girl students who had similar adjustment problems at home or at school run away from home jointly. All these contribute to several types of psychosomatic disorders. Therefore, one of the main hypothesis of this study was: there is positive association between adjustment problems and psychosomatic disorders. It is found that the relationship is highly significant at 0.01 level. Those adolescent girls who have adjustment problems have also developed psychosomatic problems correspondingly. Those who had no adjustment problems were free from psychosomatic disorders.

The maladjusted girl students or those girls who had more adjustment problems were also found to be emotionally upset. Such frequent instances might become the cause of psychosomatic illnesses. The hypothesis based on this was accepted as the results were highly significant. Among the three groups (well adjusted, moerately adjusted and maladjusted, Table 18.6) the well adjusted girls were found to be emotionally stable and were with least psychosomatic disorders, whereas the maladjusted girls had more emotional stress and severe psychosomatic disorders. The moderately adjusted group had some emotional upsets and moderate psychosomatic problems. Therefore, it may be stated that in the case of adolescent girls students, more adjustment problems, more emotional instability or emotional stress and severe psychosomatic disorders go together. There were no studies made earlier using adjustment problem as the independent variable and psychosomatic disorder as the dependent variable. The emotional stress is used in this study as the minor dependent variable. Therefore, this is one of the important new results borne out by this enquiry. This hypothesis can be verified in the population of adolescent girls of any culture.

It is also interesting to see that these three groups differ from each other significantly at various levels of psychosomatic disorders (Tables 18.6 and 18.8). In one of the studies conducted at Annamalai University (1984), it was observed that students who participate in games and sports when emotionally maladjusted developed psychosomatic disorders.

The economic status or the financial positions of the families were not without any effect in the adjustment problems and psychosomatic disorders of the adolescent girls. The enquiry revealed that girls from affluent families were better adjusted and had the least psychosomatic disorders than those girls who came from impoverished families. This study has also highlighted that the lower the income the higher the psychosomatic disorders were and the higher the income the lower problems and this result was found to be significant at 0.01 level (Table 18.9).

Generally, the adolescent students are highly sensitive and critical to life event. Girls from impoverished or economically deprived families go to schools with great difficulties and live in the midst of many domestic problems. They will have to do all the household works, take care of the younger ones, take care of themselves, go to schools in time which are far away from their homes and also do their home works. Because of those commitments they could not do better in schools as they develop emotional stress and susceptible to psychosomatic disorders. But this is not the state of affair of the girls who come from affluent families. Therefore, they may be emotionally stable free from psychosomatic illnesses and can do better in schools. Since the differences are significant at one percent level this may be tried to generalize in any population. This state of affair may prevail in any culture in India among the adolescent girls.

5. CONCLUSIONS

This part of the report mainly depends upon the length of the discussion. If the discussion is very short, then conclusions may be combined with discussion. In such case the heading also can be "Discussion and Conclusions". But if the discussion is fairly long, then conclusions may be stated under separate heading. Conclusions may be generalized statements based upon the data of the experiment. Conclusions may be brief and numbered statements, summarising the data. State what purpose has been fulfilled and what has been proved or disproved.

Let us cite some conclusions from the model illustrations stated in the preceding sections.

1. There is a positive association between adjustment problems and psychosomatic disorders in the case of adolescent girl students.
2. The well adjusted adolescent girl students are emotionally stable and are least prone to psychosomatic disorders.
3. The maladjusted adolescent girls are emotionally unstable and are more prone to psychosomatic disorders.
4. The moderately adjusted adolescent girls have moderate adjustment problems and suffer from psychosomatic disorders moderately.
5. Adolescent girl students from low income groups suffer from psychosomatic problems whereas girls from high income groups are not.

6. REFERENCES

This is the last section of the paper. It is a list of books and journals provided at the end.

The paper prepared on the basis of the experimental data should provides evidences or authority for the statements made in the text of the paper. There should not be any general or sweeping remarks or statements. Whatever an important citation is made it should have proper reference to an author who has made such a note. The reference may help the reader or researcher to find out the original source of the material from books or journals and can get more information relating to his/her work. References include, only research papers and books cited in the text. The APA has provided a standard format for citations, which is followed in the write-up of all psychological studies all over the world.

The author of the paper should make it a point that every relevant reference to the studies, given in the text, should be made citing the name of the author or authors and the year of publication within bracket. If the name of the author is associated with the subject matter of the text then, only the year should be cited within the bracket. All the references cited in text of the paper should be arranged alphabetically. Any reference given within quotation, having more than three words should have the page numbers from the journal or from the book.

After having arranged the author's names alphabetically, begin within names of the authors of the book or paper with initials. Secondly, write the title of the book, thirdly, place of publication, fourthly, publisher's name and lastly, the year of publication. If page number is involved put the page numbers after the year. The title of the book should be underlined. This is the format and order of the items for books. In the case of journal the order of the items vary little. The (last) name of the author or authors should come first with initials. Secondly the title of the study without any abbreviation, thirdly, name of the journal in full which should be underlined or italicized, fourthly, year of publication of the study, fifthly, volume number which also should be underlined or italicized — all must come in the same order. If the issue number of journal is to be cited, it should be cited within bracket after the volume number. Lastly the page numbers of the study involving the first page and the last page numbers should be cited. Few examples of the references for books and journals are given here :

Book – Single Author

Allport, G.W. *Becoming* — New Havel, Conn : Yale University Press, 1955.

Book — More than One Author

Anderson, M.S. and Savary, I.M. *Passages : A Guide for Pilgrims of the Mind.* New York; Harper and Row,1972.

Journal — One Author

Duncan, D.S.Multiple range and multiple F-tests. *Biometrics*, 1955, *11*, 1-42.

Journal — More than One Author

Langer, E.J., Bashner, R.S. and Chanowitz, D. 'Decreasing prejudice by increasing discrimination'. *Journal of Presonality and Social Psycholgy*, 1985, *49*, 113-120.

IV. MATTERS OF STYLE

The report writer is to follow certain style in presenting the matters of the study. The experimental findings should be presented in a systematic manner, so that the reader could form an idea about the presentation of the matters. The step by step sequential procedure should not be changed on any account. Once a deviation from the order takes place in one instance another deviation in another place is unavoidable. Then the format is disorganized and the write-up looses its scientific treatment. Some of the researchers or the report writers who are very much interested in preparing papers are not viewing the style and order in a serious manner and they write-up the paper in whatever form convenient for them. For example, the report writer may not be giving the due importance to the 'Method' (methodology) section and straightaway start 'procedure' after giving a brief introduction in few lines. The writer may state the sample or instrument without adequate information. The reader will not make out anything from such papers. Research reports prepared with such shortcomings will not be entertained by scientific journals for publication. Therefore, the format and style laid down by the scientific journals should be strictly followed by the contributors. The Publication Manual of American Psychological Association (1974) provides clear guidelines to the report writers and to the researchers who wish to prepare and publish papers.

Regarding the matters of style, it is difficult to establish fixed guidelines for preparing and writing a report of experimental findings. However there are some commonly accepted stylistic procedure that can be found in most of the psychological literature. The abbreviation, SE, and O for Subjects, Experimenter and Observer are no longer used in the journals published by the American Psychological Association. The use of generic terms such as participants, children, rats, pigeons etc. are better to describe the experimental group rather than subjects.

Further, abbreviations to the units of measures should be used only when they are accompanied by values. For example it should be written like this : The measurement of a piece of gold is given in "millimetres" and *should not be written as in "mm"*. But when the same is accompanied by values it *should be written as "25 mm, 50 mg, 100kg"* etc. Since it has become customary for people in everyday life to indicate measures in abbreviations, researchers and report writers are no exemption to this type of mistakes.

In interpreting the experimental data some report writers used to write : "The difference between the groups is significant at 0.01 percent level". This is not correct way of stating it. It should be "............ at 0.01 level" or it should be ".........significant at 1 percent level", or "one percent level".

The report writer or the experimenter should always use the past tense in his/her report or write-up because the experiment has been completed by the time he/she writes the report. The only exception to use present tense in his/here report is, when he/she interprets the data and discusses them in the results and discussion sections.

In writing the report of the study the clarity is more important and not the language. It is not a test of language ability or the proficiency of the report writer. It should be in a simple language explaining the subject matter meaningfully. It is observed in many research papers that the clarity of the language is given the least importance. Many ambiguity statements are added which do not have anything to do with the subject matter. There are also grammatical mistakes in sentence construction. Such shortcomings can be avoided if the report writer goes through the manuscript once or twice and also by getting the opinion of some experts before it is sent for publication in some scientific journal. Then the typing mistakes also can be avoided. The typing of the matter should not be in a cramped or croweded manner. It should be always in double spacing with sufficient margin, so that corrections can be done without retyping the matter.

If the typing is in a cramped manner, there are chances for the composer of the matter to omit certain lines, which may result in delaying the printing of the paper. Psychologically it causes much strain on the part of the printer. It is because of these problems that every research journal has formulated certain strict conditions and specifications for the preparation of research papers. Journal authors often complain that contributors do not pay serious attention to the problems involved in preparing research papers.

V. CONDUCTING AND PERFORMING THE EXPERIMENT

This section, 'conducting and performing the experiment' is with special reference to psychology class rooms where experiments are conducted for training the students at graduate level or at post-graduate level. In conducting and performing the experiment, organizing and preparing the students of the whole class should be done with all seriousness by the teacher who holds the class. The teacher who conducts the practical class of the experimental psychology should inform the students in the previous class the experiment he is going to conduct, for which he must give the introduction, the plan and procedure. The teacher should dictate the whole matter relating to the experiment and the students should write down the whole thing. While dictating the matter of the experiment, the teacher should also explain certain important aspects of the experiment. Printed or cyclostyled materials of the experiments also may be available. The students should not be asked to copy such materials for the experiment. Because there may be some changes in the procedure or in the instrument the teacher is going demonstrate, may be different type of instrument and in the readily available printed material a different type instrument might have been suggested.

For example in the areas like, learning and memory, perception, lots of improvements in instruments have been made. Computerized system is introduced in the experiments, materials are presented in the Television screen through VCR tapes. Therefore, it is always better to dictate the experimental procedures. Another advantage is, that the students by way of hearing the words and terms from the teacher and by writing the material once in their observation note book, they get certain amount of familiarity with the concept and the procedure. Having done this the teacher should ask the students to come with preparation to the next class to perform this experiment.

Then students of the whole class should be organized into pairs and should be made to sit at the appropriate places. Students should not be left out to have their own partners as they like by moving here and there for conducting the experiment. This would spoil the seriousness of the experiment. We must take examples from Zoology or Botany Department Laboratories regarding the calm performance of the experiments.

The teacher himself/herself can assign the pairs to avoid too much of familiarity between the students. In a pair, one student may be the experimenter and the other participant and *vice versa.* Each pair of students should be made to sit at a reasonable distance without causing any inconvenience or disturbance to another set to students who also may be performing the same experiment or another experiment in the same hall. If possible screen should be placed between two pairs of students to avoid the visibility. Any doubt if the student experimenter had, he/she should refer only to the teacher and not to another student experimenter.

The experiment may be, conducting a performance test or paper-pencil test. Whatever it is, the seating arrangements should be made properly. If it is not possible to engage the whole class of students into one sitting, the class may be divided into two groups and work may be assigned to each group on different dates or times. The students should be informed in advance to bring the essential requirements to the experimental psychology class. The observation notebooks, (any notebook should not be used as an observation notebook) compass box, two lead pencils, one foot scale, eraser etc. should be 'the must' and stressed in every experimental psychology class.

It is also important that the student is expected to go with preparation to the experimental psychology class to perform the experiment on the date fixed for him. The designed experiment should be understood by the student correctly. It is better that the teacher who holds this class should check up whether the students have understood the correct procedure of the experiment they are going to perform. The procedure should be faithfully reproduced and all the experimental conditions as outlined in the design should be sincerely followed. Some students who are not familiar to psychological laboratory, however may have some difficulty in following the experimental directions accurately. Therefore, the teacher who handles this class should observe whether the beginning students are carefully and continuously striving to carry out the procedures exactly as they prescribed. While the performance of the experiment is in progress even a casual remark or conversation may constitute a disrupting feature producing variation in the result which may spoil the experiment. Therefore, it is absolutely essential to maintain the conditions rigidly as they are set down in the experimental design or method. The student experimenter, on any account, should not move from the assigned place during the course of the experiment unless and until he/she completes the task. The experimenter should make all the entries of his/her experimental data in the record notebook and treat the data statistically as suggested by the teacher and get his/her signature with date in the record notebook.

Whether the courses are conducted according to Semester pattern or annual pattern, in awarding of sessional marks to the students in the internal assessment for experimental psychology, the teacher who handles this class should note down the proficiency of each student for every experiment and maintain a permanent record for the final assessment. By this means the teacher may create a sense of responsibility among the students and a kind of morale in performing the experiment in the class room.

VI. ASSESSING PERFORMANCE AND THE RECORD NOTEBOOK

The University Grants Commission has been conducting workshops for various academic purposes. In one of the workshops sponsored by the U.G.C. it has been pointed out that pyschologoical experiments were not conducted in the colleges and universities with all seriousness. The students after conducting one or two experiments go out with an impression that it is "a leisure time activity". In conducing and performing psychological experiment, which is a part of the curriculam there should not be any scope for such impression in the minds of the students. They should be made to know that every task performed in the experimental psychology class is assessed and marks are awarded on the basis of the accuracy of performances.

To substantiate this idea, marks should be awarded to every practical performed and written in the record notebook. The practical record notebook should be submitted by the students before they attend the next practical class. There should not be any delay in submitting the record notebook unless it is an extraordinary circumstance.

The teacher who handles the practical class should go through every practical record note book and make corrections, and marks should be awarded for a total mark of ten. This may vary from one to any number below ten on the basis of the standard and quality of the record. Diagrams and graphs should be drawn wherever necessary. Tables should be drawn and numbered by the students as suggested by the teacher. Similarly, the diagrams and graphs also should be numbered according to the procedure. The teacher should assess various aspects of the records like, the neatness, accuracy of the data, nature of interpretation, diagrams, graphs, tables and the presentation of the data, the introduction, review of literature, critical thinking of the students, all should be assessed and on the basis of all these marks should be awarded.

If a student has not done it perfectly, the teacher should write his remarks at the end of the last page of the record notebook and this should be rectified by the student in the next experiment. The teacher also should check whether he has corrected his mistake. It is also important that the teacher *should maintain a separate attendance register for the practical class.* For awarding marks in the internal assessment the total marks for all the practicals performed in the classroom and the attendance in the practical class should be taken into account. At the end of the semester or year the students should be fully familiar with all the experiments performed in the classroom. They must know at least few names of the authors and the titles of some books in the field of experimental psychology. The concerned teacher should conduct a short orientation periodically with regard to these aspects in order to familiarize with the names of eminent experimental psychologists like Woodworth, Steveson and so on and also the titles of the books published by them.

Therefore, in order to promote efficiently in performing the experiments and to obtain accurate data, it is absolutely necessary that every experiment should be demonstrated to the student according to the design of the experiments by the teacher who handles the class. The experiments should be conducted with all seriousness and the experimenter should have the spirit that he/she is finding out something new in this experiment.

In conducting the experiment, the experimenter should know the instructions given to the participant are equally important. The instructions to the participant involve certain amount of control in the experimental situation. The participant is to carry out the instructions and perform the task and nothing more. Under this condition, the behaviour or the participant's performance is observed and assessed. These instructions should have a uniform pattern. All the experimenters should give the same instructions, otherwise the purpose of the experiment may be defeated.

Further, the experimenter should obtain the willingness and the cooperation of the participant in performing the task. Any successful experimentation depends upon the cooperation of the participant. Whether the person is an outsider or the experimenter's classmate who serves as a participant and also plays the role of an experimenter should carry out the instructions sincerely and should not ignore them on the ground that he/she knows them already.

REFERENCES

Ackner, B. Discussion on physiological measurements of "emotional tension". *Proce.roy.Soc.Med.*, 1958, *51*, 76-78.

Attneave, F. Dimensions of similarity. *Amer.Jl.Psychol.* 1950, 63, 516-556.

Berg, R.L. and Beebe-Center, J.C.Cardiac startle in man. *Jl. exp.Psycholgy.*, 1941, *28*, 262-270.

Boas, E.P. and Goldschmidt, E.F. *The Heart rate*. Springfield, Ill: Thomas, 1932.

Boring, E.G. *A history of experimental psychology* (2nd ed.), New York : Appleton Century- Crofts, 1950.

Bower, T.G.R. The visual work of infants. *Sceintific American*, 1966, 215; 89-92, 132.

Brown, C.H. and Van Gelder, D.Emotional reaction before examinations. I: Physiological Changes. *Jl. Pyschol,* 1938, *5*, 1-9.

Bugalski, B.R. *A first course in Experimental Psychology,* New York : Henry Holt and Company, 1951.

Buhler, R.A. *Stress and flicker fusion.* In W.H. Ittelson & S.B.Kutash (Eds.), Perceptual Changes in Psychopathology. New Brunswick, N.J. : Rutgers University Press, 1961.

Candland, D.K.*Classical Psychophysics and Scaling*, (Eds.) Manning, S.A. and Rosenstock, E.H. New York : McGraw-Hill Book Company, 1968.

Candland, D.K. *Pyschology : Experimental Approach*, New York : McGraw Hill Book Company, 1968.

Champanis, A. How we see : A summary of basic principles. *In Human Factors in Undersea Warfare*. Washington, D.C.: National Research Council, 1959, pp. 3-60.

Christman, R.J. *Sensory Experience* (2nd Ed.) New York : Harper and Row Publishers, 1979.

Cleary, A. *Instrumentation for Psychology* New York: John Wiley & Sons, 1977.

Carmer, T.Uber die Bezichung des Zwischen mediums zur deu Transformations and Kontrasterscheinungen. *Z.Sinnasphysical*, 1932, *54*, 215-242.

Culler, E. Studies in Psychometric theory. *Jl.exp. Psychol,* 1926, *9*, 271-279.

D'Amato, M.R. *Experimental Psychology : Methodology, Psychophysics and Learning*, New York : McGraw-Hill Book Company, 1970.

Darrow, C.W. Continuous records of systolic and diastolic blood pressure. *Arch. Neurol. Psychait*, 1937, *38*, 365-370.

Delboeuf, J.Etude psychologique Recherches theoriques et experimentales sur la measure des sensations et specialement des sensations de lumiere et de fatique. Brussells, 1873, 155 PP.

Delov, V. Analysers (Sense Organs), *In Textbook of Physiology.* Ed. K.M. Bykov, Moscow : Peace Publishers.

Easton, D.H. *Mechanisms of body functions* (second edition). New Delhi :Prentice-Hall of India Private Limited, 1978.

Edridge-Green, F.W. *Colour blindness and colour perception.* London: 1891.

Edwards, A.L.*Techniques of Attitude Scale Construction.* Bombay : Vikas, Feffer and Simons Private Ltd. , 1969.

Fantz, R.L. The origin of form perception, *Scientific American*, 1961, *204*, 66-72.

Fechner, G.T. *Revision der Heuptpunkte der Pyschophysik.* Leipzig: Breitkppf Und Hartel,1882.

Fechner, G.T. *Elements of Psychophysics* (H.S. Langfeld, Trans) In B. Rand (Ed.). The Classical Psychologists. Boston: Houghton Mifflin, 1912, pp. 562-572.

Fullerton, G.S. and Cattell, J.MCK. On the perception of small differences. *Pub. University.Pa.Phil.Ser.*, 1892, No. 3.

Galanter, E. Contemporary Psychophysics. In R. Brown, E. Galanter, E. Hess and G. Mandler, *New Directions in Pyschology*, New York : Holt, 1962.

Galton, F. *Inquiries into human faculty and its development* London: Macmillan, 1883.

Galton, F. *Memories of My Life*. London : Metheun, 1908.

Garrett, H.E. *General Psychology* (2nd ed.) New Delhi : Eurasia Publishing House (Pvt.) Ltd. 1975.

Geiger, P.H. and Firestone, F.A. The estimation of fractional loudness. *Jl. Acoust.Soc. Amer*, 1933, *5*, 25-30.

Geldard. F.A. The description of a case of total colour blindness. *J. Opt. Soc Amer.*, 1933, *23*, 256-260.

Geldard F.A. *The human senses,* New York:Wiley,1953.

Gibson, J.J. *The perception of the Visual World.* Boston: Houghton Mifflin, 1950.

Granit, R. and Harper, P. Comprative studies on peripheral and central retina : II. Synaptic reactions in the eye. *Amer.J.Physiol.*, 1930, *95*, 211-218.

Granit, R. *Sensory mechanisms of the retina,* New York : Oxford, 1947.

Grossman, S.P. *Text Book of Physiological Psychology*. New York : John Wiley & Sons, Inc., 1967.

Guilford, J.P. The method of paired comparisons as a psychometric method. *Psychol. Rev,* 1928, *35*, 494-506.

Guilford, J.P. Some empirical tests of the method of paired comparisons. *J.Gen. Psychol.* 1931, *5*, 64-76.

Guilford, J.P. *Psychometric methods*. New Delhi : Tata-McGraw-Hill Publishing Co. Ltd., 1954.

Guilford, J.P. and Frutcher, B. *Fundamental Statistics in Psychology and Education* (6th edition). International Edition Singapore, McGraw-Hill International Book Co., 1987.

Harvey, W. *Anatomical studies on the Motion of the Heart and Blood.* Springfield, Illinois : Charles C. Thomes Publisher, 1931.

Hecht, S., Peskin, J.C., and Patt, M. Intensity discrimination in the human eye: II. The relation between I/I and intensity for various parts of the spectrum. *J.Gen.Physiol.*, 1938, *22*, 7-19.

Helmholtz, H.Von. *Helmholtz' treatise on physiological opitics* (J.P.C. Southhall, Trans, & Ed.) Vol. II, pp. 449, New York : Dover, 1962.

Helson, H. Fundamental Problems in colour vision I. The Principle of governing changes in hue, saturation and lightness of noe-selective samples in chromatic illumination. *Jl.exe.Psychol.* 1938, *23*, 439-476.

Helson, H. Adaptation-level as frame of reference for prediction of Psychophysical data. *Amer.Jl.Psychol.* 1947, 60, 1-29.

Helson, H. Adaptation-level as a basis for a quantitative theory of frames of reference. *Psychol. Rev.* 1949, *55*, 297-313.

Helson, H. *Adaptation-level theory* : New York : Harper and Row, 1964.

Henry. F.A. A Direct reading Cardio-chronoscope. *Jl. Exp.Psychol*, 1938, *22*, 598-601

Hering, E. Zur Lehre Vom Lichtsinn. *Nein Akad.Wiss, Sitzbr.*, 1874,69, 85-104.

Hevner, K. An empirical study of three psychophysical methods. *Jl.Genl. Psychology*, 1930, *4*, 191-212.

Hilgard, E.K., Atkinson, R.C., and Atkinson, R.L. *Introduction to Psychology*, New Delhi : Oxford and IBH Publishing Co., 1975.

Ishihara, S. *Series of Plates designed as tests for colour blindness*. Tokyo : Chicago: C.S. Stallting, 1920.

Jones, L.A., and Lowery, E.M.Retinal sensibility to saturation differences. *Jl.opt.Soc. Amer.*, 1926, *13*, 25-34.

Jung, C.G. *Studies in World Association* (M.D.Eder, Trans.), London :

Heiuemann, 1919.

Kellogg, W.N. An experimental comparison of psychophysical methods, *Arch. Psychol.* New York : 1929, 17, No. 106.

Kelley, K.H., Havland, C.I., Schwertz, M., Abalson, R.B. The influence of judges' attitudes in three methods of attitude scaling, *J.Soc.Psychol.*, 1955, *42*, 147-158.

Kerlinger, Fred. *Foundations of Behavioural Research.* New York : Holt, Rinehart and Winston, 1965.

Kimble, G.A., Garmezy, N., and Zigler, E. *Principles of Psychology* (6th Edition) New Delhi : Wiley Eastern Limited, 1985.

Kleitman, N. *Sleep and Wakefulness*. Chicago : Chicago University Press, 1939.

Klineberg, F.L. Studies in measurement of the relations among sovereign states. *Psychometrika*, 1941, *6*, 335-352.

Knox. G.W. Some psychological factors in flicker and fusion. *Am. Jl. Optom.* 1950, *28*, 221-226.

Konradi, G. Circulation, In K.M.Byknov (Ed.). *Text book of Physiology.* Moscow : Peace Publishers.

Kuppuswamy, B. *Elementary Experiments in Psychology.* Madras : Oxford University Press, 1954.

Kutash (Ed.), *Perceptural changes in psyschopathology,* New Brunswick. N.J.Rutgers University Press, 1961.

Landis, C. Changes in blood-pressure during sleep as determined by the Erlanger method. *Amer. J.Psychol.* 1925, *73*, 561-555.

Landis, C. and Gullette, R. Studies of emotional reaction-III : Systolic blood-pressure and inspiration-expiration ratios. *Jl.Comp. Ps.choi.,* 1925, *5*, 221-253.

Landis, C. Studies of emotional reactions V: Severe emotional upset. *Jl.Comp. Psychol.,* 1926, *6*, 221-242.

Lane, H.L., Cataria, A.C. and Stevens, S.S. Voice level: Autophonic scale, perceived loudness and effect of side tone. *Jl.Acoust. Soc. Amer.* , 1961, *33*, 160-167.

Lane, H.L. Psychophysical parameters of vowel perception, *Psychol. Mnogr.* 1962, *76,* No. 44.

Lange, C.G. *Om Sindsbevagelsar, et Psycho.fysiolog* Studie. Copenhagen: Kroner, 1985.

Lawson, R.D. *et el. Experiments in Psychology.* London : Oxford University Press, 1975.

Leukel, F. *Introduction to Physiological Psychology.* Saint Louis : The C.V. Mosby Company, 1968.

Lindsley, D.B. Psychophysiology and perception. *In current trends in description and analysis of behaviour.* Pittsbergh, Pa : University of Pittsbergh Press, 1958.

Loewi, O. On the Humoral Transmission of Heart-Nerves. In *Great Experiments in biology* (ed.) by M.L. Gabrial and S.Fogel. Englewood Cliffs, N.J.: Prentice Hall, Inc.,1955.

Lomonosov, M. *Discourse on the Origin of Light Presenting a New Theory of Colours*, 1956.

Macey, R.I. *Human Physiology*. New Delhi: Prentice-Hall of India Private Limited, 1973.

Marcus, A. Krupp, *et el. Physician's hand book* (Maruzen Asian Edition) 19th Ed. Singapore : Lange Medica Publications, 1979.

Matheson, D.W., Bruce, R.C. and Beamchamp, K.L. *Experimental Psychology* (3rd Edn.). New York : Holt Rinehart and Winston, 1971.

McCormick, E.J. and Bachus, J.A. Paried comparison ratings. I.Autophonic scale, perceived loudness and effect of the side tone. *Jl. Accoust.Soc.Amer*, 1961, *33*, 160-167.

McCormick, E.J. and Tiffin, J. *Industrial Psychology* (6th ed.) New Delhi : Prentice-Hall of India Private Limited, 1979.

McGuigan, F.J. *Experimental Psychology : A Methodological Approach* (3rd edition), Englewood Cliffs, New Jersey : Prentice Hall, Inc., 1978.

Mueller, C.G. *Sensory Psychology*. New Delhi : Prentice Hall of India Private Limited, 1969.

Muller, C.E. *Zur Grundlegung der Psychophysick.* Berlin : Friefen, 1878.

Murphy, G. *An Introduction of Psychology*. New Delhi: Oxford and IBH Publishing Company, 1964.

Newhall, S.M. An interpolation procedure for calculating thresholds. *Psychological Review*, 1928, *35*, 46-66.

Osgood, C.E. *Method and theory in experimental Psychology*. Fair Lawn, N.J.: Oxford, 1953.

Parry, J. and Adiseshiah, W. *Experimental Psychology*, Bombay : Allied Publishers Private Limited, 1977.

Peryam, D.R. and Haynes, J.G.Prediction of soldiers food preference by laboratory methods. *Jl. Appl. Psychol*, 1957, *41*, 2-7.

Pickford, R.W. *Individual differences in colour vision.* New York : Macmillan, 1951, 254-255.

Plateau, J.A.F. Sur la mesure des sensations physiques at Sur la loi qui lie l' intensite de ces sensational' intensite de la cause excitants. *Bull.Acad.Roy.Belg.*, 1872, *33*, 376-388.

Polyak, S.L. *The retina.* Chicago : University of Chicago Press, 1941.

Postman, L. and Egan, J.P. *Experimental Psychology : An Introduction:* Ludhiana: Kalyani Publishers, 1949.

Poulton, E.C. The new psychophysics : Six models of magnitude estimation. *Psychological Bulletin*, 1968, *69*, 1-19.

Publication Manual of the American Psychological Association (2nd Edition), Washingtion, D.C. American Psychological Association, 1974.

Purkinje, *Text-book of Physiology*.

Rabideau, G.F. Difference in visual acuity measurements obtained with different types of targets. *Psychological Monograph*, 1955, *69*, No. 10.

Rajamanickam, M.and Mercy Arunmozhi, R. Adjustment Problems in Relation to psychosomatic disorders among the adolescent girls. *Journal of Community Guidance and Reseach*, 1992, *9*, 2, 151-179.

Rayleigh, J.W.S. *Experiments of colour Nature*, 1881, *25*, 65-66.

Richardson, M.W. Multidimensional Psychophysics. *Psychol. Bull*, 1938, *35*, 659.

Ruckmick, C.A. *The psychology of feeling and emotion*. New York : McGraw Hill, 1936.

Samraj, P. and Rajamanickam, M. Neuro-Psychiatrics and psyschosomatic symptoms in athletes and non-athletes. *Indian Journal of Community Guidance Service*, 1984, *Vol. 1*, 3, 55-63.

Seitz, C.P. Effects of Anoxia on Visual Functions, a study of Critical frequency, *Arch-Psychol.*, 1940, 38, No. 257.

Sheehan, M.R. A study of individual consistency in phenomenal consistancy. *Arch.Psychol.*, 1932, No. 22.

Sherphard, J.F. Organic changes and feeling. *Amer. J. Psychol.* 1906, *17*, 523-584.

Shephard, J.F. *The circulation and sleep with atlas*. New York : Macmillan, 1914.

Sheridan, C.L. *Methods in Experimental Psychology*, New York, Holt Rinehart and Winston, 1979.

Simonson, C and Enzer, N. Measurement of Fusion Frequency of Flicker as a test of the fatigue of *Central Nervous System.* Observation on laboratory technicians and office workers. *Jl. Industrial Hyg. And Toxical* 1941, *23*, 83-89.

Simonson, Enzer and Benton, R.W. Influence of Mascular work and fatigue on the state of Central Nervous System. *Jl.Lab.Clin. Md.* 1943, *23*, 1555-1569.

Spearman, C. The method of 'right and wrong' cases without formula.

British Journal of Psychology, 1908, 2, 227-242.

Spielberger, C.D. and Perry London. Raga Boomerange – A key to preventing Coronaries is emerging : Learn to handle anger and avoid seven deadly responses. *Indian Journal of Community Guidance Service*, 1984, *1*, 15-19.

Stevens, S.S. On the theory of scales of measurement, *Science*, 1946, *103*, 35, 695.

Stevens, S.S. (Ed.). *Hand book of experimental psychology*. New York : Wiley, 1951.

Stevens, S.S. On the Brightness of lights and the loudness of sounds, *Science*, 1953, *118*, 576 (Abstract).

Stevens, S.S. and Stone, G. Finger Span: Ration scale category scale and JND scale. *Jl.Exp.Psychol.*, 1959, *57*, 91-95.

Stevens, S.S. and M. Guirao, Loundness, reciprocality and partition scales. *Jl. Acoust. Soc. Am.* 1962, 32, 1446-1471.

Stevens, S.S. and M.Guirao, Subjective scaling of length and area and the metaling of length to loudness and brightness. *Jl. Exp.Psychol,* 1963, *66*, 177-186.

Stevens, S.S. *Psychophysics* (Ed.) by Geraldine Stevens, New York : John Willey & Sons, 1975.

Stovkis, B.A. Method for the uninterrupted registering of blood pressure as a psychophysiological research technique for the study of psychic stimuli on the blood pressure. *Jl.Exp.Psychol.* 1938, *22*, 365-376.

Surendra Kamat. *Flicker-Fusion Appartus Manual.* Bangalore : Electronic Measurements, Mimec Pvt. Ltd.

Teuber, H.L. Battersley, W.S. and Bander, M.B. *Vision defects after penetrating missile wounds of the brain.* Cambridge, Mass: Harrand, 1960.

Thorndike, E.L. Handwriting. *Teach. Coll.Rec.* 1910, 11, No. 2.

Thorndike, R.L. and Hagen, E. *Measurement and Evaluation in Psychology and Education* (4th Edition). New York : John Wiley, 1977.

Thurstone, L. L. A Law of comparative judgment. *Psychol. Rev.,* 1927, *34*, 273-286.

Thurstone, L.L. Psychophysical analysis. *Amer. L. Psychol.*, 1927, 38, 273-286.

Titchener, E.B. *Experimental Psychology*. Vol. II, Pts., I and II, New York : Macmillan, 1905.

Torgerson, W.D. *A theoretical and empirical investigation of Multidimensional scaling.* Princeton N.J. : Educational Testing Service, 1951.

Torgerson W.D. *Theory and methods of scaling*. New York : Wiley, 1958.

Turnbull, C.M. Some observations regarding the experiences and behaviour of the Ba Mbuti Pymies. *American Journal of Psychology*, 1961, 74, 304-408.

U.G.C.workshop reports, 1975.

Uhrbook, R.S. and Richardson, M.W. Item analysis. *Person. Jl.* 1953, *12*, 141-154.

Underwood, B.J. *Psychological Reseach*: New York : Appleton Century Crafts, 1957.

Underwood, B. J. *Experimental Psychology*. Bombay : The Times of India Press, 1965.

Urban, F.M. *The Application of Statistical Methods of Problem of Psychophysics*. Philadelphia : Psychological Clinic Press, 1908.

White, P.L. *Human infanats : Experience and Psychological Development*, Englewood Cliffs, N.J.: Prentice-Hall, 1971.

Whithord, J.C. Kaufman, M.R. and Thoma, J.M. Heart rate in relation to emotional disturbances. *Arch. Neurol.Psychiat*, 1935, *33*, 712-731.

Whithord, J.C.and Richter, H. Unsteadiness of the heart rate in psychotic and neurotic state. *Arch. Neurol.Psychiat*. 1937, *38*, 62-70.

Woodworth, R.S. *Experimental Psychology*. London : Metheun and Co., 1938.

Woodword, R.S. *Experimental Psychology*, New York : Holt, 1947.

Woodworth, R. S. and Marquis, D. G. *Psychology*. London : Methuen & Co. Ltd., 1952.

Woodworth, R. S. *Experimental Psychology*, London : Metheun & Co. Ltd., 1950.

Woodworth, R. S. and Scholsberg, E. *Experimental Psychology*. New York: Henry Holt, 1954.

Zeigler, H.P. and Leibowitz, H. Apparent visual size as a function of distance for children and adults. *American Journal of Psychology,* 1957, *70*, 106-109.

INDEX